STUDIES IN EVANGELICAL HI

Laws of the Spiritual Order

Innovation and Reconstruction in the Soteriology of
Thomas Erskine of Linlathen

STUDIES IN EVANGELICAL HISTORY AND THOUGHT

*A complete listing of all titles in this series
will be found at the close of this book.*

STUDIES IN EVANGELICAL HISTORY AND THOUGHT

Laws of the Spiritual Order

Innovation and Reconstruction in the Soteriology of
Thomas Erskine of Linlathen

Don Horrocks

Foreword by Trevor Hart

PATERNOSTER

Copyright © Don Horrocks 2004

First published 2004 by Paternoster

Paternoster is an imprint of Authentic Media,
9 Holdom Avenue, Bletchley, Milton Keynes, MK1 1QR, U.K.
and
P.O.Box 1047, Waynesboro, GA 30830-2047, U.S.A.

10 09 08 07 06 05 04   7 6 5 4 3 2 1

The right of Don Horrocks to be identified as the Author of this Work
has been asserted by him in accordance with Copyright, Designs and Patents
Act 1988.

All rights reserved. No part of this publication may be reproduced, stored in a retrieval system, or transmitted in any form or by any means, electric, mechanical, photocopying, recording or otherwise, without the prior permission of the publisher or a license permitting restricted copying. In the U.K. such licenses are issued by the Copyright Licensing Agency, 90, Tottenham Court Road, London WIP 9HE.

British Library Cataloguing in Publication Data
A catalogue record for this book is available from the British Library

ISBN 1-84227-192-X

Typeset by Don Horrocks
Printed and bound in Great Britain for
Paternoster
By Nottingham Alpha Graphics

STUDIES IN EVANGELICAL HISTORY AND THOUGHT

Series Preface

The Evangelical movement has been marked by its union of four emphases: on the Bible, on the cross of Christ, on conversion as the entry to the Christian life and on the responsibility of the believer to be active. The present series is designed to publish scholarly studies of any aspect of this movement in Britain or overseas. Its volumes include social analysis as well as exploration of Evangelical ideas. The books in the series consider aspects of the movement shaped by the Evangelical Revival of the eighteenth century, when the impetus to mission began to turn the popular Protestantism of the British Isles and North America into a global phenomenon. The series aims to reap some of the rich harvest of academic research about those who, over the centuries, have believed that they had a gospel to tell to the nations.

Series Editors

David Bebbington, Professor of History, University of Stirling, Stirling, Scotland, UK

John H.Y. Briggs, Senior Research Fellow in Ecclesiastical History and Director of the Centre for Baptist History and Heritage, Regent's Park College, Oxford, UK

Timothy Larsen, Associate Professor of Theology, Wheaton College, Illinois, USA

Mark A. Noll, McManis Professor of Christian Thought, Wheaton College, Wheaton, Illinois, USA

Ian M. Randall, Deputy Principal and Lecturer in Church History and Spirituality, Spurgeon's College, London, UK, and a Senior Research Fellow, International Baptist Theological Seminary, Prague, Czech Republic

The Rev. John McLeod Campbell remarked concerning his dear friend Thomas Erskine that he "felt more fellowship with him in what seems to be his life, and what I desire may more and more be my own life, than I ever feel with any other man."

*This book is dedicated to my wife
Stephanie who has unfailingly challenged me
by her own life to remember what and who all this is for.*

Contents

Foreword xiii

Preface and Acknowledgements xv

Abbreviations xvii

Chapter 1: Introduction 1
    Perceptions of Thomas Erskine 1
    Erskine's Scottish Setting 9
    Erskine and John McLeod Campbell 13
    Objectives of this Book 15

Part 1: Thomas Erskine as Eclectic Soteriological Innovator 19

Chapter 2: Introducing Erskine's Soteriological Thought 21

Chapter 3: Re-educating Perceptions of God 27
    Introduction 27
    The Cruciality of Divine Character 28
    Relational Trinitarianism 33
        Eternal Sonship 36
        The Holy Spirit 38
        Divine and Human Relationality 41
    Summary 44

Chapter 4: Revelation and the Location of Authority 46
    Introduction 46
    The Nature of Evidence 49
        Conscience 53
        Laws of the Spiritual Order 58
            Salvific Knowledge 66
    The Nature of Saving Faith 69
        Faith, Knowledge and Understanding 77
        Hermeneutical Implications 79
        Justification by Faith 81
    Doctrine, Bible and Creed 88
    Summary 93

Chapter 5: Salvation – Its Extent and Nature 94
Introduction 94
Universal Pardon and Assurance 96
The Doctrine of the Atonement 101
    Introduction 101
    The Nature of Atonement 105
    Suffering and Sacrifice 110
    Propitiation 117
    The Nature of Sin 120
The Place of Election 126
Summary 130

Chapter 6: Erskine and Theological Controversy 131
Introduction 131
Scottish Reaction–J.A. Haldane 132
The Soteriological Role of the Spirit 135
    Newman's 'Rationalistic' Concerns 145
    Erskine's Theology of Conversion 149
Summary 159

Part 2: Erskine's Reconstructive Eclectic Soteriology in its Wider Setting 163

Chapter 7: Erskine and his Nineteenth-Century Context 165

Chapter 8: Erskine's Sources 172
Introduction 172
Mystical Theology 176
William Law 180
    William Law and the Influence of Edward Irving 187
Summary 192

Chapter 9: Erskine in a Reconstructive Victorian Context 194
Introduction 194
The Divine Purpose 195
Erskine and Nineteenth-Century Incarnational Soteriology 203
    R.H. Hutton 205
    F.D. Maurice 209
    Moral Idealism 211
The Notion of Sacrifice 217
    Horace Bushnell 219
    F.W. Robertson 220

Contents xi

       F.D. Maurice and R.S. Candlish 221
  Summary 224

Chapter 10: Erskine in a Reconstructive Continental Context ... 225
  Introduction 225
  The Extent of German and Romantic Influence 226
  Erskine and the Continent 230
  Erskine's Relation to German Theology 235
      Augustus Tholuck 238
      Richard Rothe 239
      Erskine's Assimilation of German Thought 244
      Charles Hodge 250
  Summary 251

Chapter 11: Concluding Comments.................................. 253

Appendices

Appendix 1: Thomas Erskine and Kant in the Nineteenth Century 265

Appendix 2: Thomas Erskine, William Ellery Channing and the Unitarians 268

Appendix 3: Thomas Erskine and Biblical Criticism 272

Appendix 4: Thomas Erskine and the Implications of Sandemanianism 278

Appendix 5: Thomas Erskine and Moral Government............. 289

Bibliography 297

Index of Subjects 349

Index of Persons 357

Foreword

Thomas Erskine is an odd figure in the history of British theology. He had one of the most fertile minds of his generation, yet his works (some of which ran into eight or nine editions and were translated into French and German) are hardly ever read today. He was not even a cleric, let alone a theologian by training, but a lawyer, and one compelled to relinquish his profession at an early age to assume responsibility for the family estate at Linlathen in Forfarshire. Yet Erskine's classical education combined with a close knowledge of Scripture (he read a portion of his Bible in the original languages each day) and a passion for the Christian gospel to make him much more than an 'amateur' theologian. Through his published writings and his circle of personal contacts, Erskine certainly made his mark on nineteenth century religious sensibility and established his place as a respected cosmopolitan figure among the educated and literary classes of Britain and Europe. Among the best known of those who became his friends and correspondents were Madame de Broglie, Thomas Carlyle, Thomas Chalmers, John McLeod Campbell, Charles Kingsley, F. D. Maurice, Adolphus Monod, Prévost-Paradol, A. J. Scott, J. C. Shairp, Dean Stanley, John Tulloch and Alexandre Vinet.

Erskine's books cover a wide range of themes, some heavily expository and others reflecting sophisticated awareness of the challenges and opportunities presented to Christian faith by movements in contemporary European philosophy. He has been called the 'Scottish Schleiermacher'; but, while Erskine certainly eschewed what he saw as an arid intellectualism in the Calvinism familiar to him from his upbringing and emphasised the importance of faith as a moral reality and the importance of religious experience over mere credal subscription, he was no parent of the theological liberalism which emerged later in the century. Theologically, while eclectic, he was nonetheless broadly orthodox and biblical, concentrating his doctrinal attentions upon the incarnation, the atonement, and the unconditional freeness of the Gospel of grace. Some of his published views, though, set him in direct opposition to the general tenor of the *Westminster Confession of Faith* (which was and remains the chief subordinate doctrinal standard of the Church of Scotland) and conflicted directly with the ascendant interpretation of it in the so-called Federal theology of popular Calvinism. Erskine cared little about being perceived orthodox in these terms, and defended himself exegetically. If, as a layman his outspoken criticism of the tradition caused him no professional difficulty, it did cost him in personal terms; he was asked (reluctantly) to leave the small independent chapel congregation to which he and his mother and sister belonged. Later, Erskine openly embraced the hope that God would finally redeem all his creatures through the atonement made by Christ. While such a hope certainly fell well outside the boundaries of traditional orthodoxy, Erskine's reasons for hoping it were nonetheless ones drawn directly from the gospel itself. If God freely accepts even the worst of sinners, he mused, how can we suppose that he should at the last breach the logic of his own grace and impose a temporal condition upon their salvation?

Erskine is certainly a complex figure. Religiously, he straddles the Calvinist and the Episcopal traditions in Scotland, and the divergent influences of each can readily be discerned in his views. Culturally, he tries to hold together the Christian gospel (with its decidedly counter-cultural aspects) and much that he himself learned from his study of classical literature, history and philosophy. He flirted in a significant way with charismatic renewal on the West Coast of Scotland, but later eschewed his involvement in it, and notably had little place for the Holy Spirit in his own theology, preferring to emphasize the Logos of God, and making a typically nineteenth century appeal to conscience as the place where God lays hold of human beings and reshapes them. His writings, though, while they sometimes reveal the strains which such differing influences placed on him, remain a rich resource and contain some great insights of both a theological and a spiritual sort. They deserve to be widely read, and it is an enormous pleasure to see Don Horrocks' first rate study of Erskine now available to the theologically interested public. His is a reliable guide in largely unfamiliar territory. Let us hope that it will serve as a stimulus for others to explore that territory for themselves.

Trevor Hart
Professor of Divinity
University of St. Andrews

Preface and Acknowledgements

This book represents the substance of my 2001 PhD thesis originally entitled *The Soteriological Eclecticism of Thomas Erskine of Linlathen: Perceptions of Theological Innovation in an Age of Reconstruction.*

The name of Thomas Erskine of Linlathen meant absolutely nothing to me when I first heard of it during my undergraduate theological studies involving John McLeod Campbell. I was intrigued that this shadowy figure who had apparently made such an impression on so many of his contemporaries and had so helped to inspire McLeod Campbell himself was now relatively unknown. There appeared to be no shortage of scholars keen to produce eminent studies of John McLeod Campbell. But interest in Thomas Erskine seemed commensurate with a general tendency to view him rather paternalistically and dismissively as a well-meaning amateur of marginal importance.

What a different picture emerged from my three years engagement with this charming, saintly, intelligent and far-seeing man. I am now more convinced than ever of the supine underrating of the transitionary importance of this nineteenth-century theological figure. If this study contributes in some way to re-establishing the significance of Thomas Erskine of Linlathen as a serious contributor to, if not shaper of, nineteenth-century theological development, I shall be more than satisfied.

One important feature of this work has been the extensive compilation of the first seriously comprehensive bibliography comprising primary and secondary material relating to Thomas Erskine and his times. Accordingly, no apology is made for its requisite length. Re-discovery of previously neglected manuscript material housed at the National Library of Scotland, has been particularly useful in extending our knowledge concerning the scope of Erskine's sources and influence.

I gratefully acknowledge my supervisor Graham McFarlane's initiative in inviting me to pursue research to uncover clearer perspectives on the role of Thomas Erskine of Linlathen. It has truly been a journey of delightful discovery. Despite the acknowledged difficulty of Erskine's style, I have nevertheless unwaveringly found him to be a fascinating subject. I remain in Graham's debt for introducing me to Scottish theology, for his friendship and enthusiastic interest, and for so readily offering motivational support and encouragement along the way. I also pay tribute to faculty members, staff, and fellow research students at London Bible College for affording a motivational and spiritually encouraging working atmosphere and facilities, and for acting as inspirational sounding boards for debate. Our weekly research seminars were a consistently stimulating influence for serious theological reflection, developing maturity, and academic aspiration, as well as being hugely enjoyable. I pay particular tribute to the memory of Mike Crowley, a doughty debating colleague, who was tragically killed shortly after completing his own doctoral studies.

I have made use of many library facilities during my research. However, I should single out the staff at Cambridge University, and especially New College, Edinburgh, for their patience in the face of repeated demands for access to restricted rare items and manuscript collections, often during unsociable hours. Special tribute must go to Sally Harrower of the National Library of Scotland in Edinburgh for her remarkably good-humoured help, co-operation, and painstaking work over a period of several months to identify and organise the systematic microfilming of assorted manuscripts. The staff of my own local, tiny public library in Chalfont St. Peter, Buckinghamshire, deserve special mention for their interest, patience and good humour during the many times when I certainly taxed their book location capacity.

Finally, of course, my deepest thanks go to my wife Stephanie, and my teenage children, Philip, Katherine and Luke, who had to get used to my being unavailable for domestic and parental responsibilities, and watched me disappear gradually into a remote academic world. Their love, understanding, and unflagging support helped keep me going. I hope they agree it was all worthwhile.

Don Horrocks
Chalfont St. Peter
November 2002

Abbreviations

ANCL	Alexander Roberts and James Donaldson, (eds.), *Ante-Nicene Christian Library,* Vol. IX (Edinburgh: T.&T. Clark, 1868).
Baxter	Thomas Erskine, *Introductory Essay to Baxter's Saints' Rest,* [Combined Edition] (Edinburgh: David Douglas, 1878).
CD	Karl Barth, *Church Dogmatics,* G.W. Bromiley and T.F. Torrance (eds.) (Edinburgh: T.&T. Clark, 1956-75).
CHA	The Thomas Chalmers Manuscript Collection, New College, Edinburgh
DHT	*The Dictionary of Historical Theology*, Trevor A. Hart, (general editor), (Carlisle: Paternoster, 2000).
DSCHT	Nigel M. de S. Cameron, David F. Wright, David C. Lachman, Donald E. Meek (eds.), *Dictionary of Scottish Church History and Theology* (Downers Grove, Illinois: IVP, 1993).
ECI	*The Edinburgh Christian Instructor*
Election	Thomas Erskine, *The Doctrine of Election and its Connection with the General Tenor of Christianity, illustrated from Many Parts of Scripture, and especially from the Epistle to the Romans* (London: James Duncan, 1837).
Evidence	Thomas Erskine, *Remarks on the Internal Evidence for the Truth of Revealed Religion,* [10th combined edition] (Edinburgh: David Douglas, 1878).
Ewing-I	The Right Revd Alexander Ewing, Bishop of Argyll and the Isles (ed.), 'Some Letters of Thomas Erskine of Linlathen', in *Present-Day Papers on Prominent Questions in Theology,* Third Series, [first edition] (London: Strahan & Co., 1871); [supplementary edition] (London: Daldy, Isbister & Co, 1878). [1871 edition used except where stated].
Ewing-II	The Right Revd Alexander Ewing, Bishop of Argyll and the Isles (ed.), 'Some Further Letters of Thomas Erskine of Linlathen', in *Present-Day*

	Papers on Prominent Questions in Theology, Third Series, [first edition] (London: Strahan & Co., 1871); [supplementary edition] (London: Daldy, Isbister & Co, 1878). [1871 edition used except where stated].
Extracts	*Extracts of Letters to a Christian Friend, by a Lady. With An Introductory Essay by Thomas Erskine, Esq., Advocate* (Greenock: R.B. Lusk, 1830).
Faith	Thomas Erskine, *An Essay on Faith* [5th edition] (Edinburgh: Waugh and Innes, 1829).
Freeness	Thomas Erskine, *The Unconditional Freeness of the Gospel: in Three Essays* [2nd edition] (Edinburgh: Waugh & Innes, 1828); [new edition] (Edinburgh: David Douglas, 1879). [2nd edition used except where stated].
Gambold	Thomas Erskine, *Introductory Essay to the Works of the Rev. John Gambold, A.M., Late one of the Bishops of the United Brethren*, [Combined Edition] (Edinburgh: David Douglas, 1878).
Gifts	Thomas Erskine, *On the Gifts of the Spirit* (Greenock: R.B. Lusk, 1830).
Gurney	Ellen Mary Gurney (ed.), *Letters of Emelia Russell Gurney* (London: James Nisbet & Co., Limited, 1902).
Institutes	John Calvin, *Institutes of the Christian Religion*, John T. McNeil (ed.), translated by Ford Lewis Battles, in The Library of Christian Classics, Volumes XX and XXI (Philadelphia: The Westminster Press, 1960).
Letters-I, -II	William Hanna (ed.), *Letters of Thomas Erskine of Linlathen*, in 2 volumes; Vol. 1 from 1800 till 1840; Vol. 2 from 1840 till 1870 (Edinburgh: David Douglas, 1877).
Love	William Law, 'The Spirit of Love', in *The Spirit of Prayer and The Spirit of Love*, Sidney Spencer, (ed.) (Cambridge & London: James Clarke & Co. Ltd, 1969).
Memorials	Donald Campbell (ed.), *Memorials of John McLeod Campbell, D.D. Being Selections from his Correspondence*, in 2 volumes (London: Macmillan and Co., 1877).
MS(S)	Manuscript(s)

Abbreviations

NOTA	John McLeod Campbell, *The Nature of the Atonement and its Relation to Remission of Sins and Eternal Life*, [new edition] (Edinburgh: The Handsel Press, 1996).
NCLE	New College Library, Edinburgh
NLS	National Library of Scotland
Prayer	William Law, 'The Spirit of Prayer', in *The Spirit of Prayer and The Spirit of Love*, Sidney Spencer, (ed.) (Cambridge & London: James Clarke & Co. Ltd, 1969).
Present-Day Papers	The Right Revd Alexander Ewing, Bishop of Argyll and the Isles (ed.), *Present-Day Papers on Prominent Questions in Theology,* Third Series, [first edition] (London: Strahan & Co., 1871); [supplementary edition] (London: Daldy, Isbister & Co, 1878). [1871 edition used except where stated].
RSCHS	Records of the Scottish Church History Society
Salvation	Thomas Erskine, *Introductory Essay to Letters of the Rev. Samuel Rutherford, Late Professor of Divinity at St. Andrews,* [Combined Edition] (Edinburgh: David Douglas, 1878).
Serpent	Thomas Erskine, *The Brazen Serpent; or Life Coming Through Death,* [1st edition] (Edinburgh: Waugh and Innes, 1831); [1st edition – including an extract by Miss Rachel Erskine entitled "That Christ Suffered as our Head, to lead us through Suffering to Glory, – and not as our Substitute to dispense with our Suffering"] (Edinburgh: Waugh and Innes, 1831); [2nd edition] (Edinburgh: Waugh and Innes, 1831). [citations from the 1st edition except where indicated].
SJT	*Scottish Journal of Theology*
Sp.Order	Thomas Erskine, *The Spiritual Order and Other Papers Selected from the Manuscripts of the late Thomas Erskine of Linlathen* [3rd edition] (Edinburgh: David Douglas, 1884).

All Scripture quotations are taken from the King James Version of the Bible, in line with Thomas Erskine.

CHAPTER 1

Introduction

Perceptions of Thomas Erskine

Despite his lack of prominence, the little-known and still comparatively neglected Thomas Erskine of Linlathen (1788-1870), is nevertheless increasingly coming to be regarded as a key transitional figure in facilitating the inauguration of a new 'free-thinking' epoch in early nineteenth-century theological thought. He was a man ahead of his time, or as Charles Darwin's niece and close friend of Robert Browning, Julia Wedgwood, put it in 1870, "a lofty peak that reflected the morning light so early".[1] Erskine represented a modified evangelical stance between arid eighteenth-century Enlightenment rationalism, and the immanental shift towards inward individual experience and the 'spiritual life', which increasingly characterised nineteenth-century critique of theories of knowledge and revelation.[2]

Though initially welcomed in the early 1820s as a refreshingly innovative popular apologist for Christianity, Erskine soon came to be viewed by his reactionary Scottish evangelical Calvinist contemporaries as a respectable but idiosyncratic layman who entertained and propagated threatening and dangerously unorthodox views. They tended to associate him not only with past disputes like the Marrow controversy a hundred years earlier, but with contemporary 'heretics' such as Edward Irving, A.J. Scott, and John McLeod Campbell who were ejected from the Kirk in the early 1830s.

---

[1] "Thomas Erskine of Linlathen", in Julia Wedgwood, *Nineteenth Century Teachers and Other Essays* (London: Hodder and Stoughton, 1909), 63.

[2] Immanuel Kant (1724-1804) is generally held to have inaugurated the trend turning theology and philosophy away from abstract metaphysical and doctrinal speculation, and inwards towards the human consciousness – that psychological aspect of religious apprehension and experiential knowledge in which religion was understood to be more properly reflected in categories of practical reason, ethics and morality. (See Appendix I).

Though his main published work spanned only the years 1820-1837, Erskine has been accused by some of instigating the process of liberal theology in Britain,[3] whilst others strenuously defend his essential orthodoxy.[4] Erskine undoubtedly found the narrow 'orthodoxy' of nineteenth-century Presbyterian Scotland as disagreeable as they found his so-called 'neology'. Though at times his more broad-minded and thoughtful contemporaries found his ideas 'subtle', 'novel', 'startling', sometimes demanding uneasy acquiescence, they welcomed his pioneering, radical, constructive, and inspirational theological mind.[5]

Some have hailed Erskine in almost magisterial terms. Describing him as the "great inaugurator of the Third Scotch Reformation", the *Spectator* considered *The Unconditional Freeness of the Gospel*, published in 1825, as "epoch making" in setting in motion theological thinking that would come to be "no less revolutionary and revealing...than was the discovery of Newton in astronomy". Maintaining the hyperbole, the periodical suggested Erskine "inaugurated a method of inquiry which is more radically affecting theological thought than even the Theses of Luther himself".[6] Writing in 1890, the more measured authoritative German Tübingen scholar, Otto Pfleiderer, noted that although Erskine's views were condemned in Scotland, they were, however, "received in the soil of the Liberal theology of England", and together with his friend and compatriot John McLeod Campbell, he assessed their ideas "as the best contribution to dogmatics which British theology has produced in the present century".[7] The great Congregationalist scholar, Robert Franks, spoke of Erskine's

---

[3] In his unpublished masters thesis, John B. Logan concluded that since Erskine had been instrumental in the overthrow of traditional Calvinism in Scotland, he was justified in describing him as "one of the founders of the modern Liberal theology in Britain", 'The Religious Thought of Thomas Erskine of Linlathen' (Union Theological Seminary, 1931), 87. In his more recent study, Nicholas Needham portrays, almost in the mode of a 'decline and fall' tragedy, Erskine's 'journey' from Calvinism to "Romantic Liberalism", ending up as "a classic Victorian theological Liberal" and "Liberal Universalist", (*Thomas Erskine of Linlathen: his Life and Theology, 1788-1837* [Edinburgh: Rutherford House, 1990], 3, 9, 177, and dust jacket).

[4] Olive Brose is adamant that "at no time did [Erskine] offer what has come to be known as a 'liberal theology'", *Frederick Denison Maurice: Rebellious Conformist, 1805-1872* (Ohio University Press, 1971), 44. Trevor Hart protests that "to present him as a theological Liberal in the mould of Lessing, Schleiermacher, or Ritschl (as some have attempted) is to do Erskine a serious injustice and to do interpretative mischief to his writings" (*The Teaching Father: An Introduction to the Theology of Thomas Erskine of Linlathen* [Edinburgh: Saint Andrew Press, 1993], 2).

[5] E.g., Principal Shairp, "Reminiscences of Thomas Erskine", in *Letters-II*, 365-6.

[6] The *Spectator*, 29 December 1877, 1661; 12 July 1873, 896; 23 June 1877, 794.

[7] Otto Pfleiderer, *The Development of Theology in Germany since Kant and its Progress in Great Britain since 1825*, [2nd edition] (London: Swan Sonnenschein, 1893), 383, 382.

Introduction 3

ability to balance 'patristic', 'medieval', and 'later Calvinist' theological thought.[8]

Towards the end of the nineteenth century it began to be more widely perceived that Erskine had played a significant role in the development of Scottish, and indeed British, theology.[9] Later assessment, however, has been relatively scarce or muted. Perhaps the most positive twentieth-century commentators, Andrew Drummond and James Bulloch, considered Erskine "the most significant figure in Scottish theological thought in the quarter of a century preceding the Disruption – and perhaps in the nineteenth century".[10] Vernon Storr found it "remarkable" that Erskine, as a layman, "should have so decisively influenced the course of theological developments in [the] early years of the nineteenth century".[11] And it was not just at home that his impact was felt. Erskine has been credited with "widespread influence" on the continent and in America as well.[12]

Sometimes portrayed as an eccentric anachronism, Erskine's relative obscurity today could lend credence to those who deny his theological contribution was in any sense pioneering or innovative.[13] In contrast, others highlight Erskine's creative piety, passion, articulateness, and intelligence – a profound thinker whose "life interest was religion, as to which he displayed

---

[8] Robert S. Franks, *The Work of Christ* [1918] (London: Thomas Nelson and Sons, 1962), 661-2.

[9] Principal John Tulloch of St. Andrews said of Erskine's *Remarks on the Internal Evidence for the Truth of Revealed Religion*, that it marked "a crisis in the theological thought of Scotland", *Movements of Religious Thought in Britain During the Nineteenth Century* [1885] (Leicester: Leicester University Press, 1971), 133. Franks placed Erskine alongside Coleridge as being "instrumental in the regeneration of British theology in the nineteenth century". Regarding Erskine's *The Brazen Serpent*, Franks asserted that "the doctrine of this book is historically of great importance, in view of the later development of theology in Britain", (*Work of Christ*, 655, 657). D.J. Vaughan positioned Erskine at the forefront of four "remarkable" Scots who exercised "wide", "deep", and "everlasting" influence upon English nineteenth-century theological thought. The others were John McLeod Campbell, Norman Macleod, and Alexander Ewing, ("Scottish Influence Upon English Theological Thought", *Contemporary Review*, XXXII [June, 1878], 457).

[10] Andrew Drummond and James Bulloch, *The Scottish Church, 1688-1843* (Edinburgh: Saint Andrew Press, 1973), 194.

[11] Vernon F. Storr, *The Development of English Theology in the Nineteenth Century 1800-1860* (London: Longmans, Green and Co., 1913), 353.

[12] Andrew L. Drummond, *The Kirk and the Continent* (Edinburgh: Saint Andrew Press, 1956), 180, 191-2; Henry F. Henderson, *Erskine of Linlathen: Selections and Biography* (Edinburgh and London: Oliphant Anderson & Ferrier, 1899), ix. Several of Erskine's works were translated into French, German and Italian.

[13] Needham represents Erskine from time to time as "eccentric", e.g., *Thomas Erskine*, 120. Steve Gowler is one who rejects the view of Erskine as "a self-conscious innovator or as a leader of a movement. He was neither", ("No Second-hand Religion", *Church History* 54 [1985], 202).

a remarkable originality of mind".[14] The Dean of Wells, E.H. Plumptre, who knew and admired Erskine commented, "How far he was indebted to the teaching of any previous thinker I am unable to say. His own writings represent, almost or altogether, the workings of his own mind, without reference to or quotation from the writings of others.[15]

Sympathetic to the broadly evangelical Pietist tradition,[16] Erskine acknowledged that the two greatest influences on his life were persons of extraordinarily godly character and personal holiness – his brother James, and the saintly Duchess de Broglie, daughter of Madame de Staël, both of whom died young. Erskine's theological motivation was bound up with a similar passionate pietism. He was a saintly lay Christian apologist whose genius, we argue, was successfully to introduce into a highly reactionary environment what at the time were controversial, albeit not entirely original, theological ideas, in a novel, progressive, and visionary way. Crucially, he was not subject to ecclesiastical establishment control, his lay status unquestionably facilitating his ability to speak freely.[17] He was to occupy, for a short while, a virtually unique place which enabled him to initiate a process of new apologetic, including much-needed contextual theological reconstruction. A lawyer by training, whose Edinburgh University education at the turn of the century probably provided the background for a broad religious and philosophical awareness,[18] he applied his talent for logical argument to the field of religious apologetics in an eclectic, creative and innovative way. By all accounts, however, Erskine exercised greatest influence through his completely God-absorbed personality, holy living, and wide personal contacts, than through his pre-mortem publications.[19] A

---

[14] Bernard M.G. Reardon, *Religious Thought in the Victorian Age: A Survey from Coleridge to Gore,* [2nd edition] (London: Longman, 1995), 294.

[15] *The Spirits in Prison and other studies on the Life after Death,* [3rd edition] (London: Wm. Isbister, 1885), 210-11.

[16] Erskine's background involved both Episcopalian and Calvinist evangelical piety. Though he was constitutionally unsympathetic to Arminianism, he nevertheless appreciated Wesley and the Moravians, and visited Herrnhut.

[17] The *Spectator,* 29 December 1877, 1662, noted that Erskine's views in the 1820s and 1830s were to be regarded as especially valuable, coming from a layman rather than from a "professional theologian". In particular, "his private fortune rendered it a matter of no consequence to his outward comfort whether society accepted or condemned his utterances, and so far as the moral courage is concerned of deliberately encountering the prejudices of a whole nation, Erskine showed that he possessed it".

[18] See p.227 below, and Appendix 5, pp.292-93.

[19] Steve Gowler thinks that "Unlike Coleridge, Schleiermacher, and the German Idealists, Erskine did not wield influence through the philosophical depth or ingenuity of his thought," (*No Second-hand Religion,* 214). Those who knew him best regarded Erskine as a 'living saint', William Hanna speaking for all in describing him as "the best, the holiest man they ever knew, – the man most human yet most divine, with least of the stains of earth, with most of the spirit of heaven", (*Letters-II,* 346). To his disciples he

Introduction 5

kind of wise 'elder statesman' or spiritual nineteenth-century 'Lord Falkland', he attracted to himself a wide range of international, interdenominational, and influential friendships, which he sustained by copious letter-writing and social and intellectual gatherings for theological reflection, both at his estate at Linlathen near Dundee, and at his seasonal dwellings in Edinburgh.[20] For Alexander Ewing, Bishop of Argyll, there were "few in our or any generation whose speech and writings have equalled in spiritual power and benefit those of Mr. Erskine", for "far above the generality of men, he was occupied with spiritual things and the search after God...he brought the spirit of heaven into the things of earth...".[21]

Speaking for authentic religion with remarkable foresight into an era of religious revolution, development and reconstruction, the force and immensity of which many were initially unconscious, Erskine's life spanned an age of rapid change in which theology was to be transformed, though he himself remained 'pre-critical' in outlook. The sympathetic, innovative tendency of his own broad theological thought sought to emphasise more spiritual and ethical aspects of religion, in contrast to the legalising dogmatic, orthodox Calvinism of his native land. Allied to his pioneering association with key representatives of what came to be known as the nine-

---

was "a prophet indeed, a sacred oracle whose every word was received with veneration", (Anon., "A School of the Prophets", *Blackwood's Edinburgh Magazine*, CXXII, DCCXLIII [September, 1877], 285). Erskine's obituary in the *Spectator*, 2 April 1870, 431 affirmed that "More than anyone else whom we ever met with, [Erskine] fulfilled the idea of what Novalis called 'a God-intoxicated man'". The influential A.J. Scott told Erskine that "Everything that reminds me of God reminds me of you", (Wedgwood, *Teachers*, 74). Others, like Alexander Ewing, Bishop of Argyll, venerated Erskine. As the 'fearless exponent of his principles', Ewing "carried them into the ecclesiastical sphere...", James Cameron Lees, "Bishop Ewing", *Scottish Divines 1505-1872* (Edinburgh: MacNiven and Wallace, 1883), 360, cf., *Ewing-I*, 8.

[20] Emelia Russell Gurney, pious wife of the government commissioner Russell Gurney, and a regular visitor to Linlathen together with her mother, Mrs Batten, daughter of the evangelical, Henry Venn, announced passionately to Julia Wedgwood in 1867, "Oh, how thankful I am to be counted in that Linlathen circle!", (*Gurney*, 49). A significant catalogue of clergymen, deans, bishops, and even a future archbishop of Canterbury, benefited from hearing Erskine's views. Amongst the many distinguished names who counted him as a valued friend or acquaintance were Thomas Carlyle and his wife Jane Welsh Carlyle, Edward Irving, Thomas Chalmers, A.J. Scott, Benjamin Jowett, Charles Kingsley, F.D. Maurice, Bishop Ewing, Principal Shairp, Dean Stanley, George MacDonald, Lord Rutherford, John Tulloch, Adolphe Monod, Alexandre Vinet, Madame de Broglie, Merle d'Aubigne and César Malan. Julia Wedgwood, in referring to the many thinkers of his day who were influenced by Erskine, notes that "it was not so much by communication of thought – it was by a kind of manifestation of the invisible world – that he laid hold of those who came near him", (*Teachers*, 74).

[21] *Ewing-II* (London: Strahan, 1871), 7; (London: Daldy, Isbister, 1878), 76.

teenth-century 'Broad Church' movement, not surprisingly Erskine became indelibly linked to that group.[22]

It is impossible to separate Erskine from his context. Whilst innovative in the way in which he adapted intellectual and cultural trends to contemporary theology, he was nevertheless essentially reflecting new trends in nineteenth-century religion, such as the emergence of the 'relative' in place of the 'absolute', the primacy of the subjective and experiential, the association of belief in God with ethical values and action, and the representation of Jesus in terms of archetypal spiritual and moral consciousness. In an age of uncertainty, Erskine was effectively a creative, forward-looking apologist, motivated by the need to establish a cohesive and acceptable soteriology, and unlike others, rejecting retreat into the past at a time when traditional supports were progressively being undermined. The nineteenth century was above all an age in which an adaptive approach was necessary in coming to terms with progress and the consequent redundancy of what were perceived to be medieval religious obscurities. It is also vital to appreciate the shifting balance between what began to be regarded as human rather than divine activity. The realities of a scientific era were underlined by the reforming Charles Finney. Addressing a London audience in 1851, he extolled the "spirit of enquiry", emphasising the need for "continued investigation and change of views and practice corresponding with increasing knowledge". This necessarily involved appropriate reconstruction of

---

[22] The 'Broad Church' was less a 'movement' than a largely English theological 'mood' of the mid-nineteenth century. Tending to revolve around F.D. Maurice, it looked for its pioneering influence to Samuel Taylor Coleridge, though Erskine was revered by many of the group. Gowler unhesitatingly includes Erskine in the Broad Church group, (*No Second-hand Religion*, 202). Storr described the Broad Church as "characterised by the spirit of free inquiry in theology, by a ready acceptance of the results of biblical criticism, and by the desire to separate the kernel from the traditional husk of Christianity. All its members possessed that wider spiritual outlook which was the chief quality of Coleridge's mind", (*English Theology*, 333). John Kent suggests a wider 'Broad Church' which included Schleiermacher, Maurice, Horace Bushnell, and Kierkegaard. They were "neither strictly liberal nor strictly orthodox (the word 'conservative' would often be more appropriate)...who, when they appealed to religious experience would confirm what they still regarded as divine revelation, not provide a substitute", (*The End of the Line? The Development of Christian Theology in the Last Two Centuries* [London: SCM Press, 1982], 43). Other members of the English Broad Church 'movement' included F.W. Robertson, Charles Kingsley, the Arnolds, Benjamin Jowett, Dean Stanley, and perhaps James Baldwin Brown. From Scotland Alexander Ewing was probably its foremost representative, whilst figures such as John McLeod Campbell, A.J. Scott, Norman Macleod, and George MacDonald were entirely sympathetic. Campbell's *The Nature of the Atonement,* published in 1856, was considered almost as an 'authority', (George Smeaton, *Christ's Doctrine of the Atonement* [1870] [Edinburgh: Banner of Truth, 1991], 434). There were many close personal ties between the group's members.

theology to achieve the "Christian consistency" demanded by the century.[23] Such was the emerging scenario which challenged the pioneering spirit of Thomas Erskine in reactionary early nineteenth-century Scotland.

Though a leading systematic theologian has recently hailed Erskine as "one of the finest and most creative minds on the British theological scene in the early nineteenth century", remarkably he "has all but been forgotten".[24] This study suggests that the nature and extent of Erskine's "influence on the development of British theology in the nineteenth century has only recently been recognized and is still to be thoroughly explored".[25] Erskine has most often been compared to the nineteenth century's "great spiritual mentor" and pioneer, Samuel Taylor Coleridge (1772-1834), especially in his efforts to demonstrate the trustworthiness of human feelings and the authenticity of personal experience as a basis for reasonable faith, responding to the Enlightenment dichotomy between faith and reason.[26] But it is remarkable that Coleridge's important and influential *Aids to Reflection* was published only in 1825, well after the appearance of Erskine's significant early works, *Remarks on the Internal Evidence for the Truth of Revealed Religion* [1820] and *An Essay on Faith* [1822]. Even contemporaries who remained strongly hostile to his views nevertheless agreed after his death that Thomas Erskine was a man "whose views and influence have not yet received the attention they deserve", and that "undoubtedly, there is much in the writings of Erskine that is of great value and importance".[27]

We suggest that Erskine indeed exercised timely influence through his innovative approach to soteriological thought, and through acknowledgement and appropriation of broader strands of thought may legitimately be regarded as a significant figure in facilitating and inspiring a nineteenth-century shift towards more enlightened evangelical theological awareness. Undoubtedly he anticipated certain liberal trends. Those who, like John Henry Newman, praised Erskine's spirituality, but feared for the tendency of his ideas in the hands of others, had an important point.[28] Nevertheless,

---

[23] *Lectures on Systematic Theology* (London: William Tegg, 1851), viii, x.

[24] Hart, *Teaching Father*, 1. Mrs Oliphant suggested that although Erskine was "so very well known to all religious thinkers, [he] was not perhaps a sufficiently salient figure, to have outlived oblivion with the general", (*A Memoir of the Life of John Tulloch* [Edinburgh and London: William Blackwood and Sons, 1888], 217).

[25] David Young, *F.D. Maurice and Unitarianism* (Oxford: Clarendon Press, 1992), 131.

[26] Reardon, *Religious Thought*, 294. Henry Henderson noted in 1899 that Erskine had been described as "the Scottish Coleridge", (*Erskine*, 92).

[27] J. Stuart Candlish, "Thomas Erskine of Linlathen", *British and Foreign Evangelical Review*, XXII, LXXXIII (January, 1873), 106, 125.

[28] "Such is the theology to which Mr. E.'s principle is found to lead...a theology...which violently robs the Christian Creed of all it contains...", ("On the Introduction of Rationalistic Principles into Religion", Tract No. 73, *Tracts for the Times*, by

Erskine's vision and genius lay in creatively holding together traditional orthodoxy and post-Enlightenment thought in a rapidly transforming era, when massive winds of intellectual change were blowing in the aftermath of the French Revolution. The sheer breadth of formative impulses he took on board made Erskine a supremely eclectic thinker in what was a typically eclectic age, when novel and complex interplay between philosophy and theology was rapidly evolving.[29] Fuelled by the ideas of Kant and Schelling, Christianity was actually in danger of becoming little more than a popular form of philosophical expression, or a stage in the process of historical development towards 'universal truth'. A critical Enlightenment heritage, Unitarianism, Evangelical Pietism, Romanticism, and German 'neology', were all contributory factors.[30] In England, Pietism *succeeded* rationalistic Deism, whilst in Germany the Aufklärung movement followed and consolidated Pietism. The tendency to displace Lutheran and Calvinist forensic notions of salvation with ethical, individual, and experiential aspects of grace and conversion was encouraged by the Pietists, and taken up in England notably by Methodists, Quakers, and William Law.[31]

Erskine simultaneously embodied and transcended his context, which was not narrowly restricted to Scotland. His vision was always wider. Hitherto, his novel ideas have not been sufficiently examined and understood in conjunction with the broader theological and philosophical formative nineteenth-century context out of which they were forged. Erskine's development corresponded with the period when "the most active minds of the period were…at once emancipated and reconstructive. In the very conservatism of the time there was an element of novelty".[32] Crucially, Erskine eschewed the fashion for heterodoxy, even though he passed beyond the narrow limitations of orthodoxy as defined by contemporary Scottish Federal Calvinism. He undoubtedly retained to the end a passionate, experi-

---

Members of the University of Oxford, Vol.III, for 1835-6 [3rd edition] [London: J.G. & F. Rivington, 1838], 45).

[29] In a sardonic note entitled "Difficulty of Finding a Characteristic Name for the Followers of Mr. Erskine", the reactionary Archibald Robertson complained about those "who have embraced Mr. Erskine's system" and suggested that "to call them *Campbellites*, *Erskinites*, or by the name of any other person of notoriety among them, would be conferring too much individual honour". Rather, "they may be called *Eclectics*, for they embrace part of the sentiments of many different sects", (*A Vindication of "The Religion of the Land" from Misrepresentation* [Edinburgh: William Whyte, 1830], 245).

[30] Roy Porter has described Romanticism as "what is left of the soul when the religion has been drained out of it", *The Enlightenment* (Basingstoke: Palgrave, 2001), 66. David Young considers that none of the 'Scottish circle' of Erskine, A.J. Scott, Campbell, and George MacDonald had "an alien spirit to mid-nineteenth-century Unitarians", (*Maurice*, 8).

[31] Paul O'Callaghan, *Fides Christi*, (Dublin: Four Courts Press, 1997), 58-9.

[32] Anon., "The Church and Theology of Germany During the Nineteenth Century", *National Review*, XVIII (January-April, 1864), 194.

mental, and evangelical Christian faith. But he felt it necessary to challenge tradition by requiring it to satisfy the demands of experience, rather than vice versa. Though the mode of its outworking was very different and opposite in direction to that of Erskine, the English Tractarian movement which emerged in the 1830s, was rooted in a parallel response to the same early nineteenth-century milieu.

Essentially an 'amateur' theologian, Erskine's weaknesses included a tendency to focus intensely and exclusively on certain fixed ideas which caught his imagination. The spontaneity, intuitive reflection, and frequent augmentative repetition of thoughts, produced a consequent prolixity of literary style which makes his published works difficult both to read and to systematise. Nevertheless, he displayed remarkable creativity in responding to the challenge of the rapidly changing British and European environment, especially from within the constraints of his Scottish conservative tradition. Erskine's soteriology informed his entire theological outlook, and therefore it is instructive to evaluate the influences which particularly shaped his soteriological development, since it was here above all that he subtly began to reconstruct traditional ideas whilst seeking somehow to remain within the bounds of orthodoxy.[33]

Erskine's Scottish Setting

In the 1820's the publication of Erskine's works "fell like bomb shells into the ill defended, and poorly garrisoned theological citadel" of the Kirk.[34]

Erskine was one of the first of his generation in Scotland to articulate effectively genuine popular spiritual unrest, and voice alternatives to orthodox interpretations of soteriology, by engaging creatively with contemporary theological issues, and by questioning and clarifying what he felt had been obscured by accepted Calvinist orthodoxy – notably the nature and character of God, the atonement, biblicism, conditional salvation, and determinism. In 1897, retrospectively evaluating theological trends in early

---

[33] In 1870, reconsidering the context of Erskine's early writings, Julia Wedgwood reflected the significant shift in nineteenth-century opinion when she informed her readers "Forty years ago the ideas were not only unfamiliar, they seemed presumptuous heresy", (*Teachers*, 65). Concerning Erskine's supposed heterodoxy, Mrs Oliphant referred to his "never-ending expositions of a faith which he made every listener feel to be new, yet which one could not distinguish afterwards to be much different, except in vivid force and realisation, from ordinary Christian belief", (*Tulloch*, 217). John Tulloch himself noted Erskine's subtle approach, pointing out that he never brought about change by attacking "the dogmas of the Church", but rather "in all his writings, [he] tended quietly to subvert them", (*Movements*, 132).
[34] Anon, "Professor A.J. Scott, M.A.", *Owens College Magazine*, XIII, 3 (June, 1881), 109.

nineteenth-century Scotland, the eminent Church of Scotland theologian, Robert Herbert Story, acknowledged Erskine's innovative role, remarking that Calvinist evangelicalism was unable to satisfy

> the needs of the deepening spiritual consciousness...which could not accept as a veracious theory of the atonement, one which excluded from its scope the vast majority of human beings. The earliest, and in some respects the most deeply spiritual and original, representative of this unrest and wider outlook was a layman, Thomas Erskine of Linlathen.

Story regarded Erskine, together with John McLeod Campbell, as

> the pioneers of the movement, which has ultimately broken the gloomy dominion of the theology that had been so cramped in its growth by the shackles of Westminster that its continued influence would have, sooner or later, extinguished the spiritual and intellectual liberty without which an apostolic ministry becomes impossible.[35]

The prevalent scheme of Federal Calvinism in Scotland emphasised legalistic religion, Christ's work on behalf of the elect, and human covenant response. It tended to limit the focus on divine grace and what Christ has done for us, consequently minimising the implications of Christ's headship and solidarity with humanity through the incarnation.[36] By contrast, Erskine's innovative christology (which substantially informed his soteriology) could be viewed as 're-adherence' to a classical orthodoxy lost sight of in the Calvinist Scotland of his day.[37] He was especially concerned to rediscover the much-needed *relational* aspect of the gospel, believing the fallen condition of mankind was more accurately portrayed less in terms of offence against the majesty and law of God, and more as departure from, and forfeiture of, eternal filial relationship to God. This was fundamental to the truth concerning humanity. Erskine lamented that in the contemporary Scottish church there seemed to be a crucial discrepancy between divine salvific love as portrayed in the gospel, and the characteristically severe view of God popularly entertained, which minimised practical moral influence in peoples' lives. He particularly wanted to reverse the tendency of such an erroneous view of the character of God to cause dichotomy from the work of Christ. Rather, he sought to stress the intimate relationship be-

---

[35] *The Apostolic Ministry in the Scottish Church* (Edinburgh and London: William Blackwood and Sons, 1897), 307-8.

[36] James B. Torrance, "The Contribution of McLeod Campbell to Scottish Theology", *SJT* 26 (1973), 299-302. The *Edinburgh Review* remarked appositely, "Nothing is so heterodox as popular orthodoxy, or the complacent dogmatism in the nineteenth century which supposes itself echoing the creed of the seventeenth...", (CXLVII, 302, [April, 1878], p.389).

[37] Cf., Thomas F. Torrance, *Scottish Theology*, (Edinburgh: T.&T. Clark, 1996), 263.

Introduction

tween Father and Son and the universal love and Fatherhood of God. In 1873, the Free Church leader, J.S. Candlish, acknowledged that the type of Scottish evangelical theology prevalent in Erskine's day tended to be "too one-sidedly intellectual, and to lay too much stress on mere formal orthodoxy". He admitted it stood in stark contrast to the approach of James Fraser of Brea and the theology of the 'Marrow men' in eighteenth-century Scotland which was "warm and emotional, giving prominence to the feelings and affections of the heart as of the very essence of saving faith".[38]

Judging by his contemporary popularity (or notoriety), Erskine successfully managed to engage with traditional soteriological concepts, coherently reinterpreting them to bring out their fuller spiritual depths. After initial welcome, his approach was denounced by a threatened Scottish establishment, though he seemed to be more readily acceptable in the more liberalised England.[39] However, from about the middle of the nineteenth century Scotland began to see a shift of perspective relating to the traditional Westminster standards, hitherto regarded practically as divine authority. Still in 1843 in Scotland, "stiff credal orthodoxy was absolutely in possession, and would not brook any questioning of the Westminster Standards in the slightest degree".[40] But by 1877, John Tulloch could allude to the forces of 'liberalism' invading even "the very citadel of the Free Church itself", with "the current of free thought…running deep and sure in all the Churches".[41] Significantly, Church of Scotland historian, G.D. Henderson, regarded Erskine and Campbell, together with Schleiermacher, F.D. Maurice, Thomas Carlyle, and the Cairds, as responsible for the "collapse of the old orthodoxy".[42]

Despite earlier causes, like the Marrow Controversy of 1720, which had championed greater liberty with regard to, for example, the extent of the atonement, Erskine nevertheless lived during a "renaissance of dogmatic Calvinism"[43] in early nineteenth-century Scotland, where theology had be-

---

[38] Candlish, "Thomas Erskine", 109.

[39] Theology developed along lines "far more rich and diversified in England, not because the original theology of the Church of England is really different from that of Scotland, but because the intellectual and Christian life of England has been so much larger, richer, and more fruitful than Scotland", (Anon, *Edinburgh Review*, CXLVII, 302 [April, 1878], 389).

[40] J.R. Fleming, *A History of the Church in Scotland 1843-1874* (Edinburgh: T.&T. Clark, 1927), 7.

[41] John Tulloch, "Religious Thought in Scotland", *Contemporary Review*, XXIX (March, 1877), 544, 551; cf., Andrew L. Drummond and James Bulloch, *The Church in Victorian Scotland, 1843-1874* (Edinburgh: Saint Andrew Press, 1975), 276-7, 299-307.

[42] G.D. Henderson, "Arminianism in Scotland", *London Quarterly or Holborn Review* (October, 1932), 502-3.

[43] Drummond and Bulloch, *Scottish Church*, 215-16.

come particularly entrenched, defensive, reactionary, and polemical. Erskine was a pioneering visionary within this context:

> Living in a stormy age, an age of change, convulsion and tumult, those who framed the Church polity of Scotland clung intensely to the thought of a supreme king and governor. They took as their leading idea 'The Lord reigneth', and the whole of their theological system was pervaded by that thought. It was governmental, founded on the relation of a king towards his subjects, as that relation was understood in those days, rather than on that of a father towards his children. God was the omnipotent sovereign against whom man had raised the standard of rebellion. Only after he was reconciled to his rightful Lord, or rather after his rightful Lord had become reconciled to him, did the attribute of the sovereign merge into the relationship of the father…The theory of the atonement, with its 'forensic arrangements', the doctrines of predestination, and election, all fit naturally into a scheme of theology the underlying thought of which is 'The Lord reigneth'. Such a theological system must necessarily be of a stern and solemn character…[However] the personal relation of God to man…is before the governmental…The first men in Scotland who realised this in any vivid manner, and who took their stand upon it, were McLeod Campbell of Row and Thomas Erskine of Linlathen…[44]

Erskine and Campbell did not really belong to the ongoing classical debate between Arminians and Calvinists. They had moved on from seventeenth-century polemics, though inevitably they were liable to be misunderstood by both extremes. However, their inauguration of the period of theological transition began in the early part of the century. It got under way more slowly in Scotland than in England, but inevitably it saw the gradual undermining of the authority of Westminster orthodoxy with the emergence of a new type of intuitive religion which was essentially spiritual, rationalistic and moral. It reflected a more subjective nineteenth-century mood which emphasised affective, moral and spiritual changes deemed to be appropriate in the religious believer. Erskine was one of its chief architects, synthesising current trends, and unlike his reactionary contemporaries John Henry Newman and Andrew Thomson, appealing not to traditional extrinsic authorities of Church or Standards, but to inward authority, based on conscience, practical knowledge, ethical awareness, and deep personal experience. For Erskine, ecclesiastical institutions and traditions had to be living and serve to illuminate truth. They were not to be received merely as "authority, calling for submission". Their necessary function he saw rather as "addressing the spiritual reason, calling for sympathy and consentient co-operation".[45] If they did not achieve that aim, they might happily be dis-

---

[44] Lees, "Ewing", 359-60.
[45] "The Holy Eucharist", in *Ewing-II*, 63-4; *Sp.Order*, 91. Erskine had little sympathy with the 'authoritarianism' of the Oxford Movement, or what he referred to as "Pusey-

carded. Erskine was one of the first of his generation, certainly in Scotland, to dare openly to challenge constructively the received religion of the day.

Erskine and John McLeod Campbell

The 'Row movement' of 1828-32 in western Scotland, forever associated in Scottish theological history with Thomas Erskine, John McLeod Campbell, A.J. Scott and Edward Irving, represented an important setting for a much larger picture. It was wistfully suggested after Erskine's death that "Scotland has known no other so profound spiritual movement during the present century".[46]

The events and personalities associated with Row, where Campbell was parish minister, were vigorously condemned and rejected at the time as a threat to religious and social stability. Complaints were made about the "strange and novel doctrines...supported by benevolent pretensions and specious arguments...subversive of all established opinions" which were laid at the door of Erskine's 'system'.[47] But Row was the catalyst for a much more fundamental and reconstructive theological movement than was augured by the fleeting sensationalism which surrounded the attendant charismatic phenomena. Erskine and Campbell were soon to relativise the manifestations, and to disown the millennial authoritarianism which characterised Irving's derivative Catholic Apostolic Church. Erskine's own prophetic warning concerning the 'evil deeds' carried out by an outraged Kirk against "her best prophet", Campbell, was seen by himself and others as coming calamitously true in his lifetime in the form of the Disruption.[48] Erskine himself never forgot that "revival of religion", claiming thirty years later that "the witness which was then borne has been seed which the Lord has blessed to many".[49] Row remained a potent and inspirational symbol, evoking Romantic religious associations for Erskine until the end of his life.[50]

Together, Erskine and Campbell were hailed by their adherents in Scotland in the last quarter of the nineteenth century as having influenced the

---

ism", (Letter to Mrs Stirling, 19 January 1838, *Letters-I*, 300; Letter to an unknown correspondent, 30 January 1841, *Letters-II*, 198-203).

[46] Shairp's obituary of Thomas Erskine in the *Scotsman* (31 March 1870).

[47] Anon., *The Port Glasgow Miracles. Strictures on a Publication entitled 'The Gifts of the Spirit' by Thomas Erskine, Esq. Advocate, Author of the 'Unconditional freeness of the Gospel'* (Hamburg: Hartwig & Müller, 1830), 2.

[48] Shairp, "Reminiscences", *Letters-II*, 361-2.

[49] Letter, to Mrs Story, 28 November 1859, *Letters-II*, 275.

[50] Julia Wedgwood long remembered "the deep tones of his voice as he recalled 'the shores of the Gareloch' and his early wanderings there at a time when 'the invisible seemed pressing into the visible...", (*Gurney*, 15).

reinterpretation of Christian thought concerning the atonement and revelation "above any other".[51] Whilst this is not the place to debate the question of 'who influenced who', advocates of Campbell have, despite the chronological priority of Erskine, and the similarity of many of their views, argued strongly against Campbell's dependence upon Erskine.[52] However, church historian Alexander MacEwen, evaluating Campbell in the late 1870s, considered that "You will find his best ideas in a very readable form in the letters of Erskine of Linlathen".[53] It is notable that many of Campbell's later developed views were already evident in seed form in Erskine before they met in about 1827-28, Campbell having already read Erskine's early works.[54] During the years leading up to Campbell's deposition in 1831, he was regarded by his opponents as one of the 'Erskineites', or the

---

[51] Lees, "Ewing", 364-5.

[52] For example, Eugene Garrett Bewkes, *Legacy of a Christian Mind; John McLeod Campbell, eminent contributor to theological thought* (Philadelphia: Judson Press, 1937), 6-7. Donald Winslow's half-hearted suggestion that Erskine may have been the 'victim' or 'dupe' of Campbell seems based on a misreading of the sources, (*Thomas Erskine: Advocate for the Character of God* [Lanham, Maryland: University Press of America, 1993], 20). On the other hand, Vernon Storr affirmed Erskine was responsible for initiating the reconstruction of the doctrine of atonement and "was the inspirer of John McLeod Campbell, whose volume, *The Nature of the Atonement*, would probably have never seen the light if it had not been for Erskine's earlier writings on the subject", (*English Theology,* 355). By 1830, the *London Evangelical Magazine* regarded Campbell in terms of "his known adoption of the religious opinions of Mr. Erskine…the new Caledonian school of theology", analysing Campbell's sermons to demonstrate the 'erroneous' teachings of his "leader", (London Evangelical Magazine, (ed.), *Exposure of Certain Errors Put Forth in "Notes and Recollections of Two Sermons by the Rev. Mr. Campbell of Row," being Extracts from a Review of said Sermons in the London Evangelical Magazine* [Greenock: John Hislop, 1830], 8, 15). Campbell's own comment in a letter to Erskine in 1868 is significant, "You are (not to speak of anything else) the older friend as well as the older man, and had a name in theology when I was yet a student of Divinity", (*Memorials*, II, 208). It seems most likely that Erskine, Scott, and Campbell flowed in a kindred, mutual, albeit independently assimilated, contemporary reconstructive theological stream. Campbell remarked retrospectively, "That historical independence which we mark when two minds, working apart and without any interchange of thought, arrive at the same conclusions, is always an interesting and striking fact when it occurs; and it did occur as to Scott and myself; and also as to Mr. Erskine and me, and I believe too, as to Mr. Erskine and Mr. Scott", (Robert Herbert Story, *Memoir of the Life of the Rev. Robert Story* [Cambridge: Macmillan and Co., 1862], 152).

[53] David S. Cairns, *Life and Times of Alexander Robertson MacEwen* (London: Hodder & Stoughton, 1925), 80.

[54] Campbell had at least read *Evidence* by early 1826, Donald Campbell (ed.), *Reminiscences and Reflections, Referring to His Early Ministry in the Parish of Row, 1825-1831. By the late John McLeod Campbell, D.D.* (London: Macmillan and Co., 1873), 16).

Introduction 15

party of which Erskine was distinctly seen as ringleader.[55] The "Neology of the Erskinites" became a popular term of abuse.[56] Nevertheless, whilst we believe the evidence supports Erskine as the earlier pioneer, visionary, and innovator, nobody would argue that out of the two, Campbell was not the true 'theologian'.[57]

Objectives of this Book

The eighteenth century had bequeathed to its successor a milieu of human-centred 'progress', 'improvement', and 'innovation', though religion remained isolated, reactionary to change and resistant to new perspectives, especially in Scotland. Thomas Erskine inevitably found himself operating within a theological and philosophical context which was questioning how, and indeed whether, saving knowledge of a transcendent God could be possible. We believe that in nineteenth-century Britain, and especially Scotland, Erskine was instrumental in helping achieve "the same reconstruction of the doctrine of salvation which had been effected by Kant and Schleiermacher".[58] Somehow, Erskine was working intellectually in parallel to the great continental theological minds of the time. The aim of this study is to investigate how Thomas Erskine came to understand and reshape understanding of nineteenth-century soteriology, notably by appropriating and linking philosophical and intellectual ideas to religion, and to assess the nature and extent of its innovatory character, as measured particularly by contemporary perception. This therefore represents a historical/ contextual study of Erskine's contribution to the process of nineteenth-century radical theological reconstruction, involving the interaction of Christianity with philosophy, science, culture and society. We shall seek to demonstrate that Erskine was a fresh and independent thinker whose originality was, how-

---

[55] An anonymous article in *ECI*, XXX, IX (September, 1831), 610, was entitled, "Brainerd versus the Erskineites", and referred to "the Society for diffusing Mr. Erskine's doctrines". William Hamilton commented how his "promising and active young friend, Mr. Campbell of Row, was, by Mr. Thomas Erskine and others perverted from the truth", (James Hamilton (ed.), *Life and Remains of the Late Rev. William Hamilton,* in 2 volumes [Glasgow: Maurice Ogle & Son, 1836], I, 199). Campbell was apparently seen by many contemporaries as "propagating some of Mr. Erskine's most objectionable doctrines", (see appendix entitled "Row Heresy" attached to the British Library's copy of Peter Brotherston, *A Brief View of Faith* [Edinburgh: William Whyte, 1828], 316).

[56] Anon., "Review of 'The Morning Watch', No.VI", *ECI*, XXX, II (February, 1831), 121.

[57] See Shairp's comparison of Erskine and Campbell in "Reminiscences", *Letters-II*, 363-4.

[58] Edward Caldwell Moore, *An Outline of the History of Christian Thought Since Kant* (London: Duckworth, 1912), 201.

ever, qualified by conscious and unconscious tendencies to parallel, or draw widely on, contemporary eclectic sources to stimulate a creative genius pre-eminently employed in their interpretation and application to concurrent soteriological issues. We therefore include within our study investigation of sources considered to be formative and influential in the evolution of Erskine's thought, together with examination of relevant parallel theological developments to illustrate the reconstructive context in which he operated.

Erskine's publishing career effectively spanned the years 1820 – 1837. After a long gap, during which we have only an incomplete record of his private correspondence,[59] a collection of fragments was published posthumously at the author's request in 1871. Erskine was no systematic theologian, and the task of presenting the various elements of his theological 'system' is a complex one defying organised exposition. Neither is the task of assessing the extent of Erskine's originality straightforward. He rarely cited his sources, and we must look to close historical and contemporary parallels for evidence of apparent inspiration and influence. Previous studies of Erskine have tended to adopt a chronological form because "there is no immediately obvious point of departure, no one fundamental axiom around which all others revolve and upon which they all in turn depend".[60] Such approaches tend to be theologically restrictive.[61] The present study examines key elements of Erskine's overall soteriology, highlighting Erskine's concern with the mode of acquisition of salvific knowledge. Adopting a largely thematic approach, it seeks to get to grips with his 'system' as an internally consistent whole. Taking a broad view, we attempt to earth him in his context, appreciating in a more ordered format Erskine's historical and theological significance, identifying the forces that shaped his conceptual evolution, and assessing his anticipation of later nineteenth- and twentieth-century theological developments. Erskine's entire range of published and unpublished writing is considered, including previously neglected manuscript and contemporary review material. Attention has also been given to the significant, yet often missed, variations between the various editions of Erskine's works, especially *The Brazen Serpent*. Whilst not claiming to be exhaustive, a major bibliographical objective has been to incorporate a comprehensive record of works relating to Thomas Erskine. Though purely biographical detail is minimised, we allude to relevant historical developments to root Erskine's theological thought within its British and European context. The overall aim has been to examine Erskine's ap-

---

[59] William Hanna's version is highly edited; also many identificatory names have been removed. Sadly, most original manuscripts are lost.
[60] Hart, *Teaching Father*, 18.
[61] A comprehensive biographical and chronological study like Needham's *Thomas Erskine* found its scope necessarily curtailed, covering the period only up to 1837.

Introduction 17

proach to the challenge of championing divine revelation and salvation in dialogue with a rapidly changing and sceptical intellectual environment, whilst simultaneously seeking to remain within the bounds of orthodox religion. In particular, we investigate the novel epistemological aspects of Erskine's exploration and treatment of the dynamics of salvific apprehension. Whilst the evident chronological development within Erskine's thought is acknowledged, we consider his body of work as an integral unity, harmonising earlier ideas with later developments. Towards the end of his life, Erskine pursued elucidation and explication, both in the clearer conversation style of his private correspondence, and in the posthumous *The Spiritual Order*. Accordingly, particular use is made of these sources.

The conflation and interlocking of Erskine's major soteriological themes inevitably involved key elements of his theological scheme recurring within different contexts. Some thematic repetition is therefore unavoidable to elucidate how Erskine understood his system as holding together. It is our contention that, however much we may sometimes find Erskine's logic and approach to scriptural exposition unsatisfactory to twenty first-century ears, nevertheless he remained a largely self-consistent, popular, influential, and highly innovative interpreter and defender of Christianity at a time when few evangelicals were capable of responding seriously to the challenges posed by a sceptical, inquiring and revolutionary age. It is therefore an associated objective of this study to estimate and reassess Erskine's overall significance for the development of soteriological thought in the nineteenth century.

Part 1 of the book, representing approximately two thirds of the whole, is devoted mainly to a study of the detailed *internal* innovatory soteriological approach of Erskine, primarily concerned with how he understood God 'initiating', 'sustaining', and accomplishing the work of salvation in Christ,[62] and which to date has been neither systematically examined nor sufficiently appreciated. The extent of Erskine's perceived theological reconstruction is also gauged from contemporary reaction. Part 2 concentrates more specifically on the *external* reconstructive setting within which Erskine developed and filtered his soteriological ideas, albeit through the medium of his Scottish experience. We assess more closely those primary sources which supposedly inspired Erskine's reconstructive genius. In particular, we examine Erskine's contribution in the light of his direct or indirect connection and interrelation with his wider cultural European setting, which we believe has largely gone unrecognised. We aim to show how his work was harmonious with other concurrent developments, and requires appropriate recognition fully to appreciate Erskine's true significance.

---

[62] John McIntyre, *The Shape of Soteriology* (Edinburgh: T.&T. Clark, 1992), 17.

PART 1

THOMAS ERSKINE AS ECLECTIC
SOTERIOLOGICAL INNOVATOR

CHAPTER 2

Introducing Erskine's Soteriological Thought

The first part of the book examines Thomas Erskine's consciousness of the nature of the soteriological task of reformulating, for the benefit and demands of his contemporaries, traditional understandings of classic Christian dogmas concerning the nature and apprehension of God, location of authority, revelation, orthodoxy, nature and extent of salvation, and the doctrine of atonement. It seeks to highlight Erskine's innovative and reconstructive method, including the eclectic appropriation of theological/ philosophical concepts, concluding with a select review of both contemporary and present-day responses to the controversial issues he raised. We concentrate in Part 1 on the *internal* consistency and presentation of Erskine's soteriological approach, and observe how it was creatively designed to respond to the challenges of his era.

Reminiscing in about 1865, Erskine concisely summarised the motivation behind his context-driven quest to find in Christianity a salvifically valid presentation of divine truth:

> I must discern in the history itself a light and truth which will meet the demands both of my reason and conscience...however true the history may be, it cannot be of any moral or spiritual benefit to me until I apprehend its truth and meaning. This and nothing less is what I require...for the only real instruction is that which helps us to perceive the truth and meaning of things, not that which merely asserts that such and such things are true and insists on our accepting them as such...I was brought up from my childhood in the belief of the supernatural and miraculous in connection with religion, especially in connection with the person and life and teaching of Jesus Christ; and like many in the present day I came, in after life, to have misgivings as to the credibility of this wonderful history. But the patient study of the narrative and of its place in the history of the world, and the perception of a light in it which entirely satisfied my reason and conscience, finally overcame these misgivings and forced on me the conviction of its truth.[1]

---

[1] *Sp.Order*, 81-3.

From the publication of his first major work in 1820, Erskine passionately believed that a religion's authenticity must reside in its ability to account satisfactorily for the human condition; firstly, spiritual awareness and moral sense, as confirmed by the existence of conscience; secondly, self-awareness, necessarily involving the reality of struggle, sin and suffering. In effect, like Kant, Rousseau, and many nineteenth-century thinkers, he was motivated by the search for a satisfactory contemporary theodicy, though Erskine strove to resist its secularisation.[2]

Reflecting an Enlightenment optimism in contrast to the prevailing gloomy estimation of humanity in Calvinist Scotland, Erskine was convinced (confirmed by his study of Paul's interpretation of Habbakuk in Romans 1.16-17), of the universal, constitutional, human consciousness of a divine righteous purpose for humanity in the "higher order of things".[3] He showed that the existence of individual personality further proved there must be a *personal* divine originator of that purpose, who desired to reveal both his eternal salvific loving purpose and corresponding character. Erskine developed his conception of a God whose character and eternal unceasing objective was the pursuit of universal perfection in righteousness, which he defined as "the idea of pure unselfish love".[4] His portrayal of the divine nature was bold and revolutionary in contemporary Scotland, and necessarily underpinned his entire reconstructive soteriological framework. As the loving initiator of salvation, God did not need to be reconciled to humanity. The importance of Christ's work, and the purpose of the incarnation, according to Erskine, required a new perspective. It was a *prospective* more than *retrospective* one, emphasising the reconciling of humanity to God through ethical regeneration, not merely satisfying God's wounded sense of justice. 'Incarnation' was not to be understood merely as dogma relating to the second person of the Trinity, but as everything for which Jesus Christ stood, the redemptive nature of his life as a whole, including his sacrifice, work of atonement and resurrection. Simple evangelical belief in God's loving purpose he believed was itself salvific and transformational.[5]

In contrast to what he regarded as prevailing Calvinist emphasis on God as *Judge*, Erskine's primary understanding of God as *Father* implied a novel relational theology emphasising vital notions of love, grace and trust, with radical new implications for the balance between law and gospel. Of

---

[2] Cf., Bernard Reardon, *Kant as Philosophical Theologian* (Totowa, New Jersey: Barnes & Noble, 1988), 79-83; Mark Larrimore (ed.), *The Problem of Evil* (Oxford: Blackwell, 2001), 210-15, 224-33; Roy Porter, *Enlightenment: Britain and the Creation of the Modern World* (London: Allen Lane, Penguin, 2000), 445.
[3] *Sp.Order*, 47-9.
[4] *Sp.Order*, 235.
[5] *Sp.Order*, 247.

paramount importance was Erskine's abiding motivation to overturn and reinterpret the contemporary alienating impression in Scotland of God as 'terrible', 'fearful', 'condemning', and 'unapproachable', and to re-establish divine trustworthiness based on love. Rejecting penal, retributory or deterrent theories of punishment, he regarded the question of human-divine accountability in such a way as to minimise the judicial aspect and emphasise instead a free-will obedience emanating from a relationship of love in which the threat of punishment was not a factor influencing response and behaviour. Crucially, Erskine considered that our primary understanding of the character of God fundamentally affected our view of whether his salvific purpose towards us was 'probationary' or, as he sought to reinterpret it, 'educative'.

In the aftermath of the Enlightenment, seeking to demonstrate the essential reasonableness, moral suitability and social utility of religion offered the most promising route for Christian apologetics, though it could imply a tendency to reduce theology to ethics by collapsing distinctions between religion and morality. In this way, it was hoped, potential conflict between historical criticism, science, and religion might be avoided. Erskine regarded his task as essentially apologetic and ethical, demonstrating that Christianity conformed to the human moral conscience, commended itself to reason, answered fundamental human needs, and worked out in practice.[6]

In a radical step for Scotland, Erskine insisted religious authority was essentially inward. He remained adamant that conventional and institutional authority was ineffectual in itself to produce salvific righteousness. There could be no "true or profitable conviction possible, except through the reason and conscience", and certainly not through "any outward authority whatever", unless it clearly contained "reasonableness and righteousness" which could be profitably apprehended so as to 'do us good and sink into our soul'. Erskine saw it as his objective "always to arrive at this apprehension".[7] His essential aim was to emphasise the harmony between Christianity and the moral realities both outside us and within us. For Erskine, the proper criterion of the truth of Christianity was not primarily historical criticism or any external authority or dogma, but rather the inward awareness of 'moral obligation'. In one sense, this could sound remarkably like a 'Christianised' Kantianism. God revealed himself in the example of Christ for the purpose of our salvific moral development or 'perfection'. This necessarily involved bringing our own wills and affections into line with the divinely-originated universal sense of moral obligation to which

---

[6] In recent times, Hugo Meynell has attempted the same objective in *Is Christianity True?* (London: Geoffrey Chapman, 1994).
[7] Letter to Bishop Ewing, 3 December 1864, *Ewing-I*, 54.

humanity aspires. Hence, "the object of Christianity is to bring the character of man into harmony with that of God".[8]

In this belief, Erskine was driven primarily by an anthropology which assumed a universally redemptive incarnational christology. Principal J.C. Shairp of St. Andrews, commenting on Erskine's 'first principle' concerning 'the conscience as the Christ in each man', asserted Erskine's supreme conviction

> that all true thought about God would be found to harmonise with all that is truest and highest in the conscience and the affections of man. It was the desire himself to see and to make others see this harmony, to see that Christian doctrine was that which alone meets the cravings of heart and conscience, – it was this desire which animated him in all the books he wrote, and in all the many conversations he carried on.[9]

For Erskine, salvation was never a 'one-off' experience, or status. Rather, his re-working of the doctrine tended to equate salvation with *sanctification* – a continual 'sympathetic', responsive, existential salvific process towards entire holiness. Personal sanctification and holiness tended to blend in naturally with nineteenth-century ideas concerning progress and societal improvement.[10] Initially, therefore, Erskine was perceived creatively to appropriate contemporary thought categories in aid of a thoroughgoing Christian apologetic.

Erskine's was an essentially *relational* theology, and this also sounded a new contemporary note. His concern was to convince the world of what, for him, was traditional yet axiomatic: humanity's universal capacity to attain direct communion with God and salvifically participate in divine life, provided they would allow God to impart it by reaching out with experimental faith, acknowledging who he really is. However, Erskine introduced the controversial, novel insistence that Christ dwelt in every person by virtue of an innate, organic relationship to God, deriving from our "original constitution" in the image of God. A latent power within all human beings, Christ came to awaken it by appealing to our intuitive faculties and capacities for apprehension. Within everybody, Erskine maintained, there is a 'Jesus-light' "which is ever calling us upward out of sin into righteousness".[11] He therefore asserted, in the face of Kantian denials, the orthodox belief that direct knowledge of God was possible, not so much as a result of empirical evidence, but rather because God universally reveals himself by means of the 'higher' faculties, such as conscience, faith, and intuition or

---

[8] *Evidence*, 48.
[9] Shairp, "Reminiscences", *Letters-II,* 353, 366.
[10] David Bebbington, *Holiness in Nineteenth-Century England* (Carlisle: Paternoster, 2000), 45.
[11] *Sp.Order*, 164.

inner knowledge. Supremely, to know and believe one's true *relationship* to God was itself the gospel – "the power of God unto salvation" – necessarily involving the spontaneous release of transformational ethical power and motivation, which was of a different order to some Kantian 'moral duty'.[12] Hence, Erskine believed, further radically amending traditional concepts of retribution, 'moral evil' equated to rejection of the gospel which, because it involved self-imposed divine separation ("rejection of forgiving love", necessarily implying eternal misery) represented his only ground for conceiving the possibility of divine condemnation. God himself rejected no-one.[13]

Though unquestionably sincere, Erskine's endeavours to convince sometimes tended to leave the impression of a rather vague and ambiguous mysticism or form of pantheism which echoed similar emergent contemporary philosophical ideas concerning 'universal spirit' and 'consciousness'. He was suspected of indulging in speculative philosophy,[14] and at times appeared reminiscent of the Romantics with their idealistic concept of the human soul as a reflection of the developing universe, and their conclusion that the foundational principles of all truth were to be discovered within it. Parallels with Schleiermacher (1768-1834) were apparent, especially his concept of 'Christian consciousness' involving an experiential sense of redemption through participation and union with Christ, which he construed in terms of the harmony of the soul with the governing laws and principles of the universe.[15]

In constructing a contemporary theodicy and apologetic system, it was a short step for Erskine from controversially rejecting penal substitutionary atonement theories to embracing a revolutionary universalistic, moral, salvific vision. From this perspective, he enunciated a novel, universal, divine 'spiritual order', in contrast to prevailing human and world 'disorder', which could be embraced merely through the supernatural power of individual revelation. It reached its most mature expression in the posthumously published *The Spiritual Order*. Platonic dualism and Kantian concepts underly Erskine's eclectic, philosophical account of it.[16] To grasp his otherwise obscure and mystical spiritual dynamics, it is essential to comprehend this real divine 'spiritual order' to which humanity is necessarily organically related, and on which it should be dependent. This 'higher or-

---

[12] *Evidence*, 124, quoting Romans 1.16, cf., *Sp.Order*, 23-4, 260-1.

[13] *Freeness* [1870 edition], 157, cf., *Extracts*, 1.

[14] E.g., Andrew Thomson, *The Doctrine of Universal Pardon Considered and Refuted* (Edinburgh: William Whyte and Co., 1830), 456, 471-2 (footnote).

[15] Friedrich Schleiermacher, *The Christian Faith* [1830] (Edinburgh: T.&T. Clark, 1989), §100, 425-31; Anon., "The Church and Theology of Germany During the Nineteenth Century", *National Review*, XVIII (January-April, 1864), 210-11.

[16] *Sp.Order*, 11-15, 200.

der', theologically akin to the 'kingdom of God', contained its own laws and supernatural ethical power, the nature of which must be known and understood through the 'higher part of our being', before it could be entered into. Our 'conscious moral nature' tells us of its existence. Informing his entire soteriological reinterpretation, in effect, for Erskine, salvation became deliverance from 'disorder', rather than deliverance from 'punishment' or providential suffering, which remained intrinsically efficacious in dealing with disorder.

CHAPTER 3

Re-educating Perceptions of God

Introduction

The nineteenth century was characterised from the outset by a mood of moral approbation. Responding to contemporary questions concerning the supposed 'morality' of God's character, Erskine had a particular concern for his own countrymen to refute the prevalent notion of God as "a Sovereign without any moral attribute, [in which] man was dealt with as a mere creature of necessity, without any real responsibility".[1] He accordingly set about reformulating traditional soteriological concepts and terminology where necessary in an endeavour to re-educate popular understanding of God's character, and hence the status of salvation itself. Perceptions that he endeavoured to retain, or worse, to render flexible and ambiguous, the language of soteriological orthodoxy, whilst re-working the underlying doctrines did not, however, endear him to his critics.[2]

Despite a simultaneous revival of seventeenth-century Federal Calvinist heritage in Scotland, serious concerns relating to traditional perceptions of God had begun to arise in the early part of the century in Britain. Inspired by the *Westminster Confession,* its tendency was to portray God as a Judge and Lawgiver, who could only become a Father to human beings provided his requirements could be satisfied. Predictions that this traditional but nevertheless popular concept of God was to have "problematic and deleterious effects in later Scottish theology", were about to be fulfilled.[3] Erskine's pioneering initiative in seeking constructively to redress the theo-

---

[1] *Election*, 5.
[2] Irving's assistant, David Brown, accused Erskine, together with Irving, and Campbell, of re-defining inter alia, *Substitution, Imputation, Sacrifice, Satisfaction, Atonement, Reconciliation, Redemption,* and *Sanctification,* ("Letter to a Friend Entangled in Error", *ECI,* II, III [March, 1833], 146-7).
[3] Torrance, *Scottish Theology*, 133.

logical balance was initially almost without contemporary precedent in Scotland. But he succeeded in igniting a spark which subsequently became a flame. He suggested that the *justice* of God had become confused in the popular mind with "the justice of a sheriff-substitute", that is, it was concerned solely with "the punishment of offenders" instead of, what was axiomatic to Erskine, that God's justice was to do positively with "the righteousness and regeneration of the creature".[4] If people were ultimately to be judged on account of their responsible choices, it became imperative therefore, based on Erskine's understanding of the God of the Bible, that God should plainly be seen as a judge of equality and righteousness,

> placing himself as it were at the bar of their consciences, and claiming from them a judgment testifying to his righteousness, and clearing him of all inequality, and that not on the ground that his righteousness is above their understanding, – far less on the ground that he has a sovereign right to do as He pleases, – but on the ground that his righteousness is such as men can judge of, and because it is clear and plain to that principle of judgment within them, by which they approve or condemn their own actings, and the actings of their fellow-men.[5]

The Cruciality of Divine Character

In contrast to the previous one, the nineteenth century developed strongly dynamic immanentist ideas of God, influenced by Romantic subjectivity and evolutionary and anthropological considerations which required fundamental changes to conventional perceptions of the creator-creation relationship. Traditional static concepts of an external transcendent God who created by mere decree were declining rapidly. Erskine was sympathetic with such trends, considering it of overriding importance for the nature and character of God to be correctly understood, together with how such understanding impacted humanity. Desiring to preserve evident points of contact between God and humanity, his entire theology developed from this crucial starting-point.[6] In line with the increasingly dominant sentiment of the new century to view God less as an authoritarian figure, though still a novel perspective in Scotland, it was self-evident to Erskine, that God was a purposeful, loving and forgiving Father, whose objective had always been to

---

[4] Letter to Bishop Ewing, 14 November 1865, *Ewing-I,* 65.

[5] *Election,* 5-6.

[6] Towards the end of his life Erskine acknowledged A.J. Scott, and his own exemplary brother James, who died in 1816, as the two main influences on his developing realisation that "all Divine precepts testified to Divine character", and that all "amiable" human characteristics were attributable to God, (Letter to A.J. Scott, 11 February 1864, *Letters-II,* 146-7).

restore humanity to its righteous image through Christ. For Erskine, recognising the unconditionality of divine love was foundational and transformational. But like P.T. Forsyth at the end of the century, he insisted it was necessarily '*holy* love':

> Holy love is the great principle developed in the gospel. It is the union of an infinite abhorrence towards sin, and an infinite love towards the sinner. This mysterious history is the mighty instrument with which the Spirit of God breaks the power of sin in the heart, and establishes holy gratitude and filial dependence.[7]

The problem, as Erskine saw it, was that legalistic Calvinistic Christianity tended to propagate the wrong image of God's character and purpose, and it was this that motivated his bold and revolutionary corrective moral crusade against it:

> It supposes that God's chief relation to man is that of a judge, and that the relations of Father and teacher must suit themselves to it, in subordination to it; whereas I am convinced that it is just the contrary. The forensic system supposes that God made men that He may afterwards judge them; I believe that He judges them that He may teach them, so that His judgments are instructions. I believe that God created man that He might instruct him into a conformity with His own character, and so make him a partner of His own life, the eternal life which is His will or character.[8]

With his insistence on the reality of divine sonship through the Fatherly, universal love of God for fallen humanity, recognition of which became inherently salvific, Erskine mirrored Wesley and the Evangelical Revival,[9] though he knew that Wesley and his message had been largely rejected in Presbyterian Scotland, not least by his uncle, the leader of the Evangelicals in the Church of Scotland, John Erskine (1721-1803).[10] Nevertheless, Er-

---

[7] *Freeness*, 16, cf., Forsyth, *God the Holy Father* [1897] (London: Independent Press, 1957), 3-27.

[8] Letter to Rev. Paton J. Gloag, D.D., March 1858, *Letters-II*, 205.

[9] "The essential doctrine of Wesley was that of the universal love of God as the supreme fact, concerning human life – a fact which carried with it the assurance that all men, however sinful, were called to, might be rendered capable of, and could only be completed in, the life of God's sons. Thus every one to whom Wesley or his followers preached was not merely fallen from Divine sonship, but one still made and destined for the sonship from which he had fallen, incomplete without it, and yet able by the help of the Spirit of God – acting through the revelation to his heart of the universal love of God – to return, in and through Christ, to the wholeness of nature which he had lost by sin," (J. Scott Lidgett, *The Fatherhood of God in Christian Truth and Life* [Edinburgh: T.&T. Clark, 1902], 332).

[10] Henderson, "Arminianism", 500. The 'Marrow men' had also sought to promote the idea of the forgiving, loving, Fatherly heart of God. Officially the 'Marrow' was con-

skine shared the conviction that God's love must be a wholly incarnational experience. It was "the living, quickening principle of our moral being"[11], and Erskine metaphorically represented the divine initiative in organic terms of God seeking to permeate the entirety of human life, both individual and corporate, as a flowing fountain, or sap rising from the root of the vine. He sought to persuade Jane Welsh Carlyle that God's love was "a love that seeks not to please you, not to flatter your superficial feelings, but to bless you by entering your conscience, your will, your inmost soul, and filling you with itself – which is the life of God – the holy will of God".[12]

Erskine saw his task as convincing others of this, but his overwhelming Johannine insistence on the 'holy love of God' as the primary divine motivation towards humankind, allied to the perceived 'benevolence' of his theological 'system', soon provoked accusations of 'novelty', 'delusion', 'extravagance', 'sectarianism', 'unsoundness', 'fancies and conjectures', 'perversion' and 'misrepresentation' from establishment opponents who linked it with 'Socinianism' or 'Unitarianism'. From this basic 'misunderstanding' of God, they suggested, proceeded the subversion of every other doctrine.[13] But it was to grasp the life-changing reality of our own sinfulness and need that Erskine believed we are provided with the measuring rod of God's goodness and excellent character, which is revealed supremely through the life, atonement, and sacrifice of Christ. When this is *truly* perceived, and all may apprehend it because "God has left no man without the means of salvation", our conscience accordingly becomes fully enlightened, this revelation being itself the one necessity which can produce inner peace and happiness:

> The revelation of God in flesh means not only the revelation of the history of Jesus Christ, but the revelation of God in His relation to man's understanding and feelings and nature in general. Jesus Christ was God and man, showing that God could in a measure be comprehended by man, and that man's faculties were fit recipients of God...The image was and is the inward likeness...[14]

Correct knowledge and grasp of God's character self-generated salvation, "because the truth could not otherwise enter the mind". In Erskine's innovatory scheme, such salvific activity was typically expressed in terms of

---

demned by the Kirk. Erskine was adversely linked to the Marrow men. See e.g., Thomson, *Universal Pardon*, 478-9.

[11] Letter to Bishop Ewing, 2 March 1867, *Ewing-II*, 34.

[12] Letter to Jane Welsh Carlyle, 23 July 1855, *NLS MS* 1774-73.

[13] E.g., Thomson, *Universal Pardon*, viii-ix, 371, 374, 389, 400-1, 407, 414, 421, 444, 456-7, 462-3, 471-2 (footnote); David Brown, "Letter to a Friend Entangled in Error", *ECI*, II, III (March, 1833), 147.

[14] Letter to Madame de Broglie, 13 August (probably 1838), *Letters-I*, 324.

the immediate 'healing of the soul' through the internal operation of a type of pre-existing eternal, philosophical/ spiritual moral 'law':

> The *thing given* for the healing of the soul and fitted for it, not by any sovereign appointment, but by the eternal constitution of things, was a manifestation of the true character of God, a truth addressed to the understanding and the feelings through which alone the soul acts or perceives.[15]

Hence Erskine consistently, albeit controversially, reformulated the starting point for a correct salvific understanding of God in terms of true apprehension of God's character, rather than in the prevalent traditional eighteenth-century apologetic instruments of 'evidences' and 'miracles':

> I believe that a true explanation of what Christianity means is the only evidence on which it can be received. No miracles of whatever kind could make a man who felt in his conscience that he was called to be good, loving, righteous, believe that God was not good, nor loving, nor righteous; his difficulty is to reconcile this character of God with the facts around him – I may add, with the facts within him. The idea of judgment comes in and bewilders him. He sees sin and misery around him; he is conscious of sin and misery within himself, and God becomes to his conception a Judge and not a Father. With such a conception it is impossible that he can make any progress in moral or spiritual life...I must have...a confidence in His purpose to make me and all men LIKE HIMSELF. This is the confidence I must have in God if I am not to fear Him, or hate Him, or despise Him.[16]

This was novel thinking in the evangelical world of the early nineteenth century where attachment to miracles and legal soteriological concepts ran deep. However, despite emphasising the subjective, Erskine did not maintain that assurance in God was to be based merely on an inward subjective feeling. The orthodox objective reality of Christianity, whilst relatively subservient to ethical inwardness, nevertheless remained important. Erskine realised the dangers of pure subjective religion, expressing as his greatest desire to experience "the actual presence of the great Objective in me...something which I was sure did not depend upon myself, but would always assert its own distinct independent reality, and which could not possibly be my own imagination...".[17] Nevertheless, for Erskine, static objective, doctrinal and forensic categories undoubtedly took second place to more dynamic organic, relational, and ethical concepts, subjective though these might be, since his reconstructive focus remained on the beneficial, character-transforming purpose of God for humanity, mere apprehension of

---

[15] *Serpent*, 24-5.

[16] Letter to Professor Lorimer, 5 August 1858, *Letters-II*, 214-5.

[17] Letter to Julia Wedgwood, 19 March 1868, *Letters-II,* 319-20; Letter to Bishop Ewing, 16 April [no year], *Ewing-II*, 39.

which *in itself* contained salvific regenerational power. The essence of such apprehension was the conviction that

> God was a Father whose desire with regard to us was to train us into a participation of his own character and blessedness, and that such a belief must produce such a confidence. If I know the purpose of God toward me, if I know that it is his unchangeable purpose, I cannot but trust him.[18]

Immanental knowledge of the divine perfections, which necessarily corresponded to humanity's highest moral consciousness, was therefore fundamental to Erskine's concept of God, so that we might 'participate' in the divine character. As "there is but one kind of righteousness, namely, the character of God...therefore, in order that a man should be righteous or good, he must have God dwelling in him".[19]

Echoes of Wesleyan holiness may be discerned in Erskine's commitment to a sanctified and holy life as evidence of salvation: "...the hope for man is simply the hope that God will continue to insist upon his being righteous, until he actually becomes so".[20] He introduced the concept of a kind of natural inner 'law', in which true faith becomes the shaper of our character, whilst appreciation and appropriation of the spiritual power of Christ's atonement automatically generates ethical conformity to God's character. Erskine was to develop the concept of *character* rather than *individuality* into a revolutionary reconstructed doctrine of divine 'election' whereby "a man by changing his character, might change God's dealing towards him", for God "in very deed judges men according to their characters, and makes promises and threatenings to them simply in relation to their characters...".[21]

For Erskine, the real source of opposition to true Christianity resided not so much, as many supposed, in the area of reason, as in the moral will of the unbeliever, who, whilst often happy with abstract truths, frequently had no awareness of the necessity for Christian truth to be incarnated in the individual. The gospel's uncompromising principle of active holiness stood in marked contrast to resistant and corrupt human nature. Erskine believed much contemporary religion failed to address this vital practical moral dimension.

---

[18] Letter to J.C. Shairp, 4 October 1859, in William Knight, *Principal Shairp and his Friends* (London: John Murray, 1888), 210.

[19] Letter to Monsieur Gaussen, 7 December 1832, *Letters-I*, 289.

[20] Letter to Bishop Ewing, 25 October 1863, *Ewing-I*, 39. See pp.123-25 below.

[21] *Election*, 16-17, 20.

Relational Trinitarianism

In the increasingly moralistic and liberal nineteenth century, a classic metaphysical doctrine such as the Trinity could not be so easily 'moralised'. Its personal and social significance for 'community', so much the province of the later twentieth-century trinitarian renewal inspired by Karl Barth,[22] apparently eluded them. Accordingly, it tended to be neglected altogether.

Erskine had little use for the Trinity as a purely speculative concept. It had to be demonstratively capable of moral utility.[23] But he did not discard the orthodox doctrine of the Trinity like Schleiermacher and the Unitarians.[24] Instead, he engaged creatively with its relational soteriological implications, simultaneously identifying with the Cartesian Enlightenment movement away from the centrality of God towards the thinking subject. Fuelled by Locke, it had culminated in Kant's definition of a 'person' as a free-willed, responsible, self-conscious moral subject. The importance of the individual continued to be stressed by nineteenth-century Romanticism, but tended to give way to increasing emphasis on social and corporate humanity.[25] For Erskine, as for contemporaries like Coleridge or Maurice, the displacement of God from centre-stage and increasing focus on human psychology did not imply they were departing from Christian doctrinal orthodoxy. Rather it meant that they perceived the ethically relevant, inward revelation of truth as primary, with traditional doctrines relegated to a secondary explicatory, illustrative, corroborative function.[26]

Although many found his novel concept of 'the divine in every man' problematic, arguably Erskine remained largely orthodox and trinitarian. His real concern was to introduce a more confident, incarnational, relational Christianity, building on the foundational reality of Christ indwelling each person. This stood in contrast to the timid, static, legalistic, lifeless approach which Erskine believed dominated popular religion. In some ways he could be construed as anticipating, albeit from a limited perspective, present-day concerns about the nature of personhood and the *imago Dei*. The paradigmatic, representational person of Christ was central in his

---

[22] See e.g., Colin E. Gunton, *The Promise of Trinitarian Theology*, [2nd edition] (Edinburgh: T.&T. Clark, 1997), xv, 1,17, 19.

[23] *Evidence*, 93-4.

[24] Samuel M. Powell, *The Trinity in German Thought* (Cambridge: Cambridge University Press, 2001), 88-103.

[25] D.W. Bebbington, "Evangelical Christianity and Romanticism", in *Crux*, XXXVI, 1 (March, 1990), 12.

[26] *Sp.Order*, 32. It was as a result of his perception of the Trinity as an eternal communion grounded in the social nature of God that F.D. Maurice came to understand humanity essentially as social beings, ("On the Trinity in Unity", *Theological Essays* [1853] [London: James Clarke, 1957], 281-99).

thinking, and it was vital that Christ's life should not be separated from his teaching. Who Christ was, and the Spirit's power which enabled him to embody what he taught, were of central exemplary importance for Erskine. His vision of true religion was Christocentric, pneumatic, and experiential, mirroring trinitarian relationality. The love of God could be nothing more than a "mere benevolence, apart from the history of the life and death of Christ", and "nothing but *sonship* is a full revelation of fatherhood". His creative concept of 'sonship' had to be organically foundational to the whole of creation. As Erskine put it, all humanity was originated in Christ: "the whole spiritual creation is constituted in the Son", so that it might thereby share in the Son's relationship to the Father, and participate in the divine "Spirit and character".[27]

Erskine believed that all human conceptions of goodness could only originate in, and be derived from, God himself, since "goodness is the substance of God",[28] and therefore the divine incarnation provided the necessary relational 'pattern' or 'root' *within humanity itself*. Thus, it followed that "the right conception of God and His relation to men…when once apprehended…commends itself to the moral reason as an intelligible and necessary truth, *i.e.*, if believed on its own ground, and not on that of external authority".[29] Erskine continually emphasised the immanence of Christ within each person, so that we only need to recognise his presence by faith for his regenerating power to be actualised. This, rather than propositional dogma, was the very essence of the gospel:

> It is preaching God tabernacled in the flesh of every man. For what is true of the whole race is true of every individual in the race. Each man is a microcosm, a miniature of the world and of the race, and therefore when we hear of Christ coming into the flesh of our race, we in fact hear of his coming into the flesh of every man. When we hear of God *so* loving the world, we hear of his so loving each man of the world. It is just the root of the vine being in every one of its branches, in virtue of its fibres pervading all the branches, the withered, as well as the living. Remember, Christ came into Adam's place. This is the real substitution. The power of the gospel lies in the union between God and the fallen nature of man revealed in it, and this union is called the *mystery*.[30]

The dynamic concept of salvific relationship to God through living dependent sonship became self-evident once the compatibility of the human constitution with the divine nature was recognised through revelation to the conscience. In the early 1820s, this sounded very new and innovative, and Erskine's seminal reconstructive role was acknowledged by Maurice who

---

[27] Letter to Bishop Ewing, 31 October 1869, *Ewing-II*, 48, cf., *Sp.Order*, 120-1.
[28] *Ewing-II*, 51.
[29] Letter to Dr. Manning, 3 October 1865, *Ewing-I*, 64.
[30] *Serpent*, 104-5.

was to attribute enormous debt to him. From his earliest apologetic writings Erskine, famously followed by John McLeod Campbell, consistently expounded variations on the relational theme of the universal 'Fatherhood of God', 'sonship', and 'brotherhood', which Christ came to reveal.[31] Though a characteristic Unitarian concept, being a favourite subject of Erskine's American contemporary, William Ellery Channing,[32] it was adopted by many in the Broad Church, notably F.D. Maurice, eventually becoming a watchword of later nineteenth- and early twentieth-century liberalism, preeminently in the hands of Albrecht Ritschl and Adolf von Harnack (1851-1930).[33] In contrast, the perceptive Free Church scholar, George Smeaton (1814-89), complained in 1870 about those "Rationalists [who] have been wont, down to our day, to lay all emphasis on the universal Fatherhood of God, and to repudiate as intolerably severe and terrible every representation of God as a supreme ruler and judge".[34]

But in Erskine's hands it became a vitally experiential concept which formed an integral part of his innovatory approach to salvific awareness. Erskine was not simply a relational theologian. The consistent testimony of his private correspondence, of his friends, and even his opponents, reveals a man who *lived* in close personal relationship to God and humanity, and commended it for others.[35] Anticipating twentieth-century insights, his 'personalism' incorporated an early form of 'I and Thou' relational theology.[36] For Erskine, the vital evangelical truth of religion remained

> our own conscious meeting with God in the secret of our own hearts, and knowing Him there, our own personal God, loving us, longing over us with fatherly longings, and speaking to us so that we may hear and know His voice, and distinguish it from all the other voices within and without us.[37]

---

[31] See, e.g., *Sp.Order*, 5; Letter to Mr Craig, [no date-probably 1863], *Letters-II*, 240. For Campbell, see *NOTA*, e.g., 238-57.

[32] Gary Dorrien, *The Making of American Liberal Theology: Imagining Progressive Religion 1805-1900* (Louisville: Westminster John Knox Press, 2001), 33.

[33] Albrecht Ritschl, *The Christian Doctrine of Justification and Reconciliation* (Edinburgh: T.&T. Clark, 1900), 617-19; Adolf von Harnack, *What Is Christianity?* [1900], [5th edition] (London: Ernest Benn, 1958), 54-6, 78-80.

[34] Smeaton, *Christ's Doctrine*, 480.

[35] "[The substance]...is the living personality of God in our flesh...a personality whose presence I can recognise in my own heart...", Letter to Lady Elgin, 29 November 1833, *Letters-I*, 202.

[36] "John xvii.3 is an exemplification of the relation of thou to I as its proper complement...man by losing his knowledge of the great thou has lost everlasting life – he recovers it when he knows *thee*", (Letter probably to Dr. Samuel Brown, 30 May [no year], *NLS MS* 1890-153).

[37] Letter to Madame de Broglie, 4 June 1838, *Letters-I*, 308.

In keeping with Erskine's passion for true Christianity as an existential reality, in contrast to the uncertain "religion of the land",[38] he continually emphasised the need for each individual Christian's experience to demonstrate the living reality of the universally incarnate Saviour, so that the result of Christ being in each individual would be truly morally dynamic as humanity evolved into an extension of the life of Christ. Such universal potential was the result of God's work through Christ. The human race was the body of Christ, its Head, and union with Christ was the essence of the gospel: "Christ hath become one flesh with you, that you might become one spirit with Him. He is in you as the root is in the branch. He is your Head…".[39] Julia Wedgwood noted how Erskine tended to de-emphasise any approach that relegated the fullest meaning of Christ's work merely to his historical appearance in the world. Rather, "He was a being witnessed by the conscience, quite apart from his revelation in history".[40]

Eternal Sonship

Resisting contemporary trends to dispense with trinitarian categories, Erskine developed arguments which remarkably anticipated twentieth as well as later nineteenth-century concerns in applying the principles of reason and conscience to claim continued adherence to doctrinal orthodoxy regarding the deity of Christ.[41] By locating his convictions concerning the divinity of Christ in the concept of 'eternal Sonship', he was to reflect later divine ontological relational emphases. Having established the idea of universal divine Fatherhood, he regarded 'eternal Sonship' as a necessary but vital distinction within the divine nature, salvifically revealing the character of God and the nature of the divine – human relationship. For Erskine, fatherhood, eternal sonship and union with Christ were organic relational concepts of such importance as "fundamental principles" which 'regulate and harmonise the creation' through inculcation of the 'law of love', that they completely dominated his salvific thought:

> The revelation of the Son is the only thorough revelation of the Father; and as the Son is the Head of the spiritual creation, he of necessity communicates his own relation of Sonship to all its members; and as a common sonship is a common brotherhood, he also unites them all to each other in that bond. Thus

---

[38] *Extracts*, xxxvi.
[39] *Gifts*, 21.
[40] Wedgwood, *Teachers*, 68-9.
[41] In this context, it is misleading for Donald Winslow to allege regarding the Trinity, that Erskine "dismissed it with a word or two", (*Thomas Erskine*, 74).

love is the universal living law, originating with the Father and received by the Son, that it may by him be propagated to the whole spiritual family.[42]

Since "Jesus Christ was God, taking human nature into union with himself...Christians are men who yield themselves up to be taken into union with God, by submitting themselves to be led by his Spirit". 'Sonship' was accordingly "participation of the Divine nature, through union with the Son of God".[43] Erskine's innovatory trinitarian reflections were essentially soteriological, rooted in a theology of the nature of God which was inseparable from theologies of grace, anthropology, christology, pneumatology, and ecclesiology, based on God's overriding desire to reveal himself: "God is my Father, Christ is my head, and the Spirit proceeding from the Father and the Son is breathing into my conscience".[44]

To an extent, Erskine accepted the incorporation of elements of natural religion or the scientific and philosophical into his reconstructive system. He spoke in terms of eternal 'principles' and 'laws of the spiritual world' uniting Father and Son to each other, and organically to the created order. But 'self-sacrificing love' was the 'divine glue' which alone could "maintain order and harmony throughout".[45] Erskine's three-fold scheme of eternal sonship, justification through filial dependence, and obedient self-sacrifice, captured in essence his salvific vision, and its subsistence within the Godhead and the created order were for him the principal evidences for the truth of Christianity:

> The connection between these three great principles, (1) the eternal Sonship, (2) faith or dependent recipiency, and (3) that sacrifice of self which is the only putting away of sin, is to me an irrefragable evidence of the truth of the whole revelation. I see that sin can be put away only by this self-sacrifice; that filial trust is the only principle which can produce such sacrifice; and that this trust must exist within the Divine nature itself. And thus these three great doctrines of Christianity, the Divine nature of Christ, the righteousness of faith, and the necessity of self-sacrifice, appear to be cognate principles existing as necessary elements of the spiritual order, and in perfect harmony with the reason and conscience of man. This is the true *natural* religion, which carries God's own certificate to my reason.[46]

---

[42] *Sp.Order*, 244, cf., 249.
[43] *Election*, 411, cf., 376.
[44] Letter to Mrs Batten, 17 August 1859, *Letters-II*, 233.
[45] *Sp.Order*, 233.
[46] *Sp.Order*, 246.

The Holy Spirit

Innovation inevitably tends to be accompanied by claims of heterodoxy. Donald Winslow suggests that because Erskine's christology concentrated so exclusively on the subject of eternal divine sonship, his trinitarianism was deficient with regard to the role of the Holy Spirit, singling out Erskine's essay on "The Divine Son" in *The Spiritual Order* which he claims to be "unashamedly binitarian".[47] John McLeod Campbell evinced concern regarding Erskine's focus on the Father – Son relationship, that "the personality of the Holy Spirit might be lost sight of".[48] But Erskine frequently tended to cause misunderstanding as a result of his typically single-minded and often one-sided approach to what he perceived to be crucial points of issue. Though the Father – Son relationship was critical for his overall argument, he did not thereby intend to relativise the role of the Spirit. As he explained,

> The revelation of the eternal Sonship in the Divine nature is an opening up of the structure and organization of the spiritual order. The whole spiritual creation is constituted in the Son, that so it may partake in His relation to the Father, and may thus be also led into the participation of His Spirit and character".[49]

The Spirit's role was to manifest the Father's character within humanity, through the indwelling Christ. Despite Winslow's anxiety concerning relativisation of the Spirit, Erskine actually spoke in "The Divine Son" of divine unity as "completeness" not "singleness", and insisted that although the idea of 'God' was indeed represented by "the personalities of Father and Son", they were necessarily "united in one common Spirit".[50] It is, perhaps, more accurate, therefore, to suggest not so much that Erskine was 'binitarian', but that his concept of the Spirit was less as *personality,* and more as divine 'power', revealing, illuminating, uniting, but nevertheless unambiguously an integral part of the Godhead.

Erskine's creative approach resembled an 'enabling pneumatology'. The Spirit's function involved "enabling every one, to know God and walk with Him", to display the divine family characteristics.[51] However, there is an element of reductionism apparent in Erskine's thought generally. It is usually impossible, for example, to distinguish the presence of the Spirit from the presence of God or Christ. 'Father', 'Son', 'Christ', and 'Spirit' were freely interchangeable. He further identified the Spirit with both the in-

---

[47] Winslow, *Thomas Erskine*, 93.
[48] *Memorials*, 345.
[49] Letter to Bishop Ewing, 31 October 1869, *Ewing-II*, 48.
[50] *Sp.Order*, 36-7.
[51] *Election*, 182.

dwelling Christ and universal human conscience: "He comes down now to each man, is, as it were, again incarnate in each man's conscience, and in that conscience, the true light, the Spirit within each man, He grieves over each man's sin, agonises for it in each man...".[52] So the indwelling 'Son' was also the indwelling 'Spirit'.[53]

Erskine's radical Spirit christology is reminiscent of Edward Irving's novel concept of the incarnate Son as our pattern wholly dependent on the Spirit's enabling to manifest the character of God.[54] Although Christ represented corporate humanity in actual 'possession' of, and in 'union' with his "fallen nature", to Jesus the Holy Spirit was, however, given "without measure".[55] Like Irving, Erskine merged his understanding of Christ assuming our fallen human nature with his complete dependence on the Spirit to remain sinless:

> Jesus took the flesh, just as the 'children' have it, Heb. ii. 14; but that does not make him a sinner, for as he was without sin in a sinful world, so he was without sin in a sinful nature. And how was he so?...Was it not by a continual refusal to live to the flesh, and a continual choosing to live to the Spirit?[56]

Though it flew in the face of Calvinist doctrine, Erskine's concept of the restoration of the Spirit to the human race combined with orthodox trinitarianism underpinned his fundamental belief in the progressive divinisation of humanity. Since Christ is one with the Father, and the head of humanity, "the life that flows from him into the human race is the divine life".[57] As human beings "receive life, even eternal life, God's own life, God's own Spirit...into their souls", we become "living members of Christ".[58] Erskine's original theme of 'recipiency', by which he meant Christ's faith and ours co-operate to actualise a real exchange between human and divine nature, was explicit:

> Faith implies recipiency; the Son's faith receives out of the Father, and man is created in the Son that he may receive of the divine nature and the eternal life. Thus the creation of man necessarily supposes the purpose of Incarnation, the recipiency of the divine nature by flesh, the difference between the

---

[52] Shairp, "Reminiscences", in *Letters-II*, 356.

[53] *Sp.Order*, 162-3.

[54] *Serpent*, 46-47, 50, 107 [1st edition], 159 [2nd edition]; *Election*, 236; *Sp.Order* 138. For Irving see *The Orthodox and Catholic Doctrine of Our Lord's Human Nature* (London: Baldwin and Cradock, 1830), viii; Graham McFarlane, *Why Do You Believe What You Believe about the Holy Spirit?*, (Carlisle: Paternoster, 1998), 116-18.

[55] Letter to Monsieur Gaussen, 7 December 1832, *Letters-I*, 295.

[56] *Election*, 368.

[57] Letter to Mrs Schwabe, 14 December 1853, *NLS*, *MS* 9747–33.

[58] *Gifts*, 22.

Head and the members being this, that the Head is God assuming flesh – men are flesh receiving God.[59]

The close link between the Spirit indwelling humanity and deification was not in itself new, but like many aspects of Erskine's seemingly novel trinitarian incarnational thinking, it suggested rediscovery of Patristic sources.[60] There is undoubted resemblance to themes of *theopoiesis* in Irenaeus and Athanasius, where Christ was understood as mediating the Spirit to redeem and sanctify our humanity through his own humanity, which itself was sanctified by the Spirit. For both Irenaeus and Athanasius, what the incarnate Son assumed to himself from humanity was fundamental to their soteriology. Irenaeus regarded Jesus as both 'divinising human existence' and acting "as a revealer and new model for human existence".[61] Athanasius emphasised that redemption took place "within the mediatorial life and person of the Incarnate Son." It was Athanasius too, who established that the ground for all our knowledge of God came supremely through the mutual relation of the Son and the Father. That mutual relation necessarily included the relation of the Spirit to the Father and the Son.[62] Athanasius's trinitarian understanding of the process of divinisation was soteriologically motivated, being mediated by the indwelling life of Christ. Jesus poured out his Spirit upon humanity through the incarnation. We appropriate salvation and divine sonship through participation in the Spirit.[63] John McLeod Campbell was to follow Erskine in propounding a clear doctrine of divine participation,[64] and Erskine may further be regarded as anticipating twentieth-century reflections by theologians like Karl Rahner concerning the unifying of the 'economic' and 'immanent' Trinity, where God's self-communication as Father in the incarnation of the eternal Son through

---

[59] Letter to Mrs Gurney, 14 May 1862, *Letters-II,* 253.

[60] Echoes of eastern orthodox soteriological concepts of deification and divine union through the incarnation are apparent throughout Erskine. Erskine's study of Plato and William Law remain a likely source. There is little *direct* evidence that Erskine read the Church Fathers, though he appeared to possess impressive knowledge about them. See Samuel Gobat, *Samuel Gobat, Bishop of Jerusalem* (London: James Nisbet, 1884), 42-3.

[61] Roger Haight, *Jesus Symbol of God* (New York: Orbis Books, 2000), 251.

[62] Thomas F. Torrance, *Theology in Reconciliation* (London: Geoffrey Chapman, 1975), 229-32; *The Trinitarian Faith* (Edinburgh: T.&T. Clark, 1993), 188.

[63] Peter Widdicombe, *The Fatherhood of God From Origen to Athanasius,* [revised edition] (Oxford: Clarendon Press, 2000), 226-7.

[64] Jesus "became the son of man, that we might become the sons of God, and the one is just as literal as the other", Sermon XIII: "1 Peter I.3,4,5", Preached at Row, 16 May 1830, in *Notes of Sermons by the Rev. J. M^{c}L. Campbell, Minister of Row, Dumbartonshire, taken in shorthand,* in 3 volumes (Paisley: John Vallance, 1831), II, 3-5.

the divinising gracious presence of the Spirit highlights the essential identity of God's eternal being and salvation history.[65]

Divine and Human Relationality

For Erskine, it was the supreme work of Jesus Christ to reveal the Fatherhood of God. The corollary was revealing in Christ's own person the existence of 'eternal Sonship' within the divine nature itself. The vitally important implication for humanity was that because all were 'created in the Son', all may actually 'enter into his spirit' and share in his filial relationship, sufferings, and "dependent recipiency". Erskine described this novel but crucial revelation as the "discovery of the Son".[66] Orthodox Calvinism knew no such pre-regenerational relationship. The revelation of an 'eternal receiver' within the Godhead threw a whole new light on Erskine's understanding of human duty and responsibility. The historical life of Jesus, lived in our nature as 'the beginning of God's creation' in complete union and dependent filial relationship as *'model truster'*,[67] was the supreme motivation for Christian assurance in a loving God whose salvific purpose for all his creatures was for the same sympathetic and dependent eternal filial relationship. But the key to humanity adopting this relationship resided in the revelation that humanity actually already 'participates' in the divine nature.

The revelation of the corporate concept of Christ as the Head of humanity, uniting human beings vertically to God, and horizontally to one another so that they actually participate in both natures, was fundamental to Erskine's apologetic for the divinity of Christ. He regarded it as a 'system' or 'spiritual order' which both explained the historical life of Jesus and met the intuitive needs of humanity by appealing to their reason and conscience in presenting God as a loving Father who takes the salvific initiative. Anticipating key twentieth-century emphases, the divine pattern served as a model for human relational personhood, and may be illustrated in Erskine's rare treatment of the subject of ecclesiology and the eucharist. He believed in the concept of a universal family in which all participate and are united by the Spirit to Christ and his body. Erskine's approach to the 'visible' Church was, therefore, determined by his organic model of Christ incarnate in his body:

---

[65] Karl Rahner, *The Trinity* (Tunbridge Wells: Burns & Oates, 1970), 35-40, cf., Catherine Mowry LaCugna, *God For Us* (San Francisco: Harper, 1991), 213, 220, 230-1.

[66] *Sp.Order*, 43, cf., 193-4.

[67] *Sp.Order*, 186, cf., 43. Campbell adopted the same concept in *NOTA*, e.g., 206.

a Church is 'God manifest in flesh' of man, – the *mind of God* shown forth in the willing, conscious acquiescence and co-operation of men...the very essence of the church is the continuation of the same showing forth of light by the indwelling of Jesus in His members".[68]

Although Erskine reflected the contemporary importance of the individual, it was the individual as defined by relationship: vertically with God, where the importance of divine Fatherhood and sonship was prominent: horizontally, in mutual fraternal relationships. Erskine's vision was for a Church which mirrored the interdependence and unity which subsists in God, actualised by the Spirit. He affirmed:

> I feel the sin and misery of Individuality, and I have received the truth of Christ in our flesh as the gift of the one heart of God to the whole human race, which would bless men by uniting them all in God.[69]

Likewise, Erskine viewed the significance of the 'real', inward eucharist as recognising the "true brotherly love" which presupposes a "common Father", and receiving the actual life of Christ as the indwelling, unifying, 'connecting' presence, so that "Christ should be the Head of the Christian Family, animating all the members with His own life", and "the bond uniting man to God, and man to all men".[70]

In the twentieth century, Karl Barth was to merge his doctrine of the Trinity with that of election, regarding the incarnation of the Son as God's self-determination by which he chose love and mercy for the human race in Christ.[71] Erskine also recognised the interdependence of the two doctrines, and, like Barth after him, reformulated a new understanding of election, affirming that Jesus was God's elect man and that all humanity was elect in him. It was within Erskine's concept of 'eternal Sonship' and Jesus's self-confessed identity that his idea of 'recipiency' operated. The Father is the "eternal Giver", and the Son the 'sympathetic' "eternal Receiver of all the fullness of God", which he communicates to "the whole spiritual creation", namely the members of "the body of the Son".[72] We know there is both Fatherhood and Sonship in the Godhead because within the essential qual-

---

[68] Erskine, "Idea of the Church", in *Letters-I*, 393-4. Note strong parallels with John Owen's teaching concerning the role of the Holy Spirit to supply the presence of Christ to the Church and perform his works, *The Works of John Owen*, in 16 volumes, William H. Goold (ed.), "The Holy Spirit" [1674] (Edinburgh: Banner of Truth, 1965), Vol.III, Book II, Chapter V, 189-97.

[69] Erskine, "Idea of the Church", in *Letters-I*, 397.

[70] Letter to Mr G. Galloway, June 1848, *Letters-II*, 63; Letter to Mrs Schwabe, 9 September 1857, *Letters-II*, 119; "The Holy Eucharist" in *Ewing-II*, 62.

[71] Bruce McCormack, "Grace and Being", in John Webster (ed.), *The Cambridge Companion to Karl Barth* (Cambridge: Cambridge University Press, 2000), 98.

[72] *Sp.Order*, 37-8, 43.

ity of 'goodness' there exists both giving and receiving, trustworthiness and trust, rule and obedience. 'Recipiency', therefore, is mutually sympathetic divine perichoresis and its human counterpart. Because God is love and the source of all goodness, the aspects of 'active' and 'recipient' goodness subsist simultaneously in the divine nature. Therefore, although it worried Campbell (and more recently Winslow), Erskine concluded there must be two distinct personalities within the divine nature apart from their manifestation in humanity. Consequently, we derive the conviction of the truth that there is community in God, which extends to the divine creation. Accordingly, Erskine could speak of

> two hemispheres in the Divine nature, – upper and under, active and passive, Giver and Receiver, Father and Son. Unity is not singleness but rather completeness, and love can only, by minds like ours, be considered complete when it has sympathy. This idea of God as comprehending both the active and the passive of all goodness, distinguished by the personalities of Father and Son but united in one common Spirit, seems to me to give the perfect conception of love and of blessedness in love; and when we add the idea that the spiritual creation stands in the Son, we have the assurance that it also is intended to be included in that fellowship of love.[73]

Both Origen and Athanasius taught the eternal generation of the Son, and argued that because of the incarnation and the example of Christ's eternal 'giving' and 'receiving' relationship with the Father, we may all experience a divine filial relationship through our participation in the Son. Especially for Athanasius, the Fatherhood of God was a trinitarian relational soteriological concept. Because of the incarnation, through the Spirit we are enabled to become sons of the Father.[74] There are evident parallels with Schleiermacher's delineation of a (albeit human) Jesus whose 'glorious' status derived entirely from his growing consciousness of the nature of his special filial relationship to God.[75] Crucially, however, Erskine consistently maintained the trinitarian dimension. Together with Maurice and Campbell, he can lay claim to playing a significant role in restoring classical belief in the universal loving Fatherhood of God and corresponding sonship to a prime position in Christian trinitarian thought. Such understanding of the nature and character of God fundamentally affected the way in which soteriological doctrines were subsequently interpreted, though Erskine had no interest in associated Victorian notions of mere divine benevolence.

Significantly, in the mid-nineteenth century, the 'Fatherhood of God' was 'rediscovered' as a major theme, complementing the sensibilities of

---

[73] *Sp.Order*, 36-7, cf., Letter to Mrs Gurney, 1862, *Letters-II*, 251-2.

[74] Widdicombe, *Fatherhood*, 67, 85, 93, 101, 146, 176, 206, 222.

[75] Friedrich Schleiermacher, *The Life of Jesus* [1864], Jack C. Verheyden, [ed.], S. Maclean Gilmour, [trans.] (Philadelphia: Fortress Press, 1975), 102-4.

the times. But it became a topic of fierce and far-reaching public theological controversy between conservatives and liberals, especially in Scotland between 1865 and 1870. The principal antagonists were Robert Candlish and Thomas Crawford, both noted theological academics, who entered into an extended dialogue of conflicting lectures under the title of *The Fatherhood of God*.[76] The main area of disagreement, involving significant soteriological implications, centred on whether divine Fatherhood could be considered natural and universal. During the course of the exchange, both appealed to biblical and patristic evidence. Whilst Crawford argued, in line with Erskine, that the paternal relationship was natural and best expressed the loving character of God, the more conservative Candlish preferred to regard God's Fatherly relationship to humanity as secondary to that of Sovereign, and denied any natural organic relationship apart from that of adopted sonship through Christ. The debate continued into the twentieth century, principally through J. Scott Lidgett, who in 1902 affirmed that

> no doctrine of the relationship of God to men has assumed such prominence during the last half-century as that of His Fatherhood…it has wrought a theological transformation in many quarters. With regard to the Atonement, for example, it has brought to general recognition the truth that the sacrifice of Christ was the outcome, and not the cause, of the love of God to mankind.[77]

Summary

In this chapter we considered the cruciality for Erskine's soteriological system of his 'rediscovery' of classical concepts of divine identity, which he combined innovatively and eclectically with new intellectual ideas to reformulate into a more existential and incarnational form of practical and dependent Christianity. In Scotland particularly, his novel emphasis on universal concepts of divine love and relationality, allied to human responsibility and ethical transformation, contrasted with traditional propositional Calvinist dogma focused on divine sovereignty. Erskine's pragmatic rather than abstract trinitarianism embraced rediscovery of a dynamic role for the

---

[76] Robert S. Candlish, *The Fatherhood of God,* [5th edition] (Edinburgh: Adam & Charles Black, 1870); *The Fatherhood of God: Supplementary volume to fifth edition containing reply to Dr. Crawford, with answers to other objections, and explanatory notes* (Edinburgh: Adam and Charles Black, 1870). Thomas J. Crawford, *The Fatherhood of God Considered in its general and special aspects and particularly in relation to the Atonement with a review of recent speculations on the subject, and a reply to the strictures of Dr Candlish* [3rd edition] (Edinburgh and London: William Blackwood and Sons, 1868).

[77] Lidgett, *Fatherhood*, 1.

Spirit within the underlying concept that God in Christ redeemed and recreated a new humanity which everyone may appropriate salvifically.

CHAPTER 4

Revelation and the Location of Authority

Introduction

Erskine introduced what for his time were innovative concepts regarding apprehension of God and appropriation of salvation. To facilitate this, the credibility of claims to speak authoritatively was crucial, and he remained aware of the vital need to remain plausible in a changing world that increasingly was rejecting traditional sources of authority.

John Tulloch has described Erskine as "an apostle of the 'Christian consciousness'", referring to his pioneering role in transforming religion in Scotland from "mere formal orthodoxy" and dry rationalism towards a more subjective, conscious and experiential faith. In accordance with prevailing trends for religion to become the province of heart and will rather than head, Tulloch regarded Erskine as "*all heart*", whilst in identifying the conscience as the main locus for divine communication, Erskine was manifestly in tune with his increasingly psychologically aware era.[1] His conviction was that humanity was universally constituted in such a way that divine revelation corresponded to its deepest needs, that the human heart and conscience was therefore prepared to receive it, and that, although individuals may often not be immediately conscious of its need, nevertheless, when confronted with divine truth, they will intuitively recognise it.[2]

Erskine formed part of the post-Hume/ Kant Romantic era where 'natural theology' and 'revelation', indeed, interpretation of the very nature of religion, were undergoing reformulation in the light of human experience,

---

[1] Tulloch, *Movements*, 138-9, cf., Trevor Hart, "Revelation", in Webster (ed.), *Karl Barth*, 39.

[2] F.D. Maurice concurred that divine revelation was what "the heart and conscience of every man was waiting for", *The Gospel of St. John* [2nd edition] (London: Macmillan and Co., 1893), 240.

emotions and volition, in preference to external authority or rational argument. The traditional concept of revelation itself was seen as requiring reconstruction, given that former confidence in its truths was rapidly dissipating. The Romantic movement at the turn of the century offered a new approach to truth, perceiving the realities of religion as awaiting discovery within the sphere of universal human consciousness. This included increasing psychological awareness of the individual, legitimising investigation of human emotions and aesthetic sensibilities involving inward consciousness, intuition, and understanding. "Romanticism, whatever else the term may be used to cover, marked a re-evaluation of religion as an experience the authenticity of which must be sought within itself".[3] Truth, therefore, began to be seen as self-evidencing within the individual consciousness, requiring no validation beyond itself. Like Schleiermacher, Erskine's own approach to faith and the salvific apprehension of God was marked by similar Romantic sensibilities which built on his Enlightenment background. As he insisted, "the only revelation from without which I can acknowledge is some light which will give its full and satisfactory interpretation to that revelation within, which I already have".[4]

In the wake of Hume and Kant, and growing acceptance that religious truth was not something capable of proof, it was Schleiermacher who supremely typified nineteenth-century theological Romanticism by emphasising the individual's consciousness of God, and inward subjective religion. If truth could not be proved, it could be sensed. In ascribing pre-eminence to religious feeling and experience, Schleiermacher inaugurated an increasingly humanistic era in which authentic Christian belief and God's existence became the province primarily of what could be felt and experienced. Accordingly, the ground of authority in religion shifted from sources outside human beings to the inner human realm of divine encounter and individual experience, and external authority and supernatural revelation became relativised into the background. Corresponding to this shift from God to humanity, it became the supreme human challenge to attain its true and perfect realisation, Jesus Christ being its consummate divine ideal and example.

Almost concurrently with Schleiermacher, but in a distinctly eclectic and transitional sense, Erskine appropriated such newer concepts to tackle innovatively the inherent tensions involved in contemporary reconstruction of belief.[5] Though misunderstood, unlike some, he never actually abandoned, and indeed believed he was striving to preserve, a place for tradi-

---

[3] Bernard M.G. Reardon, *Religion in the Age of Romanticism* (Cambridge University Press, 1985), 29.

[4] Letter to Professor Lorimer, 5 August 1858, *Letters-II*, 216.

[5] Schleiermacher's first published work appeared in 1799. Erskine had written *Salvation* in 1816.

tional 'external' inputs such as divine revelation and the Bible. Whilst retaining a belief in the supernatural and a personal God of revelation, in his hands such categories, however, took on new plastic, scientific, mystical significance, tending to become 'psychologised', 'spiritualised' or 'platonised' into a 'spiritual order' of intuitive self-evidencing 'laws' based on divine/ human continuity, or 'illustrative' of 'real' innate truth or knowledge which properly resided within the conscious subject. Erskine "thought of the world of spiritual things as an actual entity, the laws of which are, quite as much as those of physical nature, the proper subjects of endless observation and inquiry".[6] He has been accused of confusing the supernatural with the natural by adopting so-called spiritual aphorisms or 'laws' as self-generating principles which informed his theology.[7] For example, it was "a law of our moral constitution, that the foundation of our confidence becomes necessarily the mould of our characters". Consequently, because the atonement is the ground of our confidence and comprises all that is spiritually excellent, "he, then, that truly and exclusively rests his hope on the atonement becomes a partaker of the character of God".[8] Frequently Erskine appeared to confuse divine workings of the Holy Spirit with natural human intuitive and responsive faculties. In his writings 'Spirit' and 'spirit' are often interchangeable. He appeared to divinise natural human faculties, for example, by exalting human conscience into identification with the supernatural indwelling of the Spirit, or of Christ himself.[9] In *The Brazen Serpent*, Erskine sought to clarify his understanding of the role of the supernatural and its relationship to natural law in describing the salvific 'healing of the soul':

> it is perhaps truer to say, that the whole matter belongs to the sphere of a higher nature, with the laws of which we are unacquainted, than to say that there [is] any departure from the laws of nature...souls [are] healed by the supernatural acting of a sovereign omnipotence, such as that which created the heavens and the earth, – the souls [are] healed by the entrance into them of a supernatural but intelligible truth concerning the character of God, and the character of his love to sinful men...[10]

It was not uncommon to 'naturalise' the supernatural from the eighteenth century onwards. Erskine was not alone in perceiving continuity between the divine, the human, and the natural, and seeking to harmonise spiritual and psychological concepts. It was an important feature of early nine-

---

[6] The *Spectator*, (2 April 1870), 430.
[7] Needham, *Thomas Erskine*, e.g., 89, 439, 452.
[8] *Evidence*, 111.
[9] "The Spirit breathes within you – that is conscience", (Letter to Julia Wedgwood, 12 June 1865, *Letters-II*, 158).
[10] *Serpent*, 25-6.

teenth-century Romantic sensibility, becoming especially prominent in the Romantic poets and in New England Transcendentalism.[11] The final authoritative nature of individual experimental engagement with God came to dominate Erskine's thought, so that the scrutiny of reason and conscience was determinant. "Direct and overwhelming encounter" with the divine became of prime salvific importance.[12] Now for Erskine, "the thing to be believed can only be known by personal experience, like light, and sound, and taste", whilst the gospel "comes with a special and direct and individual reference to each person of the world". Crucially, this gospel could not therefore be "understood nor believed except where that special reference is apprehended, just as the sun is not seen by me, except through that ray of him, which strikes on my own eye".[13]

Further anticipating Barth's twentieth-century Christocentrism, Erskine affirmed that "Jesus Christ is just the revelation of all that I have been saying. He is the Revealer of the Father, the Revealer that he is the Father of every man, and that He desires our perfect righteousness…".[14] God not only mediated truth to us "*objectively*, in Christ", but more vitally he also called on us "to experience it all, *subjectively*, in ourselves, through the operation of the Spirit of Christ received into our hearts by faith".[15] In this way Christ remained both the object and subject of Christian faith.

The Nature of Evidence

Erskine considered his task as that of apologist for true religion in the midst of a nominally Christian environment, not unlike Schleiermacher and his German 'cultured despisers'.[16] In line with assumptions inherited from the previous century, Erskine wanted to convince others that Christianity was supremely adapted to the spiritual and moral needs of human beings inasmuch as a) the principles of the gospel demonstrate the character of God is in harmony with the dictates of reason and conscience, and b) they "tend by their natural influence when believed, to mould the human character into accordance with that of God".[17] He was to develop the idea of inward Christian 'consciousness' into a salvific 'system' based on apprehension of

---

[11] Henderson, *Erskine*, 65-6, 68-70, cf., Steve Wilkens and Alan G. Padgett, *Christianity & Western Thought* (Illinois: InterVarsity Press, 2000), 31.
[12] *Evidence*, 36.
[13] *Serpent*, 28-9.
[14] Letter to Mrs Batten and Emelia Russell Gurney [no date], *Gurney*, 26.
[15] *Election*, xviii, cf., *Sp.Order*, 136.
[16] Friedrich Schleiermacher, *On Religion: Speeches to its Cultured Despisers* [1799] (New York: Harper & Row, 1958).
[17] Candlish, "Thomas Erskine", 113.

the God who actually dwells within every human being. Accordingly, he adopted a version of natural revelation, based on Romans 2.12-16, which he understood to teach universal innate awareness of moral truth. Like Schleiermacher, in his adoption of the principle of sense evidence, Erskine was standing in the later empirical tradition of Hume and Kant.[18] Especially in *The Brazen Serpent* and *The Doctrine of Election,* Erskine emphasised that true revelation and consciousness of the divine within every human being, would of itself motivate practical moral religion, and constituted the salvific process. Hume, and especially Kant, not only rejected external evidence, but affirmed that the subjective moral sense was both innate and reliable.[19]

Erskine believed it was vital for determining one's entire religious outlook to appreciate the true divine character. He therefore sought to demonstrate not only God's excellent attributes, but his essentially beneficent attitude to humankind, so that divine nature might be seen to correspond with what were conceived to be the highest human virtues founded supremely in love. He was convinced that anyone who seriously "considers the Divine character of love and of holiness which is developed in the history of Jesus Christ will discover in it the true centre of moral gravitation"[20]. As an evangelical, he believed he was engaged in a "republication of the truths of natural religion".[21] However, Erskine's insistence on 'internal evidence' introduced a significant new note so far as many evangelicals were concerned, and Richard Watson, the Methodist systematician, reasserted in direct contravention of Erskine the primacy of *external* evidence.[22] The evangelical apologetic tradition, still concerned about responding to the earlier empiricism of John Locke, remained preoccupied with 'external evidences' and miraculous authentication of revelation. William Paley, still highly influential in Erskine's day, was represented in Scotland (until Erskine facilitated a change of mind) by Thomas Chalmers (1780-1847).[23] But for Erskine, "experience [was] necessary in order to theorise justly".[24] He thought Paley's association of miracles with external evidences was wrong. Rather, miracles pointed to a personal God who dealt with human-

---

[18] Cf., the *Spectator*, (24 June 1871), 768.

[19] For Hume see *A Treatise of Human Nature* [1737-9], David Fate Norton and Mary J. Norton (eds.), (Oxford: Oxford University Press, 2000), §3.2.10, 354, §3.3.6, 394.

[20] *Evidence*, 201-2.

[21] Henderson, citing Bishop Butler, *Erskine*, 69.

[22] Richard Watson, *Theological Institutes* (New York: J. Emory and B. Waugh, 1831), 32, 39.

[23] Anon., "The Church and Theology of Germany During the Nineteenth Century", *National Review,* XVIII (January-April, 1864), 199; Candlish, "Thomas Erskine", 110-11.

[24] *Evidence*, 2.

ity in 'provinces which were higher than the laws of Nature'.[25] John McLeod Campbell was to follow Erskine closely in affirming the relative supremacy of internal evidence and the adjudication of conscience.[26]

Erskine's emphasis on 'internal evidence' has been compared to similar work on the subject by the eighteenth-century author and M.P., Soame Jenyns,[27] or considered as a reaction to the ideas of Thomas Chalmers.[28] Probably, however, Erskine was merely responding to the climate of the later Enlightenment. In particular, he paralleled those like William Ellery Channing and the Unitarians who felt as a result of modern knowledge the inevitable need to move away from Christian 'evidences' based on Paley's 'proofs'.[29]

Firstly, Erskine challenged traditional apologetic arguments by insisting that the internal self-evidencing instrumentality of reason and conscience, rather than external historical evidence, should take precedence in verifying the truth of Christian revelation. For Erskine, the doctrines of 'true' and 'real' religion will, by their inherent nature, commend themselves to our human constitution. They are therefore "self-evidencing in the light of conscience. They are self-transforming in the very act of reception".[30] Human conscience was itself the highest and ultimate *evidence*, the "verifying faculty".[31] As he put it: "I must learn to know God's character, and His relation to me in Jesus Christ, as necessary truths, independent of any authority whatever."[32]

Secondly, Erskine stressed the importance of moral change, where evidential proof resided in the effect produced in the life and character of the Christian individual. He sought to emphasise subjective and experiential knowledge of God in a way which did not dispense with the objectivity of divine truth, but nevertheless demonstrated that reliance on the kinds of external objective evidential proofs extolled by Paley were unnecessary. Hume had in any case dealt a death-blow to this type of empirical rationalism decades previously. Apart from Thomas Erskine, those who early recognised this included Schleiermacher, and Samuel Taylor Coleridge, who famously and contemptuously exclaimed,

> I more than fear the prevailing taste for...demonstrations of God from Nature, evidences of Christianity, and the like. Evidences of Christianity! I am weary of the word. Make a man feel the want of it; rouse him, if you can to

---

[25] Erskine, Letter to Principal Shairp, 24 December 1863, Knight, *Shairp*, 212.
[26] Lees, "Ewing", 368. See Campbell, *NOTA*, 36-9.
[27] Winslow, *Thomas Erskine*, 5.
[28] Needham, *Thomas Erskine*, 46-55.
[29] See Appendix 2.
[30] Tulloch, *Movements*, 136.
[31] Lees, "Ewing", 367.
[32] Letter to Bishop Ewing, December 1865, *Ewing-II*, 25.

the self-knowledge of his need for it; and you may safely trust to its own Evidence...[33]

Like Erskine, Coleridge regarded religion as both reasonable and practical, however with the basis of faith residing not in argument or doctrine, but in experience, and the truth of Christianity verifiable existentially by self-testimony. The ultimate source of our convictions about God were to be located internally in the moral and spiritual nature of humanity.[34] Internal versus external evidence was a classic eighteenth-century Deistic antithesis which had been employed to stress that natural religion written on the heart rendered external revelation unnecessary. The 'internal excellence', and 'fitness' or 'suitability' of religious truth for the benefit of mankind and society, were further Deistic criteria for judging what was morally acceptable.[35] Accepted concepts by Erskine's day, he innovatively appropriated them for his own orthodox apologetic purposes, albeit with a strongly spiritual and practical emphasis, which simultaneously looked backwards to the century of Butler, and forwards to the century of science. If Christianity was true, Erskine asserted, "it must be the only real natural religion, that is, it must explain all the true spiritual and moral consciousness within us, just as the theory of Newton, if true, must explain all the phenomena of the heavenly bodies. The fact of conscience is the great spiritual fact in man's nature".[36]

---

[33] Samuel Taylor Coleridge, *Aids to Reflection* [1825] (Edinburgh: John Grant, 1905), 363. Further echoing Erskine, Coleridge also affirmed that "the truth revealed through Christ has its evidence in itself, and the proof of its divine authority in its fitness to our nature and needs; the clearness and cogency of this proof being proportionate to the degree of self-knowledge in each individual hearer", (Samuel Taylor Coleridge, *Confessions of an Inquiring Spirit* [1840] [London: Cassell & Company, 1892], 51). Speaking of external evidence, Schleiermacher insisted that "We entirely renounce all attempt to prove the truth or necessity of Christianity; and we presuppose, on the contrary, that every Christian, before he enters at all upon inquiries of this kind, has already the inward certainty that his religion cannot take any other form than this", (*Christian Faith*, §11.5, 60).

[34] Reardon, *Religious Thought*, 47, cf., George Park Fisher, *History of Christian Doctrine*, [2nd edition] (Edinburgh: T.&T. Clark, 1896), 447-8.

[35] John Toland saw his task as proving New Testament doctrines to be "perspicuous, possible, and most worthy of God, as well as calculated for the highest Benefits of Man", (*Christianity Not Mysterious* [1696] [Stuttgart-Bad Cannstatt: Friedrich Frommann Verlag, 1964], 174). Matthew Tindal affirmed, "there's a Religion of Nature and Reason written in the Hearts of every one of us from the first Creation; by which all Mankind must judge of the Truth of any instituted Religion whatever"; "the Good of Mankind is the Test, the *Criterion*, or the internal Evidence, by which we are to judge of all [God's] laws"; "there are Things, which by their internal Excellency, shew themselves to be the Will of an infinitely wise, and good God", (*Christianity as Old as the Creation* [London: 1730], 49, 50-1, 390).

[36] Letter to Mrs Schwabe, 9 September 1857, *Letters-II*, 119.

Since the only source of goodness must be divine, Erskine argued that our idea of God was evidenced by extrapolating to infinity universal, innate, awareness of human goodness and intelligence. Accordingly, Erskine's "true natural religion" must possess the revelatory power of self-commendation both to human reason and to the moral sense of the conscience. This was to be achieved by revelation of the quality of God's character to the soul, which self-actualised inward transformation. Crucially, however, Erskine did not understand the process as merely 'natural'. Blending natural and supernatural, he insisted it remained "a supernatural revelation to the heart of every individual testifying there to what is righteous, and proving itself, by the response of conscience, to be of God".[37] Therefore, external authorities such as the Bible and Christian dogma, were of no use at all unless appropriated and divinely transmuted into vital, moral character.

Though grounded in eighteenth-century concepts, in practice, Erskine was seeking to rediscover something which he considered had been lost sight of in Scotland – a vital, living faith which, when genuinely *believed* rather than merely *acknowledged*, following the commitment of reason and conscience, would galvanise the heart, will, and emotions, or, as Erskine termed them, the 'affections'.

Conscience

The human conscience was, for Erskine, the key to religious consciousness. In emphasising conscience, Erskine reflected growing nineteenth-century psychological preoccupation with self-discovery, self-knowledge, self-awareness, and self-expression. In the Enlightenment, conscience had "proved to be a useful device for internalizing the ethical imperative as an integral element of the 'theology of the heart'…by contrast with the 'hypocrisy' of external conformity, the authentic summons to conversion and moral change was addressed to both 'your heart and your conscience'".[38] Conscience and the existence of innate ideas was also a leading principle of Scottish Common Sense philosophy founded by Thomas Reid (1710-96) at the end of the eighteenth century in response to Hume's anti-religious scepticism which questioned the objective knowability of revealed truth and shifted the focus to the subjective experience of the knower. But according to Reid, God had set within the human intellect a set of self-evident principles and logical capacities that permitted objective knowledge and true comprehension of the real world. The human mind operates according to

---

[37] *Sp.Order*, 36, 132-3.
[38] Jaroslav Pelikan, *Christian Doctrine and Modern Culture* (Chicago and London: University of Chicago Press, 1989), 158.

laws of belief inherent in human nature that make true knowledge possible in the reliable 'common sense' form of self-evident truths, conscience, or intuitive judgments and consciousness. Erskine, who almost certainly had been schooled in the Scottish philosophy,[39] understood God as the originator of laws of belief or conscience that by definition could not be false or misleading, especially as he was quite willing to attribute the self-evidencing nature of truth to the Spirit. Erskine's friend, Thomas Chalmers, was himself a strong advocate of the Scottish philosophy, well aware of the vital role it ascribed to conscience. As Boyd Hilton observes:

> That man is good – that his faculties, emotions, and intellect are ruled over by conscience – is the repetitious argument of Chalmers...the material universe may reveal God's *cleverness*, but only man's conscience – 'a mechanism of obvious contrivance' – suggests that the Creator is benevolent as well...we derive pleasure from acting virtuously and misery from being vicious. Rectitude is thus its own reward, and sin its own punishment, from which it was possible to infer 'that we lived under the administration of a God who loved righteousness and who hated iniquity'. Here Chalmers was celebrating the Butlerian idea of conscience...natural theology was thus transferred from the physical to the mental world...[40]

Which is precisely what Erskine did. There are unmistakable echoes in Erskine of Joseph Butler's "superior principle of reflection or conscience in every man", which God has fittingly tailored to the human constitution.[41] In addition, strong overtones are recognisable of Kant's 'law which orders love', and his maxim of a universal law or moral principle, the 'categorical imperative', based on the supposed awareness of a common rational 'moral sanctioning' faculty closely related to human conscience, which was able freely to approve universally 'right' or 'moral' behaviour.[42] Furthermore, in a manner reminiscent of Rousseau,[43] Erskine elevated the role of 'con-

---

[39] See Appendix 5, pp.292-93. Referring to Reid, Leslie Stephen commented, "The conscience...which guides our moral judgments, is at once, in his language, an intellectual and an active power, and its supremacy is, as with Butler, an ultimate and self-evident fact", (*History of English Thought in the Eighteenth Century* [1876], [3rd edition, in 2 volumes] [London: Harbinger Books, 1962], II, 52-53).

[40] Boyd Hilton, *The Age Of Atonement: the Influence of Evangelicalism on Social and Economic Thought 1785-1865* (Oxford: Clarendon Press, 1988), 185-6.

[41] Joseph Butler, *Fifteen Sermons* [1726] (London: G. Bell & Sons, 1964), §1.8, 38, §2.8, 53.

[42] Immanuel Kant, *Critique of Practical Reason* [1788] (Indianapolis: Bobbs-Merrill Educational Publishing, 1956), 71-3, 85-7; *Foundations of the Metaphysics of Morals* [1785], [2nd edition] (New Jersey: Prentice-Hall, Inc., 1997), 38. Butler and Kant were frequently read together in academic circles in the later nineteenth century, (Jane Garnett, "Bishop Butler and the Zeitgeist", in Christopher Cunliffe, (ed.), *Joseph Butler's Moral and Religious Thought* [Oxford: Clarendon Press, 1992], 82).

[43] See N.J.H. Dent, *Rousseau* (Oxford: Basil Blackwell, 1988), 229-30.

science' (albeit Christocentrically) to that of virtual supreme inward authority in moral and theological matters, affirming that "the conscience in each man is the Christ in each man", "the very presence of God within us", and that "the universal diffusion of conscience through all men is Christ in all men". Crucially, conscience was "the original revelation which [God] makes of Himself in every man, whether the man regards it and understands it, or not". Erskine's mission was to help the world recognise that salvation consisted of apprehending that "the great thing is to become conscious of Him, and to know Him through Himself revealed in conscience", so to become united with Christ and manifest a Christ-like life. This was close to a natural version of *imitatio Christi*, with the conscience acting as monitor. Erskine did not ever seem to acknowledge the possibility of an erring conscience. For him, conscience is universally present and divine in origin. Everyone therefore possesses an innate and original capacity for apprehending spiritual truth. Accordingly, truth 'commends itself' to conscience for belief. In practice, Erskine would only consider anything to be 'righteous' and 'true' if it thus 'commended itself' to his conscience, which, in priority to other sources of authority, was effectively his ethical guide and rule of life, what he interchangeably called the "inward" or "true" light, the "great organ of Theology", the "Spirit within each man", which it was humanity's goal continuously to apprehend.[44]

Erskine was taking a significant and novel step forward (certainly for Scottish theology) in appropriating such eclectic sources to advocate reliance on the internal power of the human mind and its faculties as a self-authenticating trustworthy vehicle, *particularly in its unregenerate state*, for comprehending the nature and character of God. This largely represented introduction into theology of a new and increasingly optimistic, lofty, view of human nature, considered to be intimately related to God's own being as *imago Dei*. In contradistinction, bleak Calvinist assessments treated human nature as totally depraved, where even conscience required regeneration.

The Unitarians had already begun to explore this area, Erskine's contemporary, William Ellery Channing, concisely anticipating Erskine in the importance attributed to the pivotal role of conscience.[45] Furthermore, like the Romantics, Erskine recognised the tension between faith, rationalism, and experience. Realising the limitations of reason and intellect, he insisted on supplementing their authority with intuition, conscience, and feeling: "I believe that all the fundamental spiritual truths are out of the sphere of the reasoning faculty, but that they are in the sphere of conscience, and that we do not apprehend them at all, unless we apprehend them in our con-

---

[44] Letter to Lady Ashburton, 30 January [no year], *NLS MS* Acc.11388/74–57b; Shairp, "Reminiscences", *Letters-II*, 353-7.

[45] See Appendix 2.

sciences".[46] It became increasingly vital for Erskine to combat what he regarded as 'false ideas' concerning the 'justice' or 'righteousness' of God, so that crucially even 'unregenerate man' should, through conscience, be able to correctly judge and appreciate the loving, righteous character of God, because of its critical salvific implications.[47] His friend and biographer, Principal Shairp, spoke of Erskine's

> absolute conviction that all true thought about God would be found to harmonise with all that is truest and highest in the conscience and the affections of man. It was the desire himself to see and to make others see this harmony, to see that Christian doctrine was that which alone meets the cravings of heart and conscience, – it was this desire which animated him in all the books he wrote, and in all the many conversations he carried on".[48]

From a critical Calvinist perspective, his friend, Adolphe Monod, suggested that Erskine "judges by feeling, and proves by imagination".[49] Erskine confessed to ambiguity regarding his understanding of *conscience:* "I have used it sometimes to signify the Spirit of God in man, and sometimes to signify the man's own apprehension of the mind of the Spirit in him".[50] Characteristically he declared, "This is the true light, which lighteth every man. My conscience is two things – first, a spiritual faculty capable of receiving that light; secondly, the presence of that light…The true light *is* the Saviour, the Redeemer…".[51] Therefore, for Erskine, *conscience*, firstly, assumed the status of an in-built faculty to recognise spiritual truth. Secondly, it was incarnate within redeemed humanity (i.e., everyone – not just regenerate Christians), and personalised as the universal indwelling Christ himself, who facilitated a life journey of education and self-development. Like Schleiermacher and William Law, Erskine may be perceived as harking back to Platonic ideas concerning innate awareness of the divine. Schleiermacher argued this was apparent in human feeling as a sense of vital relation to the whole universe, and Law referred to it 'antecedently' as "*something of Heaven hidden* in [man's] Soul". Accordingly, doctrines were mere earthly reflections of eternal truths which must be recognised

---

[46] Letter to Madame Vinet, 6 February 1839, *Letters-I,* 348.

[47] *Election,* 10-11.

[48] Shairp, "Reminiscences", *Letters-II,* 366. Significantly, Shairp had been an undermaster at Rugby with Thomas Arnold, and was an expert in Romantic literature, especially Coleridge's philosophy and religious thought.

[49] *Life and Letters of Adolphe Monod, Pastor of the Reformed Church of France,* by one of his daughters (London: James Nisbet, 1885), 51.

[50] *Election,* xxii-xxiii.

[51] Letter to Bishop Ewing, 21 May 1861, *Ewing-I,* 36.

Revelation and the Location of Authority 57

and commended by conscience.[52] Erskine believed that the entire human race was

> as one great common – constituted in Christ, as the basis of its being – and having Christ as its head. He is thus related to the whole race, as the head of a man is related to his body. With this difference that each individual man has his own individual will and responsibility. But He is the head and sensorium to all, from which spiritual life and light and power are distributed to every member, to be used and neglected on the responsibility of that member. The presence of that life is manifested in the *conscience* of every man – but until he knows whence that life comes and whither it goes, he cannot rightly understand it, nor yield himself to it...I feel that there is an unspeakable strengthening of the obligation of duty in the discovery, that conscience is not a mere faculty of our natures, but the personal presence of our loving Lord, striving with each one, as if he had no other care...[53]

Therefore the salvific key to appropriating the reality of the latent divine relationship lay in life-transforming revelation concerning the 'treasure within', and the constant surrender of self-will to 'conscience' – that divine/ human faculty which personified the indwelling Christ. The salvific fruit, if authentic, would necessarily manifest itself in ethical obedience.

In his own version of contemporary concerns to account for the universality of the moral sense, and like other Victorians,[54] Erskine personalised conscience, so that in his experiential theology the person of Christ became an innate, active, ethical presence prompting every individual, and defining the very nature of Christianity:

> Jesus Christ is God in our flesh, – and what is the voice in man's conscience, but the voice of God in man's flesh? Christianity, then, is the unveiling of the true nature of conscience, as it is in every man.[55]

By merging incarnational christology with human psychology, Erskine thus developed an innovatory scheme holding individual and corporate salvific concepts in tension. Christ became the organic divine principle within a redeemed humanity which was progressing towards realisation of its new nature, what Erskine termed "the resurrection state of man, as standing in

---

[52] Erskine was fond of Plato, notably the *Phaedo,* where the theme of innate ideas is emphasised, and was particularly struck by similar ideas expressed by the Cambridge Platonists, (Letter to A.J. Scott, 3 August 1837, *Letters-I,* 256-7; Letter to John McLeod Campbell, 2 October 1856, *Letters-II,* 111 [and footnote]). For Schleiermacher, see *Christian Faith,* §4, 12-18, §83, 341-5. For Law, see *Love,* 209-13.
[53] Letter to Mrs Schwabe, 14 December 1853, *NLS MS* 9747-33.
[54] E.g., John Henry Newman, *An Essay in Aid of A Grammar of Assent* [1870] (Notre Dame, Indiana: University of Notre Dame Press, 1979), 98-107.
[55] *Election,* 540.

the second Adam".[56] Erskine's entire belief system was concurrently based on a Christianised philosophical assumption, which he creatively translated into popular format, that everyone instinctively becomes aware of an innate capacity for apprehending the divine within them:

> we feel that our capacity of apprehending and possessing righteousness is the highest thing within us, connecting us with a spiritual order infinitely transcending the material universe and its laws.[57]

The Law, so beloved of Erskine's Calvinist contemporaries, was itself personified into Christ himself as "the righteous will of God", so that the principle of 'law', intrinsic to the conscience, was constantly seeking to "reproduce itself in the hearts of all men, and actually accomplishing its object in so far as the love which gave Christ is apprehended".[58] Unlike many neo-Kantian thinkers, however, and perhaps in deference to his Calvinist heritage, Erskine noted (with insufficient clarity for some) the impossibility of actually living a moral life without the regenerating aid of the Holy Spirit and the personal, indwelling Christ assuming one's whole existence: "The true spiritual dispensation…consists in the indwelling of the Spirit in the heart, in knowing God personally in the heart".[59] Nevertheless the near-identification at times of his thought with some less orthodox views of Christianity as mere moral duty or universalised conscience-based religion, along with the embrace of a philosophical theology, inevitably represent, for some, problematic aspects of Erskine's system.

Laws of the Spiritual Order

Erskine's contemporary apologetic agenda therefore resulted in him presenting the truth of the gospel as an answer to the 'disease in the soul of man' independent of the historical accuracy of the facts to which it testified. Historical fact was subservient to the universal moral principles it illustrated. Erskine appealed instead to the self-evidencing nature of truth which corresponded to what he regarded, like Hume and Kant, as universal innate human instincts and moral awareness: "I may be told about difficulties attending the facts, but I still insist that it is true in morals; it is true in nature, it is true in the constitution of man, it is true in the character of God".[60]

---

[56] *Election*, 40-1.
[57] *Sp.Order*, 106.
[58] *Sp.Order*, 192.
[59] Letter to Mr W. Tait, 16 October 1834, *Letters-I*, 229, cf., Letter to F.D. Maurice, 28 June 1859, *Letters-II*, 133.
[60] Letter to Thomas Chalmers, 21 November 1818, *Letters-I*, 27.

Julia Wedgwood explained that, for Erskine, "the invisible world appeared to him to be the subject of laws just as open to investigation, and far more permanent than those by which the outward universe is governed, these laws forming the object of revelation…". Furthermore, he saw that the exhibition of love existing in God was "the law of life…[which] had, it seemed to him, an actual power to kindle in the perceiving heart the love we could never awaken by any exertion of will on our part".[61] But how did this 'law of love' work, and how did Erskine conceive of a saving knowledge of God being attained? How could he confidently affirm that "the gospel presents us with a history of facts, the belief of which must by the nature of things produce this character, bringing our thoughts and wills into union with the Supreme Will, and increasing our sense of the evil of sin whilst it annihilates despair"?[62] What was the ambiguous "something in God, which cannot be known without inspiring confidence…a ground of confidence in His very nature, which requires only to be known in order to give peace"?[63]

In seeking to describe the uniqueness of Christian revelation, Erskine referred to what he termed the 'theological' and 'preceptive' elements of religion, which needed to correspond in order to appeal to human reason and conscience. By this he meant that truth which discloses the nature of God carries within itself a divine power according to the laws of the 'spiritual order' to produce divine character conformity. Christian 'theology' must therefore afford "such a representation of the relation in which God stands to us as may have a direct tendency to produce in us that character which the preceptive teaching inculcates". Accordingly, where we meet with 'preceptive' religion, such as in creeds and doctrines, we ought also

> to expect something in its theological teaching which may correspond to it as its living root. The coherent relation of the doctrines of Christianity to its moral precepts, and the dynamic efficiency of the doctrines in producing spontaneous obedience, and thus working out the Christian character, is one of the most striking evidences of the truth of Christianity.[64]

Erskine was so convinced that human happiness and fulfilment is based entirely in the will and purposes of God, that he regarded it as 'the law of his being' and 'the very law of our nature' that the human heart could not do other than respond when it recognised God's loving promptings, since the divine seed had already been universally implanted by Christ as organic Head of the human race. He consistently believed in the intrinsic power of the divine incarnation to restore human nature to God. In one of his two

---

[61] Wedgwood, *Teachers*, 68, 72.
[62] Letter to Thomas Chalmers, 21 November 1818, *Letters-I*, 26.
[63] *Extracts*, xxvii.
[64] *Sp.Order*, 15-16.

existent sermons, probably from the Row period, Erskine proclaimed that it was the work of Jesus "to manifest...*the effect on man*, when God's love is believed and allowed to produce its true fruits in his heart".[65]

This philosophical/ scientific/ theological concept of 'saving knowledge' was developed by Erskine to seek to convey understanding of the otherwise ambiguous spiritual 'law' or dynamics whereby revealed awareness of the character (or as he sometimes preferred to express it, the 'Name'[66]) of God, chiefly presented in terms of love and grace, instrumentally generated salvific belief. It was a form of 'co-operative' or synergistic *ex opere operatum*, in which divine operation and human faculties became mystically confused. Erskine drew a parallel with the Israelites who were healed by looking at the brazen serpent in Numbers 21: "As soon as the mental eye, which is faith or understanding, came in contact with the meaning of the serpent, or the character of God revealed in it, the life of the soul was healed".[67] Imaginatively appropriating scientific terminology, he suggested a spiritual 'Newtonian' law of salvation dynamics automatically operated when we "open our hearts" to receive divine goodwill, and through necessary effectual or salvific 'knowledge', acquire confidence that we are loved and forgiven. Inner peace was actualised by simple recognition of, and faith in, God's loving, righteous purpose for humanity, incorporating the ultimate defeat of evil.[68] As a result, God's character would self-reproduce in us, belief generating character, 'love begetting love'. This self-generating mechanism Erskine referred to as the 'Gospel' which is

> THE POWER *of God unto salvation*, that is, as containing the *dynamics*, so to speak, the spiritual lever, and ropes, and pulleys, and wheels by which the human spirit may be lifted out of the horrible pit and miry clay of sin and selfishness into a harmony with the mind of God, so that a real apprehension of the character of God and His purposes towards us, and our relation to Him, without any mention of the precepts, would spontaneously produce the life of them within our souls.[69]

Salvation, therefore, was not an external forensic fact but existential deliverance from within, a transformed condition of the human soul resulting from the innate, creative, power of the gospel itself to reveal 'righteous-

---

[65] "God's Welcome to the Returning Sinner", in Donald Campbell, (ed.), *Fragments of Truth: being expositions of passages of scripture chiefly from the teaching of John McLeod Campbell, D.D., with a preface by his son*, [4th edition] (Edinburgh: David Douglas, 1898), 309.

[66] "And what is the name of God? Just the *character of God* manifested in the atonement of Christ", (*Serpent*, 257).

[67] *Serpent* 24.

[68] *Sp.Order*, 153, cf., 15-16, 83-4, 92, 128-9.

[69] Letter to Lady Augusta Stanley, 11 February 1865, *Letters-II*, 151, cf., *Sp.Order*, 119-20.

ness', defined relationally by Erskine as 'the loving fatherly purpose of God'. When this was believed (necessarily involving co-operation of human receptive faculties), the gospel automatically regenerated and justified those who appropriated it, resulting in the truth itself becoming personalised within the individual.

In a further form of cross-conceptualisation, Erskine understood this "living principle" in terms of a 'physiological' law equivalent to 'justifying faith':

> I believe that one of the physiological definitions of *life* is 'the power in a thing of appropriating extraneous or foreign matter, and converting it into its own substance.' And so, when the love of God is believed, and through the door of faith enters into the heart as a life, it converts all matter, however foreign to it, into its own substance.[70]

Erskine's convictions regarding the self-contained transforming power of the gospel became increasingly accepted during the nineteenth century, concurrent with the acceptance that natural or scientific laws undergirded all cosmic processes. But there was debate regarding its locus. Did it belong to the realm of the supernatural or to the world of empirical science? For Erskine, the underlying mechanism appeared to take the spiritual form of a *moral influence* contained as a self-generating principle within the gospel itself, in which God's true character and righteous, loving purpose for humanity, when correctly apprehended, stimulated experiential Christian confidence or assurance. Erskine did not reject a supernatural element in this process, denying it was the mere result of superhuman faculties.[71] But to distinguish prevenient activity of the Holy Spirit from human intuitive capacities in Erskine often appears impossible, and this understandably generated controversy. However, probably motivated by apologetic considerations, for which he appropriated philosophical and scientific notions, Erskine seemed intent on developing soteriological understanding within the context of his innovative controlling, dynamic, philosophical, concept of 'spiritual order'. He was accustomed to speak of the 'law of love' which generated desired spiritual order and harmony within the universe.[72] Other spiritual 'laws' in the 'spiritual order' included a "moral law of gravita-

---

[70] *Serpent*, 93.

[71] Erskine actually specified 'supernatural' in preference to 'preternatural'. Whereas 'supernatural' implied "a revelation from God", 'preternatural' was "only the coming forth of a higher nature", (*Sp.Order*, 29).

[72] E.g., *Serpent*, 39-40, *Sp.Order*, 243-6. Campbell suggested A.J. Scott might be a possible source of Erskine's more developed views in this regard: "My dear late friend, Mr. Scott, used to like to dwell on the love of God in giving us love to be the law of our being; in this giving us the law of *His* own being to be the law of *our* being", (Letter to Bishop Ewing, 5 April 1866, in Ewing, "The Relation of Knowledge to Salvation", *Present-Day Papers*, 57).

tion",[73] a 'sanctifying virtue', an 'infusion of God's character', and the self-transforming power of gospel 'information'.[74] Erskine quoted from Richard Hooker, to support his idea of 'the law of righteousness' being a foundational spiritual law of the universe.[75] In his earliest essay Erskine had referred to this principle at work:

> A growing resemblance to the character thus gloriously manifested is the necessary consequence of our love for it. This is a law of our nature. The leading objects of our thoughts and affections constitute the moulds, as it were, into which our minds are cast, and from which they derive their form and character…it is only by a constant contemplation of the character of God, and by cherishing and exercising those affections and desires which arise out of this contemplation, that the Divine image is renewed in our souls.[76]

After his death, Julia Wedgwood and Emelia Gurney, both intimate acquaintances and devotees of Erskine,[77] conducted an illuminating debate concerning the accuracy of Wedgwood's portrayal of his views for a forthcoming article. Mrs Gurney, referring to Erskine's "law of gravitation of the spiritual world" (by which she believed Erskine meant "the opening the eyes to the loving purpose for each one [which] kindled the responsive love in the perceiving heart"), considered Julia Wedgwood mistaken in describing the underlying principle as implying that mere knowledge of a law automatically resulted in conformity to that law. Instead, she affirmed, "it seemed more to me as if he taught that the perception of the light and heat brought us within its action".[78]

Julia Wedgwood confirmed that, for Erskine, Christian faith was all about "awakening to a moral Cosmos governed by fixed laws", a "revelation of laws that are independent of facts", in which the gospel was itself the "dynamic force which set men right", demonstrated supremely by Christ's resurrection which Erskine believed prototypically represented the graphic vindication of a total life of recipient love, trust and dependence.[79] Wedgwood cited his repeated description of Christianity as associated "not with history so much as with science", and his understanding of Paul's

---

[73] Erskine, Letter to Principal Shairp, May 1866, Knight, *Shairp*, 241-2; Letter to Mrs Russell Gurney, 1 November 1865, *Letters-II*, 178; *Sp.Order*, 107-8.

[74] *Extracts*, xxxiv, lvii.

[75] *Sp.Order*, 106-7, citing (slightly inaccurately) *Of the Laws of Ecclesiastical Polity*, Book I, Ch. xvi. 8. See *The Works of that learned and judicious divine, Mr. Richard Hooker*, in 2 volumes (Oxford: Oxford University Press, 1841), I, 228.

[76] *Salvation*, 303.

[77] The latter referred to Erskine as 'the interpreter', *Gurney*, 26.

[78] Letter to Julia Wedgwood, 1870, *Gurney*, 79-80.

[79] 'Julia Wedgwood's Journal', *Letters-II*, 167; *Election*, 378-9.

words in Romans 1.16 [80] as the 'spiritual centre of gravitation', with the apostle himself as "the Newton of the spiritual world".[81] Erskine himself spoke in terms of the power of divine truth to influence human beings as "a system of heavenly dynamics, acting upon them, almost like the fixed laws of nature".[82] He believed that evidence for the existence of the 'spiritual order', to which humanity was created to belong, and for the 'spiritual law', which demanded our free-will response, was discernible by the operations of the "inner consciousness".[83] When challenged, Erskine explained:

> we need a law of gravitation...*no mere effort* on our part can supply what is needed. We cannot love by trying to love, we cannot trust by trying to trust. A discerned loveworthiness, a discerned trustworthiness in God, is the 'something which we need to awaken...emotions and to keep them in healthy exercise', and is that which brings us under our proper law of spiritual gravitation ...St. Paul speaks of the Gospel of Christ as the δύναμις θεοῦ εἰς σωτηρίαν, *i.e.,* as containing the divine dynamics, by which man may be lifted out of sin into righteousness, because in it there is a revelation made of the character of God and of his relation to us fitted to produce this result. When we spiritually (not merely intellectually) apprehend this revelation, we come under the true law of gravitation.[84]

The 'laws of the invisible world' therefore necessarily involved mutual reciprocity: "I cannot love God without apprehending a love-worthiness, a love-attractiveness in Him; and if salvation consists in the love of God, I can have salvation only through this apprehension".[85] For Erskine, the answer resided solely in our ongoing participation in the trusting, filial relationship of Jesus, responding to the Father's persevering, loving, purpose to 'educate' every member of the human race until his object of inculcating righteousness was fully attained.

Erskine's underlying motivation was the burning desire to recover what he believed was orthodox but lost ethical and practical truth, and present it in the light of modern theories of knowledge. He knew that his ideas were not in line with contemporary Scottish Calvinism, which he regarded as consisting largely of the obligatory acknowledgement of 'doctrines'. But he argued strongly (if, perhaps, naïvely) that he was propounding orthodox truth because intelligent thinkers everywhere (apart from his own native

---

[80] "For I am not ashamed of the gospel of Christ: for it is the power of God unto salvation to every one that believeth".

[81] Wedgwood, *Teachers*, 68, 71.

[82] *Election*, 396.

[83] *Sp.Order*, 107-8.

[84] Letter to Bishop Ewing, 23 September 1867, in Ewing, "Relation", *Present-Day Papers*, 46-7.

[85] Letter to Bishop Ewing, [undated], in Ewing, "Relation", *Present-Day Papers*, 31.

Scotland!) took it for granted already; he believed he was stating the theologically obvious. However,

> in the ordinary theology of this country…orthodox belief is almost universally considered as a duty of itself, altogether independent of its effects in producing a right spiritual relation to God, and a right conformity of our wills to his. It is not thought of as containing the *dynamics* of righteousness…I would say that the principle of believing, for believing's sake, is generally accepted. Σωτηρία is very generally understood as 'pardon', and as conditional on orthodoxy, instead of as a spiritual state produced naturally and necessarily by a spiritual apprehension of truth. Nothing but this spiritual apprehension of our true circumstances can produce this σωτηρία – no rites or ceremonies whatever; and any good which these can possibly do, must be by helping us to this spiritual apprehension.[86]

Erskine's use of Newtonian physical laws to explain the operation of spiritual truth was evidently in tune with his era, but their adaptation to theology was highly innovative. Erskine's thought categories were also inward, living, personal, organic – characteristically Romantic.[87] The eclectic mix sounded refreshingly novel and contemporary, complementing the apologetic context. However, Erskine had no wish to relativise the work of the Spirit; merely to demonstrate by analogy with modern scientific discovery that natural and spiritual laws went together. Spiritual dynamics were crucially and intrinsically ethical. As natural humanity is incapable of fulfilling its high calling of obedience to divine precepts through mere effort, something inwardly radical and dynamic was needed to produce complete divine/ human beings. Paradoxically, the self-generating 'power' was simultaneously inward, yet externally-sourced, and could not be originated by the individual. It took the form of supernaturally-inculcated, intuitively-discerned, inward ethical qualities such as humility, purity, and love:

> A principle of love – a living love, the opposite of selfishness – is the only power which can enable me to be inwardly what I feel I ought to be, and to give free and spontaneous submission to all the demands of my conscience; yet love is a power which I cannot create or command within myself, which must come to me, if at all, from some outward source.[88]

Such 'inability' was no Calvinistic moral inability however. Erskine stressed that we needed to recognise God's loving purpose for us was actually to *be* fully dependent upon him, so that we might derive a new, spon-

---

[86] Letter to Bishop Ewing, 23 September 1867, in Ewing, "Relation", *Present-Day Papers,* 47-8.
[87] The Wesleyan tradition, though similarly rooted in the Enlightenment, owed much to Romanticism, (Bebbington, *Holiness,* 57, 68-9).
[88] *Sp.Order*, 18.

taneous, *divine* ability to love. God *uses* our sense of weakness and inability to highlight awareness that an attitude of self-sufficiency hinders God's 'moment by moment' influence. Erskine's 'law of spiritual gravitation' guaranteed necessary self-generating order and harmony, providing such dependent relationship was maintained with the true divine 'centre of gravity'.[89]

Note the complex circularity of argument. For Erskine, the 'organ' by which we were meant to relate rightly to the "great spiritual Centre" was the dependent conscience. The proper operation of conscience was 'loving spontaneity' derived from God himself. We were therefore to seek it only in the 'spiritual Centre', "for love alone can give…rightness and order and blessedness".[90] As voluntary beings we *choose* this relationship, but once we do so, because we thereby fulfil the purpose of our creation, 'the law of our being' dictates that everything we do out of our relationship with God will "necessarily be right"; "it is in our relation to God, rightly observed, that our whole strength lies". We operate, therefore, under "the power of being right", and "a law of necessity". Though we have free will, if we decide to bring our will into line with God's (i.e., complete 'dependence') we *choose* the 'right centre', and thus become 'right' ourselves. But *how* do we make the right choice? Erskine answered, "By becoming acquainted with our spiritual order, that is…by learning to know God, that so we may trust Him fully and love Him fully". 'Knowing' God necessarily involved understanding and commending God's righteousness and love, because "love can be called forth only by a Being whom we can approach and know and love". Since we cannot 'love' laws and abstractions, we must therefore deal with a *personal* God who is accessible and knowable, and whose attitude towards us is manifestly loving. And it is only through loving God that we in turn can develop "the spontaneous love of right". Therefore, in God's love there is an innate "living power" which enables us to love with God's own love. God is "living righteousness" and "the very being – the living and personal fountain – of righteousness".[91]

Erskine seems here to set out an extended philosophical, mystical, and complex analogy of, or correspondence to, the supposed metaphysical and psychological consequences of the evangelical 'new birth' experience. In an evangelical sense, it mirrored a Wesleyan concept of new life through the indwelling Christ which regenerates and sanctifies, and through the Spirit "creates the subjective life of God and Christ in us".[92] In this under-

---

[89] *Sp.Order*, 20-21.
[90] *Sp.Order*, 21-2.
[91] *Sp.Order*, 23-6 (including footnotes).
[92] Melvin E. Dieter, "The Wesleyan Perspective", in M.E. Dieter, A.A. Hoekema, S.M. Horton, J. Robertson McQuilkin, J.F. Walvoord, *Five Views on Sanctification* (Grand Rapids: Zondervan, 1987), 16.

standing, Christ lives within the Christian and infuses his own love to replace our limited human capability. For Erskine, the contrast with Calvinism was vital. The Wesleyan stress on experiential faith diverged widely from the Reformed tradition where "unremitting effort was called for [and] holiness...could only be achieved by dint of regular deeds that hardened into godly habits".[93] Erskine's 'law of love' closely resembled Wesley's 'royal law' of love or 'perfection of love', enunciated within the context of inward regeneration and entire sanctification. Though he minimised eighteenth-century 'revivalism' and 'crisis experience', Erskine nevertheless echoed characteristic Wesleyan terminology in emphasising the "filial love of God", and showing that true freedom consisted in being able to love with God's own love which, Erskine maintained, he had 'shed abroad in the heart by the Holy Spirit'.[94]

In stressing that salvation necessarily involved an end to sin, there was an implied perfectionist strand to Erskine's ethical soteriology which derived from his incarnational, organic vision of a new humanity, and the inculcation of divine love as the "universal living law" within the subject.[95] A further likely influence was William Law. Erskine was impressed by his focus on the *imago Dei*, divine love, and union with Christ, and Law employed the terminology of the "eternal Law of Love" and the "Order of…Creation".[96] Law stressed that "God can have no *Delight* or *Union* with any Creature, but because his well-beloved Son, the express Image of his Person, is *found* in it". For Law, the 'Spirit of Love' was a "Necessity" for Christian sanctification and "perfect Holiness", and as a transforming divine "*Birth* in the soul" it regulated every aspect of a Christian's life because "Divine Love is a new Life, and new Nature, and introduces you into a new World".[97]

SALVIFIC KNOWLEDGE

To address issues of 'ignorance' in relation to God was a key Enlightenment concern, for "if a man can be said to have been liberated or redeemed by Christ, it is in the sense of being delivered from false conceptions of God"[98] Probably influenced by his reading of Plato, *knowledge* for Erskine

---

[93] Bebbington, *Holiness*, 62.

[94] Cf., John Wesley, Sermon IV, "Scriptural Christianity", and Sermon VIII, "The First Fruits of the Spirit", *Sermons on Several Occasions*, in 3 volumes (London: Wesleyan Conference Office, 1874), I, 43, 97, 103.

[95] *Sp.Order*, 244.

[96] William Law, *Prayer*, 58, *Love*, 269.

[97] Law, *Love*, 166, 238-9, 261, 270, cf., 168.

[98] Alister McGrath, "The Moral Theory of the Atonement", *SJT*, 38, 2 (1985), 212.

became an instrument which brought life, whilst ignorance produced death. A further related term which Erskine employed with a specialised meaning to show that gospel content has power within itself to counter the consequences of ignorance and effect salvation was *information*:

> The enmity of the natural heart, is the grand evil, the grand sin, the grand misery. Deliverance from it, is salvation. If the belief in the gospel, then, produces salvation, it must be because it contains information with regard to God, which will destroy the enmity of the heart.[99]

The transformative 'information' Erskine considered crucial involved the righteous character of God, his universal loving purposes, and the fact of Christ's deliverance of humanity from sin. Incorporating Enlightenment watchwords, the process remained both *objective*, satisfying reason, and *subjective*, satisfying conscience. However, spiritual truth was never a mere body of facts to be acquired, but always supremely an illumination within humanity itself which required actualisation based on willing response. *Light* was therefore frequently a potent mystical symbol adapted by Erskine to account for revelatory dynamics: "as the light enters into us by our eyes seeing it, so this life enters into us by our minds seeing it, i.e., by our believing it or knowing it as truth".[100] In *The Doctrine of Election* Erskine emphasised the Christocentric and incarnational nature of salvific revelation which he believed released a divine life principle within us through correct spiritual apprehension:

> when we see rightly the gift of Christ, we shall see that as he is the true *light* which lighteth every man, so also there is in Him a communication of *life* to every man...and thus, the light which lighteth every man is *a living* light – a light whereby he may live. And thus by the entrance of the word into our flesh, not only has God been brought near to us, as an *object* of trust and love, but also his *living* Spirit, the divine nature, has been communicated to us *subjectively* as a capacity of embracing God, whether we exercise it or not. I do not mean that the divine nature is in a man to his profit, unless he joins himself to it; but there it is, – in him.[101]

Erskine's efforts to remain essentially orthodox may be discerned in his concern to avoid any charge of human deification. It is reasonable to view this now as little more than an innovative explanatory re-working of traditional views concerning Christian regeneration, albeit with mystical and psychological overtones. For his time, however, it sounded revolutionary. Erskine's thinking concerning salvific knowledge was closely linked with controversial assertions concerning the ethically transformative power of

---

[99] *Extracts*, lvii.

[100] Letter to Miss Rachel Erskine, July 1829, *Letters-I*, 155.

[101] *Election*, 61.

the character of God, the universal indwelling Christ, universal pardon, assurance, and Christ's atoning work, which he acknowledged was fundamentally at variance with accepted religious precepts.[102]

Erskine's emphasis on personal interest, however, acted as a necessary orthodox corrective to pervasive eighteenth-century Deistic natural theology, which tended to reduce religion to an innate, human-centred expression of morality. By insisting on knowing God through Christ, by possessing correct 'information', Erskine ensured that revelation was essentially Christocentric in nature and intrinsically redemptive in power, and that salvific experience necessarily involved authentic transformative personal relationship with God.

Erskine's novel approach in expressing soteriological views which sounded traditional notes whilst simultaneously chiming with contemporary moral and philosophical speculative thought, was paralleled elsewhere, and confirms our view that Erskine is best understood eclectically as part of a much bigger picture. With the rise of continental idealistic philosophy, the ability of 'higher truth' to impact individuals through recognition of a universal divine 'power', which was able to authenticate itself within the individual through correspondence with the internal 'divine' faculties of reason, conscience and the moral sense, began to be recognised more widely. It was not surprising that some forward-looking thinkers recognised the potential for theological speculation concerning divine apprehension. Erskine's close friend, Alexandre Vinet, the noted liberal French Swiss theologian, whom he met at Lausanne in 1838, was denoted by George Stevens "the French Schleiermacher".[103] Vinet, strongly influenced by Erskine, in whom he found "a more liberal and congenial evangelicalism",[104] held remarkably similar views concerning the inward, subjective appropriation of truth within the human consciousness, the importance of the moral adaptation of Christianity to the human character, and the self-regenerating power of the gospel.[105] Like Erskine, Vinet considered Christian belief to be a transcription of "the historical facts of the gospel into our inward and outward life", with the gospel as "a force, a virtue that transforms those who study it".[106]

---

[102] See *Extracts*, xxx-xxxv.

[103] George Barker Stevens, *The Christian Doctrine of Salvation* (Edinburgh: T.&T. Clark, 1905), 227.

[104] Bernard Reymond, "Towards a Rediscovery of Vinet", cited by Donald Kennedy, *Alexandre Vinet Liberal Evangelical* (Belfast: private publication, no date), 173.

[105] Cf., Laura M. Lane, *The Life and Writings of Alexander Vinet* (Edinburgh: T.&T. Clark, 1890), 125; Pierre Bovet (ed.), *Alexandre Vinet: Lettres, 1813 – 1828,* in 4 volumes, (Lausanne: Librairie Payot, 1947), I, 204-5.

[106] Paul T. Fuhrmann, *Extraordinary Christianity* (Philadelphia: Westminster Press, 1964), 69, 67.

The Nature of Saving Faith

Revelation, knowledge, understanding, and faith were vitally and inextricably related in Erskine's eclectic epistemology of divine salvific apprehension. Saving faith was intimately connected, as in all his thinking, with personal "knowledge of the laws of the invisible world", especially "the great law of the dynamics of the moral world", and the essential Fatherly, loving, righteous character of God, which it was Christ's mission to reveal.[107] This was the 'divine goodness' which faith, as "the recipient organ in the spiritual being" must receive "out of Him", and was necessarily manifested ethically in righteous living. So for Erskine, faith was the 'awakening of this receptive spirit within us'.[108]

To Calvinist Scots, Erskine's novel doctrine of universal pardon made justification antecedent to faith, thereby effectively eliminating faith as the means of justification, and redefining it as little more than discovery of the fact. To those who questioned, 'if God has already pardoned everyone what is the use of faith?', Erskine replied that God's love was not conditional on belief in Christ, but that faith *consisted of* personally knowing and appropriating God's love for the individual. Such consequential confidence was the key to open the heart to receive "God's living Spirit". Again, the crucial factor was knowledge of God's pardoning character:

> The belief of this information as written in the death and resurrection of Christ is the faith of the gospel; and the use of it is, that it makes the character of God the ground of confidence...Any faith which is not personal confidence appears to me a mere fallacy.[109]

Erskine saw 'true' faith as involving two related but distinct concepts – 'belief', and 'trust' or 'confidence' – the second flowing necessarily from the first as an authenticating inner witness:

> I cannot trust in God or man, without a belief of trustworthiness. I must apprehend a character justifying and warranting my trust, before I can fully trust. A entire trust in our righteous Father, is evidently the right state of man...This trust, therefore, necessarily presupposes the belief, that God is an almighty, loving, wise, and righteous Father and Guide. Now what is my warrant for believing this?...It is surely my inward consciousness that this ought to be the character, connected with the conviction that what ought must be...[110]

---

[107] Wedgwood, *Teachers*, 71, cf., *Letters-I*, 160-1.
[108] Letter to Bishop Ewing, [no date], in Ewing, "Relation", *Present-Day Papers*, 32; Wedgwood, *Teachers*, 71.
[109] Letter to Miss Rachel Erskine, 15 September 1829, *Letters-I*, 165-6.
[110] *Ewing-II*, 58-9.

Faith, for Erskine, was much more than mere rational assent to doctrines and historical events. It was a total existential response of the human being to the revelation of God in Christ, a "total spiritual condition showing that a man had responded in his whole being to the love of God".[111] Spiritual apprehension in Erskine's hands equated to a psychological process involving the necessary 'awakening' of the inward 'receptive spirit' to the laws of the invisible world. This stood in direct contrast to the prevailing understanding in Scotland of 'faith' as the 'title-deeds' to eternal security.[112] Creatively sensitive to his scientific context, and reflecting Lockean empirical perspectives, Erskine was concerned to demonstrate that 'true' faith was not a kind of blind belief based on external received authority, and often popularly perceived to be opposed to knowledge. What mattered was internal conviction of revealed truth. Individuals must *for themselves* experientially apprehend the 'light' and 'truth' of any supposed teaching in their own reason and conscience. For Erskine, *faith* became virtually synonymous with *conscience*, being the complementary responsive faculty to revelation as the organ of 'inspiration' and 'spiritual apprehension':

> All spiritual truth is addressed to the conscience in man, and is only understood by the conscience; and if the conscience is not in action the truth is to him like light grasped by the hand instead of received by the eye...I believe that all spiritual truth is of inspiration, and that it is apprehended (as I said before) by that in man which is of the nature of inspiration.[113]

Conscience was the effective agent of salvation. Erskine insisted it must not be resisted and required complete obedience. It was the key to manifesting an existential quality of salvific faith which depended on moment-by-moment dependence on God, and made 'sympathy' with divine providence possible. The model was Christ's own free-will trust in the Father, and the process again involved *spiritual recipiency* – that sympathetic dependency, the only means by which we can "really participate with Him and make His actions our own by faith".[114] Accordingly, "*faith* and *recipiency* are one thing. The righteousness of faith is God received into man's will...but a *belief* in the inextinguishable loving purpose of God is necessary as the basis of this faith"[115]

---

[111] Duncan Finlayson, "Aspects of the Life of Thomas Erskine of Linlathen, 1788-1870", *RSCHS*, XX (1980), 34. Contrast this with suggestions that Erskine was influenced by Sandemanian views; see Appendix 4.
[112] Wedgwood, *Teachers*, 71.
[113] Letter to Professor Lorimer, 14 July 1858, *Letters-II,* 213, cf., Letter to Rev. Donald Campbell, 11 March 1864, *Letters-II,* 257.
[114] Letter to Bishop Ewing, [no date], in Ewing, "Relation", *Present-Day Papers*, 33.
[115] Letter to Bishop Ewing, 16 September 1865, *Ewing-I*, 61-2.

Unless revealed truth penetrates individuals' responsive "inner consciousness", "conscience", or "moral reason" (the terms appeared interchangeable), Erskine believed they had no real grasp of Christianity.[116] Erskine therefore radically and immanently reformulated 'faith' as that "spiritual faculty which may perceive and receive Divine truth, from whatever source it comes". Reminiscent of Hume's and Kant's 'inherent moral sense', it took the form of a universal "innate original capacity of apprehending spiritual truths when revealed, that we might find God and know Him for ourselves".[117]

External sources, like the Bible, were not meant to provide final grounds of authority in themselves. This definitively resided in the human "spiritual consciousness", where truth was 'discerned' by 'true' faith based upon "inward facts". Employing a favourite scientific analogy, Erskine argued that as humanity was able to apprehend *material* reality using *physical* faculties, so they possessed *spiritual* faculties for discerning revealed *spiritual* reality. For those exercising the 'higher faculty' of faith, the Bible became a "vehicle" or "instrument of education" revealing "spiritual discoveries". It expounded spiritual laws and intrinsic truths which necessarily corresponded with the known "outward facts" of human existence, in the same way as the discoveries of material laws 'discerned' by scientists like Kepler and Newton were accepted in due course to correspond with outward reality, even though initially resisted.[118] Hence, Erskine's radical insistence that the only satisfactory indisputable evidence was internal, and that human capacity to discern truth needed to be developed by training in spiritual understanding and knowledge *of* God, rather than knowledge *about* him.

The connection between revelation, knowledge, understanding, faith, and the moral influence of gospel content properly apprehended, was developed particularly in *An Essay on Faith*. Here Erskine was concerned to demonstrate that his object was not

> to represent faith as a difficult or perplexed operation, but to withdraw the attention from the act of believing, and to fix it on the object of belief, by showing that we cannot believe any moral fact without entering into its spirit, and meaning, and importance.[119]

Rather,

> the revelation of a spiritual truth means, *presenting and explaining it to our spiritual understanding*. It can do me no good until it comes in contact with

---

[116] *Sp.Order*, 99, 91.
[117] *Sp.Order*, 79, 83, cf., 80-1, 89-90.
[118] *Sp.Order*, 83-4, 87, 92.
[119] *Faith*, 142.

my own spiritual understanding – until I see its eternal truth and reasonableness. It is not really revealed to me till then".[120]

Particularly apposite for legalistic Scotland, Erskine insisted that the necessary consequence of believing the gospel is divine conformity, for "obedience to the law of God" and "holy love to God and man is the natural fruit of faith in the Gospel".[121] Together therefore, revelation, knowledge, and faith generate a quality of inward spiritual apprehension which necessarily motivates ethical and practical outworking, instead of mere legal or doctrinal apprehension:

> One great mistake into which man falls in the matter of religion, is that he thinks that obedience to the law is the way by which he is to arrive at a farther blessing…But the great blessing itself is, to have the law written in the heart…because the law is God's own character. And he who has God's law in his heart, is conformed to God's character.[122]

The gospel, as the right 'object of belief', incorporated within itself the necessary power to produce character transformation. In a firm statement regarding inward versus outward authority, Erskine declared:

> If I am to be saved or spiritually healed by a truth, I must have my spirit brought into contact with the quality and character and reality of that truth, so as to be affected by it in accordance with its proper nature, – and any faith which is not fitted to do this is not that which I need.[123]

Faith was therefore no mere intellectual exercise or form of mental assent, but something dynamic, experimental, and transformational. But neither did it drift away to consist merely of subjective experience, but rather of internally-applied knowledge. Erskine was convinced that "salvation by faith", or what he often termed 'the healing of the soul', "is only effected by the knowledge of the truth concerning God's love", and that "a man is saved by coming *to the knowledge of the truth* – of what is and has been always true". In this way Erskine could link faith directly with his concept of universal pardon as historical fact.[124] Nevertheless, the validity of truth overwhelmingly lay in its necessarily life-transforming power. Reflecting on the variety of human experience, he distinguished between different kinds of 'illumination', and on hearing that Lord Melbourne had enjoyed reading a favourite spiritual author, Erskine lamented: "It seems to me to imply a great defect in any work on religion, that it should be able to be

---

[120] Letter to Bishop Ewing, 16 September 1865, *Ewing-I*, 62.
[121] *Faith*, 143.
[122] *Extracts*, lvi, lviii.
[123] Letter to Bishop Colenso, [undated], *Letters-II*, 209.
[124] *Serpent*, 26, 77.

read by those who walk without God, and to be read with pleasure by them".[125] In contrast, he contended that true religion provokes a living response from the heart to the inward voice of God: "Christianity consists in...listening to and following and cleaving to the spirit testifying in the conscience; and ungodliness consists in going forward without attending to this voice of God. Our Christianity is not out of us but in us".[126]

In *An Essay on Faith,* Erskine displayed his pre-modern, empirical, and psychological preoccupation with the processes by which we understand, rationalise, and apprehend, as creatively applied to the acquisition of salvific faith. He reflected genuine nineteenth-century post-Kantian absorption in comprehending how meaning and reality are formulated by the mind:

> What is the difference between knowledge or understanding, and faith? Our understanding of a thing means the conception which we have formed of it, or the impression which it has made on our mind, without any reference to its being a reality in nature independent of our thought, or a mere fiction of the imagination: And faith is a persuasion, accompanying these impressions, that the objects which produced them are realities in nature, independent of our thought or perception...Faith, then, is just an appendage to those faculties of the mind by which we receive impressions from external objects, whether they be material or immaterial. It stands at the entrances of the mind, as it were, and passes sentence on the authenticity of all information which goes in.[127]

This sounds remarkably like a Christianised version of Locke, Hume, or Kant. In effect, Erskine eclectically reformulated traditional understanding of faith to accord with both historical and contemporary philosophical epistemological speculations. Informed by 'correct' knowledge and understanding, faith became essentially a 'divine adjudicator', authenticating mental 'truth' or 'sense' impressions. Additionally integrating Platonic and Romantic notions, it operated as a kind of 'higher spiritual faculty'.[128] Erskine, like many Romantic contemporaries, found Plato intellectually and spiritually stimulating, especially his emphasis on inquiry after truth. One of Erskine's favourite Platonic dialogues, the *Gorgias*, emphasised the close connection between knowledge and goodness.[129] Reason remained a noble faculty, but discerning truth was no mere rational exercise. Truths such as 'goodness' and 'love' also needed to be *experienced*. Nevertheless, if no impression is actually made on the mind, there cannot be faith or ex-

---

[125] Letter to Mrs Stirling, 19 June 1838, *Letters-I,* 299.
[126] Letter to Madame de Broglie, 4 June 1838, *Letters-I,* 309.
[127] *Faith,* 37, 39.
[128] Cf., Arthur F. Holmes, *Fact, Value, and God* (Leicester: Apollos, 1997), 14-16, 101-2.
[129] Edith Hamilton and Huntington Cairns (eds.), *The Collected Dialogues of Plato* (Princeton: Princeton University Press, 1961), 241-43.

ercise of belief. Furthermore, if the impression is based on 'incorrect' information the resulting belief will be false. We need 'correct' moral impressions (which for Erskine proceed uniquely from the gospel) before we can believe them. So we do not receive truth authentically "unless the impression of its moral meaning is actually made on the mind".[130] Accordingly, Erskine was able to regard 'faith' or 'understanding' as a kind of insight, intuition, or "mental eye" (perhaps appropriating Plato's "eye of the mind"), divinely appointed to suit the human constitution. On contact with something which reveals true knowledge concerning the righteous divine character, it results automatically in salvation or 'healing of the soul' when the intuition is appropriated.[131] Boundaries between human and divine spirits were apparently deliberately blurred by Erskine. The 'voice of God' interchanged as intuition, conscience, or the Spirit of Jesus.[132] Faith was inextricably involved as the 'truth adjudicator'. He was convinced that "in spiritual things logic really goes for nothing, except the gratification of the consciousness of intellectual power; intuition is everything, that is, the faculty of seeing light and recognising it to be light". Reminiscent of Hume, who rejected the primacy of reason in favour of moral subjectivity,[133] spiritual intuition was a 'higher faculty than logic'.[134] Erskine was to refine the distinction between the intellectual understanding of the mind and the inward witness of the spirit, in particular linking it to his developing ideas of 'the true light which lighteth every man' and the 'understanding' which comes from dependence on the 'great deep' of divine, as opposed to human, wisdom. Erskine saw Christians as "placed above this great deep, with an apparatus, a mental apparatus, for drawing it up". The apparatus itself he compared to creating a vacuum in a 'spiritual pump' which draws up divine wisdom only when we suspend recourse to our own human wisdom.[135]

Erskine frequently resorted to analogy and metaphor to explicate the self-evidencing process of saving faith. Asking "what is it that enters into our hearts when we believe anything?", he replied, "Is it not the thing that we believe?" The true object of saving faith was unquestionable: "God's love is the only spiritual life – the only sap of the universal vine, and it can

---

[130] *Faith*, 85.

[131] *Serpent*, 24. The 'eye of the mind' or 'eye of the soul' is a concept found especially in Plato's "Republic", Hamilton and Cairns (eds.), *Collected Dialogues*, 746, 760. It also appears in William Law's *Prayer*, 117. John McLeod Campbell also understood revelation in terms remarkably similar to Erskine, *Thoughts on Revelation*, [2nd edition] (London: Macmillan and Co., 1874), 26-7.

[132] Letter to Madame de Broglie, 4 June 1838, *Letters-I*, 309.

[133] Hume, *Treatise*, 294-5, 301-6.

[134] Letter to Rev. Donald Campbell, 11 March 1864, *Letters-II*, 255-6, cf., Letter to Julia Wedgwood, 12 June 1865, *Letters-II*, 158.

[135] Letter to Madame de Broglie, 4 June 1838, *Letters-I*, 310.

only enter, as it cannot but enter, by being believed".[136] This, then, represents the 'correct information'. Good 'knowledge' of God, when believed, of itself necessarily reproduces divine character within human beings, profoundly impacting their wills. Though today we perhaps tend to regard Erskine's confidence in a 'necessary' transformational process as somewhat naïve and unrealistic, it nevertheless resonated with the nineteenth century's predilection for universal laws. However, such a radical and innovatory view of faith had far-reaching consequences for authentic practical religion. Erskine suggested that those who viewed the atonement merely as "a means of procuring the pardon of sin", had a 'selfish', limited, and erroneous idea of it. True revelation concerning the atonement, however, necessarily involved personal appropriation of its active moral categories like 'holiness', 'obedience', and 'forgiveness'. That is, "it contains a medicine for the mind" which is entirely suited to it, since "the revelation is addressed to human thought and human feeling", enlightening the conscience and exciting the 'affections'.[137] The implications for contemporary Scottish religion were profound. Erskine's ideas were soon indignantly perceived to undermine the entire Calvinist belief structure by attacking establishment ministers for failing to preach the true gospel and condemning believers for 'selfishness' and 'self-righteousness'.[138]

Erskine seemed to understand a kind of natural/ supernatural salvific 'law' inherent to the believing process, often perceived by critics as mystical and psychological soteriological novelty and innovation:

> by *faith* as used in Scripture [Erskine] understood to be meant a certain moral or spiritual activity or energy which virtually implied salvation, because it implied the existence of a principle of spiritual life possessed of an immortal power. This faith, he believed, could be properly awakened only by the manifestation, through Christ, of love as the law of life, and as identical with an eternal righteousness which it was God's purpose to bestow on every individual soul. As an interpreter of the mystical side of Calvinism and of the psychological conditions which correspond with the doctrines of grace Erskine is unrivalled.[139]

The self-evidencing, subjective, experiential nature of the gospel was clearly equated by Erskine to salvation itself. Referring to the circumstance of the parable of the creditor and debtors in Luke 7, Erskine advised a clerical inquirer:

---

[136] Letter to Miss Rachel Erskine, May 1829, *Letters-I*, 153.
[137] *Faith*, 96, 97-9.
[138] Robertson, *Vindication*, 5; Thomson, *Universal Pardon*, 484-93.
[139] "Thomas Erskine", in *Encyclopaedia Britannica* [11th edition], XI (New York: Encyclopaedia Britannica Inc., 1910-11), 756. Andrew Thomson declared that the "novelty of a religious doctrine [was] a presumption against it", *Universal Pardon*, 343-4, 497.

> This was generous love on the part of the creditor, and the debtor, who believed the love, loved in return. Faith in the love produced love, and love, being salvation, salvation and faith saved her. Now this…illustrates the mind of God towards our whole race…there is a loving desire in the heart of God towards every man, that he should turn from all sin and become righteous. As soon as I know this, and also know something of the value of righteousness, I immediately feel myself in God's hands…as soon as I have this feeling, although I am conscious of weakness that will probably lead to falls, yet I know and feel myself to be of one mind with my Father, and therefore embraced with His forgiving smile.[140]

Erskine did not go unchallenged by contemporary Calvinists, for whom faith was generally held to *follow* belief as a divine gift. This was unacceptable to Erskine since it seemed to reward human effort and minimise divine grace. He insisted that simple belief or faith in the gospel in and of itself produced forgiveness, trust and assurance towards God:

> If a man is to get a blessing for believing a thing as a reward for believing a thing, then the thing itself need not be a matter of joy; but…the gospel is itself glad tidings which are neither made gladder nor truer by being believed, but yet can make no heart glad until that heart knows them to be true…I cannot understand how a man can ever feel quite assured that he is forgiven unless that forgiveness is contained in the message of the gospel.[141]

At one level, the innovative concept of faith promoted by Erskine seemed unremarkably orthodox. He advocated true faith in the gospel as both self-evidencing and personal. People "must hear [God's] own voice, knowing it by its own evidence in their hearts", and authenticate its life-transforming fruit by practical outworking. There was no serious challenge to Erskine concerning this. However, where he was perceived to depart from traditional understanding was in marginalising the Holy Spirit, and emphasising faith as human-centred, inward, spiritual, authority, in priority to tried and tested external authorities. Ironically, however, Erskine cited Irving's Catholic Apostolic Church in vindication, when, in 1834, it too succumbed to placing establishment authority above that of individual conscience. Erskine condemned this development as an "outward faith which acknowledged God's appointments and ordinances, but did not meet Himself, [therefore it] is not the faith of the new covenant".[142]

---

[140] Letter to Rev. Thomas Wright Mathews, 19 August 1854, *Letters-II*, 396.

[141] Letter to Rev. Thomas Wright Mathews, 18 January 1854, *Letters-II*, 394-5.

[142] Letter to Mr W. Tait, 16 October 1834, *Letters-I*, 227-8.

Faith, Knowledge and Understanding

Erskine believed faith was itself "the humble acknowledgement of authority", but he apparently failed to consider that subjective categories such as conscience, intuition, and moral approbation might themselves be inconsistent and unreliable authorities. Instead, he tended to acknowledge the defects of external authorities, justifying internal authority on the basis of its 'proper' emphasis on personal responsibility.[143] Also, since true faith produces genuine fruit, Erskine constantly challenged contemporary religion to check the ethical authenticity of its own faith. How much was it concerned with mere abstract words and symbols, and how much with substantial "things" which embrace "the spirit and meaning"? In contrast to popular perceptions, he continued to insist that the real purpose of faith was not for the mere sake of believing, or to show our submission to God's will, "but because the objects which are revealed to us for our belief have a natural tendency to produce a most important and blessed change on our happiness and our characters. Every object which is believed by us operates on our characters according to its own nature".[144]

Replying to accusations that his object in seeking to persuade people to "wait on God for the instruction of His own spirit in their consciences" was to afford himself incontrovertible subjective authority, Erskine responded that for those who genuinely rely on God's spirit

> religion does not consist in receiving information about God, however true, – or on whatever good authority, – but in having the life of God in the heart – the well of water there springing up into everlasting life – and in as much as they know, that no truth coming from without, can thus become life in the soul, until it meets a living thing in the soul, which recognizes its truth and its importance, and unites with it, communicating to it, its own life...nothing is truly religion, in them, or matter of faith, in them – until it is thus met and sealed and quickened from within – by a spiritual presence of God.

Drawing an analogy from the realm of academic learning, even there Erskine suggested that for any knowledge or information to be authentically appropriated by an individual,

> it must meet a light within him, which recognizes it – and enables him so to enter into the principles of it, as to apprehend the truth in it – independently of all men and all books – and to stand above the risk of being deceived by, mistakes in his teacher, and typographical errors in his book.

Proceeding to make a vital distinction between mere religious 'understanding' and true spiritual apprehension – what he termed "the confounding of

---

[143] *Sp.Order*, 89-92.
[144] *Faith*, 87, 94.

the intellectual witness in our minds, with the more inward spiritual witness" – Erskine continued:

> This is God's teaching to the *understanding* of man – which would make a man stand alone against an ignorant multitude, without losing confidence. And if He thus teaches the *understanding* to escape the mistakes of the eye and the ear does He leave the *spirit* of man to depend on outward instruction, without giving it any test, whereby it may escape from the mistakes of the understanding (which assumes to be its teacher) – either in other men or in that mind where it is itself placed?[145]

When applied to religious faith, Erskine seemed to place the emphasis on first-hand experiential knowledge as opposed to mere second-hand assent:

> This is the difference between *information* and *faith*. Many have much information about God, who have never yet thought of listening to His voice, to and in themselves. And so they have no true religion, no religion which *they themselves know to be true*, from having received it *direct* and at the *first hand*.[146]

In distinguishing between knowledge or understanding as mere intellectual assent, and a 'higher' direct form of knowledge which produces dynamic, self-evidencing faith, Erskine not only appeared to echo Calvin's concept of "faith as higher knowledge",[147] but also to parallel Jonathan Edwards's distinction between knowledge which was 'speculative' or 'natural', and knowledge which was 'practical' or 'spiritual'.[148] Importantly, it also corresponded with Coleridge's famous distinction between understanding and reason. For Coleridge, 'reason', which he described as "the Power of Universal and necessary convictions, the Source and Substance of truths above Sense, and having their evidence in themselves",[149] took the form of a 'higher faculty' which transcends 'understanding'. The latter is only able to apprehend provisional physical realities, being dependent on the fallible human senses, whilst 'reason', which in conjunction with 'conscience' Coleridge described as "the Light within me",[150] opens up for us the realm

---

[145] Letter to Jane Stirling, 8 April 1837, *NLS MS*, Acc.11388/120.

[146] *Election*, 90.

[147] Calvin, *Institutes* III. ii. 14. Campbell was also to describe faith as "that highest capacity of knowledge...the truest and most absolute knowledge", (*Thoughts on Revelation*, 33).

[148] "there is a difference between having a right speculative notion of the doctrines contained in the word of God, and having a due sense of them in the heart", Jonathan Edwards, "Christian Knowledge: or, the Importance and Advantage of a Thorough Knowledge of Divine Truth", in *The Works of Jonathan Edwards*, in 2 volumes, Edward Hickman [ed.] (Edinburgh: Banner of Truth, 1974), II, 158.

[149] Coleridge, *Aids*, 189-90.

[150] Coleridge, *Aids*, 125, quoting Cambridge Platonist, Henry More.

of ultimate and metaphysical reality. Where the divine and human met was in the moral will or nature, that *"essential"* of the common humanity.[151] It was therefore through 'reason', according to Coleridge (who in this regard seems to have been influenced principally by Kant[152]), that we gain access to moral and religious truth, and by means of our moral sense and will express both our freedom and responsibility within a sphere which goes beyond the mere senses.

Both Coleridge and Erskine broke with Romantic sensibilities in continuing to attribute humanity's 'spiritual disease of the will', which prevented the exercise of 'reason' or 'faith', to the orthodox doctrine of the fall, which they regarded as impacting humanity in its entirety.[153] However, in insisting on the co-operation and interdependence of the voluntary and cognitory functions, they reflected increasing trends in the nineteenth century to follow Kant in stressing human capacity, freedom of the will, and hence personal responsibility in determining the salvific process.[154]

Hermeneutical Implications

The apprehension of truth by a subjective 'higher faculty' raised significant implications, not only for authority, but for biblical hermeneutics, and the validity of interpretations variously formed by the human intellectual understanding and the inward spiritual witness. Erskine's commitment to a universal organic law which stipulated that any 'correct' religious truth must 'commend itself to one's own moral consciousness', allied to a corresponding hermeneutical approach, meant that highly subjective novel scriptural interpretations could result. Consequently, Erskine frequently came under strong pressure to justify what were considered to be peculiar and contrived renderings of biblical passages. He enunciated a revolutionary type of existential, spiritual, or 'reader-response' hermeneutic which outraged his Calvinist critics, in which, though multiple meanings were valid, yet the inward spiritual witness afforded a higher level of life-impacting truth which transcended interpretations based on mere traditional understanding. Though Erskine admitted the existence of differing levels of truth, there is no mistaking which he considered most valuable:

---

[151] Coleridge, *Aids*, 119.

[152] See Samuel Taylor Coleridge, *Biographia Literaria* [1817] (London: J.M. Dent, 1906), 76-8. In his 1819 lecture on German philosophy, Coleridge praised Kant for showing that the will and the conscience belonged to a higher sphere of reason than the intellect, J. Robert Barth, S.J., *Coleridge and Christian Doctrine* (New York: Fordham University Press, 1987), 26.

[153] See Coleridge, *Aids*, 122; Erskine, *Freeness*, 89, 141.

[154] Barth, *Coleridge*, 27.

There is certainly only one true interpretation of any passage of Scripture – but yet we know that almost every passage might be interpreted many different ways, without entirely losing sight of the truth of God. And those who are listening to the inward voice, may be wandering far from that true critical interpretation of the passage – and yet they may be drinking water of life out of it – whilst the correct interpreter may be drinking nothing, but self-satisfaction at his own superior knowledge...I never would think of saying that I had the inward spiritual witness that the meaning of a passage was such and no other – but I could say that I had the inward witness that the meaning which I attached to it, was a living truth of God in my soul.[155]

Erskine's biblical interpretation was widely regarded as "ingenious", but often "born from within his own thought, rather than gathered from impartial exegesis".[156] Critics considered its novelty undermined his overall credibility. John Nelson Darby remarked:

I think Mr. Erskine (though in many respects useful, and that *extensively*) is entirely wrong, if judged properly by scripture, and wrong for pursuing his own thoughts without just subjection to scripture, conceiving them new, when many, very many, have held them faithfully without mistake.[157]

Erskine's wearisome Greek word studies and tortuous hermeneutics applied to Paul's letter to the Romans in *The Doctrine of Election* and *The Spiritual Order* often involved what were perceived to be long-winded, free, forced, and generally unsatisfactory alternative translations and exegeses, implying that centuries of Protestantism had not properly understood 'Paul' and 'justification by faith'. Whilst Erskine brought a refreshingly creative and original approach to interpreting Scripture, it could nevertheless appear dangerously subjective and selective. Internal consistency was therefore achieved at the cost of some hermeneutical inaccuracy, since interpretative principles were dictated by overriding motivations, for example, to present God as a loving Father. The repeated impression is that Erskine too often attempted to impose his desired intuited interpretation on the text, under the justification of satisfying his 'reason' and 'conscience' and complementing his theological system. Nevertheless, he succeeded in convincing many contemporaries that a freer understanding of Pauline theology was warranted, and sometimes his questioning of traditional biblical interpretation yielded significant gains.

---

[155] Letter to Jane Stirling, 8 April 1837, *NLS MS*, Acc.11388/120, cf., *Sp.Order* 104-6, 198 (footnote 1).
[156] Shairp, "Reminiscences", *Letters-II*, 363.
[157] "Reflections upon the Prophetic Inquiry", *The Collected Writings of J.N. Darby*, Prophetic I, William Kelly [ed.] (London: G. Morrish, no date), 29-30.

Justification by Faith

True faith was considered by Erskine as firstly, apprehending the free grace of God thereby permitting simple reception of the gift of the gospel, since belief of good news involved no meritorious work or moral qualification. Secondly, it facilitated the psychological operation of gospel power as the "instrument of sanctification". Accordingly,

> pardon could not be enjoyed by those whose characters are unrenewed; and faith is the only instrument by which a spiritual change can be effected...it is the enlightened belief of this pardon which heals, and purifies, and elevates the faculties, by bringing them in contact with the attributes of God, of which it is an intelligible and energetic manifestation.

Erskine concluded logically that it was entirely morally reasonable to argue that 'justification' and 'faith' were intimately connected, since faith by its very nature had to do with "a restoration to that spiritual character, which alone can fit for communion with God, or the happiness of heaven".[158] 'Walking by faith' therefore consisted in having "the cross and the glory of the Saviour ever present to the heart as the springs of holy love and holy hope...[looking] to him continually for abundant supplies of his comforting and quickening Spirit...[considering] ourselves as blood-bought children of our Father...[feeling] that our eternity has already begun".[159]

Jesus Christ, for Erskine, was both the subject and object of faith. Firstly, our faith was to consist of the faith OF Christ, based on Erskine's own novel interpretation of Romans 3.22,[160] in the light of Hebrews 12.2.[161] Coleridge, Campbell, and Maurice shared this view, which highlighted the nature of the dependent, recipient faith by which Jesus himself lived as a son, and which we are called to 'enter into' or 'adopt'.[162] It recognised as a priori fact that as human beings we are "created in the Son" already, *not* that we must attempt to 'make ourselves sons'. This emphasis on the need for "filial trust in God – the faith of Jesus himself – [as] the right or right-

---

[158] *Faith*, 139.

[159] *Faith*, 141.

[160] "Even the righteousness of God which is by faith of Jesus Christ unto all and upon all them that believe."

[161] "Looking unto Jesus the author and finisher of our faith".

[162] See J. Gerald Janzen, "Coleridge and 'Pistis Christou'", *Expository Times*, 107, 9 (June 1996), 265-8; John McLeod Campbell, Sermon XXI: "Psalm XXVI", Preached at Row 10 April 1831, in *Notes of Sermons*, II, 13-14; Letter from F.D. Maurice to Thomas Erskine, 13 January 1868, *Letters-II*, 311-12. See also Erskine's reply to Maurice of 16 January 1868, (*Letters-II*, 313). The concept of the faith *of* Jesus became a favourite theme of nineteenth-century liberal theology, associated with the Fatherhood of God and the brotherhood of man, (W. Barnes Tatum, *In Quest of Jesus* [Nashville: Abingdon Press, 1999], 95).

eous state for man", was modelled on Christ's own life and death, which were "just manifestations of this faith".[163] Secondly, faith also consisted of belief in the person and work of Christ. As Erskine saw it, "The value of the first [i.e., the faith which Jesus lived by] is that it constitutes spiritual life, whilst the value of the second consists in its furnishing and explaining and illustrating the ground on which the first rests". So Erskine regarded those who attained assurance of God's loving Fatherhood, believing that his purpose was to train them into "a participation of His own righteousness and blessedness", as 'possessing true faith' – "the faith which Jesus had".[164]

Erskine shared with Schleiermacher the radical concept of a fully 'dependent', 'God-conscious' Jesus, with 'God-consciousness' demonstrating the existence of the divine within human nature. It was also closely related to Irving's presentation of Christ dependent on the Spirit.[165] Christ was for Erskine the "eternal truster". It therefore followed, as F.D. Maurice acknowledged to Erskine, that Jesus was "the source of trust in all the race".[166] Hence Erskine's emphasis on humanity being *in* Christ. Salvation itself consisted in a "real union with God" which must be actualised by "a true apprehension of the Divinity". For although the life of God really was given *to* everyone, it did not become life *in* the individual until they apprehended the light.[167] Whether believers or not, Erskine insisted that "Christ is in our decayed fallen family, the hope of glory, though little appreciated, and he is in each one of the family, though unknown and unnoticed".[168] Since Christ dwelt in each individual, 'salvation' effectively became experiential revelation and discovery of the fact. The indwelling Christ was therefore "the universal condition of humanity", which Erskine equated to being 'in the image of God'. What was necessary to actualise that salvific presence was again 'recipiency', Erskine's expression for 'dependent' recognition and 'reception' of God's loving purpose of righteousness for humanity. On this basis, in Erskine's interlocking system, true faith became "the law of spiritual gravitation, the spiritual nexus of the universe".[169] Accordingly, Erskine could now synthesise his new perception of faith with his convictions about the 'spiritual order' and Christ as the organic head of

---

[163] *Sp.Order*, 120; Letter to Bishop Ewing, [undated], in Ewing, "Relation", *Present-Day Papers*, 32.

[164] Letter to Rev. John Young, 18 February 1867, *Letters-II*, 249; *Sp.Order*, 59, 159.

[165] See pp.39-40 above.

[166] *Sp.Order*, 202; Letter from F.D. Maurice to Thomas Erskine, 13 January 1868, *Letters-II*, 311.

[167] Ewing, "Reconciliation", in *Present-Day Papers*, 23, cf., *Serpent*, 82, 88-9.

[168] *Serpent* [2nd edition], 103; cf., *Election*, 58.

[169] Letter to Rev. John Young, 18 February 1867, *Letters-II*, 249-50, cf., Letter to Bishop Ewing [undated], in Ewing, "Relation", *Present-Day Papers*, 31-2.

humanity, and lay the foundation for a wholly novel understanding of *justification by faith* based on 'dependence' and 'character', rather than 'position' and 'legally imputed righteousness':

> I believe that filial trust is our true righteousness, and that *it* is founded, and can only be founded, on the fact that we are sons of God by birth, being originally created in the Son. But until we know this fact we cannot have that trust which is our righteousness, our right state in relation to God and all His creatures.[170]

> Justification by faith means the rectification of a man's spiritual and moral nature in relation to God and man, produced by a belief of God's fatherly purposes concerning all men…[171]

Parallels with Schleiermacher's understanding of justification as necessarily involving 'laying hold believingly on Christ' to appropriate antecedent "forgiveness and adoption", are immediately apparent.[172]

The sense of soteriological conflation/ reduction was exacerbated by further close association with *sanctification*. Being 'set right' with the Father through ongoing 'trust', 'belief', and 'sympathy' with God's purposes was the 'real' significance of *justification by faith*. Since true faith is necessarily the mould of divine character, holiness becomes inevitable. According to Erskine, the traditional forensic view, which emphasised the obtaining of a favourable status before God by subscribing to "an artificial and very conventional dogma", was based on complete misapprehension of Paul. Within Erskine's reformulated complementary system, 'filial trust' was itself equivalent to 'the righteousness of faith', simply because 'trust' or 'dependency' was the 'right' state for humanity in relation to God. It was a state of 'recipiency' in which as a consequence of God infusing his own righteousness, sinful behaviour ceased. It followed that the value and power of the biblical gospel lay in its presentation of the supreme filial relationship, so that Erskine could speak of salvation itself consisting of filial trust, since "Christ saves us from sin, by revealing to us the trustworthiness of the Father".[173]

The conflation of faith, trust, justification, and sanctification in Erskine's soteriological scheme, set within a framework of ethical personal transformation with perfectionist implications, closely paralleled developments in evangelical Pietism and Wesleyanism.[174] There was a close link between

---

[170] Letter to Bishop Ewing, 28 February [no year], *Ewing-II*, 36.

[171] *Sp.Order*, 102.

[172] Schleiermacher, *Christian Faith*, §109, 503.

[173] *Sp.Order*, 243, cf., 112-14, 120-1,159-60.

[174] Although he took pains to separate justification and sanctification, Wesley's own understanding of justification as 'pardon' and 'acceptance' showed similar disapproval

Pietist understanding of justification and Enlightenment re-evaluation of the doctrine in terms of moral exemplarism:

> Pietism…tended in spite of its best intentions to gradually *displace faith* and confidence in God by a concentration on the practice of piety and ethical integrity. A virtuous *imitatio Christi* became not only the result and demonstration of justification, but in a sense its cause, in practice if not in theory.[175]

Erskine's overall objective remained to show "the sanctifying influence of the truth, as the end and design of faith", and that moral obedience is produced not by knowledge of the 'law', but by faith in the gospel. So also the forgiving mercy of God, according to Erskine, was not a precept to be learned, or an authority to be assented to, but a dynamic principle which operates upon the mind by faith and "by its natural influence it moulds the character".[176]

In this way, 'pardon', though it existed independently of the believer as a result of the finished work of Christ, only became effective when believingly appropriated. It could then also be called 'justification', which was "the particular application of the general amnesty" already declared, and which can only be appropriated by faith.[177] 'Universal pardon', the leading innovatory theme of Erskine's earlier work, was developed into the inherently salvific concept of "conscious spiritual sympathy"[178] with the universal 'purpose' of God to make all humanity righteous. Recognising God's purpose necessarily involved reproducing in human lives Christ's filial dependent trust and self-denial, which, in a circular process, was only possible through assured belief that God is in reality a loving, forgiving Father. The person of Christ was our model, for he "*declared* in *His words* that God is our Father, but *in His own person* He *revealed* the Father as our Father", so that "when we see Him, we see what the Father desires and purposes that we should be". When this recognition of God's purpose in Christ is actualised within the new humanity "we are thus *put right* by *trust, justified* or *put right* by faith in the loving fatherly righteous purpose of God towards us".[179] 'Justification' for Erskine, therefore, became a con-

---

of forensic concepts and excluded the concept of imputation, John Wesley, "Justification by Faith", *Sermons on Several Occasions*, I, 61-4.

[175] O'Callaghan, *Fides Christi*, 59.

[176] *Faith*, 106.

[177] *Faith*, 139.

[178] *Sp.Order*, 91. Erskine may have borrowed the principle of 'sympathy' from Hume, who identified it with conscience or the innate moral sense. See Hume, *Treatise*, e.g., 393-5.

[179] Letter to Bishop Ewing, 31 October 1869, *Ewing-II*, 47-8; Letter to Dean Ramsay, 19 October 1869, in E. B. Ramsay, *Reminiscences of Scottish Life and Character* [1858], [27th edition] (London: Gall and Inglis, 1875), lxxxvii–lxxxviii.

tinuous salvific process of faith, trust, and dependent, self-denying response to the will of God.[180] Elements of Erskine's account of justification anticipate Barth's ontological notion of *Rechtfertigung*. Based on Christ's inauguration of a new humanity, "Justification...is to do not simply with the law and our standing before it, but fundamentally with God's purpose as Creator and Lord of the covenant, and our fulfilment of the same". Barth, like Erskine, highlights the ontological, as distinct from the forensic, nature of justification, which encompasses our transformed, existential, human 'history', not just our 'position' or 'state', whilst simultaneously grounding the doctrine firmly in the 'history' of Christ, in whom God has justified his new creation.[181]

Erskine's reconstructed concept may be perceived as reflecting Enlightenment critique of traditional doctrines of justification, emphasising in contrast the autonomy of human beings as individual moral and ethical agents, and also Kant's later insistence on the cruciality of the moral consciousness.[182] Erskine's antipathy to the traditional Protestant doctrine of forensic imputation, also shared much in common with historic Roman Catholic understanding, where justification assumed the character of a regenerating 'infusion of righteousness' into human beings. The individual 'becomes' or is 'made' righteous, rather than is 'accounted' or 'declared' righteous as a result of the 'Great Exchange'.[183] 'Justification by faith', or what he called man being "put into his right state by trust in God",[184] meant in practice for Erskine a practical, applied 'recipiency'. That is, filial, dependent, trusting acceptance that adverse providential life events (what he termed divine 'punishment'), actually proceeded from a loving God whose purposes were ultimately beneficial, a view which sounded very different from traditional Augustinian understandings of suffering and punishment resulting from the fall.[185] Convinced that God's eternal purpose for humankind involved being "*partakers of His own righteousness*", Erskine believed that this divine purpose demonstrated *love* in its highest expression as "the self-

---

[180] Shairp, "Reminiscences", *Letters-II,* 360.

[181] Trevor A. Hart, *Regarding Karl Barth* (Carlisle: Paternoster, 1999), 52-3, 61-2.

[182] Alister E. McGrath, *Iustitia Dei* [2nd edition] (Cambridge: Cambridge University Press, 1998), 323, 336.

[183] William Cunningham noted that Tridentine theology "errs by...comprehending renovation as well as forgiveness under the head of justification", *Historical Theology: A Review of the Principal Doctrinal Discussions in the Christian Church Since the Apostolic Age*, in 2 volumes (London: Banner of Truth, 1960), II, 18.

[184] Letter to the Bishop of Argyll [undated], in Ewing, "Relation", *Present-Day Papers*, 31.

[185] Letter to Rev. John Young, 18 February 1867, *Letters-II,* 249-50, cf., Richard Swinburne, *Providence and the Problem of Evil* (Oxford: Clarendon Press, 1998), 38, 43; Larrimore, *Problem of Evil*, 53, 140.

communicating principle, – the longing for sympathy, giving and receiving".[186]

Hence, within the relational context of the 'Fatherhood of God', 'righteousness' assumed a quite distinct educative significance within the 'school of life', compared to the bare legalistic meaning attributed to it by Calvinism. A lover of the classics, Erskine admitted that Plato's *Gorgias* had inspired his "doctrine of the atonement in its principle applied to the conscience, better than any religious book I have ever read. I mean the principle of 'accepting punishment', which is the *fond* of the doctrine".[187] He also "learned the meaning of justification by faith" as a universal principle from Plato's *Gorgias* before he "saw it in St. Paul". Erskine was referring to the dialogue between Socrates and Polus, in which Socrates (who, according to Erskine, not only taught the 'doctrine' as an 'apostle' before Paul, but was himself *justified* by the same faith as Paul, because he trusted in the rightness of Athenian authority as the 'type' of universal law) argued that punishment should actually be welcomed for its remedial beneficial role in the restoration of wrong-doers.[188] The 'righteousness of God' had therefore little to do with forensic concepts such as 'administration', 'judgment', and 'imputation', but rather involved organic relationship with God, spiritually apprehended by faith in "God's eternal, unchangeable, and unalterable purpose of making all men righteous".[189] Once again, we note the motif of belief in the object necessarily conforming the believer to its likeness:

> Faith, confidence, dependence, is the name for man's turning from himself to God...This faith is man's right condition, and it is the righteousness of Christ, as the sap in the branch is the sap from the vine. When I entirely trust in another, so as to surrender myself to his guidance, the righteousness of that other is communicated to me. This is, I believe, the δικαιοσύνη which is on all men whether they believe it or not, the manifestation of the loving purpose of God toward them in Jesus Christ, but which does not become δικαιοσύνη, righteousness, until it is received by faith, the spiritual apprehension.[190]

Perhaps one of Erskine's most significant achievements, though it made him unpopular with critics, was successfully to engineer a radical shift in traditional theological terminology, to encompass broader understandings.

---

[186] Letter to Bishop Ewing, 2 March 1867, *Ewing-II*, 34.

[187] Letter to A.J. Scott, 21 April 1837, *Letters-I*, 253-4.

[188] Letter to Rev. John Young, 18 February 1867, *Letters-II*, 250, cf., *Sp.Order*, 115-18, 132-3. See "Gorgias", Hamilton and Cairns (eds.), *Collected Dialogues*, 256-64.

[189] Letter to Bishop Ewing, 24 August 1865, *Ewing-I*, 59.

[190] Letter to Rev. Paton J. Gloag, D.D., March 1858, *Letters-II*, 204. F.D. Maurice commended Erskine's 'insight' on justification by faith, and expressed indebtedness to it, (Letter to Mr. Erskine, 13 January 1868, *Letters-II*, 312).

Simultaneously, he managed to conflate theological categories. Henry Henderson thought that although Erskine was not particularly 'logical' he nevertheless had "the logician's liking for unity, for reducing the many to the one."[191] According to Principal Shairp, though Matthew Arnold criticised Erskine,[192] he nevertheless shared Erskine's understanding:

> With you, he lays his hand on righteousness as the central thought of all the Apostle's teaching, the longing to be really intrinsically right in heart and will, not with a forensic or artificial righteousness, but with a rightness real and deep as the universe.[193]

Erskine rejected 'imputed righteousness' in its classical Lutheran formulation of *iustitia alienum* and *iustitia extra nos,* because he saw it as a legal "fiction",[194] implying that people must be believers *before* God can love or forgive them. He was responding to what he regarded as the danger of distortion of traditional orthodox truth from ethical dynamic religion into Calvinist legalism. 'Imputation' therefore needed to be re-defined in relational terms. Rather than *Christ's* righteousness which is 'imputed', it became *God's* assessment:

> *Imputation*...means the same thing as *estimate.* This is God's estimate of the creature's confidence in the Creator, – He says that such confidence is righteousness, – He imputes it, or reckons it, or accounts it, or estimates it to be righteousness".[195]

Liberal theology has generally been more comfortable with dynamic, organic, semi-mystical relational language to describe the meaning of Jesus's life and death than with orthodox forensic categories. Moral influence theories prefer to understand redemption in terms of increased 'God-consciousness' than as legal 'satisfaction'. Schleiermacher was happy to call his soteriology 'mystical'.[196] Through the presence of Christ's 'life', or 'Spirit', or 'seed' within us comes the active *impulse* to fulfil God's will and experience living fellowship and communion with Christ in a morally

---

[191] Henderson, *Erskine*, 65.

[192] See Matthew Arnold, *Literature and Dogma: An Essay Towards A Better Apprehension of the Bible* (London: Smith, Elder, 1886), 200. Note that Arnold has apparently misunderstood Erskine concerning his view of the role of doctrine.

[193] Shairp, Letter to Mr. Erskine, 3 December [no year], Knight, *Shairp*, 215.

[194] Erskine's own terminology, e.g., in *Election*, 328. The term was distinctive of the Enlightenment, and employed by Kant, (see McGrath, *Iustitia Dei*, 339). It was also a favourite expression of William Law, e.g., "A Religion that is not founded in Nature is all Fiction and Falsity and as mere a nothing as an *Idol*," (*Spirit of Love*, 251).

[195] *Serpent* [2nd edition], 257, cf., Letter to Rev. Thomas Wright Mathews, 23 January 1829, *Letters-II,*, 390-1.

[196] Keith Clements, *Friedrich Schleiermacher* (London: Collins, 1987), 57.

effective way. For Schleiermacher, Erskine, and proponents of moral influence concepts, this is the only sense in which the 'imputation of Christ's righteousness' can be spoken of.[197] It also legitimates individual response to God's love within the context of what otherwise could amount to a vague universal parenthood of God and brotherhood of humanity. Platonic overtones are evident. Schleiermacher was a student and translator of Plato, as were most of the Broad Church. Both Erskine and Schleiermacher, as theological representatives of their era, pioneered the reformulation of concepts of suffering and punishment in Platonic terms as non-retributory, beneficial, and educatory. This provided a basis to further reconstruct understanding of the atonement.[198]

Doctrine, Bible and Creed

Insistent that faith did not remove penalty or produce pardon, Erskine asserted that the proper salvific use of faith was to add to the pardon already declared, "a moral influence, by which it may heal the spiritual diseases of the heart".[199] He repeatedly stressed that "the knowledge communicated by revelation is a moral knowledge, and it has been communicated in order to produce a moral effect upon our characters"[200]. Apart from the corrupt will of humanity which hindered acceptance, the actual offer of salvation, when indispensably accompanied by an exhibition of God's excellent moral qualities, was by its very nature morally transforming. Erskine helped pioneer the nineteenth century's radical approach to traditional preceptive authority by insisting that any religious doctrine which purported to reflect truth must likewise contain such moral revelatory power:

> The reasonableness of a religion seems to me to consist in there being a direct and natural connexion between a believing of the doctrines which it inculcates, and a being formed by these to the character which it recommends. If the belief of the doctrines has no tendency to train a disciple in a more exact and more willing discharge of its moral obligations, there is evidently a very strong probability against the truth of that religion. In other words, the doctrines ought to tally with the precepts, and to contain in their very substance some urgent motives for the performance of them; because, if they are not of this description, they are of no use.[201]

---

[197] John Driver, *Understanding the Atonement for the Mission of the Church* (Scottdale, Pennsylvania: Herald Press, 1986), 47.
[198] For Schleiermacher, see *Christian Faith*, §101, 432-38.
[199] *Freeness*, 22.
[200] *Evidence*, 94.
[201] *Evidence*, 58.

Since fallen human will was the major obstacle in persuading humankind of the gospel, Christ's saving work was designed specifically to impact those human 'affections' which generate ethical transformation. Accordingly, it "must excite love", and so "must produce resemblance"[202]. Similarly, Erskine believed regarding true Christian *doctrine* that

> there is an intelligible and necessary connexion between the doctrinal facts of revelation and the character of God, (as deduced from natural religion,) in the same way as there is an intelligible and necessary connexion between the character of a man and his most characteristic actions; and farther, that the belief of these doctrinal facts has an intelligible and necessary tendency to produce the Christian character...[203]

Since Erskine argued the essence of all Christian doctrines is already universally present in human hearts as latent divine light, then all true religion must necessarily be adapted to the nature and constitution of humanity, and recognisable through the authenticating faculties of reason and conscience. Traditional religious authorities like Bible, Church, and dogma must therefore be secondary to the morally sanctifying effect of true knowledge of God. Christian doctrines must accordingly not only convey principles of "eternal and necessary truths" to be recognised by our "spiritual understanding" (because "no principles whatever...can really be believed unless their truth is apprehended"), but must also inherently possess an ethical sanctifying influence.

So it was of paramount importance that Christian character and lifestyle must never be separated from Christian doctrine.[204] Genuine Christian doctrine will, by definition, embody ethical Christian truth. Erskine was therefore adamant that "the habit of viewing the Christian doctrines and the Christian character as two separate things, has a most pernicious tendency". Vital *principles,* which were intrinsically able to excite and animate performance, were to be distinguished from mere unproductive assent to *doctrines*. Rather, "the doctrines of revelation form a great spiritual mould, fitted by Divine wisdom for impressing the stamp of the Christian character on the minds that receive them". That is, they must be understood 'spiritually' to be authentically 'believed' and therefore impact character.[205] As Erskine lamented, "The great argument for the truth of Christianity lies in the sanctifying influence of its doctrines; and alas! The great argument

---

[202] *Evidence*, 71.
[203] *Evidence*, 19-20.
[204] Letter to Dean Stanley, 4 April 1864, *Letters-II,* 148, *Sp.Order*, 85-7, 258-9.
[205] *Evidence*, 137, cf., *Sp.Order*, 40-1.

against it lies in the unsanctified lives of its professors".[206] He proceeded to lay down ground rules for judging doctrinal authenticity:

> When, therefore, we are considering a religious doctrine, our questions ought to be, first, What view does this doctrine give of the character of God, in relation to sinners? And secondly, What influence is the belief of it calculated to exercise on the character of man?[207]

In insisting that the real test of the truth of a doctrine lay in its moral appropriateness for the human condition, Erskine was reflecting nineteenth-century sensitivities regarding the object and design of religion as preeminently one of moral improvement, rather than subscription to dogmatic propositions. Coleridge also reflected this mood by questioning the role of 'dogma' in *Aids to Reflection:* "Will the belief tend to the improvement of any of my moral or intellectual faculties?"[208]

Whilst passionately concerned for biblical truth, Erskine unsurprisingly had little in common with the 'external evidences' school. Acknowledging that apologetic arguments for the Bible and Christianity based on mere *external* evidence were susceptible to rejection on grounds of reason, the *internal* evidence of biblical revelation seemed to offer a more unassailable approach. Erskine remained convinced that a cynical person could be persuaded by serious unprejudiced study of the Bible itself, but only when they discovered its "moral mechanism, which, by the laws of our mental constitution", tended to reproduce the divine character.[209] As John Tulloch recognised, Erskine "had no argumentative or historical turn. His genius was purely spiritual. If he was to receive Christianity at all therefore, it must come to him as an internal light, flooding his soul – conditioning his whole life".[210]

Erskine's approach was consistent. The Bible served to confirm that right perception of the excellent character of God necessarily coincided with the human condition. Like Schleiermacher, who regarded the Bible as a record and presentation of 'Christian piety', Erskine found in it "a historic record of conscience, and in Christ the universal conscience of the

---

[206] *Evidence*, 111-12. Erskine's aversion to doctrinal acquiescence as the basis for determining authentic Christian profession was paralleled by Schleiermacher's refusal to allow revelation to be limited to cognitive assent; see *Christian Faith*, §10, 50.

[207] *Evidence*, 96.

[208] Coleridge, *Aids,* 165. Coleridge further echoed Erskine's characteristic themes of religion being adapted to humanity, and life as a form of education, (*Aids*, 163-4).

[209] *Evidence*, 182.

[210] Tulloch, *Movements*, 138.

race...".[211] Erskine would have commended Schleiermacher's assertion that the tradition of scripturally proving doctrine was valid only if it expressed original and authentic truth concerning faith, so that doctrine itself could be understood as authoritative only so long as it "belongs to Christianity" rather than because it is "contained in Scripture".[212] Shairp recorded Erskine as stating: "The Gospel history is the consciousness I find within me expressed outwardly"; "The Bible is the great interpreter of consciousness, and of conscience. Conscience is not mine, I am its". Accordingly, if Erskine encountered something in the Bible or in dogma which did not accord with his conscience as witnessing to the righteousness of God, he effectively suspended judgment until further light should be forthcoming, or until the demands of reason and conscience allowed the passage beneficially to 'sink into his soul'.[213]

The Bible therefore remained 'profitable', but most importantly, by showing us the Christ who both revealed and himself trusted the Father, it had to "awaken within us a corresponding form of our inward spiritual consciousness", in order that we may 'know' with a deep inner certainty its truths to be 'true' "by conscious experience, and not merely on the outward authority of the Book".[214] Erskine believed that, when from a genuine, open-minded examination of the Bible we realise how the moral character of God is presented as perfectly suited to the hearts of humankind, and how it illustrates and energises the abstract concepts of God already confirmed by reason and conscience, the natural response will be one of conviction prompting personal character transformation. For Scripture to produce this salvific impact, disciplined study and proper understanding of it was vital. It was therefore a two-way process: "in order, then, to believe the gospel, we must understand it; and in order to understand it, we must give it our serious consideration".[215] It was a contradiction in terms to Erskine for someone to claim, for example, that they believed the miracles of the Bible without at the same time incarnating within themselves the principles of the gospel: "the regeneration of the character is the grand object; and this can only be effected by the pressure of the truth upon the mind".[216] Accurate and deep knowledge of truth incorporated a life-changing power through its impact on the mind, if we would only examine it authentically. Orthodox

---

[211] Erskine, Letter to Principal Shairp, 13 January 1854, Knight, *Shairp,* 177. For Schleirmacher's concept of scripture, see *Christian Faith,* especially §128-133, 591-611.

[212] Schleiermacher, *Christian Faith,* §128, 593.

[213] Shairp, "Reminiscences", *Letters-II,* 356, 360; Letter to Bishop Ewing, 3 December 1864, *Ewing-I,* 54.

[214] *Election,* 524.

[215] *Evidence,* 189.

[216] *Evidence,* 190.

assent to truth alone was not enough. Continual and experiential heart knowledge remained essential for 'spiritual health'.

However, Erskine's convictions undoubtedly underwent development, forged particularly through the many trials and sufferings he observed in his own and others' experience. In later life he was able to look back and affirm

> One of my earliest convictions, when I first apprehended the meaning of Christianity, was that, however much we might learn truth from the Bible, as soon as we had learned it, we found that we held it on a much deeper and more unshakeable ground than the authority of the Bible, namely, on its own discerned truthfulness. This idea was the origin of my first publication on 'The Internal Evidences of Christianity', although I failed in bringing it out, because I did not fully understand my own thought.[217]

Erskine's reconstructive approach to biblical authority was highly innovatory, especially in Scotland, but others, like the Unitarians, had begun to think on similar Kantian lines in the early nineteenth century. Coleridge, in *Confessions of an Inquiring Spirit* (published posthumously in 1840) saw the Scriptures as a mere reflection of the "Light higher than all", and similarly reformulated the Bible's authority in terms of its power to address the innermost needs of the human self, partly fuelling later developments in moral reflection.[218] William Ellery Channing himself had in 1819 insisted that interpretation of Scripture must be in accordance with "the known character and will of God, and with the obvious and acknowledged laws of nature...we therefore distrust every interpretation which, after deliberate attention, seems repugnant to any established truth".[219] Of course, such radical approaches to the Bible were highly controversial. Frequent complaints of 'Socinianism' and 'subjectivism' resulted from traditional Calvinists against whose 'Biblicism' it was aimed.

Erskine's new and forward-looking approach to external authority was to stand him in good stead in the face of intense historical and scientific critical attack against the Bible later on in the century. His innovative views concerning biblical criticism were perceived directly to have contributed to theological change in late Victorian Scotland.[220]

---

[217] Letter to J.C. Shairp, 2 June 1863, Knight, *Shairp*, 211.

[218] Coleridge, *Confessions*, 13-16.

[219] William Ellery Channing, "Unitarian Christianity", in *Unitarian Christianity and Other Essays*, Irving H. Bartlett (ed.) (New York: Bobbs-Merrill Company Inc., 1957), 7.

[220] See Appendix 3.

Summary

Chapter 4 covered the wide-ranging question of revelation and authority in conjunction with Erskine's treatment of the salvific apprehension of God. Reflecting eclectic contemporary intellectual currents, such as Enlightenment thought, empirical philosophical epistemology, the Romantic movement, and scientific laws and concepts relating to psychology and physiology, we noted how Erskine innovatively appropriated some of their notions and conventions in furtherance of his evangelical Christian apologetic agenda. In many ways, Erskine attempted to spiritualise Calvinism and synthesise philosophy, science, and theology to produce a coherent metanarrative for relating to God, though at times, he seemed to approach an almost Hegelian mode of understanding God and religion in terms of "consciousness alongside psychological, ethical, and aesthetic experience".[221] We observed how many of his ideas seemed to be derived from, or paralleled in the thinking of, historical predecessors and contemporaries ranging from Plato, Wesley, Law, and Butler, to Hume, Kant, Schleiermacher, Rousseau, Coleridge, Edwards, Channing, and Irving. In particular, we noted Erskine's relativisation of external religious authority in favour of a turn inward to the individual human being, in which he mirrored the contemporary fashion to invoke the human consciousness. We also noted how Erskine sought creatively to retain an orthodox expression of Christianity based on universal moral principles and experiential religion, whilst endeavouring to preserve historical objective truth in the face of the challenge of modern knowledge. In this objective, his novel redefinition of traditional soteriological terminology was crucial, though he did not meet with universal approval, especially in Scotland. In his far-sighted attempts to neutralise the impact of biblical criticism, Erskine inevitably became identified with less constructive trends to relativise Scripture. In certain circles, he may therefore be perceived as anticipating subsequent liberal agendas.

---

[221] Peter C. Hodgson, (ed.), *G.W.F. Hegel: Theologian of the Spirit* (Edinburgh: T.&T. Clark, 1997), 5.

Chapter 5

Salvation – Its Extent and Nature

Introduction

God's loving Fatherly purpose for humanity and the incarnational work of Christ were fundamental to Erskine's soteriology. Indirectly, he drew on neglected traditions of the past and interpreted and applied them creatively to the demands of a new century. Erskine believed the concept of salvation needed to be freed from narrow, evangelical, dogmatic shackles and the confines of selfish needs for security, and replaced with a grander, life-changing vision, no less than the restoration of divine qualities to humanity through Christ:

> This restoration of the image is salvation. Salvation is not forgiveness of sin; it is not the remission of a penalty; it is not a safety. No, it is the blessed and holy purpose of God's love accomplished in the poor fallen creature's restoration to the divine image. And as this could only be effected by God dwelling in man, so the work of Christ has been God's taking possession of a part of the fallen nature and uniting Himself to it…and in that part working perfect righteousness, and so ordering it that this part of the nature so possessed by God should become the new root and head of man, from which the Holy Spirit given to Him without measure might flow forth seeking entrance into every part of the nature, wherever it can find an open heart.[1]

In his earliest apologetic work dating from 1816, Erskine had already indicated that salvation was more than the mere removal of judicial penalty. Primarily it involved a holistic renewed health of the soul, necessarily evidenced by transformed will and character. God's glory and character was to be recognised in his proactive loving *deliverance* of the human race from sin, rather than in retributive punishment without any greater meaningful objective. Since God's ultimate loving purpose in the believer was confor-

---

[1] Letter to Monsieur Gaussen, 7 December 1832, *Letters-I,* 294-5.

mity to his own character, belief must be ethically dynamic: "The sole object of Christian belief is to produce the Christian character, and unless this is done nothing is done". The effect could not exist without the cause. "To resemble God is the great matter...".[2]

In Erskine's thought, *salvation* and *sanctification* became virtually synonymous. He radically transformed traditional concepts of 'punishment' or 'penalty' into indispensable elements in the educational process of divine conformity within God's "great school of existence".[3] Contrary to popular conceptions, it was vital for Erskine's scheme that individuals were *not* delivered from this refining process, since a deep sense of forgiven sin was crucial for the existence of salvific filial trust. Because it was a pre-existent "permanent fact in the Divine nature, and a permanent element in the relation of God to man", Erskine affirmed that forgiveness was already "man's permanent condition".[4] A loving, forgiving, paternal God therefore used 'punishment' in a prospective sense to teach us not to sin: "there is *never* removal of penalty, for penalty is a healing process".[5] Accordingly, forgiveness was not an end in itself, but 'a means to an end'. Rather than "deliverance from a penalty or the reversal of a sentence", *salvation* was innovatively presented by Erskine in terms of a continuous divine education programme, with the objective of producing ultimate righteousness "*even through the infliction of the penalty and the execution of the sentence*".[6]

Since, however, Erskine believed that right perception of God's character was itself salvific and transformational, his starting point in understanding 'salvation' resided in personal confidence regarding the loving, Fatherly, character of God towards him:

> What...is to make me rejoice in God? A sight of God's heart as loving me, a knowledge of God's goodwill concerning me...[Jesus] came to seek and save the lost, by declaring to them the Father's heart, and as soon as they know that heart they are glad, they rejoice in salvation; but whilst they continue ignorant of God's heart, they continue to be without eternal life in them...God's heart is a heart of forgiving love to us before we believe, but we cannot enjoy God, which is full salvation, without knowing or believing what His heart is to us.[7]

---

[2] *Salvation*, 310. It was composed in 1816, but not formally published until 1825 as an introductory essay to *Letters of the Rev. Samuel Rutherford*.
[3] Letter to Lady Ashburton, 20 January [no year], *NLS MS* Acc.11388/74.
[4] *Sp.Order*, 244, 240.
[5] *Ewing-II*, 52.
[6] *Sp.Order*, 140. John McLeod Campbell felt that Erskine forgot that God not only "punishes...to save and bring to the truth". He also "punishes...directly and immediately to testify His displeasure at sin", (Letter from Principal Shairp to Donald Campbell, *Memorials*, II, 343).
[7] Letter to Monsieur Gaussen, 7 December 1832, *Letters-I*, 293.

This formed the effective starting point for Erskine's reconstruction of what he believed constituted the Christian understanding of salvation.

Universal Pardon and Assurance

Whilst Erskine's Calvinist contemporaries initially welcomed his refreshing apologetic approach, they soon parted ways over the issue of 'pardon'. In his most controversial publications, *The Unconditional Freeness of the Gospel* (1828), and the introductory essay to *Extracts of Letters to a Christian Friend, by a Lady* (1830), Erskine stridently proclaimed what was implicit in his earlier work, his opposition to the prevailing 'selfish', 'narrow', and 'individual' Calvinist understanding of the process of salvation. Instead, he introduced what was then regarded as a radical, novel, and unorthodox doctrine which he called 'universal and unconditional pardon'. Erskine was determined to combat the prevalent idea that the gospel was an *offer* of pardon that those who sought for it were called to believe or accept. By contrast, he was adamant that until one believed that the gospel was not an offer of pardon but an offer of '*enjoyment of the pardon*', it amounted to denial of it.[8] This conviction derived from his fundamental soteriological belief that the gospel proclaimed the universal purpose of divine love devoted to the "restoration of the ruined race"[9]. It was probably confirmed and developed by his reading of William Law, who himself came to embrace the notion of universal redemption and restoration based on the gospel of 'Divine Love'.[10]

Taken up and developed by the Row movement, and particularly by John McLeod Campbell, who considered the absence of assurance amongst his flock to be his major pastoral issue,[11] the concept of universal pardon was most clearly enunciated in Erskine's 1830 revolutionary essay, published at the zenith of his brief polemical phase. In a bold attack on contemporary religion and those who encouraged it, he uncompromisingly highlighted what he perceived as the contrast between true and false religion, setting out provocative, radical views concerning the 'correct' salvific apprehension of God. Predictably, he provoked a strong backlash, with even the esteemed moderate Calvinist, Ralph Wardlaw (1779-1853), who knew and respected Erskine, suggesting he and his followers had been car-

---

[8] *Extracts*, xvi-xvii.

[9] *Freeness*, 110.

[10] See pp.180-86 below. On Law's concept of universal restoration, see, e.g., *Love*, 294 (and footnote 17); Stephen Hobhouse (ed.), *Selected Mystical Writings of William Law* (London: C.W. Daniel Company, 1938), 350-3.

[11] J.S. Candlish called it "the theory started by Erskine, and adopted by Campbell of Row", ("Thomas Erskine", 116).

ried away by love and zeal to the point of delusion and rebellion.[12] Erskine's essay was the main pretext for the book itself, whilst the anonymous female author provided the occasion for his argument. Unlike most Christians in Scotland, Erskine declared approvingly that she was one who knew for sure she was included in God's universal love:

> she believed that her forgiveness, as well as the forgiveness of the whole race, was a past act of God, declared and sealed by Christ's sacrifice – and thus, her peace rested on the unchangeable foundation of God's truth, and not on the variable foundation of her own feelings, or of her estimate of herself.[13]

Erskine's unshakeable belief in God's universal loving educative purpose for humanity evolved into the novel and unorthodox conviction that eventually nobody would continue to resist the gospel, either in this life, or if necessary, the next. They would then take their place in "the great organized body of the humanity of which Christ is the Head". Erskine boldly insisted that "this purpose implies forgiveness of past sins; and thus *they are under the forgiveness of God whether they know it or not*". He made the distinction (insufficiently clear for many) that this did *not* mean that "men *were saved* whether they knew it or not" – rather that humanity could be divided only into those who had or had not appropriated divine forgiveness[14] – a truth he perceived in the Old Testament analogy of the brazen serpent, and which provided the motivation and title for his 1831 book.

At one level, Erskine was merely developing the arguments propounded in the eighteenth century by the Marrow men to the effect that God's grace was logically a priori to human repentance and faith, which should be understood not as its cause, but as response to it:

> forgiveness must precede belief, for it is the very thing believed, and…salvation must follow belief, for salvation is nothing else than the love which is produced by the knowledge of God's forgiving love already bestowed".[15]

Accordingly, 'pardon' was not the *object* of Christian calling, but rather the *instrument* by which we become salvifically related to God, the *antecedent*, not the *consequent* of faith in Christ as Saviour.

---

[12] Ralph Wardlaw identified the main objection to Erskine being that he had condemned as 'selfish' and 'the religion of man' "all who, in their preaching, connect pardon with the faith of the gospel", (*Two Essays: I. On the Assurance of Faith: II. On the Extent of the Atonement, and Universal Pardon,* [2nd edition] [Glasgow: Archibald Fullarton, 1831], vii, 324). More recently, Nicholas Needham continues to regard Erskine's idea of universal atonement as "eccentric", (*Thomas Erskine*, 120).

[13] *Extracts*, vi.

[14] Letter to Bishop Ewing, 16 September 1865, *Ewing-I*, 61, 63.

[15] *Extracts*, xliii.

'Universal pardon' was not to be confused with the idea of 'general' or 'sufficient' pardon accepted by some Calvinists to refer to the atonement of Christ as notionally available for all humanity. Erskine regarded each member of humanity as unconditionally pardoned already.[16] But even for those Calvinists who did accept a general atonement but with particular reference, Erskine's novel notion nevertheless appeared to abrogate the revered doctrines of judgment, retribution and limited atonement, whilst devaluing personal confession and repentance. Neither was 'universal pardon' the same as 'universal salvation', though often confused with it by Erskine's opponents. Some discerned that Erskine's 'pardon' did not necessarily include 'salvation', but rather that *by the believing of it* humanity might *attain* salvation. The *Edinburgh Christian Instructor* correctly recognised that "the belief, however, of the fact that he is forgiven, as it implies new perceptions of the character of God, is fitted to change his character, and it is in the change produced in this way that salvation properly consists".[17] The problem for Calvinists focused on the validity of belief in pardon when evidence of regeneration remained absent.

However, other equally discerning critics realised that Erskine's concept of universal pardon inevitably *tended towards* universal salvation. John Smyth, Minister of St. George's Church, Glasgow, declared "that the doctrine of universal pardon unavoidably leads to that of universal salvation", and was one of the first to prophesy that Erskine's concept of universal pardon would inevitably lead him to the doctrines of "universal salvation" and "universal restitution to happiness".[18] Thomas Chalmers himself expressed similar reservations when in 1829 he spoke approvingly of Erskine's *The Unconditional Freeness of the Gospel*, but expressed a deeper concern: "I fear, I do fear that the train of his thoughts might ultimately lead Mr. Erskine to doubt the eternity of future punishments. Now that would be going sadly against Scripture".[19] Erskine increasingly found the logic of his theological system under pressure to account for why, if all were pardoned, some were not actually saved, a question which orthodox Calvinism readily answered by reference to the sovereign election of God and limited atonement. His wrestling with this issue led him virtually to abandon Calvinism altogether in 1839 when, having radically reconstructed the doctrine of election, he quietly began to embrace universalistic belief.[20]

---

[16] *Extracts*, xvi-xix.

[17] Anon, "Review of *The Gairloch Heresy Tried* by Dr. Robert Burns", *ECI,* XXIX, II (February 1830), 105.

[18] John Smyth, *A Treatise on the Forgiveness of Sins as the Privilege of the Redeemed* (Glasgow: Thomas Ogilvie, 1830), 122, 125.

[19] William Hanna, (ed.), *Memoirs of the Life and Writings of Thomas Chalmers,* in 4 volumes (Edinburgh: Thomas Constable, 1851), III, 247.

[20] See Needham, *Thomas Erskine*, 448-51.

Erskine crucially linked the necessity of *assurance* to his concept of pardon, in contravention of official Calvinist dogma that assurance could not be 'of the essence of faith'. But the ground of a person's salvific confidence *had to be* universal pardon through Christ, because of Erskine's novel insistence that the very concept of pardon was founded in the eternal nature of God, which accounted for its self-embodiment in the form of salvific moral influence.[21] As Erskine robustly reminded Chalmers, a priori pardon was the very essence of the gospel:

> You know that I consider the proclamation of pardon through the blood of Christ, as an act already past in favour of every human being, to be essentially the gospel. I consider this to be the only gospel, because this is the only intelligence the belief of which will immediately give peace to creatures under condemnation, when they know their true condition.[22]

It was the lack of peace and assurance amongst his fellow countrymen which largely inspired Erskine's zeal for such a message of hope, and was similarly cited by John McLeod Campbell as the motivation for his own pastoral concerns.[23] Erskine complained that "nothing stirs up the enmity of men more than maintaining that personal assurance is necessary to salvation; and this is just because they have no personal assurance, as indeed according to their religion they cannot have it".[24] The general Calvinist insistence that God's love and forgiveness were only available to those who already had faith, and the denial of the validity of personal assurance of salvation, were for Erskine scandalous – "the leprosy which has overspread the land".[25] He fearlessly condemned the popular preachers of the established church for perpetuating this "false gospel",[26] and for hindering the peoples' need for assurance by insisting on the introspective Puritan doctrine of 'evidences' or 'fruits of the Spirit': "A religion which does not declare sin already forgiven, but which promises pardon as the consequence of believing something, or doing something…places the ground of the sinner's confidence in himself and not in God".[27] In defiant polemical response, Erskine insisted that peoples' eternal salvation was at stake:

> Nevertheless, personal assurance is necessary to salvation, – for personal assurance is nothing more or less than the faith of the Gospel…In the gospel then, forgiveness of sins through Jesus Christ, is declared *to every man*; and therefore faith in the gospel is each man's belief that *his sins* are forgiven

---

[21] *Extracts*, xxix.
[22] Letter to Thomas Chalmers, 20 October 1829, *Letters-I,* 167-8.
[23] *Memorials*, I, 50-51; Donald Campbell, (ed.), *Reminiscences,* 18-19, 24-8.
[24] *Extracts*, xxxv.
[25] *Extracts*, xxiii.
[26] *Extracts*, xxxv.
[27] *Extracts*, xxviii.

through Jesus Christ's finished work. He that does not believe this, does not believe the gospel – he is yet an unbeliever. And thus personal assurance is not an advanced stage in the Christian life, it is the very first step out of unbelief.[28]

Arguably, Erskine's view of assurance as 'of the essence of faith' (i.e., "to believe God's expressed love and to be assured of it are the same thing"[29]) could be regarded as in fact more in line with Calvin's teaching than his Scottish contemporaries. Much debate has centred on the question of the faithfulness of subsequent Calvinist doctrine to Calvin himself, and it has been argued that Calvin saw faith located passively in the mind as a kind of certain knowledge of salvation based outside ourselves in the person and work of Christ:

> "Scottish theology, on the other hand, gradually came to teach that faith is primarily active, centred in the will or heart, and that assurance is *not* of the essence of faith, but is a fruit of faith, and is to be gathered through self-examination and syllogistic deduction, thereby placing the grounds of assurance *intra nos*, within ourselves".[30]

In presenting the gospel, not as "a diagnostic report of...sensations [but]...a simple setting forth of eternal principles...especially...the proclamation of the fact and principle of the forgiveness of sin", Erskine was perceived outside Scotland to be a "mere layman...threatening to throw down the time-honoured tradition-walls between the favoured few and the far-off many, and publishing a doctrine of non-favouritism".[31] His views on universal and unconditional pardon and assurance being of the essence of faith were in direct challenge to the religious establishment in Scotland, and provoked furious reaction from defenders of the traditional Calvinist standards.[32] If, as Erskine insisted, belief in forgiveness and removal of condemnation was essential for salvation, most contemporary doctrine was by definition undermined. Many rushed into print to refute the 'heretical' or 'antinomian' opinions of Erskine and his followers. Several tried to ar-

---

[28] *Extracts*, xxxvi-vii.

[29] Lees, "Ewing", 361.

[30] M. Charles Bell, *Calvin and Scottish Theology: The Doctrine of Assurance* (Edinburgh: Handsel Press, 1985), 8. The 'Calvin versus the Calvinists' debate has continued unabated since the publication in 1981 of R.T. Kendall's *Calvin and English Calvinism to 1649* (Carlisle: Paternoster Press, 1997).

[31] The *Spectator*, "Ewing's Latest Teachings", (12 July 1873), 896.

[32] *The Westminster Confession of Faith* maintained that "assurance doth not so belong to the essence of faith, but that a true believer may wait long, and conflict with many difficulties, before he be partaker of it", (Chapter XVIII, Section III, Robert Shaw, *An Exposition of the Westminster Confession of Faith* [1845] [Fearn, Ross-shire: Christian Focus Publications, 1992], 189). This gave rise to the widespread practice of 'evidence-seeking.'

gue that Erskine had failed in his attempt to render pardon unconditional since belief was still necessary to actualise it, though this tended to miss Erskine's main distinction that whilst the one required trust in *God's* character, the other implied dependence on *self*. Andrew Thomson was one of several establishment leaders who delivered and published series of sermons to protect the 'faithful' from perceived revolutionary attempts by Erskine and his 'school' to "break the constitution of the gospel into pieces".[33]

Erskine's understanding of universal pardon remarkably anticipated Karl Barth's twentieth-century view of the decisive work of redemption or salvation as belonging in the past history of Christ, whilst awaiting its full manifestation in, and appropriation by, human beings. For Barth, God's saving initiative was fulfilled in the incarnation and atonement of Christ, which reconciled humanity to God, 'whether they realise it or not'. Like Erskine, Barth saw the Spirit's work as alerting people to this salvific reality to bring them into the realm of God's purposes as manifest in Christ.[34]

The Doctrine of the Atonement

Introduction

Horton Davies has identified three main trends in nineteenth-century attempts to restate soteriological thought. Firstly, a humanising and moralising of the meaning of the atonement to free it from 'crude' and 'immoral' traditional orthodoxy. Secondly, a recognition of the atonement as a saving act of cosmic reconciliation which has effected a fundamental transformation in God's relationship to the whole of fallen humanity, not just for repentant individuals. Thirdly, a strong social emphasis linked to a growing incarnational understanding of the church as the actual body and community of Christ.[35] In evident keeping with his era, each of these elements clearly underlie Erskine's innovative approach to understanding and reinterpreting the atonement.

Erskine believed the atonement to be "the corner-stone of Christianity, and to which all other doctrines of revelation are subservient…".[36] But he regarded traditional presentations of it as wholly inadequate. In accordance

---

[33] Thomson, *Universal Pardon*, 361-3.
[34] See, e.g., Barth, *CD*, IV, 3 (i) (Edinburgh: T.&T. Clark, 1961), 269; *CD*, IV, 1 (Edinburgh: T.&T. Clark, 1956), 229-30.
[35] Horton Davies, *Worship and Theology in England:* Volume IV, *From Newman to Martineau, 1850-1900* (Grand Rapids: Eerdmans, 1996), 197-8.
[36] *Evidence*, 95.

with his concept of God, the divine scheme of salvation and the design of atonement were "to make mercy towards this offcast race consistent with the honour and holiness of the Divine government".[37] But the conscious thrust of Erskine's revolutionary atonement theology went much further than some superficial adherence to increasingly popular rectoral atonement theory.[38] Christ did not just die to redeem humankind from the punishment of sin, but organically to create at root a transformed, renewed humanity in whose hearts and lives the true character of God is evident. God's character was supremely demonstrated in, and mediated by, the atonement. Erskine portrayed it in terms of divine light penetrating the moral darkness of the soul of humanity to restore life and spiritual health. Such a view of atonement was radically removed from a purely objective, forensic, governmental, or sovereign understanding towards something far more inward, subjective, corporate, participative and dynamic:

> The truth concerning God's character is an immortal and glorious principle, developed and laid up in Jesus Christ; and God imparts its immortality and glory to the spirits in which it dwells. This truth cannot dwell in us, except in so far as the work of Christ remains as a reality in our minds. We cannot enjoy the spiritual life and peace of the atonement, separated from the believing remembrance of the atonement, as we cannot enjoy the light of the sun separated from the presence of the sun.[39]

This Abelardian emphasis was characteristic of later nineteenth- and early twentieth-century writing on the atonement by theologians who followed Erskine, notably Campbell, Maurice, Horace Bushnell, and Hastings Rashdall. B.B. Warfield summarised it as a major shift in focus on the saving power of Christ from what he does *for* us to what he does *in* us.[40] It was not enough merely to acquiesce to the truth of the atoning work of Christ. It had to become incarnated within us:

> the atonement was not a mere *opus operatum, a mere act* on account of which God blesses man, but it was and is a living principle, reproducing itself in the hearts and lives of those that receive it...the atonement must be reproduced in each heart...[41]

---

[37] *Evidence*, 100.

[38] Nicholas Needham considers Erskine in terms of moral government theology; see Appendix 5.

[39] *Evidence*, 106-7.

[40] Significantly, Warfield's examples included Schleiermacher, Richard Rothe, and F.D. Maurice, Benjamin Breckinridge Warfield, *Studies in Theology* (Edinburgh: Banner of Truth, 1932), 267-8.

[41] *Election*, 373.

To be effective, the doctrine of Christ's saving work must be an ever-present sanctifying influence in the heart, rather than a remote, separate category of mental assent. It is by 'rejoicing' in the atonement that we share God's heart, enjoy communion with God, and thence become conformed to his moral likeness: "the same truth which gives peace produces also holiness".[42]

Erskine appreciated the danger of being perceived to overturn dearly-held beliefs by relegating traditional ideas of substitutionary expiatory atonement through Christ's vicarious death to the status of "human invention opposed to the true character of God".[43] Anxious to retain strong elements of orthodoxy, he did not deny the unique and objective retrospective aspect of Christ's atonement in dealing with past sins.[44] However, because his contemporary reconstruction of salvific Christianity involved identifying God as a Father whose loving purpose was to bring all of humanity into conformity with his Son, it was essential that Erskine demonstrated divine mercy to be a gracious, free-flowing attribute of God's character, rather than requiring reluctant release through prior satisfaction. The incarnational life of Christ, which, like John McLeod Campbell, Erskine regarded as foundational to a correct understanding of the atonement, was accordingly the revelation of God's pre-existent loving heart. It confirmed that the introduction of sin into the human condition had not affected God's eternal loving purpose towards humanity, demonstrated by God himself adopting fallen flesh: "the union of the two natures in Christ – the union of Jehovah with our fallen flesh...This is the gospel – this is that great truth of the fallen humanity of Jesus...".[45] Because sin was spiritual and personal, which in its most radical form consisted of "disbelief" of God's love" and the "want of filial trust", it could only be eliminated by the inculcation of righteousness within the same individual. Accordingly, Christ did not act *instead of* humanity, but representatively *for* them, so that "by what he does his spirit may be reproduced in them".[46]

Erskine reflected early the nineteenth-century tendency to reject any idea that by the substitutionary suffering by another individual of a penalty properly due to us, sin could be removed. It was in an organic, restorative sense as the Head of humanity that the representative saving work of Christ was properly to be viewed: "When, therefore, it is said that Christ did or does things for us, it is not meant that he did or does them as our substitute, but as our head. He does them for us, as a root does things for the branches,

---

[42] *Evidence*, 108.
[43] *Sp.Order*, 151.
[44] *Election*, 376.
[45] *Serpent*, 129. For Campbell's emphasis on incarnational soteriology see *NOTA*, 19-23.
[46] *Sp.Order*, 182.

– or as a head or heart does things for the body."[47] By his example and the saving power of his life of filial trust reproduced in us, every individual might participate in his relationship to God and, in a novel restatement of *imitatio Christi*, effectively 'recapitulate' what Christ did as the self-denying, obedient representative and Head of the human race. In this way redemption of the entire creation would eventually result:

> Salvation in its highest sense must be a personal and individual thing; and therefore in order to attain it each man must himself participate in the filial trust of Christ which is righteousness.
>
> But although Christ's work is not substitutionary or, in the ordinary sense of the word, vicarious, still it is work done *for* man in a sense applicable to the work of no other human being. He does nothing *instead of* us – nothing, that is, to save us from doing it; he does things *for* us that we also may in him have power to do them. He did not die to save us from dying, but that we might, in the power of an endless life, die with him, that we might by partaking in his death – by surrendering our life as he did into the hand of the Father in loving confidence – be also partakers of his resurrection. When he assumed our nature under all its evil conditions he *lived by faith,* he accepted sorrow and death in faith, it was the cup his Father had given him to drink, and in doing so he overcame death and him who had the power of death, thus by his example giving guidance and encouragement to every child of man. And further, he did this not as an individual but as the Head of the race; thereby lifting all humanity along with himself up from the bondage of corruption into the glorious liberty of the children of God. None certainly can enter into his victory except by partaking in his trust, but in that general elevation of the nature there must be contained real help for every man in his special work, as well as a pledge that He who has raised Jesus to His own right hand will not cease His labour of love till He has raised thither also the last and least of his members. In the victory of our Head He has given us an all-sufficient foundation for the most absolute trust, as well as a manifestation of the certain effects resulting from its exercise. None but a Son could have made this revelation, and none but those who are created in the Son could be capable of apprehending or receiving it. He came to draw and guide the hearts of the children back to the Father, and he did so by his own life of filial trust.[48]

Note the organic, relational emphasis. Only 'sons' are able to apprehend the significance of Jesus' life and death. This concept of Christ as representative, rather than substitute, of the entire human race, placed Christ's saving work right into the inward sphere of the subject. Accordingly, it carried far-reaching implications for traditional Calvinist soteriology, involving the nature of atonement, imputation, original sin, the fall, and the supposed depravity of humanity.

---

[47] *Serpent*, 38.
[48] *Sp.Order*, 154-5, cf., 151-4.

The Nature of Atonement

Controversially, Erskine closely identified Christ's incarnation, atoning work, and resurrection with the redemption of human nature itself:

> He came into it as a new head, that he might take it out of the fall, and redeem it from sin, and lift it up to God;[49]

> Now *how* did the fall come *through* Adam? Was it not by the actual communication of his corrupted nature to the rest of the race?...therefore...the restoration has come also by the communication of the nature of Jesus Christ to the rest of the race;[50]

> It is the redemption of humanity by its purgation in its root – the God-man, through His death and resurrection.[51]

> eternal life that rests on Christ, is extended...by the extension or propagation of his nature...[52]

> as it is by His death that we are reconciled to God, so it is by His life that we are saved.[53]

> But God...[sent] *His own Son* into the condition and nature of the sinner, to help him out of that evil condition, and to cure the disease of his nature...[he] was raised from the dead, bearing with him the human flesh made clean, and holy, and immortal; and he became a fountain-head of spiritual life, united with the human nature, from which a rill flowed to every one of the race...".[54]

> Christ has redeemed the whole humanity, the whole capacities and faculties of man, so that all our doings should be holy.[55]

This unconventional means of linking atonement with incarnation, and regarding the events of the entire earthly life of Christ as "belonging to the innermost essence of the atoning mediation he fulfilled between God and mankind", has sometimes been categorised as the 'physical theory' of redemption, which assumes Athanasius's statement "For he became man that we might become divine", to imply that human salvation was accomplished

---

[49] *Serpent*, 35.
[50] *Election*, 313.
[51] Letter to Bishop Ewing, February 1861, *Ewing-I*, 30.
[52] *Election*, 315-6.
[53] *Election*, 253.
[54] *Election*, 365-7.
[55] Letter to Mrs Burnett, 17 March 1840, *Letters-II*, 195.

by the incarnation of itself.[56] Whilst a classic two-nature christology is apparent in Erskine's presentation of the union of the divine and human, he developed the concept to include purification and effective recreation of human nature itself following its assumption by the divine. Because of his close identification of incarnation with atonement, Irenaeus is frequently appealed to in this context.

Scholars have debated to what extent Irenaeus adopted Greek speculative ideas involving the infused redemption of human nature itself through the physical union of divine and human natures in some kind of mechanistic manner. Thomas Torrance has shown this to be "a serious misrepresentation, for it overlooks the fact that as the incarnate Logos Christ acts for us personally on our behalf, and that he does that from within the ontological depths of our human existence which he has penetrated and gathered up in himself".[57] Trevor Hart believes that a correct understanding of Irenaeus suggests that, though Christ's ontological solidarity with fallen human nature was vital, it was through his obedient human life that Christ 'recapitulated' human history in himself as the 'firstfruits' of a new humanity which he thereby sanctified. We are therefore included in Christ's obedience and righteousness by virtue of our union with him. Significantly, there is no suggestion in Irenaeus of consequent universalism. Indeed, the vital salvific necessity for the response of faith is emphasised.[58] Whilst Erskine undoubtedly stood close to the classical tradition, his insistence on the necessity for the repetition of human 'recapitulation', his relatively mechanistic view of the redemption of human flesh, and his consequent universalism, perhaps tend to place him somewhat nearer to the 'physical' camp. However, his understanding of salvation ultimately rested on the need for humanity to recognise its true redeemed condition and respond in faith. Conversely, condemnation equated to refusal to abide in the revealed reality that all of humanity is in fact corporately delivered from sin and organically united to Christ already, because Christ's incarnate life has purified sinful human flesh as the pioneer Head of a new redeemed humanity:

> all of us stand under the righteous head – as members of the one colossal man, who, in the person of Christ the head, has accepted his punishment to the glory of God, and has become partaker of the uncondemned life; and thus, whilst this dispensation lasts, we are all free from that condemnation on sin which would bar the sinful creature from the enjoyment of God's love;

---

[56] Torrance, *Trinitarian Faith*, 167, cf., 155-6; Athanasius, *De Incarnatione*, Robert W. Thomson (ed.) (Oxford: Clarendon Press, 1971), §54, 269; cf., Trevor A. Hart, "Irenaeus, Recapitulation and Physical Redemption", in *Christ in Our Place: The Humanity of God in Christ for the Reconciliation of the World*, Trevor A. Hart and Daniel P. Thimell (eds.) (Exeter: Paternoster, 1989), 154.

[57] Torrance, *Trinitarian Faith*, 156, 167.

[58] Hart, "Irenaeus", in *Christ in our Place*, Hart and Thimell (eds.), 152-181.

because we have a righteous head, and in him a righteous life, in which we may appear before God uncondemned. The oneness of the flesh unites all men with the head, whether they are believers or unbelievers, just as the continuous texture of the vine unites the branches with the root, whether they be living branches or dead. The oneness of substance in the root and the branch, puts the branch in the condition of receiving the sap from the root – if this oneness did not exist, the branch could not receive the sap of the root, and could not be justly blamed for being sapless. The condemnation of the dead branch lies in its oneness of substance and texture with the root. So it is the oneness of the flesh that puts the member in the condition of receiving the life from the head – and it is this same oneness which is its condemnation, if it is found without life.[59]

Erskine believed that although Christ's death historically had uniquely achieved full *pardon* for a new humanity by representing them as its Head and accepting the righteous divine condemnation of death for the old fallen flesh, the sinful nature of human life demonstrated that the *penalty* of sin was evidently not removed. This was something which he believed human beings were required to deal with existentially. Accordingly, Erskine introduced a novel development of the classical concept of *imitatio Christi* which insisted that Christ's prototypical historical life and death be consciously, albeit metaphorically, 'recapitulated' in every detail by each human being. He explained, "we really do not and cannot understand the outward history of Christ until we recognise its correspondence with this inward history. The very same mysteries which appear in the outward history of Christ are to be found in our own hearts".[60] As Henry Henderson observed of Erskine, objective truth must be mirrored in subjective experience: "each individual man is a little world in himself in which the tragedies of the Betrayal and Crucifixion are being enacted and reproduced". "All the moments in the history of Christ – the Incarnation, the Crucifixion, the Resurrection, the Ascension – are merely the outward manifestations of an inward universal experience. The truest incarnation takes place within ourselves".[61]

Henderson called these inward experiential analogies "flights into the realm of mysticism", drawing historical comparisons with the theological spiritualising of Johann Arndt, (1555-1621), the Lutheran mystic venerated by German Pietists, who was translated by Boehme.[62] Albert Schweitzer labelled Arndt "a prophet of interior Protestantism".[63] He was notable for his movement away from a forensic view of the atonement to focusing on

---

[59] *Serpent* (2nd edition), 54-5.
[60] Letter to Madame Forel, 19 November 1838, *Letters-I*, 336-8.
[61] Henderson, *Erskine*, 37, 65-6.
[62] Henderson, *Erskine*, 67.
[63] Cited by Peter Erb in his introduction to Johann Arndt's *True Christianity* (London: SPCK, 1979), 1.

the work of Christ in the human heart. However, though Erskine knew and read Boehme, there is no evidence he actually read Arndt.

Because Erskine's view of atonement was *existential* rather than *transactional* – Christ assumed fallen human flesh to redeem and heal it to effect a real reconciliation of human *existence* to God – he believed that, since Jesus was "the organic Head of the race...everything which he did is in its principle to be reproduced in us".[64] Erskine's understanding of the atonement, therefore, was both *objective* and *subjective*, though the innovative subjective element came strongly to the fore. This 'double' salvific scheme involved Christ's work both in an objective *retrospective* sense, by removal of the condemnation for sin in the human race through the cross, and in a *prospective* sense, through the ongoing subjective experience of 'condemning sin in the flesh' by sharing in Christ's sufferings and death through the same enabling "holy Spirit".[65] What was at issue for Erskine was the crucial need for salvific appropriation of the new human nature available through Christ's life, death, and resurrection:

> it is the will of God...to restore and to glorify the fallen nature by filling it with his own spirit, his own eternal life, – in order that the work which has been accomplished in the head, may also be accomplished in the body...it is only through the actual death of the flesh, that [one] can be personally fitted for the presence of God, and [one] can have fellowship with God in the spirit, only in so far as he is separated from the flesh; he will therefore...enter into God's plan of crucifying it.[66]

Erskine, therefore, radically demanded not only that divine forgiveness of sins must be believed and inwardly appropriated, but that everyone must also experience for themselves the suffering and death of Christ, and by the operation of the same 'Spirit of Christ' to be received into their heart by faith, walk their own journey to the cross, even including the spiritual inward 'shedding of their own blood'. The latter expression served as a euphemism for yielding up our independent wills to embrace the will of God, in imitation of Christ who showed us how to surrender self-will in complete dependence and obedient trust of the Father.[67]

The implications were revolutionary for Calvinist soteriological dogma. Undermining what he acknowledged to be traditional and precious doctrines (though justified by the higher objective of 're-educating misunder-

---

[64] *Sp.Order*, 160, cf., 252-3; Letter to an unknown correspondent, 15 January 1830, *Letters-I*, 286-88; *Serpent*, 54-5, 115-16.

[65] See *Serpent*, 60, 115-6. Erskine introduced the concept and terminology well before John McLeod Campbell significantly developed it in *NOTA*, chapters VI, 114-26 and VII, 127-50.

[66] *Serpent* [2nd edition], 52.

[67] *Election*, xviii-xix; *Sp.Order*, 252-3.

standing'), Erskine affirmed our faith was therefore not to rest in any supposed intrinsic saving power of the blood of Christ, because "it was not his blood which made the propitiation, but his faith in shedding it". Instead, salvation consisted of emulating Christ's self-sacrifice, which was what constituted the 'shedding out of the blood of his self-will'.[68] Controversially, Erskine attributed no salvific efficacy to the death of Christ in and of itself. It was merely a measure of, and the most appropriate form for, the expression of God's love, as opposed to any necessary act, payment of debt, or expiatory sacrifice. It supremely demonstrated how all of humanity may become righteous through embracing a similar process of 'dying' as the inevitable result of sin. So what the death and resurrection of Christ actually achieved was a pioneering triumph over death and sin, and the injection of his life and 'Spirit' into the human race by way of a "new spiritual commencement" which every individual may appropriate. Salvific 'efficacy' therefore lay in apprehending God's love through Christ's death, which necessarily involved a yielding of self to subjective participation in both his death and resurrection life as a member of the race of which he was Head. For support, Erskine appealed to his interpretation of Romans 5.10 and 6.11.[69] The blood of the cross therefore could not itself possess any intrinsic salvific efficacy, "for it is not the shedding of Christ's blood which sets us right with God, but our trust in the love which shed it". Convinced that the principle of self-sacrifice was "the fullest and most perfect manifestation of the loving dependent recipiency by which the creature becomes partaker of the righteousness of God", Erskine repeatedly emphasised the importance of willing self-denial, our being crucified, dying and rising with Christ, and the need to surrender ourselves in complete dependence "to be punished with sorrow and death" as an ongoing experience.[70]

Given this model, the traditional transactional and forensic concepts of *atonement, imputation,* and *justification* found little place in Erskine's system. But that did not mean he dispensed with the traditional terminology; he simply attached new notions to it. In effect, Erskine held his innovative scheme together by redefining, reconciling, linking or conflating traditional theological language and doctrinal concepts into existential categories. He neatly concluded that

> the Atonement and the Righteousness of faith, are connected in this way –
> the Atonement being the objective view of the doctrine, and the righteousness of faith the subjective, – so that the Atonement, when experienced by

---

[68] *Sp.Order*, 157, cf., 149-60; *Election*, 370-1; *Ewing-II*, 52.

[69] "For if, when we were enemies, we were reconciled to God by the death of his Son, much more, being reconciled, we shall be saved by his life"; "Likewise reckon ye also yourselves to be dead indeed unto sin, but alive unto God through Jesus Christ our Lord". See *Sp.Order*, 174-6, 188-9, 240.

[70] *Sp.Order*, 174, 157, cf., 133-4; *Election*, 297.

ourselves, is the righteousness of faith; and the righteousness of faith, when viewed out from ourselves, in Christ, is the Atonement. Thus to die with Christ, or to be partakers of His death, or to have His blood cleansing us from all sin, means the same thing as to be justified by faith, or to have the righteousness of faith, – and thus also the blood of Christ, when taken subjectively or experimentally, means the shedding out of the life-blood of man's will, in the Spirit of Christ, inasmuch as no one can know the blood of Christ purging his conscience, in any other way than by personally shedding out the life-blood of his own will.[71]

Erskine was careful however to avoid pursuing his theme of identification with Christ to the extent of risking blatant and offensive unorthodoxy. Accordingly he affirmed some distinction:

Jesus Christ was God, taking human nature into union with himself – and he made the atonement. Christians are men who yield themselves up to be taken into union with God, by submitting themselves to be led by his Spirit – and thus they become righteous. Christ's atonement was righteousness – but their righteousness is not atonement, for it did not bring the Spirit of life into them; it was produced in them by their receiving the Spirit, the gift of righteousness, which had been brought to them through the atonement of Christ, and their righteousness does not put away their past sins, for it is founded on the forgiveness of sins declared, through the atonement of Christ. Jesus Christ was alone in the atonement, to show that the work of redemption was God's own work, in which man could have no share, except as a receiver.[72]

In this sense, Erskine continued to regard Christ's atonement as special, although our identification and participation with Christ in his atoning death remained closely connected. He showed Christ's atonement was unique inasmuch as it alone dealt with *past* sins and inaugurated a new humanity. We are consequently enabled to receive Christ's 'Spirit of life', which in turn produces 'righteousness' in us. This represented Erskine's *retrospective* and *prospective* aspects to the atonement. So though we are responsible for 'condemning sin in the flesh' we do not in fact *participate* in Christ's actual work of redemption, we just 'receive' it.[73] Erskine's genius for finely balancing orthodoxy and innovation was here undoubtedly stretched to the limit.

Suffering and Sacrifice

The nineteenth century saw significant theological innovation through emphasis of redemptive psychological aspects of the atonement, with interest

---

[71] *Election*, xviii-xix.
[72] *Election*, 376.
[73] *Serpent*, 116.

in understanding Christ's (and by extension the individual's) motivations and emotions in the context of suffering. It has been described as the "age of atonement", in which evangelical notions were integrated into society in such a way that concepts like 'sin' and 'regeneration' became coupled with the idea of earthly life as a journey of progress towards the production of character through trial and suffering. One significant outcome was the protestant work ethic.[74]

In line with his understanding of the character of God, Erskine developed his own innovatory theodicy or theology of suffering which he presented (in contrast to traditional Calvinist conceptions of life as a 'test', 'trial', 'judgment', or 'probation') in terms of God's beneficial and salvific 'education process' through the providential events of life, good or bad. Erskine saw the idea of education versus probation as an innovative key to a right understanding of all classic soteriological doctrines. Even sin itself was providentially designed as a learning experience, another novel perspective Erskine shared with the Unitarians.[75]

Erskine was strongly motivated to remove ideas of the necessary infliction by God of penal suffering on Christ from the doctrine of the atonement because, like Schleiermacher, and increasing numbers of his contemporaries, he found the idea morally unacceptable. Anticipating key aspects of John McLeod Campbell's *The Nature of the Atonement*, he therefore conceived that the only valid way of accounting for Christ's willing suffering and acceptance of 'punishment' was to transpose it into a response of love towards God and humanity, presenting it in the Abelardian form of an exemplary and educational human existential theodicy in which the life and death of Christ are re-enacted in the believer's life:

> for the sight of that love is the very spirit of Jesus, and will, in those who see it, work even as it did in Jesus. *Accepting our punishment,* is just being of one mind with God, in hating and condemning sin, and longing for its destruction. It is submitting ourselves to the process of its destruction, and setting our seals to the righteousness of God in the process. *It is the death-pang of the crucified head thrilling through the member, and accomplishing in it what it did in the head.* This is a mighty thing, a mighty truth, reader, which may the Lord make life to us...No creature that has sinned against God can have fellowship with Him again, except by *accepting the punishment of sin.* The thrill of this pang is the sin-consuming power of the Spirit, and until it passes through the creature, the power of sin remains in it, and must exclude it from God. To dispense therefore with this would not be merely a departure from righteousness, it would be a departure from the eternal constitution and necessity of things.[76]

---

[74] Hilton, *Atonement, passim.*

[75] "[W]e are tried that we may be educated, not educated that we may be tried", (*Sp.Order*, 59). See also Letter to Rev. John Young, 1866, *Letters-II*, 247; Appendix 2.

[76] *Serpent* (2nd edition), 48-9, cf., *Sp.Order*, 75.

Based on his own reinterpretation of Christ's atoning work, which human beings were to imitate or 'recapitulate', Erskine reformulated traditional concepts of 'punishment', redefining 'penal suffering' in the process. Christ suffered in order to 'condemn sin in the flesh' in sympathy with God's condemnation of sin. As a result of his sufferings, Jesus was resurrected, thereby perfecting human nature and effecting divine-human reconciliation. Sin was forgiven, but its punishment was not remitted; therefore the ongoing presence of sin in the flesh must continue to be 'condemned'. As an 'eternal self-executing principle', necessarily belonging to 'the eternal constitution of things', penal suffering must be experienced, not just by Christ, but by every Christian. Viewed in this way, suffering was actually a blessing from a loving God, to be welcomed rather than avoided. Like Jesus, we are to be 'made perfect' through suffering.[77] But since natural humanity is unable to apprehend the love of God in the midst of suffering, we needed to have our thinking and our lives salvifically transformed by recognising how the 'uncondemned life' of Christ grasps God's loving purposes through 'punishment':

> Now, this is the great thing which Christ has accomplished by suffering for us; he has become a head of new and uncondemned life to every man, in the light of which we may see God's love in the law and in the punishment, and may thus suffer to the glory of God, and draw out from the suffering that blessing which is contained in it.

Through his sufferings Christ's human nature

> became capable of containing the glory of Godhead, and was made a Fountain-head of eternal life to all the rest of that nature. This eternal life was never under condemnation – it had always access to God, and fellowship with him. And thus being itself uncondemned, but coming into the condemned human nature, it takes part with God in his condemnation of the flesh.[78]

Erskine therefore sought to reconstruct traditional understandings of why Jesus had to suffer and die, by showing that suffering is necessarily linked to sin, and that sympathetic acquiescence through faith to the loving and ultimately beneficial nature of providential suffering or divine 'punishment' is itself salvific and reformatory. John McLeod Campbell was later to develop this concept in depth, stressing the spiritual rather than the physical and penal value of the sufferings of Christ. But Erskine was the innovator in formally proclaiming that no longer was Jesus' suffering to be understood as *of itself* atoning, penal, retributory, and redemptive in the

---

[77] Hebrews 2.10.
[78] *Serpent* (2nd edition), 41, 43-4, cf., *Serpent*, 115-6; *Sp.Order*, 193.

traditional sense. The 'penal' nature of the sufferings resided in the fact that Jesus partook of human fallen nature and 'vindicated' God by 'sympathising' with his verdict against it, acknowledging and even confessing sin as if it was his own to obtain forgiveness:

> why was this suffering of our nature in the person of Jesus needful? It was a *fallen nature;* a nature which had fallen by sin, and which, in consequence of this, lay under condemnation. He came into it as a new head, that he might take it out of the fall, and redeem it from sin, and lift it up to God; and this could be effected only by his bearing the condemnation, and thus manifesting, through sorrow and death, the character of God, and the character of man's rebellion; manifesting God's abhorrence of sin, and the full sympathy of the new Head of the nature in that abhorrence, and thus eating out the taint of the fall, and making honourable way for the inpouring of the new life into the rebellious body. Because *thus* only there could be an open vindication given of the holiness and truth of God, against which the fall was an offence, and who were pledged to its punishment; and *thus* only could it become a righteous thing in God, – in consideration of this new Head of the nature, who had, in that nature, and in spite of its opposite tendencies, vindicated the character of God, and fulfilled all righteousness, – to declare the race partaking of that nature forgiven, and to lay up in him, their glorious Head, eternal life for them all, which should flow into each member, just as he believed in that holy love of God, which was manifested in the gift and work of Christ.[79]

In Erskine, the Calvinist doctrine of 'equivalence' therefore became thoroughly redundant.[80] Like Schleiermacher,[81] Erskine saw Christ's sufferings as exemplary in his complete identification and sympathy with the fallen, sinful human condition. However, integrating both soteriology and christology, he was careful to maintain simultaneously Christ's own divinity and perfect sinlessness. Christ's willing embrace of suffering through the incarnation therefore acts as our model. The Saviour's suffering performed a unique pioneering function as the "first-fruits of the whole humanity", in the sense that it allowed him to overcome sin in human flesh and be resurrected to prove that humanity as a race had been eternally 'justified'.

---

[79] *Serpent* (2nd edition) 33-4, cf., *Election*, 235. See also pp.117-18 below. John McLeod Campbell also rejected the penal concept of the death of Christ and the atoning value of sufferings 'as sufferings'. His presentation of the sympathetic vicarious repentance of Christ was a significant development of Erskine's psychological and representative approach to Christ's sufferings. See *NOTA*, 105-13, 116-26, and Chapters XI and XII.

[80] Alexander Ewing lamented as late as 1871 the continuance of 'equivalence' as that "terrible conception" of Calvinism. Its 'error' proceeded from the fact that "When the sufferings of Christ came to be regarded as the object of the incarnation, it inevitably followed that their value was centred in themselves, and that if they were that which warranted man's salvation they had a negotiable value, and if so the greater the amount the better", ("Reconciliation", in *Present-Day Papers,* 17).

[81] Schleiermacher, *Christian Faith*, §101, 436-7.

Through what Thomas Torrance has called "the redemptive reversal of human suffering in Christ", as God he "penetrated into our passion, our hurt, our violence, our condition under divine judgment, even into our utter dereliction", and was made perfect, becoming in the process the Head of a new humanity, making possible our 'deification'.[82] This was "the atoning exchange", the 'vicarious humanity' of Christ, "a humanity which becomes the basis for a renewed and restored humanity". It was to be understood soteriologically, for "to see the humanity of Christ is to see the revelation of who God really is".[83] Erskine was to elucidate this revelatory, epistemological, salvific process employing his favourite organic imagery:

> The fall drew forth [the] full manifestation of [God's] character. And as that manifestation is made *in* a *man,* who is the root of the nature, and so connected with every individual of the nature, the character so declared is more than a manifestation; it becomes an infusion; it is a new sap. It is laid up *in that man,* as in a fountain, that it may flow through the rest of the members, just as they open their mouths to receive it. In this way whatever is manifested of God in his dealings with us, when *known,* enters into us, and becomes *life.* And thus it is that life eternal consists in the *knowledge* of the only true God, and Jesus Christ whom he hath sent. And thus also it is that we become partakers of the divine nature, even now, through the knowledge of those promises, which declare the character of God.[84]

Erskine understood the vicarious humanity of Christ as the basis for atonement. When we recognise it, we are thereby enabled to become partakers in his holiness because through the incarnation we can now share his perfect humanity, and consequently may conform to his suffering life through faith. Abelardian overtones are apparent here, though, as F.W. Dillistone has pointed out, the medieval mystical tradition, as reflected in Bernard of Clairvaux, also emphasised the redemption of human nature by incarnate divine love. Individuals, who may or may not be conscious they have been brought within the scope of redemption, merely needed to recognise, accept, and identify with what had been made possible through divine grace, thereby entering into union with God. Erskine perhaps tended to identify more with what Dillistone denotes as this more passive role for

---

[82] Torrance, *Trinitarian Faith*, 152, 184-89.

[83] Christian D. Kettler, *The Vicarious Humanity of Christ and the Reality of Salvation* (Lanham: University Press of America, 1991), 121, 133. Morna Hooker uses the term "interchange in Christ" for her related Pauline studies in *From Adam to Christ* (Cambridge: Cambridge University Press), 1990.

[84] *Serpent*, 245-6, cf., Letter to an unknown correspondent, 15 January 1830, *Letters-I,* 286-88.

the individual, compared to the more 'active' and 'passionate' devotional response of Abelard, though it is no less total and life-consuming.[85]

Anticipating potential misunderstanding that by speaking of 'suffering' and 'punishment' as 'necessary', and life as the 'furnace' for the 'purging away of sin', we are in any way to make up for the (incomplete) atoning work of Christ, or that our salvation depended on how much we suffer, Erskine offered reassurance that Christ has already fully remitted sin and brought righteousness right into the human condition. Stressing that it is the 'Christ-spirit' (to be identified with the Holy Spirit) by which we live 'in Christ' which is the crucial factor, Erskine elucidated that we do not, in fact, *atone* for our own sin through any process of suffering. This was properly the refining process of *sanctification*, which he identified with *salvation* itself:

> I am not speaking of atonement, but of the purifying of the nature which is produced by sorrow received in a godly sort. And even with regard to this need of suffering – I do not mean to say that any amount of suffering is necessary to salvation. It is the suffering spirit of Jesus in us that is necessary. Now every one who really knows Christ, does according to the measure of his faith receive that spirit of Christ which suffered in Christ, and which in Christ accepted the punishment of sin, and gave God glory as its punisher – and he by that same spirit accepts his punishment, giving God glory therein...The entrance of that Holy Spirit into the heart of the sinful creature is the entrance of the purifying fire which withers and consumes the flesh...*The punishment is always in our flesh,* and the entrance of the spirit of Christ at once discovers to us the presence of the punishment, and teaches us to accept it. Every pain that we suffer arises from sin – for nature is a suffering nature, simply because it is a fallen nature. This is true, whether the suffering be mental or bodily...Punishment, lovingly received, is the process by which we are sanctified. This process began in our Head, and must descend into every member. Christ's sufferings made the atonement, because through them the life was let into the body – through them Christ became the head of life to the body – and it is only by that life in us, that we can lovingly receive our punishment, putting to our seal, that God is righteous in it. Any sinful creature that accepts his punishment is necessarily saved, because, in fact, such acquiescence is salvation, one-mindedness with God.[86]

Erskine sought to highlight what Tom Smail has recently described in terms of Christ's work on the cross 'remaining within the realm of possibility and mere potentiality until it is actualised and made real by our participation in it'. For Smail, the salvific 'decisive moment' consists of

> the moment of our participation rather than the moment of Christ's action on our behalf. The new humanity needs no action or response on our part to

---

[85] F.W. Dillistone, *The Christian Understanding of Atonement* (Welwyn: James Nisbet, 1968), 324-5.
[86] *Serpent* (2nd edition), 56-7, cf., Thomson, *Universal Pardon*, 482-4.

move it out of the realm of possibility into actuality. It became real and actual at Calvary, and remains for ever real, actual and powerful at the right hand of the Father, whether we know of it or not, trust ourselves to it or not. The question is not how it can gain reality and actuality by being joined to us, but rather how we can attain ultimate reality and actuality by being joined to the risen and ascended Jesus whose humanity it is.[87]

Erskine believed that everyone participated in the glorious 'bond' which linked them through the incarnation to Christ. The fact of Christ's universal indwelling of humanity by assuming their fallen nature was the gospel of 'hope'. However, it required actualising by the Spirit so that a second 'bond' would be forged, that of Christ indwelling the believer by faith. Erskine's 'double incarnational' concept was therefore essentially soteriological. His objective was for human beings to achieve that perfect state "when it is no more we that live, but Christ living in us", i.e., nothing less than union with Christ. How this was attainable in practice was through sharing in the sufferings of Christ, and battling moment by moment against the forces of evil:

> The process by which this is accomplished, is a continual fellowship with the sufferings of Christ; a continual rejection of evil, or grieving over its power; – a continual protest for God, against the devil, and the world, and the flesh. This, I say, is the *process* by which it is accomplished. But the *power* by which the process is carried on, and the work is accomplished, is "Christ in you the hope of glory." This is the supply – this is the provision of life and strength. It is neither life nor strength to the man who disbelieves it, as the sun is not light to the man who shuts his eyes – but yet it is life and strength given to him, and which he may use if he will, and for the use of which he will be judged. "Christ in you the hope of glory," then, is the gospel to every man, for it is the description of the first bond, namely, that of the flesh, by which every individual of the race is united to Christ. "Christ dwelling in your hearts by faith," is the second bond, namely, that of the Spirit, by which those only who believe in the truth are united to him; and without which the other bond will at last bring against unbelievers the charge of love, and power, and bliss rejected – when the time of judgment comes. This union of God with the whole fallen nature in the person of Christ, is the great matter in God's dealings with men.[88]

Participation in Christ, including his sufferings, was therefore seen by Erskine as indispensable to salvation. It also afforded a satisfactory innovative theodicy in an age which encountered theological problems with the idea of suffering. The purpose of 'punishment' was in reality 'a voice of divine love' which, when correctly apprehended and responded to, enabled the sinner so to love God's law and hate sin, that divine 'punishment' is

---

[87] Tom Smail, *Once and for All: A Confession of the Cross* (London: Darton, Longman & Todd, 1998), 153.
[88] *Serpent*, 88-9.

actually commended. 'Judgment' therefore effectively became the means by which we recognise our sin and fallenness, and acts as an incentive to seek God. It represents 'spiritual education'. Accordingly, the only 'condemnation' Erskine recognised was the result of refusing the divine education process. The pain of suffering in life was therefore to be welcomed as necessarily educative in dealing with sin and bringing one's life into 'spiritual order'.

Propitiation

Erskine's logical linking of his new understanding of Christ's representative atonement with human sanctification necessarily involved radical departure from traditional orthodox ideas relating to Christ's 'substitution':

> Throughout the whole course of his life on earth, Christ was just accepting his punishment, as the head of the sinful nature; and that eternal life which his believing members receive out of him, is continually doing in them what it did in him. Christ suffered then for a purpose directly opposed to the purpose which is implied in the doctrine of substitution, he suffered not to dispense with our suffering, but to enable us to suffer, *as* he did, to the glory of God, and to the purification of our natures. And here then is the simple connexion between the atonement of Christ and the sanctification of his members. The atonement consisted in Christ's accepting the punishment of sin as the head of the nature; and the sanctification of his members consists in their accepting it also in the power of his spirit dwelling in them.[89]

It is important to recognise Erskine's insistence that the sufferings of Christ themselves were not 'sacrificial' or 'propitiatory' in the traditional sense. He was determined to remove any suggestion that the death and sufferings of Christ were in any way 'propitiating' God's wrath. Rather, they served as the example for us to work out our own 'sacrifice' and 'propitiation', for "God desires to see that propitiation in all men".[90] In Erskine's innovative, reconstructive terminology 'propitiation' now equated to Christ's self-sacrifice, his God-dependent surrender of self-will, his sympathetic confession of sin, his acceptance of God's loving 'punishment', and his righteousness, all of which we were to imitate incarnationally. Anticipation of John McLeod Campbell is again evident:

> God had set forth that sacrifice, by which Christ the head had made propitiation for the whole race, as a pattern of the righteousness to which every individual of the race is called, and of which every one is made capable...Jesus

---

[89] *Serpent* (2nd edition), 49.
[90] *Sp.Order*, 157-8.

truly partook of that same flesh and blood of which the children were partakers, and on which the righteous sentence of condemnation lay; and that, therefore, in his sacrifice, he was the real Head and not the mere substitute of the sinful race, and did what he did, as the right thing, becoming and fitting himself to do, as a partaker of that nature, and what would have been right for all men to do, and what must still continue right for all men to do...in the Psalms we find Jesus continually confessing sin as one of the sinful race on whom the Lord had laid the iniquities of all, although he had no personal sins; and casting himself on God as the faithful God who forgiveth sin, and forsaketh not those that trust in Him. Jesus confessed sin, and the Father was faithful and just to forgive him his sin. He accepted his punishment, and God remembered the covenant of life and raised him from the dead. And, indeed, His propitiation consisted much of these two things, confession of sin, and acceptance of punishment...his official righteousness was founded on the forgiveness of past sin, and a forgiveness exactly similar to that which is bestowed on us, namely, a forgiveness which does not remit the punishment of sin, but which carries us through it, into eternal life, on the other side of it...the way by which Jesus made reconciliation for the race, as its head, should be also the pattern of the righteousness to which every individual of the race is called; as it is certain that it is only by yielding ourselves to that same Spirit in which Jesus lived and offered his sacrifice, and which He brought as a fountain of righteous life into our fallen nature, that any of us can become righteous, so that our righteousness must be essentially the same as His, being, in fact, only a rill out of His fountain.[91]

Here Erskine creatively united several themes, presenting Jesus as the representative *Head* of the sinful human race rather than its *substitute*. Jesus is made to confess sin and obtain forgiveness from God in the same way as us. Because he sacrificed his own will and accepted his 'punishment', God raised him from the dead, and fallen flesh, having been 'purgated in its root', became acceptable to God, for Jesus "gave the Father to see something in the human nature in which he could be well pleased, and over which he could rejoice".[92] Erskine's scheme therefore required radical (and arguably excessively literal and extreme), innovative reinterpretation of 'propitiation' and 'sacrifice' as something we are all to do in imitation of Christ by ourselves 'confessing sin' and 'accepting punishment'.

However, there still remain as a consequence nagging ambiguities regarding the extent to which Erskine regarded Christ's sacrifice as unique:

the sacrifice of Christ was truly the sacrifice of self at the very root of the humanity...sin consists in self-seeking; and sin can therefore be put away by no other means than the sacrifice of self – a sacrifice, however, which must be reproduced in every soul of man before he is individually delivered from sin. Christ's sacrifice cannot be unlike anything else in the world – it is the

---

[91] *Election*, 234-6.
[92] *Serpent*, 50.

very type of what must be done by the spirit of Christ in every human being.[93]

Erskine was not suggesting that Jesus did not carry out a 'sacrificial' work of 'propitiation'. He merely redefined the terminology and shifted the emphasis, removing the less acceptable aspects of 'satisfaction', and extending its application to human beings for execution in the same 'Christ-spirit'. However, Erskine's understanding of 'propitiation' as "faith carried to its highest power", that is, trust in the loving purposes of God even whilst shedding life-blood, contained no suggestion of placating divine wrath, and to all intents and purposes he completely undermined the established doctrine.[94]

Erskine was bothered by suggestions that he was responsible for undermining traditional truth, and he frequently defended himself against the charge, claiming people misunderstood him. But his tendency to focus on one aspect of truth to the exclusion of others, and the ambiguous nature of his self-confessed tortuous style and lawyer's logic, which many, friends and opponents alike, found difficult to follow, did not help. This applied particularly when faced with charges of excess subjectivity, detracting from the unique objective work of Christ, and even of ascribing sin to Christ. Thomas Chalmers was one of several who reacted to *The Doctrine of Election* with profound disquiet, though a frustrated Erskine passionately protested that even the great man himself had not comprehended him. He was forced to elucidate his 'real' meaning for Chalmers' benefit and the preservation of his evangelical credentials, though much damage had irreparably been done:

> I desire much not to be misunderstood by you, therefore I would remind you, that in the view which I gave of the propitiation, I [did] not mean to exclude that which I do not dwell on, namely, the idea of Christ actually bearing the sins and punishment of all mankind – but that I have thought it my duty to dwell on a part which seems to me to have been much overlooked in it, namely, that in as much as it consisted in the shedding out of the life of man's will, by Jesus Christ, in the filial spirit – it is the very prototype of that very righteousness which is required in every man, and which it is the object of Christianity to produce in every man."[95]

---

[93] Letter to Bishop Ewing, 9 January 1861, *Ewing-I*, 27, cf., *Sp.Order*, 250.
[94] "The faith spoken of in the 25th verse [of Romans 3] is I believe Christ's own trust in the Father – the trust which sustained him *even in the shedding out of his life-blood*", (*Sp.Order*, 155-7).
[95] Letter to Thomas Chalmers, 28 October 1838, *NCLE MS CHA* 7.2.12.

The Nature of Sin

As the nineteenth century became increasingly sensitive to issues concerning evil and suffering, sin tended to be viewed more as something from which humanity would progressively and educationally free itself, "thus treating a moral as though it were a physical defect". Stressing the essential dignity rather than depravity of humankind, self-centredness, self-dependence and a failure to recognise the true potential of human nature began to replace traditional ideas of sin as 'disobedience'.[96]

Erskine mirrored this anthropological trend in his reinterpretation of atonement as the redemption of human nature. Wrestling with the problem of reconciling God's love with the existence of evil and suffering, in accordance with his own self-consistent theodicy, Erskine tended to view sin as a 'disease' of human nature needing continual healing, rather than mere reliance on any supposed forensic removal of guilt through the cross. Further echoing Abelard, it became the therapeutic moral influence of the character of God as revealed through Christ which was divinely fitted to perform the work of deliverance and its necessary adjunct, sanctification:

> Sin is a disease of the mind which necessarily occasions misery; and, therefore, the pardon of sin, unless it be accompanied with some remedy for this disease, cannot relieve from misery. This remedy, as I have endeavoured to explain, consists in the attractive and sanctifying influence of the Divine character manifested in Jesus Christ. Pardon is preached through him, and those who really believe are healed; for this belief implants in the heart the love of God and the love of man, which is only another name for spiritual health.[97]

In Erskine's complementary scheme the effects of the 'disease' also constituted 'divine punishment':

> We see on one side, life, health, happiness; and on the other, death, disease, pain, misery. The first class furnishes us with arguments for the goodness of God; but what are we to make of the opposite facts? The theory on this subject which is attended with fewest difficulties, is founded on two suppositions, – first. That moral good is necessary to permanent happiness; and second, That misery is the result of moral evil, and was appointed by the Author of Nature as its check and punishment.[98]

---

[96] L.E. Elliott-Binns, *English Thought 1860-1900: The Theological Aspect* (London: Longmans, Green and Co., 1956), 250-1.

[97] *Evidence*, 192.

[98] *Evidence*, 49, cf., 70.

Left to itself, therefore, sin becomes its own punishment. What was needed was revelation that God's condemnation of sin was something to be welcomed, for

> when I understand that His condemnation contains within it an unchangeable purpose to draw me out of my sin, I can accept His condemnation and bless Him for it. It seems to me that the Gospel of Jesus Christ is just the full and living manifestation of this purpose, – that it means this or nothing.[99]

'Sin', for Erskine, properly constituted failure to resist temptation and accept punishment which was divinely intended to be reformatory:

> It is no sin to have selfish, sensual, violent propensities, – *the sin is to yield to them*. Resistance to the evils within us and without us constitutes the education of man; the sense of our own incompetency for the task is intended to lead us to take hold of God's strength.[100]

This concept fuelled Erskine's novel conviction in his earlier work that any final 'condemnation' could result solely from individuals' rejection of free pardon. It could not be on account of *sin* (for which pardon has already been granted), but only "the condemnation at last for the rejection of the gospel, and the penalty of the second death".[101] As his universal scheme of divine education took hold, and the question of the fate of those who continued to resist the gospel exercised his mind, Erskine was eventually to produce his own version of the doctrine of predestination. He conceded that even determined refusal of the gospel would finally be overcome in the eternal love of God, since his conception of God could not admit he would ever "bring into existence any spirits which he foresees will finally resist His desire":

> We have each one of us been created to be educated into a fitness to fill a particular predestined place in the great body of the Son; and until we attain that fitness we must suffer the misery of disorder, and anarchy, and conscious guilt, in not yielding ourselves to the true Light; but I believe that God will not be overcome of evil, but will overcome evil with good ultimately, and that He...will wait, with much long-suffering, for the perfecting of His spiritual offspring.[102]

---

[99] *Sp.Order*, 242-3.

[100] Letter to Mrs Blackwell, 23 June 1862, *Letters-II*, 263.

[101] *Extracts*, xxxv. In Erskine's earlier work the 'Second Death' refers to the fate of those who reject the true gospel, since Christ has pardoned all forgivable sin already. So rejection of the gospel became a kind of 'unforgivable sin', though Erskine does not employ that phrase.

[102] Letter to Rev. John Young, 1866, *Letters-II*, 246-7; Letter to the Bishop of London, later Archbishop of Canterbury (Archibald Campbell Tait), 11 July 1863, *Ewing-II*, 57-8, cf., Letter to Mr Craig, [no date – probably 1863], *Letters-II*, 237-44.

Therefore the existence of evil and suffering was closely related to God's loving purposes. Erskine commented in regard to the exodus wanderings of the Israelites that "their sufferings did not proceed from any lack of love in God, for that the very infliction itself by which sin was punished, was in the purpose of God to become the source of *new life*".[103] Sin was accordingly intimately related to Erskine's theology of suffering and atonement:

> [Jesus] did not suffer the punishment of sin, as the doctrine of substitution supposes, to dispense with our suffering it, but to change the character of our suffering, from an unsanctified and unsanctifying suffering, into a sanctified and sanctifying suffering.[104]

Erskine acknowledged there were implications in his ideas for difficult questions concerning the origin of evil. But his concept of God's remedial use of sin and affliction to instil righteousness was remarkably close to Schleiermacher's understanding of the human sense of sin as the tension caused by the awakening of God-consciousness, and therefore ordained to be within God's overall redemptive purpose.[105] Erskine's radical shift from an objective to a more subjective, human-centred interpretation of sin and punishment can be seen as reflecting his broad background. Enlightenment theologians sensed a kinship with Abelardian soteriological concepts, especially moral atonement theory. As Alister McGrath has demonstrated, representatives of the German *Aufklärung* defined the work of Christ

> in terms of the promotion of human happiness and perfection...the divine dispensation towards mankind is totally concerned with the promotion of a 'supremely excellent and complete morality' which finds its personification in Jesus Christ. God demands nothing of man which is not directly and totally beneficial to man himself; the object of the Christian religion is to meet the religious and moral needs of mankind.

With regard to sin, humanity was not so much ontologically alienated from God, as alienating itself by acts which worked against its own happiness and perfection. So the essence of sin was deemed to reside in the damage it caused to human beings themselves, rather than by directly affecting God:

> Sin, it must be noted, is most emphatically *not* understood as an offence against God, for which an appropriate satisfaction is required. If Christ's death is to have *any* significance for man, this must therefore be *located in the effect which it has upon man himself*. This important conclusion finds its most natural expression in an exemplarist or moral theory of the Atonement, which is characteristic of the later Enlightenment theologians...for these

---

[103] *Serpent*, 31.

[104] *Serpent* (2nd edition), 39.

[105] Schleiermacher, *Christian Faith*, §67.2, 274, §80.2-3, 327-9, §81.1-3, 330-5.

theologians, the predicament from which man requires to be delivered is not that of bondage to sin or demonic powers, but *ignorance or misunderstanding concerning God*.[106]

This clearly identifies Erskine as a 'late Enlightenment theologian'. For him, 'knowledge' was dynamic power and the key to deliverance from sin. Mere knowledge of duty was not enough: "The love of God must be rooted in the heart; and this can only be accomplished by habitually viewing him in all the amiableness of his love and of his holiness"[107] Living knowledge and love of God's character were essential to produce the necessary desired conformity, "because this conformity of character is the living principle of union which pervades and binds together the whole family of God and capacitates the meanest of its members for partaking in the blessedness of their common Father".[108]

Erskine, therefore, tended to restate sin in terms of ignorance, independence, or unwillingness to accept Christ's incarnational work in human flesh together with its implications in the work of sanctification. The 'wicked', for example, became "those who know not, or who forget, that God hath forgiven sin through an atonement".[109] There was little suggestion in his work of acceptance that 'the wicked' were, in fact, guilty perpetrators of sinful deeds. By not relating 'sin' to sinful activities but rather to failure to appropriate antecedent forgiveness, Erskine was open to the charge of holding a low view of sin. He acknowledged some might accuse him of minimising the seriousness of sin, but he nevertheless justified his approach by emphasising his revolutionary concept of the salvific efficacy of sin itself. He considered there to be

> a teaching through sin, an instruction in righteousness through sin, which perhaps could not be given in any other way. The conviction of the rightness and blessedness of a perfect trust in God may be more efficiently taught through the conviction of the sin and misery of self-trust and self-seeking than through simple spiritual apprehension".[110]

George Smeaton regarded Schleiermacher and the 'German Tendency' as responsible for what he lamented as the reconstructed understanding of sin which so 'deleteriously' influenced the Broad School. Schleiermacher "repudiated all allusion to law or divine wrath, and merged the judicial aspect of theology in the ethical...the watchword of this tendency...is spiritual

---

[106] Alister McGrath, "The Moral Theory of the Atonement", *SJT* 38, 2 (1985), 206, 210-1, cf., Robert Letham, *The Work of Christ* (Leicester: IVP, 1993), 166-7.

[107] *Evidence*, 164.

[108] *Evidence*, 165.

[109] *Serpent*, 256-7.

[110] Letter to Rev. John Young, 1866, *Letters-II*, 247.

life, not expiation, the renewal of the nature, not the acceptance of the person; in a word, a mere moral redemption". He sardonically remarked, "According to Schleiermacher sin is a mere defect in the consciousness of God, and the atonement is a mere readjustment of the natural and divine consciousness of man".[111]

Nonetheless, according to his friends, Erskine entertained a deep personal sense of the seriousness of sin. The *Spectator* affirmed with regard to *The Spiritual Order* that "the sense of sin, and the punishment of sin, is in every page".[112] But he undoubtedly sought to re-define its traditional connotations, tending, like Schleiermacher and F.D. Maurice, to regard sin in terms of self-centred individualism and alienation. 'Sin' effectively became refusal to acknowledge our true relationship in union with God as sons, and to live independently and unconscious of God.[113] Both Erskine and Maurice were utterly convinced that salvation was from 'sin' itself understood in this way, rather than from what they regarded as the Calvinist concept of salvation from the punishment of sin.

Erskine believed God's aim was to combat sin and eradicate it through consciousness of God, positive sanctification, and holiness of life. Through the incarnation, Christ had introduced a new, radical, element into the human race itself, which, when acknowledged, worked existentially to produce a fundamental change within individual human nature to deal with sin at its very root. Because "a belief in Christ is just the same thing, as a belief that sins are forgiven", the only reason for guilt remaining could be for unbelief, failure to believe the gospel.[114] If 'sin' was essentially self-centredness, by contrast, 'righteousness' was putting *God* at the centre, recognising Jesus as the supreme example of filial trust, self-denial and self-sacrifice. The power of Jesus' example, when personally appropriated, effected inward transformation by promoting Christian character and conformity to Christ, an education process which delivered humanity from the sin which impeded spiritual development and progress:

> what is the signification of ἁμαρτάνειν? It is to *miss the right mark*. It does not require that you should either commit murder or adultery, or even have any definite evil purpose. The right mark is to have the mind of Christ, to love God with the whole heart, and our neighbour as ourselves…seeking that which is gratifying to the tastes and appetites as the object of life, and making it our object to avoid that which is ungratifying to them IS SIN. Hunger-

---

[111] Smeaton, *Christ's Doctrine*, 482-3, 486.

[112] The *Spectator*, (24 June 1871), 770.

[113] *Election*, 241, cf., Schleirmacher, *Christian Faith*, §66, 271; Frederick Maurice (ed.), *The Life of Frederick Denison Maurice Chiefly Told in His Own Letters,* [2nd Edition], in 2 volumes (London: Macmillan and Co., 1884), I, 450.

[114] *Extracts*, xxxvii-xxxviii.

ing and thirsting after righteousness is the exact opposite, and is what our Lord calls 'blessed'.[115]

Sin, suffering, atonement, and sanctification were therefore interdependent. Erskine was concerned to stress that Christ was our 'Forerunner' and 'Leader' in showing that the real nature of suffering atonement lay in 'sympathising' with God's evaluation of sin, for "Jesus himself suffered the punishment of sin, acquiescing in its righteousness".[116] John McLeod Campbell similarly was to emphasise the 'impossibility of regarding Christ's sufferings as penal'. Rather, they represented the sympathetic suffering of "seeing sin and sinners with God's eyes, and feeling in reference to them with God's heart". They were the "sorrows of holy love endured in realising our sin and misery".[117] For Erskine, the cross, when rightly and sympathetically appropriated in the light of its manifestation of God's character, afforded a correct estimation of the nature of humanity and the guilt of sin. The felt awareness of God's view of sin, should, in genuine imitation of Christ, reproduce in us a sympathetic "sin-hating, sin-destroying love", which 'condemns sin in the flesh'. This therefore represented "fellowship in Christ's sufferings".[118]

Schleiermacher also tended to regard liberation from sin as an incarnational rather than an atoning work, effected more through Christ's union with humanity than through the blood of the cross. He also considered Christ's sufferings as evidence of his sympathetic identification and relationship with sinful humanity, rather than penal. Christ was the 'ideal man' in whose God-conscious, sin-hating humanity we can all share, and so progressively die to sin.[119] Schleiermacher's concept involved a strong moral and ethical approach to soteriology, but it incorporated the idea that sin was not so much offence against a holy God involving a necessary incurring of divine wrath, but "a lower stage in the progress of human nature from which it is raised by union with Christ. Only in such union does the sinner become conscious of sin and strive to put it away".[120] Erskine himself never adopted the later liberal tendency to regard sin as the result merely of error, limitation, and social forces, though the liberal 'solution' to sin of moral and ethical education could be interpreted as a logical development of his views.

---

[115] Letter to Bishop Ewing, August 1860, *Ewing-I,* 25.

[116] *Serpent*, [2nd edition], 44,

[117] Campbell, *NOTA*, 107, 116.

[118] *Serpent*, 114-6.

[119] Schleiermacher, *Christian Faith*, §104, 457-62.

[120] L.W. Grensted, *A Short History of the Doctrine of the Atonement* (Manchester: University Press, 1920), 331.

The Place of Election

Notions of divine control and creaturely submission to providence, along with particularity and mercy for the few, became increasingly morally and politically unacceptable to nineteenth-century sensitivities. Coleridge, for example, reflected the growing inclusive mood when he insisted that divine grace was not restricted but "offered to all".[121] Schleiermacher reformulated the traditional idea of election to cohere with his concept of the restoration of all things.[122] Similarly, Erskine not only reconstructed classic soteriological doctrines of propitiation and sin but, prompted by what he regarded as the moral unacceptability of Calvinistic predestination and limited atonement, he innovatively sought to accommodate these historic, deeply held articles of faith into a wholly new conceptual framework more in tune with the century.

With the publication in 1837 of *The Doctrine of Election*, Erskine came formally to reject and reformulate that ultimate Calvinist bastion, its doctrine of predestination and irresistible grace. Until 1830 he had largely avoided the subject, fearing offence or rejection. But Andrew Thomson's challenge for Erskine to spell out the implications for his theological system of the doctrine of election was inescapable.[123] The intervening years had therefore been spent silently struggling to harmonise his developing views on the divine purpose and the 'larger hope' with his still revered evangelical native religion: "I often feel fettered by not feeling myself permitted more plainly and fully to introduce the final purpose of God towards all men, as the explanation of His present dealings with them".[124] He found the task immensely challenging:

> I find it very difficult to say what I wish to say without giving more offence than is necessary...I am afraid that [*The Doctrine of Election*] will have very great faults as a work...it is, throughout, in direct opposition to the received views of Christianity. So that I cannot doubt but that the most truly religious people in the land will be startled, and even shocked, by many things in it.[125]

The result was a radical reinterpretation of the Calvinist doctrine of election designed to cohere with Erskine's overall soteriological outlook. *The*

---

[121] Coleridge, *Confessions*, 11-12.

[122] Schleiermacher, *Christian Faith*, §117-20; "Appendix on Eternal Damnation", 720-22.

[123] Thomson, *Universal Pardon*, 390-1, 397-8.

[124] Letter to A.J. Scott, 21 April 1837, *Letters-I*, 252-3. Erskine's final abandonment of the Calvinist position on election may actually be dated by reference to a personal debate and correspondence with the Genevan pastor, Louis Gaussen, culminating in Erskine's letter of 7 December 1832, *Letters-I*, 288.

[125] Letter to Mrs Stirling, 23 June, 1837, *Letters-I*, 254-5.

Doctrine of Election immediately received a generally hostile reception, even from friends who found it difficult to understand and potentially misleading. Madame Vinet wrote to Erskine counselling him that as both concepts of election and universal love were in the Bible, it was best to leave them alone without trying to reconcile them.[126] Stung by the criticism, though resolutely continuing to stand by the substance, six years later Erskine was still stating his intention to re-write and transform the book into an improved select resumé of all his previous works.[127]

Erskine's reinterpretation of election was based on the analogy of "two cords attached to every heart". This emphasised his conviction that 'election' and 'reprobation' were not eternal destinies but a spiritual 'tug-of-war' between opposing 'powers' or 'character-types' dwelling as 'seeds' or 'principles' within each individual. One cord was held by Satan, pulling towards the flesh and the self; the other was held by God, pulling towards the Spirit and the things of God: "Thus man, in all his actings, *never has to originate any thing*; he has only to follow something already commenced within him; he has only to choose to which of these two powers he will join himself".[128]

Accordingly, for Erskine, election became a psychological, dualistic matter of 'God-consciousness' and human, rather than divine, choice. It was therefore from the idea of an internal struggle between two masters for domination, 'Adam' versus 'Christ', or 'flesh' versus 'spirit', that he neatly developed his own peculiar innovative incarnational concept of election in which God 'elects' the humanity and righteousness of Christ. Individuals, responding to internal revelation, must willingly 'choose' either the elect racial Headship of Christ or the reprobate headship of Adam. Erskine's virtual identification of election with *justification* became readily apparent:

> in opposition to the fall through Adam, there is a gift of grace through Christ, which fully meets the fall, and extends as widely as the fall...the gift bestowed was the nature of Christ, which, wherever it entered, carried with it the seal of God's approbation and blessing...the gift only enters into *those who accept it*...consequently such only as accept it, shall reign with Christ in life eternal...although the natural birth of man, is a thing entirely independent of his own volition, it is far otherwise with his regeneration or spiritual birth, which cannot be effected without his own consent and co-operation. Here then we see, that the doctrine of righteousness, and the doctrine of election, are one and the same thing. We see that the nature of Adam is the unrighteous nature, which God reprobates, and that the nature of Christ is the righteous nature, which God elects, – we see that they are both in every man, and that though the old evil nature has an advantage over the new, by being, as it were, first in possession of us, in consequence of our being born in its life,

---

[126] See letter to Madame Vinet, 6 February 1839, *Letters-I*, 348.
[127] Letter to Rev. Thomas Wright Mathews, 8 October 1844, *Letters-II*, 398.
[128] *Election*, 58-9.

yet the new nature, as a seed of God, is given to every man in the gift of grace, and continues within his reach during his life, whatever his offences may have been, so as to be a full counterbalance, in the judgment of eternal wisdom, to the weakness and the condemnation brought on by the fall; – we see that, whilst we are walking in our first natural life, and not accepting the gift, that is, not living to God by faith, which is the nature of Christ, we are still under the reprobation, and that it is *only by accepting the gift, which personal act God lays upon us to do, as our part in the work of salvation,* that we come under that election which ever rests, and exclusively rests, on the righteous nature of Christ, and on all who join themselves to it.[129]

Erskine's ingenious reconstruction of the doctrine of election involved the organic corporate idea of Christ as 'the elect' and Adam as 'the reprobate'. The identities of the 'elect' or 'reprobate' were not individuals but modes of existence or character, corresponding either to the 'new humanity' chosen by God to be instituted by Christ, or the 'old humanity' belonging to Adam, now superseded. To illustrate the concept, Erskine employed his favourite Romantic metaphor (probably adapted from William Law), of a tree with two roots, Adam and Christ, with the new sap expelling the old. Most significantly, Erskine introduced the idea that, rather than election belonging to the realm of divine pre-determination, human freedom and responsibility in response to the voice of conscience was now pre-eminent, for "every man in some sense has the election in him, and has it in his power to make his election sure, whether he uses that power or not".[130] Erskine referred to this crucial, universal, latent, divine/ human ability variously as 'divine grace', 'the power of joining', the "*all-important step,* by which man is called on to connect himself with God's predestination". Such choice was closely related to willingness to imitate Christ in his suffering, since "God's electing love is limited to these who consent to partake in Christ's death, namely, the spiritually-minded". So effectively *we* choose to co-operate or not with God's prevenient grace, to be part of God's 'election', or to resist it and remain in his 'reprobation'.[131] Erskine asserted that

> as Christ was really given to men immediately after the Fall, all are elect in Him, he being in them all, and all are reprobate or rejected in the first Adam; but…we can make either our election or our reprobation sure by joining ourselves either to the one party or the other. I believe that God takes the first

---

[129] *Election*, 321-3, cf., *Election*, 45-53, *Sp.Order*, 248.

[130] *Election*, 77, cf., 122-4.

[131] *Election*, 114-15, cf., 87, 145-6, 411. F.D. Maurice, who regarded *Election* highly, followed Erskine in his approach to election, holding that, though all humanity is elected in Christ, some accept their election whilst others deny it, (Ellen Flesseman-Van Leer, *Grace Abounding: A Comparison of Frederick Denison Maurice and Karl Barth* [London: King's College, 1968], 35-6).

step to every man by His Spirit, and that man's part is acceptance and yielding.[132]

Introducing an innovative and subtle development, which formed a vital step towards ultimately inevitable universalist conclusions, Erskine effectively switched 'predestination' from a doctrine focusing on the predetermined divine selection of individuals to the formation of human character conformed to Christ by means of a synergistically enacted, eternally conceived, divine plan of education, discipline and training in "the school of Christ – the school of willing scholars".[133] In this way, though internally consistent for Erskine, the parameters for classic understandings of justification, sanctification and election became thoroughly blurred.

Erskine's insistence that "Jesus is the one Elect, and…those who by thus taking part with Jesus become members of his body become also members of the election, and that those who continue to resist Him shut themselves out from the election",[134] remarkably has received little analysis in direct comparison with Karl Barth's similar association of revelation with election.[135] In Barth's thought the significance of Jesus as the elect subject supremely demonstrates the loving, universally gracious, nature of God as revealed in Christ. For Barth, like Erskine, the 'event' of revelation involved recognition of the fact of God's gracious election of the human race in Christ, but also the responsibility of human decision: "what is decided in the revelation-event is not whether the individual is elect or not, but whether she will respond to her election in faith and obedience; whether, in other words, she will live as one who is elect (and, therefore, on the basis of the truth of her existence) or as one who is reprobate (and, therefore, on the basis of a lie)".[136] Of course, in Barth, Jesus also chooses to be the Reprobate, so the precise analogy with Adam does not follow; however, in Erskine this equated to the self-sacrifice of Christ in subjecting himself as the incarnate God to 'taste death for every man'.[137]

---

[132] Letter to Madame Forel, 19 November 1838, *Letters-I*, 337.

[133] *Election*, 398-403.

[134] Letter to Madame Forel, 19 November 1838, *Letters-I*, 337.

[135] David A.S. Fergusson appears to be almost alone in acknowledging Erskine's 'prefiguring' of Barth. Not only was Erskine "probably the first Scottish theologian since the Reformation to launch a frontal attack upon the doctrine of double predestination", but his work on election has been "unfairly neglected", ("Predestination: A Scottish Perspective", *SJT*, 46, 4 [1993], 470).

[136] Bruce L. McCormack, *Karl Barth's Critically Realistic Dialectical Theology* (Oxford: Clarendon Press, 1995), 373, 459, cf., Barth, *CD*, 1.1. §5 [2nd edition] (1975), 156-62.

[137] *Sp.Order*, 169.

Summary

Chapter 5 dwelt on Erskine's reconstruction of the crucial soteriological doctrines of pardon, atonement, sin, and election. Driven by a contemporary climate unfavourable to Calvinism, Erskine brought an innovative, eclectic, synthesising genius to the challenge of reconciling the classic doctrines of salvation with modern sentiment which was rejecting perceived harsh forensic emphases on divine sovereignty, human depravity, and penal substitution. Instead, Erskine was instrumental in introducing more hopeful, dignified, human-centred concepts of divine/ human love and reciprocal sympathy, personal responsibility, and redeemed human nature. Christ became a representative example to be emulated, rather than a sacrificial object, whilst the incarnational nature of his atonement placed individual destiny in human rather than divine hands. We noted that Erskine not only paralleled developments elsewhere, especially in Germany, but in many ways pioneered nineteenth-century reassessment of soteriological thought, and offered a new basis for approaching difficult questions of theodicy and suffering. To help inspire a megashift in ingrained traditional convictions, Erskine's powers of innovatory adaptation were stretched to the limit. For many he overstepped the dividing line between evangelical orthodoxy and error, particularly as he was driven inexorably in the direction of universalism. His redefinition of key soteriological terminology was either enlightened and creative, or sheer heresy, depending on one's viewpoint. Nevertheless, we suggest that Erskine not only appropriated contemporary, eclectic, intellectual currents of thought, seeking to harmonise them within a radical but internally consistent orthodox theological framework, but he occupied a pioneering role, especially in Scotland, in introducing broader, free-thinking methods and concepts into mainstream religion, which others were emboldened to follow. Recognition of his anticipation of soteriological aspects of Karl Barth's theology has largely been neglected.

Horrocks overlooks Romanticism once again.

CHAPTER 6

Erskine and Theological Controversy

Introduction

Theological innovation inevitably implies controversy, but controversy is invaluable for highlighting specific elements of perceived novelty. Virtually from his earliest publication Thomas Erskine found he disturbed and subsequently antagonised conservative forces of evangelical orthodoxy. It is therefore illuminating to appreciate how and why crucial controversial soteriological issues raised by Erskine provoked reaction by virtue of their innovatory implications.

Immediately before, during, and after the Row controversy in Scotland, Erskine was highlighted as a dangerous subverter of orthodox evangelicalism. Even today he is viewed in some quarters as dispensing with "the Evangelical scheme of salvation in which [he] once believed", and constructing a God "in his own likeness".[1] This chapter therefore concentrates on prominent orthodox critical responses to Erskine's soteriological thought which throw further light on the tension between innovation and orthodoxy. Though Erskine excelled in the art of synthesising traditional theology with eclectic contemporary thought, he lacked the careful balancing skills of a trained theologian like John McLeod Campbell. Accordingly, he was prone to distortion which caused misunderstanding and still generates critical response. Despite the radical nature of much of his theological innovation, we argue that Erskine nevertheless largely succeeded in remaining within an orthodox apologetic framework, at least, as judged by less rigid present day standards. We further seek to affirm that Erskine resists attempts to classify him within rigid heterodox categories.

Initially Erskine's early work was positively received as an important contribution to Christian apologetics. *Remarks on the Internal Evidence for*

---

[1] Needham, *Thomas Erskine*, 453, 458.

the Truth of Revealed Religion (1820) went through ten editions. However, by *An Essay on Faith*, published in 1822, serious opposition began to materialise insinuating Erskine's subtly subversive, creeping, departure from evangelical orthodoxy. This set the pattern for controversies which dominated the later part of the decade, and on into the 1830s. By the time *The Doctrine of Election* was published in 1837, though friends continued to stand by him, Erskine had been widely condemned, especially in Scotland, as dangerously doctrinally heretical.[2]

Scottish Reaction – J.A. Haldane

The publication of *The Doctrine of Election* provoked considerable anxiety amongst certain of Erskine's friends, including Thomas Chalmers who wrote in 1838 expressing disquiet concerning the development of Erskine's views on revelation, authority, and propitiation. There followed a strained and theologically confrontational exchange of correspondence, resulting eventually in Chalmers's reluctant admission of satisfaction with Erskine's explanations.[3]

Chalmers was relatively pacified. Others, however, were not so easily placated. Time had elapsed since the height of the Row controversy, but despite the appending of a sort of recantation concerning spiritual gifts in *The Doctrine of Election*, Erskine, already condemned as a propagator of serious error, was now considered by many to have gone completely off the rails into fanciful mysticism and sheer doctrinal heresy. The orthodox Calvinist *Quarterly Christian Magazine*'s review of *The Doctrine of Election* (almost certainly authored by its editor, J.A. Haldane) was savage. Castigating Erskine for Quaker and Irvingite notions, it claimed

> he has departed farther from the doctrine of the word of God than in his former publications, although in many respects they were very unscriptural. One error naturally leads to another…we shall be surprised if he long retains his present position. Of one thing we are sure, that *his* gospel is not the gospel of Christ, but another gospel.[4]

Highlighting his embrace of the 'heretical' idea of Christ's 'fallen flesh', and objecting to the epithet 'sinful', Haldane predictably rejected Erskine's

---

[2] The *Evangelical Magazine* was typical in praying for Erskine's recovery, "that his gifted mind may be led, in all simplicity, into the truths from which he has so far wandered", Anon., 'Review of *The Doctrine of Election*, by Thomas Erskine', XVI, New Series (1838), 119.

[3] See Chalmers's letter of 9 October 1838, *NCLE MS CHA* 3.15.68; note Erskine's reply dated 24 October 1838, *NCLE MS CHA* 7.2.12.

[4] Anon., "Erskine's Doctrine of Election, and its Connexion with the General Tenor of Christianity", *Quarterly Christian Magazine*, IV, No.24 (January, 1838), 352.

argument that Jesus was born into and experienced humanity's fallen condition.[5] Deploring Erskine's presentation of Jesus as the *Head* of the sinful human race rather than its *substitute*, and implications that Jesus was 'sinful', Haldane expressed outrage at the notion that Jesus 'confessed sin', needed 'forgiveness by God', and 'accepted his punishment' in order for God to raise him from the dead. The suggestion that Jesus 'sanctified' human flesh as a result of his resurrection was equally objectionable. Identifying him with the despised ideas of Irving, Haldane attacked Erskine's hijacking of traditional terminology, protesting that his views of "the human nature of Christ necessarily lead him to set aside the atonement, although he retains the word…Mr. Erskine rejects the scriptural doctrine of atonement, and substitutes a figment of his own".[6]

Robert Burns, Minister of St. George's, Paisley, similarly arguing that "Erskinism and Christianity [were] two very *different religions*", had already declared in 1830 that "Mr. Erskine knows nothing of a righteousness *imputed*". Rather, "his is a righteousness, or *love, revealed*. He recognises not a righteousness *received by faith*; his is a *love* believed already to have *taken effect* in favour of the sinner".[7] Haldane now also highlighted the dangerous implications of Erskine's denial of the traditional understanding of *imputation*, both in the sense of Adam's sin being 'imputed' to the whole of humanity, and of Christ bearing our 'imputed' sin and Christ's righteousness being 'imputed' to us. For Haldane, "the denial of the imputation of Adam's sin, and Christ's righteousness, subverts the gospel".[8] In contrast, Erskine had demonstrated he preferred the wholly distinct concept that Christ redeemed human nature itself.

Erskine had been widely regarded as deriving from Edward Irving the idea that atonement was made apart from the shedding of Christ's blood by the union of the fallen human and divine natures manifested through the incarnation. Haldane was no exception, and he believed a seriously deficient theology of the fall was involved. The Calvinist federal idea of *imputation* relating to Adam's sin (as distinct from Christ's righteousness) was reflected in the *Westminster Confession* which regarded Adam as humanity's representative head.[9] Adam's sin of disobedience caused him to fall from original righteousness, and he became dead in sin with a wholly corrupt human nature. Adam's guilt was imputed to all humanity, along with an inherited corrupt nature. Haldane accused Erskine of denying that sin

---

[5] For Erskine's teaching that Christ adopted "the likeness of sinful flesh", see *Election*, 364-8, *Sp.Order*, 241.

[6] *Quarterly Christian Magazine*, 353.

[7] Introductory essay to Joseph Bellamy, *Letters and Dialogues between Theron, Paulinus, and Aspasio* (Glasgow: George Gallie, 1830), xviii, xix.

[8] *Quarterly Christian Magazine*, 354.

[9] *Westminster Confession,* Chapter VI; Shaw, *Exposition*, 73-83.

was *imputed* as a result of the fall, and claiming instead that the fall *revealed* the corruption, with sin *propagated* by the corrupt human nature, so that it became an 'inherited internal corruption' which Christ then cleansed and redeemed through assuming the nature. Haldane wished to demonstrate the heretical nature of Erskine's views insomuch that he "considers imputation of sin a fiction".[10] The notion that *imitation* could be substituted for *imputation* in advocating that we follow Christ's example as free and responsible agents, thereby co-operating with God in our own salvation, was liable to condemnation in 1838 Scotland as essentially Pelagian, ignoring the disabling consequences of the fall.

Though far from denying an objective aspect to the work of Christ, Erskine had nevertheless emphasised the necessarily *subjective* aspect of his salvific work through the indwelling presence of Christ, since "righteousness cannot be vicarious". He therefore spoke not in terms of our sin being 'imputed' to Christ, and Christ's righteousness being 'imputed' to humanity, but preferred the wholly distinct and innovative concept of Christ redeeming human nature itself, so that the life and power which generated it was salvifically available to us as members of the organic body of which he was Head, operating through the conscience. Therefore we are "put into Christ's standing that we may receive his spirit and his character". Although Christ was to be the "pattern" of our righteousness, Erskine stipulated that we could not simply imitate him "slavishly", nor was our righteousness to be "self-originated". Rather Christ's righteousness and character were to be "communicated to us" or reproduced "livingly" within us "by the indwelling of his Spirit".[11]

As we have seen, Erskine reformulated 'justification' into a felt sense of being in a right familial relationship to God, as son to Father, and to humanity as brother. In Erskine's conflated terminology, this filial trust was in itself *righteousness* or *justification*, and the traditional meaning of *imputation* became redundant. Similarly, although Christ's sacrifice on the cross was acknowledged to be an objective fact, Erskine was concerned to stress the need for an essentially *subjective* appropriation of its significance, in the sense that the cross manifested the divine character. The reproduction in the life of the believer of Christ's self-sacrifice, death, suffering, filial trust, resurrection, and righteousness was, for Erskine, the natural outcome of 'spiritually apprehending' the mind and purpose of God in the sacrifice of the cross, and that purpose was transformational and ethical, rather than forensic and transactional:

> although He is essentially and eternally a Father, a God of mercy and goodness and blessing, – His goodness *cannot* bless us until we yield up our

---

[10] *Quarterly Christian Magazine*, 354.

[11] *Sp.Order*, 162-5. Note further parallels with John Owen; see p.42, note 68 above.

hearts to Him, that is, until we are spiritually-minded. This transformation of heart is accordingly the great object of all His dealings with us, an object which He will never cease to urge by all means, in this and every stage of our being until it is accomplished.[12]

In complete contrast to Haldane, therefore, Erskine unashamedly warned his readers not to rely on 'fictitious' legalistic concepts such as 'imputation'. His passionate concern was to stress the paramount need for a righteousness which was "*really righteousness*, the right condition of man's heart and mind before God, and not a mere conventional thing, consisting in forms or ceremonies, or opinions, or points of doctrine". Such a state of the heart was the condition "in which alone salvation consists".[13]

The association of Erskine's teaching with Irving, especially that Christ needed to obtain the same forgiveness and experience the same punishment as us, sharing with humanity the same need for the crucifixion of fallen flesh in order to redeem it, persuaded Haldane of Erskine's essential heterodoxy. The implication that salvation was attributable directly to the 'infusion' of a 'good principle' within the race and our consequent imitation of Christ's example, rather than our sin being imputed to Christ and his righteousness being imputed to us has remained completely repugnant to orthodox Calvinists. Such emphasis on immanency and exemplarism has nevertheless continued to appeal to Protestant liberalism.

The Soteriological Role of the Spirit

Probably the earliest critic to recognise worrying tendencies in Erskine was not a Scot but the English, Methodist, systematic theologian, Richard Watson (1781-1833), who recorded initial censure of Erskine in 1823 for obliterating in *Remarks on the Internal Evidence for the Truth of Revealed Religion* the distinctions between natural and supernatural revealed religion, and relativising the external witness by making internal evidence the primary test of revelation. In making human beings the arbiters of revelation, miracles and the supernatural were thereby rendered unnecessary. Watson further criticised Erskine for building "so much truth on the sand" of a "false principle" ("the sense of moral obligation"), and for suggesting that the excellence of Christianity was demonstrated by the way it embodied "in intelligible and palpable action" the abstract principles of natural religion – what he called "a gratuitous and unsubstantial foundation".[14]

A principal area of controversy centred on Erskine's perceived representation of the role of the Holy Spirit. Again, it was not so much from his

---

[12] *Sp.Order*, 217, cf., 163-5, 237-9.
[13] *Election*, 412.
[14] Watson, *Theological Institutes*, 39, 83.

native Scotland, but from Watson himself, that the earliest attributed and sustained perceptive reaction to Erskine's innovative soteriological system came, setting the agenda for subsequent wariness relating to Erskine's work. It took the form of a perspicacious review of *An Essay on Faith* in the evangelical *Wesleyan-Methodist Magazine,* prompted by the generally favourable impression made by his first publication, *Remarks on the Internal Evidence for the Truth of Revealed Religion.*[15] Whilst not doubting his sincerity, Watson considered that although Erskine offered helpful insights and pious sentiments, nevertheless the overall *tendency* of his thought was misleading, unorthodox, and potentially dangerous. Considering Erskine 'ingenious' in his innovative apologetic attempts to 'harmonise the scriptural doctrine of faith with reason and philosophy', he was nevertheless to be regarded as 'false', 'unscriptural', 'mistaken' and 'mischievous'. Treating theology 'like the sciences' by glorifying the human intellect and empirical powers, "in order to meet the philosophers he…sacrifices the Divines".[16] Accusing him of 'novel interpretations' forced upon the Bible, Watson voiced serious objections concerning Erskine's leading ideas (dressed up in "a philosophic garb") that "faith, or belief of the truth, does, by a natural process, grounded upon the manner in which God has constituted our nature, produce all the moral effects ascribed to it in the Gospel", and that 'salvation' means 'moral healing', rather than "deliverance from the condemnation of sin". Erskine's contrived philosophical 'laws of necessity', such as 'making faith to follow necessarily from knowledge' – contemptuously dismissed by Watson as "philosophico-evangelical Christianity" – belonged properly to the Spirit's province:

> the healing power of the Gospel is to be attributed, not to sentiment, the grand error of the author; not to the supposed moral efficacy of the knowledge of facts, such as the love of God to man, by meditating on which the heart is to be warmed into indignant feeling against sin, and into the love of holiness; but to the 'mighty working' of God in the heart by his Holy Spirit, without whose aid, all knowledge, all mere belief, is fruitless…[17]

Summarising objections to Erskine's new soteriological system, Watson registered six main points of contention:

> 1. "It confines saving faith to the mere intellectual reception, or *crediting* of the truth of the Gospel; and excludes *personal trust* from its definition", whereas the

---

[15] Richard Watson, 'Review of *An Essay on Faith* by Thomas Erskine', *The Wesleyan-Methodist Magazine,* VII, Third Series (August, 1828), 531-545.
[16] *Wesleyan-Methodist Magazine,* 532.
[17] *Wesleyan-Methodist Magazine,* 535-6, 539, 543.

latter is, in fact, essential for the correct apprehension of saving knowledge.

2. "It makes faith to follow necessarily from knowledge". But this is not a valid deduction.

3. It rejects the evangelical view of faith as a gift of God and work of the Spirit in the heart.

4. "It ascribes that moral efficiency to knowledge and belief which is in Scripture ascribed solely to the *direct* agency of the Spirit of God; and it thereby diverts our confidence from God, to ourselves. It makes regeneration an intellectual and sentimental process, instead of a supernatural one. According to Mr. Erskine, man is born again of his enlightened understanding; and not according to our Lord, who says, 'He is born of the Holy Ghost'".

5. It makes faith both the efficient cause and effect of sanctification – an essential contradiction!

6. Erskine is accused of making faith human-centred: "the indication of spiritual fullness in the creature", whereas Scripture makes it "a sense of entire spiritual want and dependence".

Watson suggested that traditional and orthodox views of faith accepted that mere belief may result from rational evidence and examination of Christian evidences. However, he insisted that after that Scripture nowhere views "the work of grace in the heart…to be carried on by the natural operation of these credited truths". On the contrary, the ensuing change of mind is ascribed to "the quickening influence of the Spirit", which may be resisted.[18]

Watson was responding in 1828 to Erskine's earliest publications when their serious implications were beginning to sink in. He was alarmed that an assumed orthodox evangelical apologist was actually subtly presenting a reductionist 'philosophical' version of Christian belief. Whilst it is important to understand the issues as they were perceived at the time, the concerns Watson highlighted were repeatedly raised by subsequent Erskine critics, usually revolving around the crucial role of the Holy Spirit. Significantly, Connop Thirlwall (who knew Erskine) confirmed towards the end of the century that "the great intellectual and religious struggle of our day turned mainly on the question whether there was a Holy Ghost".[19]

As Watson noted, Erskine appeared to diminish the traditional salvific work of the Spirit, which orthodox evangelicals regarded as indispensable for convicting of gospel truth, and tended to confuse divine and human

---

[18] *Wesleyan-Methodist Magazine*, 543-4.

[19] Cited by Elliott-Binns, *English Thought*, 236.

spirits. Nearly fifty years later, J.S. Candlish lamented the fact that Erskine's useful early work on internal evidence was not accompanied by a more enlightened recovery of the vital role of the Spirit, which he thought had become generally neglected in Erskine's day:

> It is to be regretted...that the doctrine of the Spirit's Testimony had at that time so much fallen out of sight, that Erskine had not the guidance which it would have afforded him to a more thorough solution of his doubts than he ever actually attained.[20]

Though the Protestant Reformers acknowledged the possibility of a natural knowledge of God, they insisted that it must necessarily be supplemented by supernatural divine revelation. They regarded the role of the Spirit, together with the word, as crucial in the context of Christian authority.[21] However, they believed that the Spirit did not so much reveal new truth, but rather illuminated Scripture to the believer through the *testimonium internum Spiritus Sancti*. What they regarded as the 'self-authenticating' nature of Scripture in reality was the supreme authentication of the Holy Spirit: "those whom the Holy Spirit has inwardly taught truly rest upon Scripture, and that Scripture indeed is self-authenticated".[22] But following the Reformation, Protestant orthodoxy tended to demote the authenticating role of the Spirit, replacing it with a corresponding emphasis on the propositional inerrancy of Scripture, despite Pietist/ Methodist attempts to emphasise both Word and Spirit. Since most Protestants tended to minimise the role of natural theology, regarding human reason as corrupted by sin and requiring restoration by divine grace in order to grasp divine truth, the role of natural reason in salvific knowledge was marginalised. The eighteenth century, however, mindful of the religious extremism of the previous century, and encouraged by the Deists, experienced a general reaction of dissatisfaction and scepticism concerning any approach to religious authority involving special revelation.[23] Accordingly, natural reason was seen generally as a safer path to religious unity, and both external propositional truth and the internal witness of the Spirit tended to be superseded.[24]

Erskine's educational background, where the emphasis on moral philosophy reflected eighteenth-century assumptions, strongly influenced his reconstructive approach to apologetics. He was conscious that unless Christianity could be shown to be eminently reasonable and universal in terms of

---

[20] Candlish, "Thomas Erskine", 112.

[21] Alister E. McGrath, *The Making of Modern German Christology 1750-1990* (Leicester: Apollos, 1994), 24, cf., Smeaton, *Holy Spirit*, 328-9.

[22] Calvin, *Institutes*, I. vii. 4 and 5.

[23] E.g., John Toland strongly objected to beliefs based solely on "the illuminating and efficacious Operation of the Holy Spirit", *Christianity Not Mysterious*, 45.

[24] Roger E. Olson, *The Story of Christian Theology* (Leicester: Apollos, 1999), 521-2.

Enlightenment criteria which expressly rejected narrow sectarian, confessional, doctrinal, and mysterious/ supra-rational religion, he would not appeal convincingly to an increasingly sceptical and critical world. Erskine therefore needed to introduce updated modifications. Though he may consequently have relegated or reassigned the traditionally primary role of the Spirit, or introduced philosophical notions which confused his meaning, he did not, however, neglect the trinitarian concept of the Holy Spirit. From the first, he indicated that he regarded the Spirit as integral to the tranformative salvific process:

> We are not to expect any mechanical or extraneous impression separate from that which the truth makes; for it is by the truth alone, known and believed, that the Holy Spirit operates in accomplishing that sanctifying work, which is itself salvation.[25]

Erskine regularly reaffirmed that he regarded the Spirit as vital in the acquisition of faith in the gospel, in regeneration, and in sanctification. In *Remarks on the Internal Evidence for the Truth of Revealed Religion* he insisted "that the belief of the gospel is, in every instance, the work of the Holy Spirit, no one who believes in the Bible can doubt", whilst he later confirmed that "no man can come to God except in the Holy Spirit".[26] The work of 'resemblance' was clearly attributable to the indwelling Spirit:

> it appears to me clear from Scripture that the blessing which God holds out to man through the work of redemption is a real and substantial restoration to the image of God, which is to be effected by man becoming the habitation of God through the Spirit.[27]

Since obedience and conformity to Christ cannot be self-produced, Erskine insisted that we need the divine Spirit's agency: "An absolute, and childlike dependence on the Holy Spirit for light, and strength, and comfort, is a constituent part of the Christian character. The work of restoration, in all its parts, and in all its glory, is God's."[28] Erskine here perhaps even parallels traditional Roman Catholic unease regarding the tendency of the classic Protestant formulations of justification and imputation to undermine the ethically transforming role of the Holy Spirit.

Though in *The Brazen Serpent* Erskine's Enlightenment background was apparent in his affirmation of the two main ways in which we apprehend the world, through the 'senses' and through 'reason', he nevertheless intro-

---

[25] *Salvation*, 303.
[26] *Evidence*, 152; Letter to Monsieur Gaussen, 7 December 1832, *Letters-I*, 297.
[27] Letter to Monsieur Gaussen, 7 December 1832, *Letters-I*, 289.
[28] *Faith*, 144.

duced what he claimed was a third dominant category necessary for the apprehension of 'divine things' or the 'kingdom of God':

> The Spirit of God in a man...is the power in him, which corresponds to, and is necessary for the understanding of, the kingdom of God in the universe – that third and chief element in everything.[29]

Notwithstanding such apparently contrary indications, Erskine's publications nevertheless gave the overall impression to many that the Spirit was relegated to a collateral function merely supportive of natural faculties. His assertion that "the Spirit of God brings these [natural] causes to act on the mind with their natural innate power" implied a significant shift in the Spirit's role to one that was more immanent, less direct, and conformable to Enlightenment categories.[30] Nineteenth-century Romantic and Idealist philosophy, and subsequently liberal theology, were themselves to 'hijack' the Christian notion of 'Spirit' or *Geist*.[31] Ironically, Calvinist discontent with Erskine's pneumatology was enhanced when the events at Row concentrated attention on the supposed work of the Spirit. His ideas received close scrutiny, especially in the light of the perceived critical and emotive issues of universal pardon and assurance as the essence of faith. Some of the earlier objections raised by the Methodists were pursued, particularly following Erskine's defiant re-statement in 1830 that everyone possessed an innate power to believe the gospel, and that "sanctification is produced by the Spirit of Christ dwelling in the man – for that spirit is said to enter into the heart, only after the heart is opened by the belief in Jesus".[32] Though Erskine clearly addressed the subject of *sanctification* here, combined with statements elsewhere he caused confusion and outrage by suggesting that the Spirit united human beings to Christ *after* they believed:

> [A man] has just to acknowledge or believe what God has done. And this belief will open his heart to let in the life, the spirit. And thus he becomes connected with Christ by the bond of the Spirit.[33]

Though he did not deny the Spirit's role in drawing human beings to Christ, Erskine's primary stress on the Spirit's salvific role in sanctification encouraged his detractors to accuse him of inviting people to believe they could come to God by their own strength, without "the gracious operation

---

[29] *Serpent*, 6 (footnote).
[30] *Evidence*, 149.
[31] Cf., Reardon, *Romanticism*, e.g., viii, 59.
[32] *Extracts*, xliv.
[33] *Serpent*, 78.

of the Holy Spirit", and by means of a 'faith' which was little more than 'passive belief'.[34]

Similar concerns had surfaced somewhat earlier in a little-known Calvinist publication. This apparently earliest formal Scottish objection to Erskine's 'speculative' ideas appeared in 1827 as an anonymous pamphlet.[35] It took Erskine to task for *An Essay on Faith* which the author regarded as presenting a view of regeneration which excluded the Spirit, and teaching that salvation is possible by mere intellectual belief on the part of unregenerate individuals. Erskine, according to the alarmist author, was guilty of "substituting the knowledge of religious truth in the place of saving faith, and hence of underrating the extent and necessity of divine agency in its production". It was further claimed he had effectively reduced the role of the Spirit and divine agency in believing faith by equating it to the exercise of natural faculties, so that "supernatural aid is not necessary to enable us to obtain the knowledge and belief of the truth". Erskine was effectively accused of shrinking faith to a human act without any need for divine aid of the Spirit, and denying the "necessity of divine grace in the sanctification of sinners", so that "the divine agency is really practically rejected". In contrast, 'orthodox Calvinism' maintained that only those previously regenerated by the Spirit of God could truly exercise faith. Instead, Erskine was making man naturally look "to himself for the regeneration of the moral part of his nature", thereby relying on himself rather than God in the believing process.

What alarmed such critics was the supposed detection of signs that Erskine might be resurrecting classic, semi-Pelagian, monergistic/ synergistic disputes regarding human versus divine agency in bringing about salvation. Erskine was to address the question of the freedom of the will more fully in *The Doctrine of Election*, where he continued to insist that Christians were to be "fellow-workers" with God in working out their own salvation, and implying that the regenerating work of the Spirit was subservient to human 'consent'.[36] The anonymous pamphleteer, well aware that similar battles for the truth had been fought in the past, was understandably fearful concerning Erskine's 'dangerous' tendency "to induce unregenerate men to consider themselves true believers", and to make "any people universally believers [who] feel rich and have need of nothing". Consequently, opponents caricatured Erskine's provocative teachings in extreme terms as "a new growth of heretical weeds which have been grubbed up by the roots

---

[34] Robertson, *Vindication,* 168-9; Anon, "Review of Publications on the Row Heresy" *ECI,* XXIX, V (May, 1830), 342-3.
[35] Anon., *An Essay on the Extent of Human and Divine Agency in the Production of Saving Faith* (Edinburgh: William Blackwood, and London: T. Cadell, 1827). Citations are from pp. 3, 6, 95, 219, 222, 228-34.
[36] *Election*, 139-40.

twenty times since the Reformation", leading to the creation of a 'sect' deluded by self-perception as the "only believers", committed to the "denouncing all others as Atheists", maintaining "an high opinion of themselves, and a supercilious despising of others".[37]

The Calvinist-Arminian debate involving the Wesleyan concept of prevenient grace and human ability to respond by assuming some role of responsibility for one's own salvation remained a contentious subject in early nineteenth-century Scotland. Erskine was himself convinced that

> the Spirit of God is always present to [man], and that he may take hold of that strength if he will. I believe that the first step is made by God towards all men, but that they may and do accept or refuse according to something in themselves, – a personal choice which belongs to the very essence of their natures.[38]

This cut right across Calvinist thinking, stirring up 'Arminian' fears by suggesting that every person possessed an innate, latent, divine life 'principle' which becomes awakened when they 'rightly see' God's gift of righteousness in Christ. The implication of a consequent 'subjective capacity' enabling individuals to appropriate the Spirit and to 'embrace God and righteousness' if they chose to exercise it was equally unacceptable. Erskine's response proceeded from his answer to the question 'why did God not make us necessarily righteous?' He maintained, in contrast to common forensic notions, that

> the very meaning of righteousness is *choosing* to be righteous – it lies in the *will* – a man who does not choose to be righteous is not righteous – he cannot be made righteous – he must *become* righteous by *choosing* to be righteous – a man made righteous, whether he will or not, is really not righteous – we must be ourselves co-operators, fellow workers with God in this work. We are therefore created with wills, that we might learn with these wills to choose righteousness…the meaning of unrighteousness is self – it is *choosing to be our own centre*…in our right or righteous state, that self is *subordinated* to *love* bending us to God as the object of our chief desire and chief delight…[39]

Erskine remained cautiously ambiguous. He was careful to avoid stating that humanity universally has the divine nature already 'profitably' or 'beneficially' within them, but he nevertheless implied everyone has the divine nature 'potentially' or 'dormant' within them. This could seem a merely convoluted way of describing the operation of prevenient grace.

---

[37] Brotherston, *Brief View,* Appendix, 314, 316.

[38] Letter to Madame de Broglie, 21 July, probably 1838, *Letters-I,* 319, cf., *Serpent,* 228-30.

[39] Letter to Lady Ashburton, 8 March [no year], *NLS MS* Acc.11388-74–57d.

Wesley himself identified "preventing grace" with conscience.[40] But Erskine was anxious to make the concept cohere with his convictions about salvific potential universally residing in redeemed humanity, and this awareness tended to dominate other aspects of his theological thinking, so that he appeared to diminish the Spirit's salvific role. His insistence that human beings must exercise their will and *choose* God *before* the co-operative agency of the Spirit, resulted from his commitment to an individual and corporate, universally available, ethical soteriology. Consequently he downplayed any deterministic, sovereign view of salvation in which the Spirit took a prior decisive role. Erskine continued to hold doggedly to a synergistic soteriology which allowed room for a kind of 'ennabling pneumatology', but this was not enough to avoid charges of capitulation to contemporary philosophical tendencies.

What Alan Sell has called the "immanentist-pantheising approach" of the Romantic movement strongly impacted pneumatological thinking.[41] George Smeaton recognised what he regarded as the general nineteenth-century trend to reduce the personality of the Holy Spirit whilst elevating and idealising the inward, spiritual influence of the person of Christ, and ascribed its origins to Schleiermacher and the German 'mediating school'. Linking it to Schleiermacher's rejection of external scriptural authority, he regarded the suggestion that "the Christian consciousness is the source of spiritual knowledge, [as], in fact, a Quaker principle – defective and one-sided. It puts the Spirit within instead of the word without, the only full expression of the Spirit's mind". Smeaton associated it with what he termed 'Sabellianism', 'Pantheism' and 'Platonism'.[42] Concerned at the tendency of Schleiermacher's followers to make the Holy Spirit the mere "union of God with the Christian Church", and the "common Spirit", Smeaton lamented their dogmatic antipathy which led to replacement of a personal Holy Spirit with 'Christian consciousness'.[43] Schleiermacher had stated that the expression 'Holy Spirit' really meant "the vital unity of the Christian fellowship as a moral personality", what he termed the "common spirit", the "common consciousness", or the "absolutely powerful God-consciousness". Insisting that this was an inward process which everyone could self-actualise, it was "not at all to be understood…that some new and special thing happens to a regenerate person when he becomes a partaker in

---

[40] John Wesley, "On Working Out our own Salvation", *Sermons on Several Occasions*, in 4 volumes (London: J. Kershaw, 1825), III, 416.

[41] Alan P.F. Sell, *The Spirit our Life* (Shippensburg, Pennsylvania: Ragged Edge Press, 2000), 8.

[42] George Smeaton, *The Doctrine of the Holy Spirit* [1882] (London: Banner of Truth, 1958), 161, 358-9.

[43] Smeaton, *Holy Spirit*, 358, 362-3.

the Holy Spirit".[44] Seen against this background, Erskine's emphasis, with Schleiermacher, on the soteriological importance of the realisation of divine sonship could easily be seen as part of an overall trend to threaten trinitarian doctrine. Smeaton summarised the issue, protesting that

> They build on a Sabellian foundation, and yet retain the theological nomenclature in a sense entirely different from that which was usually accepted by their predecessors. What testimony of the Spirit can there be, and what Christian consciousness in any right sense of the expression can there be, without the regeneration of the Holy Ghost renewing the heart and occupying it by a true inhabitation? It can have no underlying reality, and amounts only to a figure of speech. Their whole style of thought on the Christian consciousness is a mere phrase...[45]

More recently, Nicholas Needham has resurrected the charge that Erskine presents a defective view of the orthodox doctrine of Christian regeneration, reducing it to an overwhelmingly natural process which largely dispenses with the Holy Spirit. Following the lead of Richard Watson, J.S. Candlish, and J.H. Newman, Needham alleges Erskine departs from orthodoxy in what he terms his 'psychological' account of the process and effects of believing, suggesting he has deposited faith, regeneration, and sanctification together into the realm of 'natural psychology'.[46] He further argues that Erskine adopted a 'Sandemanian' concept of faith which he links to what he regards as Erskine's 'psychologising' approach to saving belief and regeneration.[47] He also connects this with what he considers to be Erskine's "moral government understanding of the atonement", whilst expressing himself at a loss to explain why Erskine should align himself with moral government theology in general.[48]

However, we believe the evidence does not support Erskine's supposed embrace of such relatively narrow sectarian views. By contrast, it actually bears out his essentially eclectic intellectual approach. Detailed examination of the issues of Erskine's alleged 'Sandemanianism' and 'moral government theology' merely confirms Erskine was suspected of relativising the role of the Spirit in favour of a philosophical account of the faith process. He also reflected the century's preference for non-retributory presentations of divine justice, and the general prevalence of moral influence theories. The issue of Sandemanianism itself succeeded in raising in Calvinist minds the spectre of long-standing controversies associated, not only with Robert Sandeman, but with Jonathan Edwards, Walter Marshall, James

---

[44] Schleiermacher, *Christian Faith*, §116, §123, §124, 535, 536, 573, 574.
[45] Smeaton, *Holy Spirit*, 362.
[46] Needham, *Thomas Erskine*, 83.
[47] Needham, *Thomas Erskine*, 82, 13.
[48] Needham, *Thomas Erskine*, 61, 42-4.

Hervey, Joseph Bellamy, and the Marrow men, relating to the nature of the agency of the Holy Spirit in saving belief.[49]

Newman's 'Rationalistic' Concerns

J.S. Candlish acknowledged that Erskine did not ignore, and certainly did not deny, "the necessity of the enlightening work of the Spirit, in order to the perception of the truth". But he complained that Erskine regarded the gospel too much "simply as a manifestation of the true character of God, which if only believed and understood, tends of itself to impart peace and holiness to men", and hardly allowed the Spirit "its due weight and influence", giving the overall impression that it is "the power of the truth to commend itself to the understanding and conscience". His fear, which he shared with John Henry Newman, was the dangerous *tendency* of Erskine's innovative thought. Although his seeking of authoritative truth in internal evidence was valid,

> yet unless there be a clear recognition that it is only to a spiritually renewed and enlighted soul that this inherent evidence is apparent and convincing, the effect of bringing it forward will be, to make natural reason and conscience the supreme standard of truth in religion.[50]

Newman was an early admirer of Erskine, quoting him in his sermons, acknowledging him as "the source of his ideas on the atonement", and even attributing an entire sermon to the inspiration of Erskine's *Remarks on the Internal Evidence for the Truth of Revealed Religion*.[51] But it was in the context of biblical authority that Newman accused Erskine of 'Rationalism' in one of the series of Oxford tracts in about 1835.[52] John Tulloch was to call it 'intuitional Rationalism' (which he associated with Schleiermacher), and voiced concerns that the arbiter of religious truth was in danger of becoming "the supposed *primary feelings or intuitions of the soul, or higher nature in man*", and "certain higher principles, or peculiar moral judgments, which are supposed to constitute an *inner religious light* in every man". As a consequence "the special and pre-eminent authority of Scrip-

---

[49] The 'Sandemanian' and 'moral government' questions are examined in some detail in Appendices 4 and 5 respectively.
[50] Candlish, "Thomas Erskine", 113.
[51] Roderick Strange, *Newman and the Gospel of Christ* (Oxford: Oxford University Press, 1981), 98-9; Francis McGrath, *John Henry Newman* (Tunbridge Wells: Burns & Oates, 1997), 35 (note 52).
[52] Newman, "On the Introduction of Rationalistic Principles into Religion", (Tract No. 73), 15-33.

ture is...entirely set aside...".[53] Newman highlighted the 'dangerous tendency' of what he described as Erskine's 'rationalism', by which he meant reduction of Christian mysteries to the scrutiny and approval of human reason and conscience. Erskine strenuously denied he was "a mere rationalist".[54] But Newman opposed any reduction of religion to 'system'. Erskine's 'system', Newman suggested, laid

> exclusive stress upon the *character* of God, as the substance of the Revelation. It considers Scripture as a *Manifestation* of God's character, an intentional subjecting of it in an intelligible shape to our minds, and nothing more.

Newman attributed Erskine's ideas on the atonement, whereby it is viewed "not as a wonder in heaven, and in its relation to the attributes of God and the unseen world, but in its experienced effects on our minds, in the change it effects where it is believed", to a 'popularist evangelicalism' which owed its peculiar form to an idiosyncratic philosophical development of the eighteenth-century revival of religious feeling. Its arch exponents he considered to be Erskine and Schleiermacher.[55] Newman regarded systematisation of religion, which reduced 'mystery' to what was intelligible (thereby making intelligibility a condition of belief – what Newman called liberal 'manifestation' theology and 'Sabellianism'), and popular evangelicalism, which reduced it to mere feeling, as forms of *rationalism,* equating such rationalistic spirit with what he termed *liberalism*, defined as "the anti-dogmatic principle and its developments".[56]

Furthermore, it was part of an unfortunate contemporary novel trend to draw on eclectic sources to present Christianity in terms of philosophic and scientific theory. Newman denounced any suggestion that revelation may be authenticated simply through perceiving its excellence by the light of human reason. This was to confuse the natural and the supernatural. He insisted on maintaining a clear distinction between natural and revealed religion. Despite acknowledging his noble apologetic intentions to present Christianity coherently, Newman saw Erskine as responsible for encouraging the trend towards dissipation of this vital distinction. Transcendent divine revelation would be threatened if, to be accepted as true, it must conform to human ideas of what is excellent and be rejected if it did not. Erskine's elevation of the more 'experiential' or 'affective' doctrine of the atonement (whilst marginalising the more 'abstract' doctrine of the Trinity

---

[53] John Tulloch, *Theological Tendencies of the Age: An Inaugural Lecture Delivered at the Opening of St. Mary's College, on Tuesday, the 28th November, 1854,* [2nd Edition] (Edinburgh: Paton and Ritchie, 1855), 16-24.

[54] Letter to Madame Forel, 19 November 1838, *Letters-I,* 336.

[55] Newman, (Tract No. 73), 19, 13, 54.

[56] Newman, (Tract No.73), 45 and *passim*; John Henry Newman, *Apologia Pro Vita Sua* [1864] (London: Dent, 1966), 67.

due to its limited impact on the understanding, emotions and moral conscience) was, for Newman, a classic example of the dangerous tendency to judge truth subjectively on the basis of whether or not it was 'morally useful':

> For Newman, Erskine's tragedy was that he had unwittingly accommodated his theology to the spirit of the age. Newman presented liberalism as a modern way of being religious, which sacrificed ancient truths to modern prejudice and was preparing the ground for outright atheism. Erskine, in swimming with the stream, was, Newman argued, contributing to the process whereby revealed religion would eventually be swept away altogether.[57]

In 1883, Newman recalled,

> I knew, when young, Mr. Erskine's first publications well. I thought them able and persuasive; but I found the more thoughtful Evangelicals of Oxford did not quite trust them. This was about the year 1823 or 1824. A dozen years later I wrote against them or one of them, in the Tracts for the Times, and certainly my impression still is that their tendency is antidogmatic, substituting for faith in mysteries the acceptance of a 'manifestation' of divine attributes which was level to the reason.[58]

Though Newman never questioned Erskine's religious orthodoxy, commending his personal piety and desire to broadcast the message of the love of God, his concern was with what he foresaw as the logical consequences of his theological method, which included the inevitability of universalism.[59] What is apparent is that by the time Newman first deemed it necessary to respond to Erskine's growing influence in the mid-1830s, his impact had become revolutionary and widespread.

It is significant that many of his early critics contrasted Erskine's eclectic 'philosophical', 'psychological', or 'mystical' understanding of salvation with what they regarded as orthodox salvific activity through the sovereign work of the Spirit. Though it was to some extent a question of emphasis and perception, Erskine's critics had undoubtedly pinpointed a serious weakness. Erskine was certainly aware of the potential for what he regarded as misunderstanding since he acknowledged that it was vital for him to distinguish "between the living God and a metaphysical abstraction",[60] whilst in his personal correspondence he sought to dispel any doubts con-

---

[57] Stephen Thomas, *Newman and Heresy* (Cambridge: Cambridge University Press, 1991), 115-6.

[58] Letter to George T. Edwards, 2 January 1883, Charles Stephen Dessain and Thomas Gornall (eds.), *The Letters and Diaries of John Henry Newman,* Vol. XXX, *A Cardinal's Apostolate, October 1881 to December 1884* (Oxford: Clarendon Press, 1976), 168-9, cf., 204.

[59] Newman, (Tract No.73), 24.

[60] *Serpent*, 98.

cerning the importance he attributed to the trinitarian Spirit's work in humanity.[61] But the inevitable influence of contemporary philosophical ideas, especially those aspects of early nineteenth-century thought which emphasised dynamic divine immanence in humankind, and understood revelation in terms of the immediacy of experience, clearly made their mark on his thought categories. And Erskine's innovatory genius tended to disguise his lack of the essential theological skills of overview, balance and moderation. The contrast with traditional evangelical doctrines which stressed God's transcendence and insisted that he dwelt only in believers was all too apparent to Erskine's sensitive critics. The idea that "the divine and the human existed as one spiritual continuum" was, however, characteristic of the newer immanental thought which anticipated nineteenth-century idealistic philosophy, and fostered a climate which elevated human faculties at the expense of a reduced or minimal role for the supernatural Spirit.[62] Coleridge, like Erskine, believed that the divine was already immanent in every human being "prior to and independent of, any written record", and that we simply needed the divine light and life within to 'burst into flame'. In this view, 'conversion' became the actualisation of our innate God-consciousness, whilst scriptural truth, once illuminated, became self-authenticating.[63] This equated naturally to Erskine's fundamental idea that everyone possessed a God-given ability to respond to the gospel through a universal inner light. The merging of speculative philosophical, scientific, psychological, and mystical concepts was so close that Erskine could quite easily be associated with any. Since a ubiquitous role for the 'Spirit' could readily be accommodated into such a system, it inevitably led to questions of ambiguity in the face of classical dogmatic trinitarian scrutiny.

The charismatic episode at Row in 1830 caused Erskine to emphasise for a time the experiential role of the Spirit, when he even pressed what subsequently became a classic distinction between "the work of the Spirit in regeneration" and receiving "the gift of the Holy Ghost, which appears to be the sealing".[64] The fact that the events at Row did not fundamentally affect Erskine's understanding of the Spirit's role is significant. They appeared to fit logically into his system, serving as a counterweight to those who have been keen to assert Erskine's 'reductionist' pneumatology. He had enthusiastically embraced the charismatic revival in Row, characteristically hailing it as an in-breaking of the invisible into the visible realm, the immedi-

---

[61] E.g., Letter to Monsieur Gaussen, 7 December 1832, *Letters-I*, 289.

[62] H.D. McDonald, *Ideas of Revelation* (Grand Rapids: Baker Book House, 1979), 149-151.

[63] Coleridge, *Confessions*, 52; Coleridge, "Notes on the Book of Common Prayer", in *Confessions*, 98; H.D. McDonald, *Theories of Revelation* (Grand Rapids: Baker Book House, 1979), 174.

[64] *Serpent*, 182-3.

ate, experiential outworking of "God's own life, God's own Spirit" in individuals' souls,[65] though in 1837 he was obliged to confess his subsequent disillusionment publicly. However, this did not affect Erskine's ongoing conviction concerning his "abiding readiness for the supernatural", and that "it would be perfectly natural to find the Divine within the world unveiled to the eyes of those who needed to be convinced of the very existence of the Divine".[66]

Nicholas Needham refers to a discussion between Erskine and Chalmers in 1832 in which he suggests Erskine was 'abandoning faith as intellectual comprehension and assent to the truth' for irrational belief in the spiritual gifts, and concludes his mind had become unbalanced.[67] But this unwarranted speculation misses the point that the Spirit, for Erskine, was above all the incarnate presence of Christ within humanity.[68] It was the logical outcome of his trinitarian incarnational theology, of the indwelling humanity of Christ and the Spirit, and was further attested by the fact that it was *for theological reasons* Edward Irving himself found his attention drawn to Row for validation of his own parallel teaching concerning Christ's human nature.[69] Erskine was never to abandon his theoretical expectation of the restoration of the gifts of the Spirit. It complemented his controlling belief concerning the incarnational divine presence within humanity.

Erskine's Theology of Conversion

Negative reaction to Erskine's perceived insistence on the 'necessary' salvific impact of understanding God's character took various forms. The usually moderate Brethren missionary, Anthony Groves, read *The Unconditional Freeness of the Gospel* together with other Erskine publications. Like Richard Watson, he strongly denounced them for their contrived nature and apparent antipathy to the sovereignty of God: "I have lately read several of Erskine's works, or little portions of his writings, and never did I see the pernicious effects of system displayed more legibly than in several of his most interesting, but as a whole, most delusive of publications". Groves singled out Erskine's emphasis on "spreading the beauty of the Lord Jesus, and the excellency of God's love...as the cause of spiritual life in the unregenerate by being believed", concluding that "this appears to me

---

[65] *Gifts*, 22.
[66] Julia Wedgwood, cited in *Gurney*, 15-16.
[67] Needham, *Thomas Erskine*, 370-3.
[68] E.g., Shairp, "Reminiscences", *Letters-II*, 356.
[69] See Gordon Strachan, *The Pentecostal Theology of Edward Irving* (Peabody, Mass: Hendrickson, 1973), 61-75.

a radical and fundamental error". Lamenting Erskine's failure to offer what he regarded as a proper theology of conversion, Groves continued:

> What he says of the effects of love, in moulding the soul to the likeness of the object beloved, is most true; but in order to the existence of this love, not merely faith in God's love seems to be necessary, nor the reality of the things promised, but such a new creation in the soul, as shall see a desirableness in it and them...Without being thus begotten from above, though you could display all the beauties of him who is the chief among ten thousand, the altogether lovely, though you could display all the Father's love to the church from the day he commanded his gathering it, till this day, it would be as powerless as spreading the most sumptuous banquet before the dead.[70]

Such was the strength of Groves's antipathy to Erskine's ideas that his editor (none other than Erskine's friend A.J. Scott) felt obliged to add a lengthy appendix to Groves's journal, defending Erskine's novel views, and tactfully pointing out how he considered Groves to be mistaken in his critique.[71]

Erskine's most difficult task in presenting an innovative yet coherent salvific system was to maintain a valid distinction between universal pardon and individual appropriation of that pardon, without falling into the extremes of universal salvation on the one hand, and pre-determination on the other. As we have seen, he was obliged to conflate ideas of salvation and election, whilst seeking to maintain the principle of personal responsibility and conditionality:

> Most assuredly there is in Jesus Christ a *general* salvation for the whole race, inasmuch as in Him they are lifted again into that state of probation from which in Adam they had fallen, and provided with spiritual strength to go through their probation, whether they use that strength or not: but none becomes *personally* a partaker of salvation, except by personally turning to God. And, in like manner, there is in Jesus Christ, a *general* election for the whole race – inasmuch as, in Him, they are lifted out of that state of reprobation into which, in Adam, they had fallen; but no one becomes *personally* elect, except by personally receiving Christ into his heart.[72]

As an evangelical, Erskine unquestionably accepted the importance of personal response to the gospel. However, it tended to become muted and metamorphosed into a concept of power being given to humanity, in Jesus, of living to God.[73] This power of freedom of choice Erskine reformulated

---

[70] Anthony N. Groves, *Journal of a Residence at Bagdad, during the years 1830 and 1831*, [edited with an introduction and notes by A.J. Scott] (London: James Nisbet, 1832), 102, 103-4.
[71] Groves, *Journal*, 289-295.
[72] *Election*, 142-3.
[73] *Election*, 141-2.

into his peculiar concept of universal divine 'grace': "He then who is saved, is saved by grace, but by a grace which every man is free to use – and he who is lost, is lost by refusing grace, which he might have used".[74] The traditional evangelical process of conversion via the *ordo salutis* of confession and repentance appears rarely in Erskine's publications, notwithstanding evident interest in his private correspondence in death-bed conversions and accounts of sudden transformations in response to the gospel. Erskine did not totally ignore aspects like 'repentance' and 'confession', but when he mentioned them he tended to display a reductionism which reflected a contemporary sensitivity to evangelical terminology, and his instinctive dislike of defined dogmatic categories attached to traditional theological vocabulary. Hence, for example, in a rare published sermon, he tended to redefine 'confession' in terms of existential, restorative, sympathetic response to God's view of the gravity of sin:

> Thus, confession of sin is not an act done once for all, which draws down on a man God's favour, and *inclines Him* to forgive; rather, it is the contemplation of God's free forgiveness which calls forth the confession; and ever as that free forgiveness is actually received into the heart – *fed upon* (if we may use the expression), – does the confession – the discernment and abhorrence of evil – become deeper and more abiding.[75]

Similarly, 'repentance' "is just faith in the gospel...true repentance and faith are just the same thing".[76] De-emphasis on formal repentance, coupled with stress on universal pardon may be interpreted as a form of accommodation to contemporary dislike of traditional 'hard' teaching about the cross, leading to later liberal tendencies to downplay the cross altogether. Although these were trends of which Erskine himself disapproved, such revolutionary elements within his own apologetic approach reveal him as a product of his age and context.

Erskine preferred to emphasise Enlightenment concepts of the ongoing self-authenticating, 'morally therapeutic' nature and impact of truth,[77] whilst adding a strongly practical and existential dimension. With the gospel therefore considered to evince its own truth, provided a person's life exhibited the desired necessary outcome, Erskine apparently saw little need to argue specially, in an apologetic context, for a doctrine of personal crisis and conversion along classic evangelical lines. His preference was therefore for an educational rather than conversion soteriological model. He was

---

[74] *Election*, 145.

[75] "The Righteousness of God in the Heart of Man", in Campbell (ed.), *Fragments of Truth*, 277.

[76] *Extracts*, lxi.

[77] Mainly through reason and conscience; see Stanley J. Grenz, and Roger E. Olson, *Twentieth Century Theology* (Carlisle: Paternoster Press, 1992), 21-23, 31.

wary of any process which forced people to answer questions like 'Are you saved?', or 'are you a believer?', because it removed the focus of trust from its 'correct' object, continuing dependent trust in the Father's forgiving love as revealed in Christ, to self-trust and the individual's "performance of the task of believing". Erskine considered "self-trust is the root of all sin, being the substitution of self for God".[78] It also encouraged concentration on the consequences of sin and how to escape them, rather than on inculcating moral righteousness. Anything which caused people to regard Christ's life and death in terms of "a propitiation to Divine justice" in order to obtain mercy, instead of a manifestation of God's love and righteousness which they were to receive, Erskine rejected out of hand.[79]

At the same time, however, Erskine was concerned not to displace traditional concepts of divine holiness and the seriousness of sin. Rather, he subtly shifted the emphasis of the associated terminology. He reaffirmed God's hatred of sin, though he believed that a common mistake was to emphasise this without simultaneously stressing the divine purpose to *deliver* humanity from sin. Humanity's relationship *status* to God was not in question. All were children of God already by origin. But God's ultimate purpose was to produce *righteous* children, and Erskine believed that divine education included not only the remedial use of suffering but also, as we have noted, the corrective experience of sin itself. Since he directly identified God's *justice* with his *mercy*, Erskine's conflated system necessarily involved a theodicy in which, to achieve his goal of producing righteousness in human beings, God made use of any means, however painful they might be, to bring it about. Divine justice therefore was not *retributory* but *restorative,* and as an essential component of the salvation process, not to be escaped, but embraced. God's *wrath* crucially became an instrument of divine love and righteousness, not of retribution, and even the effects of the fall were seen to be within the remedial purpose of God in bringing about a greater good.[80] Within a wider setting, Erskine could perhaps be understood as reflecting Benthamite/ Utilitarian secular contemporary concerns regarding the gradual reformation of mankind, albeit reinterpreted within a theological context.[81]

Though unquestionably displaying creativity in engaging with and reflecting his humanistic nineteenth-century context, today Erskine seems remarkably naïve and unrealistic in his over-optimistic assessment of human nature. This probably owed much to exaggerated reaction against pre-

---

[78] *Sp.Order*, 63, 67.

[79] *Sp.Order*, 64.

[80] *Sp.Order*, 255-6, cf., 71-4, 130, 179-80, 193-4, 218-9. The idea of sin becoming its own punishment is an increasingly popular contemporary concept for understanding the wrath of God. See e.g., Smail, *Once and For All*, 81-3.

[81] See Hilton, *Atonement*, 282.

vailing Calvinist emphasis on human depravity. However, Erskine's incarnational stress on the regenerative power of the divine within humanity, and conviction that the gospel would naturally find ready-prepared receptivity within the human heart and conscience, inevitably resulted in an understanding of regeneration which amounted to something rather less than the radical salvific 'conversion' or 'encounter' traditionally associated with evangelicals. Erskine consistently maintained a fundamental conviction that salvation consisted not merely of cognitive assent, but of a continuous life-changing existential encounter with God which must result in nothing less than a total response of love and willing obedience towards God. Nevertheless, it was within an epistemological framework which supposed the human conscience to have already been illuminated by Christ and merely required 're-awakening'. Because Erskine elevated the role of conscience within humanity to the status of an ever-present divine internal light which acted as "the goodness of God leading him to repentance", this largely explained why he felt justified theologically in relativising the need for a classic evangelical personal crisis experience in which the Holy Spirit, rather than conscience, was the salvific agent.[82] Rather, Erskine tended to synthesise the concept of *conversion* with that of *sanctification*. Effectively, 'sanctification' represented a continual inner contest, monitored by the conscience in 'co-operation' with God, of good against evil, leading inevitably to the ultimate victory of good. This involved a continuous process of sympathetic sorrow for sin, obedient righteous choice, and surrender of self-will in response to the ongoing experience of divine 'education' throughout life's circumstances. Since Erskine regarded all humanity as having Christ 'in' them already as a 'light' or 'seed', the only effective difference between the converted and the unregenerate was that the latter remained in the state of potentiality and were not yet actually "living by the life of Christ".[83]

One of Erskine's few early published allusions to the traditional concept of 'conversion' (though it typified the sort of statement which provoked Anthony Groves) occurs in *Remarks on the Internal Evidence for the Truth of Revealed Religion* where Erskine characteristically focused on the power of recognition of true divine character as the foundation of belief: "It is thus that the faith of the Gospel produces that revolution in the mind which is called in Scripture conversion, or the new birth".[84] In *The Gifts of the Spirit*, Erskine reaffirmed that to "be born from above" simply meant to "receive into our souls God's own life, which is the *eternal life*, through the

---

[82] *Sp.Order*, 68. Erskine also identified conscience with the indwelling Spirit, e.g., see Shairp, "Reminiscences", in *Letters-II*, 356.
[83] Letter to Bishop Ewing, 25 October 1863, *Ewing-I*, 39, cf., *Gifts*, 21.
[84] *Evidence*, 109-10.

knowledge of His love to us in Christ Jesus".[85] When asked to pronounce on the genuineness of 'sudden conversions' in the 1859 Irish revival, Erskine was not especially interested in judging their authenticity. His concern was not so much for the immediate experience of 'conversion', but rather to shift emphasis to what he regarded as the more salvifically crucial aspect of *perseverance* – an ongoing sustained life of faith and trust in God. He preferred to correlate 'true conversion' with more existential concepts of salvific Christianity as exemplarist, incarnational, sanctified, participative life lived close to God. Erskine's favourite reconstruction of salvation remained in terms of relating to God as Father, surrendering one's own will to God's, and accepting divine 'punishment' or 'training':

> A conversion, that is to say a true conversion, implies a knowledge of God, and of the relation in which we stand to Him in His Son. It implies a knowledge of God as a holy, loving Father, who desires for us that we should be partakers of his own holiness and His own blessedness…God lives by and in His own Will, that Will is the eternal life of God, and when a created spirit receives God's Will into its will, it becomes partaker of the eternal life. This I conceive is salvation; I don't understand any other meaning of salvation. This is what I believe man was made for; his danger, his temptation, is self-will, – making himself the centre. This is sin, that separates a man from God and his fellow-creatures. This then is the salvation of Christ: I don't believe that He came to deliver men from any penalty. I believe that every penalty which God has inflicted on men has been for good, so that deliverance from it would be an evil. I cannot see any distinction between salvation and the conformity of the will to God…I should expect more lasting results from a silent conversion than from a more excited one, still it is the actual turning to God which is the important matter…the birth of the spirit, the birth from above, is just to receive the eternal life, to receive the will of God, instead of the will of the flesh, or of self-will.[86]

With evident similarities to Schleiermacher, salvation became more of an existential, continuous process of dependent choice based on a person's understanding of the character of God, determined by constant 'trust', 'dependence' and 'abiding' in relation to God and his will, rather than a 'one-off' crisis decision. Erskine's repeated theme was total, free-will *obedience*: "this is salvation – when a man uses his individual will merely as the recipient of God's will".[87] Orthodox evangelicals ascribed the work of conversion to the Holy Spirit, though Erskine anticipated other nineteenth-century evangelicals who began increasingly to attribute cruciality to the

---

[85] *Gifts*, 22.
[86] Letter to Mrs Batten, 17 August 1859, *Letters-II*, 232-3, cf., Letter to Mrs Burnett, 24 October, 1859, *Letters-II*, 134.
[87] Letter to Madame Forel, 24 April 1862, *Letters-II*, 236.

individual's own will.[88] This flowed from a desire, expressed clearly by Erskine, to establish the principle of freedom with responsibility:

> Moral goodness really means *choosing to be good*, and no man can be *made* to choose, or made as *having chosen*; he must himself choose ...every... personal creature is necessarily called on continually to choose between its own will and God's.[89]

Erskine's synergistic view of humans as morally responsible beings effectively determined his reshaped soteriology. This often attracted the labels *Arminian* and *Pelagian*, the terms being virtually synonymous for Calvinists (though in fact Erskine disliked Arminianism as a 'religion of man' because of its emphasis on the pursuit of individual pardon as a 'selfish' objective). Erskine, however, sought to preserve a balancing role for divine sovereignty by insisting that though the mode both of initial 'conversion' and perseverance was a continual process of apprehension by faith mediated through conscience, "neither conversion nor perseverance in good is man's own act. They are the voluntary yielding of man to the actings of God...Man...must be in a continual state of trustful dependence. We are to be fellow-workers with God, I suppose and believe, for ever."[90]

Erskine did allude to the need for human beings to be 'born again', and made direct gospel appeals.[91] But he has been criticised for a deficient doctrine of the Spirit in personal regeneration,[92] leading to later liberal notions of conversion as a "humanly contrived work".[93] This perhaps has its origins in the innovative organic, corporate, incarnational soteriology that Erskine was openly affirming by 1829. A fundamental Calvinist tenet was that regeneration is logically prior to faith. We are saved that we may believe; we do not believe that we may be saved. Regeneration, therefore, was the production of a divinely-inspired transformation of the human heart, introducing a new inclination towards God. But for Erskine, 'regeneration' of the human race was a virtually accomplished fact. So any distinction between 'regenerate' and 'unregenerate' was effectively reduced to acceptance of, or resistance to, the indwelling, regenerating Spirit of Christ. Some of Erskine's friends protested at his implication that the unregenerate or unconverted indiscriminately possess the indwelling Christ or Holy Spirit. Er-

---

[88] David Bebbington, *Evangelicalism in Modern Britain: A History from the 1730s to the 1830s* (London and New York: Routledge, 1989), 8.

[89] Letter to Bishop Ewing, 23 January 1861, *Ewing-I*, 28-9.

[90] Letter to Mrs Batten, 17 August 1859, *Letters-II*, 234-5.

[91] E.g., "Reader, are you prepared for these things? Are you on the Lord's side? Are you born again? Are you watching for the return of your Lord?", (*Serpent*, 199).

[92] E.g., Needham, *Thomas Erskine*, 83-4.

[93] Bruce Demarest, *The Cross and Salvation* (Wheaton, Illinois: Crossway Books, 1997), 237.

skine responded that, because God evidently holds us culpable for rejecting the gospel, and since divine truth can only be attained by those who have the Spirit, fairness therefore dictates that all must possess a measure of the Spirit, even though we may choose to resist Him.[94] It was in this amended sense, therefore, that Erskine regarded the soteriological role of the Spirit as crucial, preferring to describe the process of regeneration ambiguously as the 'infusion' of a new nature by the indwelling Spirit, through the self-evidencing laws of revelation and appropriation of saving knowledge. Spiritual law analogies were again useful here:

> Except a man be born from above; except a man get the life from above – an entirely new principle of life, he cannot see the kingdom of God. If you would have a branch bring forth fruit different from the natural fruit of the tree, you must first infuse a new sap, for the old sap must produce the old fruit, it can produce no other...this new life is no modification of that fleshly life which we have by our natural birth, but an entirely different subsistence; that it is a spiritual life: and as the source of fleshly life is the flesh, and every stream from that source partakes of its nature, so the source of this new life is the Spirit, and every stream from that source, in like manner, will partake of its nature.[95]

> Whatever we learn from God by His Spirit's teaching in our own hearts is true knowledge and eternal life...the regeneration of fallen man consists in his own inward ear being opened to hear and know the voice of his God.[96]

> When a man opens his eyes upon the sun, he necessarily appropriates his share of its light, and he cannot look upon the sun without making this appropriation. In like manner, no man can look upon the sun of righteousness, which is the love of God manifested *in the making and the accepting of a propitiation for the sins of the world,* without appropriating his own share of its blessed light.[97]

The soteriological role of the Spirit for Erskine could simply not be confined to the narrow theological categories or defined *ordo salutis* prescribed by Calvinist dogma. More in line with new Romantic trends, his reinterpretation was considerably broader. In *The Doctrine of Election* and elsewhere, Erskine consistently affirmed that the Spirit played a vital all-encompassing, sanctifying role as the life-giving presence of God, addressing human beings through conscience, actualising the knowledge, consciousness, and mind of God, and creating the capacity to respond to God, apprehend his righteousness, and enjoy liberty by sympathetically embracing his purpose of self-denial and crucifixion of the flesh:

---

[94] Letter to Mrs Burnett, 17 March 1840, *Letters-II,* 196-8.
[95] *Serpent,* 4-5.
[96] Letter to Mrs MacNabb, 23 January 1834, *Letters-I,* 206.
[97] *Freeness,* 136-7.

no man knoweth the things of God, but by the Divine Spirit...I must, therefore, have the Spirit of God, in order to fit me to enter into God's purpose...[98]

it is in the Spirit alone, that we can apprehend righteousness, as distinct from all selfish ends...it is only whilst we live in the Spirit, that we have true liberty...for it has the mind of God...[99]

Erskine's ambiguous theology of the fall and original sin was modified by his revolutionary insistence that humanity was created 'in Christ' from the beginning, so that Christ as Head "was latent in humanity". Although his 'Headship' was not 'manifested' until his 'personal appearance' in this world, Christ's incarnation apparently existed prototypically from creation since "both before and since that time [i.e., of his appearance] He has been, as it were, diffused through humanity, lying at the bottom of every man as the basis of his being".[100] Erskine rejected contemporary Calvinist and Arminian conceptions of the fall where humanity was either in a depraved condition, unable to respond to God, or where conscience was a purely human faculty and remnant of the Edenic state. Instead, his new scheme required that after the fall (which Erskine considered, almost in a kind of supralapsarian sense, 'advantageous' for all humanity through God's planned "higher dispensation" to bring greater good out of evil) the universal, 'latent' Christ became what he termed "the Spirit of the Word" or the "seed of regeneration" within human nature, thereby potentially connecting each person with their own divine, indwelling, salvific life force if they chose the 'Christ' rather than the 'Adam' nature.[101] Though Christ's appearance in flesh was exemplary, it was also incarnational in the fullest sense, that is, it effected our new status 'in Christ' by mere virtue of our shared humanity. Christ's indwelling of humanity is recognised through the voice of conscience making us aware of sin and righteousness, pointing us to the Father, and showing us through every detail of his exemplary history how to live in complete dependence on the Father, by surrendering self-will and embracing God's will through suffering, sacrifice and death. This amounted to Erskine's all-embracing, radical reinterpretation of conversion and sanctification, rolled into one.

Significantly, in the following century, Karl Barth, in terms reminiscent of Erskine, understood conversion as already effected in the history of Christ, so that "In His death there took place the regeneration and conver-

---

[98] *Election*, 556.
[99] *Election*, 560, cf., 533-44, 561.
[100] Shairp, "Reminiscences", *Letters-II*, 357.
[101] *Election*, 445, 567-8, cf., 312.

sion of man".[102] Conversion, for Barth, was also not a once-for-all decision, but rather the self-actualising of the new, universally available freedom, since all are, in a sense, already 'in Christ', as a result of his representative embodiment of humanity. Thomas Torrance concurs that a 'correct' understanding of 'regeneration' in the New Testament sees it as applying rather to what occurred through the incarnation and life of Christ, than to mere human-centred active repentance and belief. Torrance, like Erskine, emphasises that it was in the act of taking on our fallen humanity that Christ redeemed it and gave it new birth through his death and resurrection:

> In other words, our new birth, our regeneration, our conversion, is what has taken place in Jesus Christ himself, so that when we speak of our conversion or our regeneration we are referring to our sharing in the conversion or regeneration of our humanity, brought about by Jesus in and through himself for our sake. In a profound and proper sense, therefore, we must speak of Jesus Christ as constituting in himself the very substance of our conversion, so that we must think of him as taking our place even in our acts of repentance and personal decision, for without him all so-called repentance and conversion are empty. Since a conversion in that truly evangelical sense is a turning away from ourselves to Christ, it calls for a conversion from our in-turned notions of conversion to one which is grounded and sustained in Christ Jesus himself.[103]

The idea of God regarding humanity salvifically only 'in Christ' represents one of Erskine's major innovative themes, which he repeated and developed in various forms. Positioning the work of conversion immanently within mankind as a result of the incarnation and the gift of universal pardon, Erskine may be regarded as propounding a radical soteriology of *anakephalaiosis*. That is, we merely need to recognise what God has already done in Christ on behalf of the entire human race, in which the new headship of Christ has superseded the old headship of Adam and, through his recapitulatory soteriological work undone the sin and fall of Adam. That revelation alone contains the power within itself to regenerate us because of the new life which Christ imparts through his own life being released into humanity. Jesus Christ, for Erskine, is the true and highest example of humanity, and it is through the (trinitarian) incarnation that we gain our fullest salvific revelation of the nature of both God and humankind. This innovative theme was to dominate later nineteenth-century soteriology. Though the latter part of the century was dominated by subsequent liberal trends towards reductionist and adoptionist ideas of Christ as a man who most demonstrated how a God-centred life should be lived, Erskine's system was nevertheless distanced from such un-trinitarian developments.

---

[102] Barth, *CD*, IV, 2 (Edinburgh: T.&T. Clark, 1958), 291.
[103] Thomas F. Torrance, *The Mediation of Christ* [revised edition] (Edinburgh: T.&T. Clark, 1992), 85-6.

It fell to those later Victorians, like Charles Gore, to seek to rescue the orthodox understanding of the incarnation from such distortions. Erskine may therefore fairly be described as an innovative 'mediating' theologian who sought to reconcile Reformed and orthodox views of God and Christ with the changing sensitivities of his world.

Summary

In Chapter 6 we noted how Erskine was deemed by many critics to have fallen into the trap of doctrinal error in seeking to attain the otherwise laudable objective of a viable nineteenth-century apologetic. They tended to admire his personal piety and evangelical motivation, whilst deprecating his apparent resort to moral speculative philosophy and the blurring of categories between theology and philosophy. The more perceptive observers realised Erskine's new ideas were helpful, but could lead to liberalism in the wrong hands. Newman's selection of Erskine in one of the *Tracts for the Times* to exemplify his concerns regarding the dangers of accommodating evangelical theology to the eclectic and rational spirit of the age, confirms the extent of Erskine's novel yet popular impact, which reflected the contemporary mood, and was consequently generating widespread debate.

In particular, anxiety centred on Erskine's apparent relativisation of the Spirit's role, and comparative emphasis on natural faculties, like reason and conscience, for apprehending God, together with his appropriation of philosophical, mystical, scientific, and psychological concepts. We have argued that Erskine's pneumatology remained largely orthodox, though perceptions of deficiency are understandable given the relative space he devoted to natural epistemological ideas in his desire to encompass contemporary categories of thought. His Scottish critics, as well as more recent commentators, have sometimes sought to link Erskine to specific doctrinal positions or movements. In response, we suggest that Erskine resists narrow or exclusive categorisation, that in fact his association with other 'neologies' actually reinforces our main contentions concerning his essentially eclectic innovatory technique. In this regard, Erskine significantly shifted the focus of key traditional Christian soteriological understandings concerning, for example, evangelical conversion, by attempting to reconcile or synthesise orthodox and contemporary emphases from sovereign deliverance towards more synergistic and incarnational aspects of redemption. Though consequently opening himself to accusations of human contrivance and even misrepresentation, Erskine's reformulation was often subtle in his use of contemporary concepts and spiritual law analogies to redefine traditional religious terminology.

In the first part of this study we noted Erskine's deep apologetic consciousness of the need for a viable interpretation and presentation of salvation in a questioning yet reactionary age. We examined his innovative reformulation of the key themes of perception of God, revelation and authority, and the extent and nature of salvation, which he regarded as crucial for presenting a credible soteriology appropriate to his era.

With perceived revolutionary implications, Erskine reinterpreted the gospel as a universal proclamation of forgiveness, not in any sense as a reward for faith, even less for good works, but as a free, unconditional, divine gift to humanity through their representative Head, Jesus Christ. Everyone was free to appropriate this gift of forgiveness, which, however, was not in itself salvation, but rather the means to it. Accordingly, Erskine understood salvation not so much in terms of future benefit, but more as renewed relationship and fellowship with God through his 'holy love' which embodied the spiritual dynamics to sanctify human character. As a result of 'entering into God's mind and purpose concerning us', we "become conscious and willing fellow-workers with Him in working out that great salvation which consists in the spiritual rightness of all humanity".[104] Erskine's concept of free unconditional pardon was remote from the 'antinomian' concerns of his opponents. Pardon was not salvation, for Erskine did not consider salvation something to be awarded freely and unconditionally. Neither did it belong to the realm of creeds and doctrines. Rather, pardon could be of use only so far as it was appropriated for sanctification along with the internal revelation of the loving character of God, so that the law of holy sacrificial love became the effective power and principle of personal holiness and ethical living in the 'spiritual order', which is itself salvation. Therefore salvation was conceived in existential terms of fellowship with God and holiness of living, which Erskine called the state of 'heaven'.[105]

We have noted in Part 1 parallel currents of thought which were prevalent in Erskine's formative period, and have shown how he applied creative and novel thinking, inspired by a wide appreciation of current new ideas, to key theological questions. Though in the process his innovatory reconstructive approach simultaneously aligned with other seminal thinkers, Erskine was uncomfortable with exclusivity, though he remained outside any narrow sectarian grouping. His popularity, combined with perceived theological novelty, inevitably brought him into controversy and conflict with established conservative beliefs.

Having suggested that Erskine was an important transitional theologian of significant insight and standing, who made a major and insufficiently recognised contribution to nineteenth-century soteriological development by detailed examination of his thought, the second part of the book takes a broader contextual perspective in seeking to establish Erskine's relative

---

[104] Letter to Mrs Schwabe, 27 April 1856, *Letters-II*, 269.
[105] *Freeness*, 8-9, 11.

theological status in the nineteenth century. In particular, we investigate his apparent reliance on, and innovative use of, supposed sources, and assess his anticipation of, and influence on, later theological developments. Our objective is to demonstrate, by reference to the wider British and continental nineteenth-century scene, how Erskine was an eclectic product of his broad context, and how he functioned as an innovatory catalyst for the application and dissemination of both mystical and idealistic theological and philosophical ideas in Victorian Britain. Continuity with Part 1 is evident through ongoing analysis of Erskine's key innovative ideas. However, in Part 2 we seek to show further how those ideas fitted into, and indeed manifested the spirit of, a wider contemporary transformation in European and American soteriological thought.

PART 2

ERSKINE'S RECONSTRUCTIVE ECLECTIC SOTERIOLOGY IN ITS WIDER SETTING

CHAPTER 7

Erskine and his Nineteenth-Century Context

In Part 1 we examined how Erskine's innovatory approach to the reconstruction of soteriological thought involved eclectic inspirational and motivational factors derived from a complex pattern of theological, philosophical, scientific and cultural sources. In this second part we devote greater attention to the alleged eclectic sources and contexts themselves and assess possible connections. Whereas Part 1 concentrated on the *internal* nature and consistency of Erskine's creative appropriation of soteriological concepts, Part 2 seeks more specifically to locate Erskine within the wider *external* setting of theological innovation and reconstruction characteristic of his era. Accordingly, we examine the potential influence of contemporary intellectual and cultural forces, appraise possible origins of Erskine's innovatory thinking, suggest how and why Erskine's ideas were taken up or paralleled by others, and demonstrate how he emerged as a pioneering representative of soteriological transformation.

Erskine lived during a climate of unparalleled freedom of investigation, when "new schools of thought [were arising] in all directions, in philosophy, ethics, and theology".[1] John Tulloch highlighted the years 1810-1830 as especially notable for the springing up of "a great variety of new influences", and in Scotland it was Thomas Erskine whom he singled out. Erskine was 'prominent' both in stimulating "excitement and novelty in Scottish religion", and in anticipating and directly or indirectly influencing movements for theological development, or 'heresies', depending on one's viewpoint.[2] By way of example, we have suggested that Erskine's impact on John McLeod Campbell was greater than is often acknowledged. Others, like F.D. Maurice, were quick to acknowledge Erskine's influence. But Erskine was himself the product of eclectic influences which shaped his

---

[1] Tulloch, *Movements*, 2-3.
[2] Tulloch, *Movements*, 10, 128-45.

own creative development, some of which we have already noted, some he openly acknowledged, and many of which he was probably only half-aware.

We again warn against attempting to classify Erskine over-simplistically within narrowly-defined theological systems, as some have sought to do. At another extreme, Otto Pfleiderer unrealistically inferred that Erskine had arrived at his views completely independently from mere personal Bible study.[3] We suggest, however, that far from operating in an intellectual and cultural vacuum, Erskine was influenced more subtly and generally by the revolutionary, vibrant, intellectual milieu in which he was educated, lived and moved. It is therefore vital to consider potential sources whose relevance and influence has hitherto been underestimated or insufficiently demonstrated. Erskine evidenced an eclectic and independent mind in his writings, rarely quoting from the works of others. It was common at the time for sources not to be acknowledged or attributed, hence it is frequently from Erskine's surviving private correspondence that we derive what clues exist to the wide range of formative factors which were involved in the development of his thought.

It has frequently been noted that Erskine, Campbell, Scott and Irving all arrived at similar 'novel' theological ideas at more or less the same time, though apparently by independent routes. This has never been satisfactorily explained, particularly since it has generally been believed that none of them apparently had substantive contact with similar concurrent developments in Germany, the most obvious source for new theological ideas in the nineteenth century. Likely explanations doubtless lie within the general mood and inquiring nature of the times. Many were seeking to grapple with pressing epistemological questions, and currents of German thought seeped gradually into British theological consciousness. John Tulloch remarked concerning the 'new birth' experience of Thomas Carlyle in 1826 that "it is a date...fertile in religious thought. At centres wide apart, and tending to very different issues, the Divine impulse was moving many minds in those years – Coleridge, Arnold, Milman, Thirlwall, Newman, Erskine, McLeod Campbell".[4] In fact, most of these sooner or later came into contact with German thought. It is therefore entirely likely that, together with Scott and Irving, they were reflecting a newer form of theological awareness or 'neology' which was becoming generally evident in educated circles, owing much of its influence to the new Romantic mood impacting Britain. British theological interest in Germany dates from the 1790s, where Romantic Platonism, as in England, had been influenced by Jacob Boehme and Pietism. Schleiermacher was himself a noteworthy Platonic Pietist and both he and Kant, together with Hegel, owed much to the German mystical tradition

---

[3] Pfleiderer, *Theology*, 378.

[4] Tulloch, *Movements*, 184.

flowing from Meister Eckhart. In eighteenth-century England, William Law had been a major transmitter of Boehme's thought, and was admired by both Coleridge and Erskine, who were students of Plato in their own right.[5] The results tended towards a type of simultaneously backward- and forward-looking mysticism.

Eclecticism was fashionable in the late eighteenth and early nineteenth centuries.[6] Erskine combined an intellectually and theologically eclectic outlook with a strong streak of independent thought, allowing new ideas to stimulate his own questioning of traditional forms of religious expression. In ecclesiology as well, Erskine remained stubbornly eclectic, never subscribing to one particular church. Raised in Episcopalian surroundings (he knew Hooker's *Laws of Ecclesiastical Polity*), Erskine attended a Congregational church, frequently visited the Church of Scotland, claimed to be a Calvinist until his death, and received Anglican communion at the end of his life.[7]

There were many largely unacknowledged sources of influence which arguably contributed towards shaping Erskine's thought. Though he was recognisably a product of the eighteenth-century Enlightenment, at the same time he demonstrated a kindred spirit to the increasingly influential Romantic movement which itself emerged in reaction to the previous century, becoming an increasingly significant "vehicle for religious thought".[8] It is not surprising, therefore, that Erskine manifested the continuous and combined effects of both Enlightenment and Romantic influences, most apparent in his confidence in individual judgment, freedom from central control, authority and power, dislike of religious systems, and his evident sense of liberty in religious inquiry and innovation.

Erskine's embrace of the autonomy of internal human authority (rather than external sources) as the arbiter of truth which becomes self-evidencing at the bar of reason and conscience, was a clear development of Enlightenment principles.[9] His emphasis on ethical inward religion also reflected Enlightenment tendencies to regard religious knowledge and the existence

---

[5] David Newsome, *Two Classes of Men: Platonism and English Romantic Thought* (New York: St. Martin's Press, 1972), 8-11.

[6] The onset of the Victorian era coincided with the remarkable growth phenomenon of the secular and religious press. The Eclectic Society was formed in 1783 largely by evangelical churchmen and dissenters, and their organ, the *Eclectic Review*, commenced a new series in 1814. See L.E. Elliott-Binns, *Religion in the Victorian Era*, [2nd edition] (London: Lutterworth Press, 1946), 328-37.

[7] Bishop Ewing recounted the story that Erskine had on one occasion been refused Holy Communion by a Scottish bishop, (Lees, "Ewing", 386).

[8] Bebbington, *Evangelicalism*, 80-1.

[9] For example, in *Christianity as old as the Creation*, the deist, Mathew Tindal, had suggested that "there are some things whose internal excellence sufficiently proves their divine origin", (cited by Stephen, *History*, I, 119).

of God as self-authenticating to the free-thinking individual by virtue of their 'reasonableness', evincing qualities inherently fitted for human 'happiness', and corresponding with universal awareness of the moral law within. Enlightenment thinkers had found there was little practical difference between religion and public morality, and consequently stressed the need for moral duty as dictated by conscience. All this stood in contrast to mere external revelation, which came to be regarded as unnecessary.[10]

Despite reflecting many Enlightenment assumptions, Erskine, however, rejected earlier Enlightenment rationalism, which by his time had translated into an outmoded evangelical emphasis on external evidences, even though Paley's associated Christian apologetics remained popular. It would appear that Erskine had somehow come to share, and innovatively interpret, the findings of Kant, and subsequently Schleiermacher (both still largely unknown in Britain in 1800), that God could not be discovered by proofs and evidences, but only by individuals for themselves. The authority for faith was not to be located *outside* the believer, in the Bible or in special revelation, so much as *inside*. In Germany, unlike Britain, the Aufklärung had *followed* the Pietist movement, and whereas English Deism had tended to *destroy* traditional belief, in Germany serious intellectual endeavour aimed to *reshape* the Christian faith.[11] By some means, Erskine became associated more with this continental, reconstructive, mediating approach than with its English expression.

The radical theological concept of 'unconditional freeness' was vital to Erskine. His focus on universal pardon, and faith as a higher faculty of reason, was a necessary result of it. Reflecting Kantian and Coleridgean ideas of human freedom, he typified early nineteenth-century thinking, clearly mirroring the increasingly free spirit of the age. In asserting human freedom against divine determinism Erskine inevitably came into conflict with the Augustinian tradition which he in turn endeavoured to reshape.[12] Erskine seemed somehow to have acquired a working knowledge of Kantian ideas which prompted the overall thrust of his thought. Kant's definition of freedom had emphasised the autonomy or freedom of the will, i.e., the ability to be governed by reason, for it was the rational person who is free to choose. From this Kant had developed the sense of obligation and duty (but not compulsion) which was fundamental to his moral outlook. Morality was now to be located in the free motivation of human action, resulting in the elevated nineteenth-century ideal of the person of reason and goodwill. The concept of human freedom dependent on self-determined action was

---

[10] See Stephen, *History*, I, 121; James Byrne, *Glory, Jest and Riddle: Religious Thought in the Enlightenment* (London: SCM Press, 1996), 111-12.

[11] McGrath, *German Christology*, 18.

[12] Colin E. Gunton, *Theology Through the Theologians* (Edinburgh: T.&T. Clark, 1996), 25-6.

becoming a forceful influence in Erskine's day. Erskine appropriated the concept, adapting it for his own apologetic purposes, albeit risking association with what were often construed within the limited horizons of his religious opponents as Arminian and Pelagian heresies.

But Erskine also manifested significant differences from Kant. In particular, he rejected any suggestion that humanity could pursue truth apart from the direct sanctifying work of a personally knowable God working within an individual's life. His emphasis on the immediacy of 'felt' religion, and his embrace of "the principle of dynamic organicism which replaced the static mechanism of the previous century", rather indicated the increasing influence of Romantic sensibilities.[13] These largely originated with Rousseau who, whilst not minimising reason, stressed that it is by *feeling* that we know the things of God, together with the *conscience*, which is a 'form' of feeling.[14] In comparison, traditional religious 'doctrine' seemed as cold and arid as Enlightenment 'reason'. Romanticism was a potent, catalytic, transitional influence, requiring new responses to theology and experience, in which history was increasingly seen as a 'process' through which God was educating the human race. The Bible and doctrine were considered part of that process, but to be able to interpret them aright a new understanding of inspiration based on the self-conscious individual was needed. It was the superseding of a mechanical by a dynamic philosophy, with priority transferred to feeling, to the inward, rather than the outward. In anticipating such perspectives, Erskine shared many characteristics of an early Romantic thinker, though with evident Kantian foundations. He could well be epitomised as a serious, eclectic, transitional figure, with roots in two centuries.

For Kant, morality became the essence of true religion, and 'moral' or 'practical' reason the grounds for determining what is indispensable. Kant emphasised the inner (moral) subjective witness of the (human) spirit to determine what true religion is, an approach paralleled closely by Erskine, in which the dividing line between human and divine remained intentionally ambiguous. In line with Kantian epistemology, the Romantics, and in theology notably Schleiermacher, pursued the idea that it was through the

---

[13] Young, *Maurice*, 110. Reardon comments, "he is a true Romantic when he sees society as an organism and religion as the life-blood of that organism", (*Religion*, 12).

[14] John Kent, "The Enlightenment", in *Companion Encyclopaedia of Theology*, Peter Byrne and Leslie Houlden (eds.) (London: Routledge, 1995), 267; Reardon, *Romanticism*, 27. Vernon Storr highlighted the following distinguishing features of Romanticism: a) awareness that humanity is not merely an intellectual creature, but a being of instinct, passion and emotion. Reason was something larger than mere logical argument, rather a creative and unifying faculty for the totality of the human being. b) reawakening of a sense of the infinite and the spirit of wonder and mystery in man and nature. c) importance of the imagination working in tandem with reason in the creative task. d) a sense of sympathy between man and nature, (*English Theology*, 126-34).

non-cognitive faculty of feeling, intuition, or imagination that the human soul was brought into immediate contact with the 'Spirit of the universe', leading to a type of 'natural theology' of mystical religious experience, involving corresponding de-emphasis of special revelation.[15] Erskine is very reminiscent of Kant in his insistence on identifying a moral basis for truth and reality, rather than from mere acceptance of revelation or dogma. According to both, we gain entrance to the spiritual world rather through the medium of our free response to the universal, internal, moral impulse, the liberty of the individual conscience being tempered by a final accountability which remained a necessary postulate of moral reasoning and an ethical religious base. Erskine passionately believed reason must harmonise with experience. Correct appreciation of the role of the Bible and doctrine was essential in the light of this. The consequence would necessarily be moral living:

> The perfect moral tendency of its doctrines is a ground on which the Bible often rests its plea of authenticity and importance. Whatever principle of belief tends to promote real moral perfection, possesses in some degree the quality of truth. By moral perfection, I mean the perception of what is right, followed by the love of it and the doing of it.[16]

As we have seen, Erskine repeatedly insisted that the evidence for the truth of a religion must be demonstrated apart from all *external* evidence by its conformity with the moral constitution of the human mind, its effect on the character of the believer, and its coincidence with the practical circumstances in which humanity exists. Doctrines should reveal aspects of the divine moral mind, character and government, therefore it was the *moral* tendency of doctrines which proved their authenticity. Christ himself became the flesh and blood working model for us of absolute moral truth:

> Jesus came from heaven to show forth the character of God. He knew the Father and he came to show Him forth to us; to show Him, not by words alone – His *life* revealed the Father, for His life was a life of love…[17]

Whilst this all sounded very reasonable and persuasive, the danger was that Christianity could easily begin to take on the character of an abstract or philosophical idea, leading to a natural, humanist religion modelled on Jesus Christ as moral ideal. Alan Sell regards Kant as responsible for distinctly 'muffling' the sound of the gospel:

---

[15] Bruce A. Demarest, *General Revelation* (Grand Rapids: Zondervan Publishing House, 1982), 21.
[16] *Evidence*, 13-14.
[17] "God's Welcome to the Returning Sinner", in Campbell, *Fragments of Truth,* 308.

An inherently unknowable God, who is the projection of autonomous man's reason is not the holy creator before whom man stands as sinner. Hence the exemplar Christ will suffice; and in the result the Christian life is not a joyous life of fellowship with the risen Christ and his people, but rather a lonely attempt to attend to one's duties understood as divine commands.[18]

Erskine was well aware he needed to retain a strong balancing commitment to the evangelical emphasis on a personal Christ with whom a living relationship was to be maintained. It is in this area that his creative genius was applied. Can we discern particular influences which helped direct Erskine's thought in the concurrent tasks of theological innovation and preserving evangelical orthodoxy? The following chapter examines the most likely sources for Erskine's soteriological thought, both acknowledged and unacknowledged.

---

[18] Alan P.F. Sell, *Theology in Turmoil: The Roots, Course and Significance of the Conservative-Liberal Debate in Modern Theology* (Eugene, Oregon: WIPF & Stock Publishers, 1998), 15.

CHAPTER 8

Erskine's Sources

Introduction

Whilst Erskine remained independent and idiosyncratic, owning no formal allegiances, despite evident theological reconstructive creativity, we argue he was not, however, entirely original. We reject suggestions of 'isolated amateur originality'. Rather, he appeared passionately pious, intelligent, with a sharp lawyer's mind, well-read, well-informed, and well-educated (though not particularly scholarly), and as a theological eclectic, with numerous connections, drew upon, often apparently indirectly and unconsciously, wide-ranging contemporary and historical sources. Our dilemma remains, however, that Erskine only rarely acknowledged any direct authorial influence, and in his earlier years close personal friendships seemed to be his most important acknowledged developmental sources.[1] In this chapter we therefore seek to compare Erskine with selected key parallel theological approaches, both historical and contemporary, to assess their potential influence, and to appreciate further Erskine's place in the overall evolving context of Victorian theological development.

We have consistently noted evidence in Erskine of Enlightenment thought patterns, and parallels with developing Romantic ideas in the early nineteenth century, together with repeated correspondence with Erskine's near contemporary Schleiermacher. The century also saw renewed historical interest in the patristic tradition, and further significant parallels may be traced between Erskine and the Church Fathers, particularly Irenaeus and Athanasius.[2] Despite apparent parallels and circumstantial data however, there is little direct evidence suggesting either that Erskine was an expert

---

[1] Notably Erskine's brother, John (d.1816), Charles Stuart of Dunearn (d.1826), and later, A.J. Scott (d.1866). They produced relatively little written material.

[2] Franks, *Work of Christ*, 661; Pelikan, *Christian Doctrine*, 262-3. See p.40 above.

on the Fathers, or knew Schleiermacher.[3] In his day, Erskine was most frequently associated by critics with Quakers and mystics, Edward Irving, and William Ellery Channing and the Unitarians. Nevertheless, so far as Erskine himself was concerned, all remained largely unacknowledged in terms of influence.

Erskine corresponded with Unitarians, some of whom felt a general kinship with him. He praised J.J. Tayler and James Martineau. But he was not in full sympathy with them, considering them dry, lifeless, and even plain wrong.[4] However, during the nineteenth century, Unitarians were extremely influential, and strongly paralleled Erskine's shift of emphasis to internal religion, as opposed to a religion based on external evidences.[5] Multiple correspondences exist between Erskine, William Ellery Channing (1780-1842) and the Unitarians. The *Edinburgh Christian Instructor* highlighted a letter to the editor under the heading, "Mr. Erskine's Doctrine hailed by the Unitarians",[6] whilst the *Presbyterian Review* made a detailed comparison of Erskine's views with those of "that modern champion of the Unitarian school, Dr. Channing".[7]

Erskine knew Jonathan Edwards's writings to the extent that in *The Doctrine of Election* he critiqued his work on the freedom of the will, fundamentally rejecting Edwards's belief that *divine necessity* nevertheless remained compatible with human free-will and responsibility. For how could humanity be free if they lay under a burden of decreed reprobation?[8] Erskine's preferred early reading included the essays of the evangelical Baptist, John Foster, and he also developed a close friendship on his early continental travels with the evangelical clergyman, Gerard T. Noel. Both apparently exerted lasting, discernible, influence. Foster, whom Erskine read as a youth, regarded eternal punishment as unjust, and has been considered a source of Erskine's doctrine of post-mortem spiritual education and uni-

---

[3] Though we know Erskine profitably read Augustine (*Letters-I*, 254), whilst Samuel Gobat thought Erskine was thoroughly proficient in the Fathers, (Gobat, *Samuel Gobat*, 42-3).

[4] See *Letters-I*, 82-5, 118-21, 164. Erskine did not appreciate Martineau's review of Campbell's *NOTA* in the *National Review* (April, 1856), 478-500, and it negatively influenced his view of Martineau, (Letter to Mrs Schwabe, 14 September 1857, *NLS MS* 9747–74, cf., *Memorials*, II, 342). A feature on Erskine's life and work by William C. Smith appeared in the Unitarian *Theological Review* (London), XII (July 1875), 353-372.

[5] Young, *Maurice*, 34-5.

[6] Anon., *ECI*, XXIX, VI (June, 1830), 409-410.

[7] Anon., "Mysticism-Erskine on Election", *Presbyterian Review*, X, III (February, 1838), 488-9. See Appendix 2.

[8] *Election*, 546-70.

versalism.[9] Erskine read his *On a Man Writing Memoirs of Himself* at the age of 17, realising, as a kind of spiritual awakening, that life was a school, and time was education for eternity.[10] Erskine travelled with Gerard Noel in Europe, featuring as 'St. Clair' in Noel's travel journal entitled *Arvendel*.[11] Geoffrey Rowell believes Noel signally impacted Erskine,[12] and a reading of Noel's exceedingly moralistic sermons is remarkably reminiscent of him.[13]

Other influential sources derived from Platonic and mystical traditions which also featured strongly in Schleiermacher and Romantic circles. Significantly, the one major source which Erskine did directly acknowledge originated from this sphere. Almost certainly many of his major innovative theological ideas were inspired by the eighteenth-century devotional writer and nonjuror, William Law. Whilst Edward Irving's controversial christology is regarded by some critics as highly influential, this study adopts the view that it was from Law, rather than Irving, that Erskine gained crucial soteriological insights and motivation.

Erskine developed a theodicy of life which consisted of a universal human purificatory redemptive process in a moment-by-moment struggle between tendencies towards good or evil, encompassing a gradual education towards spiritual growth and maturity, and the vanquishing of evil by good within the overall purposes of God. This fundamental theme was not only common in the early church, but was widely revived in the eighteenth and nineteenth centuries, particularly when evolution theory offered new spiritual analogies.[14] Amongst the Church Fathers, Origen was most noted for his universalistic ideas. However, Irenaeus has been viewed in some readings as adopting a theodicy remarkably similar to Erskine's. Irenaeus regarded human beings as created originally immature and imperfect, but through providential experience of good and evil underwent moral development and growth towards divine conformity and perfection. He saw that God had planned that humanity should be "making progress day by day, and ascending towards the perfect, that is, approximating to the uncreated

---

[9] Needham, *Thomas Erskine*, 29; Leroy Edwin Froom, *The Conditionalist Faith of Our Fathers*, in 2 volumes (Washington: Review and Herald, 1966), II, 318-20.

[10] John Foster, *Essays* (London: The Religious Tract Society, undated). See Letter to Madame Forel, 29 November 1845, *Letters-II,* 51.

[11] Gerard T. Noel, *Arvendel; or Sketches in Italy and Switzerland* (London: James Nisbet, 1826).

[12] Geoffrey Rowell, *Hell and the Victorians* (Oxford: Clarendon Press, 1974), 70-1.

[13] See, e.g., 'Perceptions of Christ's love the source of moral obedience', in *Sermons, intended chiefly for the use of families,* in 2 volumes (London: John Hatchard and Son, 1826), I, especially 252-3.

[14] The latter was developed notably by Henry Drummond (1851-97).

One".[15] According to John Hick, Irenaeus offered the basis for a radical alternative to Augustinian theodicy, and played a foundational role in preparing the ground for rejection of the doctrine of eternal damnation.[16] In contrast to the Augustinian picture of the fall of Adam in catastrophic terms, with life consequently presented as a trial or probation consequent to divine punishment of Adam's sin, Irenaeus regarded the world as a training school, in which experienced good and evil were appointed in the good purposes of God with the express intention that human beings should mature towards the perfection God had planned for them.[17]

The alternative approach to theodicy suggested by Irenaeus was revived by William Law and Schleiermacher. Schleiermacher regarded salvation as consisting of a progressive awakening of our conscious relation to God by increasing awareness of the human condition of absolute dependence.[18] He taught that the development of God-consciousness was a universal responsibility which carried with it increased awareness of guilt and the need for redemption. Within the context of an evil fallen world, suffering was, in fact, a loving, divine, redemptive appointment which served to motivate us to aspire to higher states of salvific God-consciousness, for "the gradual and imperfect unfolding of the power of God-consciousness is one of the necessary conditions of the human stage of existence".[19] Schleiermacher believed that because sin was a corporate human act, and that evil was the result of sin, accordingly "the whole world in its relation to man is the proper sphere of evil, and evil the corporate suffering of the race", but that God's redemptive purposes embraced sin and evil.[20] Rejecting any idea of eternal damnation according to the Augustinian-Calvinist tradition, Schleiermacher was to assert, like Erskine, the ultimate universal efficacy of Christ's educative redemptive work.[21]

Before turning to William Law and Edward Irving for closer comparative study, we initially examine claims that Erskine's 'neology' was influenced by mysticism, to the extent of him being a 'closet Quaker'.

---

[15] Irenaeus, "Against Heresies", IV. xxxviii. 3, *ANCL*, IX (Edinburgh: T.&T. Clark, 1868), 44.

[16] John Hick, *God and the Universe of Faiths* (London: Macmillan,1973), 70; *Evil and the God of Love* (London: Macmillan, 1985), 210.

[17] Irenaeus, "Against Heresies", IV. xxxix. 1-2, *ANCL,* IX, 46-7.

[18] Schleiermacher, *Christian Faith*, §5, 18-26.

[19] *Ibid.*, §81.4, 338, §89.1, 366.

[20] *Ibid.*, §76. 3, 317, §81.1, esp. 333.

[21] *Ibid.*, §120, esp. 559-60, §162, §163, esp. 722, §169.

Mystical Theology

A review in the *Quarterly Christian Magazine,* probably authored by James Haldane, identified Erskine's concept of the universal indwelling of the Spirit in the human conscience in *The Doctrine of Election* with Quaker notions.[22] F.D. Maurice, in accord with Erskine, and acknowledging the importance of *The Doctrine of Election*, confirmed that his own sense of unity with the rest of humanity forced him, against his inclinations, to accept that the Quakers were right in respect of their doctrine of the light in every human being.[23] Robert Barclay's exposition of the inward self-authenticating nature of revelation confirms how close the Quaker concept was to Erskine's own position:

> divine revelation and inward illumination, is that which is evident and clear of itself, forcing, by its own evidence and clearness, the well disposed understanding to assent, irresistibly moving the same thereunto, even as the common principles of natural truths do move and incline the mind to a natural assent.[24]

Mystical overtones in Erskine's thought were frequently noted. Andrew Thomson was one opponent who accused him of "mystical heresy" or "raving mysticism".[25] Even friendly commentators often resorted to mysticism in an endeavour to express adequately the essence of Erskine's thought. John Tulloch concluded it was best interpreted in subjective existential terms than by means of formal 'system':

> it must be a light in his reason, a guide in his conscience – a life within his life, – a spiritual power glowing in his whole conduct. This was 'internal evidence,' – the revelation of Love to love, of Life to life, – of God to man, raising him to divine communion, and reflecting upon him the divine likeness.[26]

It was impossible to separate Erskine's thought from his life. As Bishop Ewing put it, "Should anyone attempt to write the *life* of Mr. Erskine, the difficulty must ever present itself to him that what he has to depict is spirit and not matter, that he has to convey light, to represent sound – an almost

---

[22] Anon., "Erskine's Doctrine of Election, and its Connexion with the General Tenor of Christianity", *Quarterly Christian Magazine*, IV, No.24 (January, 1838), 355.

[23] Frederick Denison Maurice, *The Doctrine of Sacrifice Deduced from the Scriptures* [1854] (London: Macmillan and Co., 1879), xix-xx.

[24] Robert Barclay, *An Apology for the True Christian Divinity* [1678], [14th edition] (Glasgow: R. Barclay Murdoch, 1886), 11.

[25] Thomson, *Universal Pardon*, 419, 485.

[26] Tulloch, *Movements*, 139.

insuperable difficulty."[27] John McLeod Campbell similarly declared, "No man is able to say to those who knew him not what he was; no man could say this to those who knew him in a way that they would feel satisfying".[28] Principal Shairp, who was eventually persuaded to pen some personal reminiscences, nevertheless felt "restrained by a sense of utter inability".[29]

It was in connection with Erskine's revolutionary subjective understanding of the atonement that for many he was associated with mysticism. Henry Henderson compared him to the great German mystic John Arndt, suggesting that Erskine found in mysticism something which met the needs of his 'intellectual' and 'evangelical' nature. However, Henderson thought his 'mysticism' was of the 'rationalistic' type: "He holds not merely that the Christ of history reproduces Himself in experience, but also that the Christ of experience explains and confirms the reality of the Christ of history".[30]

In 1838, the *Presbyterian Review* rehearsed the history of mysticism as background to its own review of *The Doctrine of Election* under the title "Mysticism – Erskine on Election". A catalogue of figures from the mystical tradition was recited for comparison purposes, including Origen, Dionysius, Thomas à Kempis, Pascal, Fénelon, Molinos, George Fox, William Penn, and Robert Barclay. Edward Irving also featured as a member of the "mystic school" with which Erskine was directly associated. The early church was reprimanded for permitting the absorption of Platonic ideas, including universal 'divine sparks' in humanity and the inward 'light within every man', which fostered notions of a universal divine faculty for apprehending truth in the place of the reliable external authority of Scripture and the inner witness of the Spirit. The reviewer concluded that Erskine "has adopted the tenets of the mystical school, and is already, in his religious views at least, a Quaker". While lamenting the decline and fall of a respected figure into 'extreme', 'extravagant', 'bizarre' and 'grotesque' opinions, the reviewer pointedly observed that it was a 'sign of the times'. Hypotheses were ventured as to why "laymen, who often excel in the practical and apologetical departments of theology, are unfitted, from the want of regular study, for managing its abstruser doctrines" and consequently slip into mystical tendencies. A four-page, point-by-point comparison between Erskine and the Quakers followed in substantiation of the charge. This highlighted some familiar themes: i) Erskine's belief in 'the light within'; ii) marginalisation of the Christ revealed in the Scriptures in favour of the 'inward Christ'; iii) his notion of 'waiting for the light'; iv) redemption by imitation and "a sort of self-crucifixion", rather than by the

---

[27] *Ewing-1*, 11-12.
[28] Campbell, Letter to Bishop Ewing, 9 July 1870, *Memorials*, II, 279.
[29] Shairp, "Reminiscences", *Letters-II*, 347.
[30] Henderson, *Erskine*, 66-7.

objective death of Christ; v) his confusion of justification, sanctification and the new birth; vi) universal redemption; vii) subordination of the authority of Scripture. The article concluded that Erskine has "contrived to weave for himself an entirely new version of the gospel", and given "the whole scheme of redemption...a different shape".[31]

Platonism enjoyed a revival both in the early part of the Enlightenment and amongst Romantics, and the influence of Platonic ideas as a catalyst for theological reformulation may often be detected in Erskine, especially involving the return to God of the divine soul innate within humanity. His critics quickly recognised the origin of affirmations in *The Doctrine of Election* such as,

> The light is come into our nature, that we may become one with it, and so may ascend with it into heaven. And we can ascend thither in no other way, than by this union...By following the leading of the light, we become one with it, and so one with the Son of man who came from God and went to God.[32]

Mystical theology regarded the work of Christ primarily in terms of inward renewal of the individual, involving not only divine identification with the human condition, but importantly elevation of the soul to God. Platonic in origin, the ultimate objective was to attain union with God and participate in the divine nature through the transforming redemptive incarnation of Christ, who came to reveal the essential divine-human unity. Jesus' achievement, therefore, was to enable us to discover the divine presence innate within each human being, and as our prototype, supremely embodying the 'inner light', show how the way of salvation is possible for all.[33]

Though at its strongest in the middle ages, mystical ideas were also prominent amongst Church Fathers like Irenaeus and Athanasius, and in the Reformation Luther himself adopted mystical elements.[34] In Britain, the seventeenth-century Cambridge Platonists famously propounded the idea that 'the spirit of man is the candle of the Lord', whilst in the eighteenth century William Law taught that all humanity possesses the internal seed of divinity, and that it is the birth of Christ within the soul rather than the sacrifice of the cross which redeems us. Erskine was almost certainly influenced by both. Besides studying Law profoundly, Erskine learned German

---

[31] Anon., "Mysticism – Erskine on Election", *Presbyterian Review*, X, III (February, 1838), 487, 491-94.

[32] *Election*, 540.

[33] Donald G. Bloesch, *Jesus Christ Saviour and Lord* (Carlisle: Paternoster, 1997), 153-4.

[34] Bengt R. Hoffman, *Luther and the Mystics* (Minneapolis: Augsburg Publishing House, 1976).

to read Boehme in the original.[35] He also read the *Select Discourses* of John Smith (1618-52), together with treatises by Henry More (1614-87).[36] Needham concludes that Erskine was a "nineteenth-century Scottish version of a Cambridge Platonist".[37]

Mysticism was revived in eighteenth- and nineteenth-century Europe, and applied to theology. Charles Hodge distinguished between 'supernatural' and 'natural' mysticism. He linked the latter with Schleiermacher in what he described as "the natural religious consciousness of men" becoming the "source of religious knowledge" rather than God.[38] Schleiermacher and other key theological figures like Coleridge and Maurice were frequently regarded as manifesting strong mystical or Platonic strands in their writings.[39] In Germany, Schleiermacher sounded distinctly mystical notes in his emphasis on the power of the indwelling Christ to generate redemptive God-consciousness.[40] Undoubtedly, like Schleiermacher and Coleridge, Erskine found inspiration and security in aspects of mystical theology in his apologetic endeavours to maintain the credibility of Christianity in offering intelligible explanations of the relationship of humanity to God in an increasingly mechanical and sceptical age. His dual urges both to conserve and to change paralleled the Romantics who started from Enlightenment revisionism and, eschewing fixed religious schemes, turned to exploration of the relationship between humanity and the natural universe of which it was part; "to sustain its authority in the new age religion had to be reassessed as itself part of the fabric of human experience".[41] However, once again, we observe that eclectically Erskine absorbed and reflected the tendencies of his era to locate precedents in historic expressions of truth. Consequently, it appears inappropriate yet again to associate him directly with any specific related movement. Although, for example, Erskine was accused of Quakerism, whilst he certainly respected its historical expression, it is over-simplistic for Marian Foster to portray him as 'coming very strongly under Quaker influence'.[42] It would be more accurate, in any case, to describe Erskine as a theologian of the 'indwelling Christ' rather than

---

[35] Agnes Maule Machar, "Thomas Erskine of Linlathen", *Andover Review*, XIV, LXXXIV (December, 1890), 475.

[36] See letters to Mrs Stirling, December 1836, and A.J. Scott, 3 August 1837, *Letters-I*, 247, 256-7.

[37] Needham, *Thomas Erskine*, 403.

[38] Charles Hodge, *Systematic Theology*, in 3 volumes (London and Edinburgh: Thomas Nelson and Sons, 1871), I, 6-9.

[39] For Coleridge and the mystics see Charles Richard Sanders, *Coleridge and the Broad Church Movement* (New York: Octagon Books, 1972), 31 and *passim*.

[40] Schleiermacher, *Christian Faith*, §11, 52-60.

[41] Reardon, *Romanticism*, viii.

[42] Marian Foster, *Representation and Substitution in Thomas Erskine of Linlathen*, unpublished Ph.D (King's College, University of London, 1992), 209.

the 'inner light', and though in a number of respects he embodied Quaker ideas, the mediated influence of William Law was probably strongest.

William Law

We have noted the revival of mystical thought within the Romantic movement. Dean Inge directly linked Erskine with an eclectic line of Christian thinkers in the mystical, Platonic, Romantic tradition, including the Cambridge Platonists, Coleridge, Wordworth, and William Law.[43] Law himself stood in close relationship to the Quakers, and his later thought owed much to the influence of the divine philosophy of Jacob Boehme, himself a precursor and stimulator of nineteeth-century ideas:

> Behmen professed to give [Law] the key to the invisible world, just when he most wanted it. Behmen's theosophy is admitted to have anticipated many of the leading principles of Schelling and Hegel...it is intelligible, therefore, that Behmen should be to Law what the later German speculation was to men like Coleridge in a succeeding generation. It seemed to him that a new spring of truth was gushing up in the wilderness of arid criticism and futile logomachy.[44]

William Law has tended to be seriously underestimated and relatively neglected as a key formative influence on nineteenth-century theological thought, especially relating to the idea of revelation and the immediacy of experience.[45] Noted as "a man of remarkable power and originality", he exercised significant influence on John Wesley. Leslie Stephen perceptively observed that Law's writings "strikingly anticipate the teaching of the later school of theology, which traces its origin to Coleridge, and has a natural affinity for the mystical element".[46] Whilst we do not know how Erskine was introduced to his later writings (though it appears he was a wide devotional reader), the early influence of William Law on Erskine was probably the most directly formative and enduring. Erskine quoted from Law's later mystical works, went back directly to Law's source in Boehme, and attracted to himself an aura of mysticism which commentators frequently noted and directly connected with Law himself.[47]

Though Erskine admitted reservations on first reading Law's *The Spirit of Prayer*, remarking that "It is not the gospel, but I think it may be profita-

---

[43] William Ralph Inge, *Vale* (London: Longmans, Green and Co., 1934), 45-6.
[44] Stephen, *History*, II, 344, cf., Stephen Hobhouse, *William Law and Eighteenth Century Quakerism* (London: George Allen & Unwin, 1927), 289, 324-32.
[45] McDonald, *Ideas*, 158.
[46] Stephen, *History*, II, 331, 344.
[47] See e.g., Henderson, *Erskine*, 26-30.

bly read by those who know the gospel",[48] towards the end of his life he personally confirmed the influential role played by Law, especially in determining his fundamental persuasion that Christianity was not to be viewed

> as a system of doctrines imposed on us by God, of which we could know nothing except from the Scriptures, but as the eternally true and natural religion to which all our spiritual faculties are adapted, and the intrinsic truth and certainty of which, though we could not have discovered it for ourselves, yet when revealed we can so apprehend, as to hold it on account of that intrinsic truth, and not on any outward authority whatsoever.[49]

Emphasising the unassailable "essential inwardness of religion as a spiritual power",[50] Law's insistence on a 'religion of nature', in which natural laws were seen to fit humanity for redemption, clearly anticipated Erskine. For Law, God was

> not the judge nor the artificer, but the all-pervading and immanent force, from whom all nature is an emanation. We recognise him by a sensibility of our nature which reveals the spiritual world; and reason is an 'impotent spectator' which only receives its materials from this supreme faculty...Religion, then, with Law, becomes subjective and emotional, when to almost all his contemporaries it was historical and rational. A sovereign faculty of intuition sets aside the common sense which they took to be the only judge in all controversies...the mechanical is superseded by the dynamical view, and we contemplate the forces by which the heart is transformed, not its arbitrary relations to an external being.[51]

Like Erskine, Law regarded *knowledge*, not merely as intellectual acceptance, but as a dynamic consciousness of truth in which intellect and will became fused: "all *real* Knowledge is *Life*, or a living *Sensibility* of the Thing that is known".[52]

Erskine seems to have been strongly influenced by Law's mystic immanental system, which was based on understanding the disorders of a fallen world in the light of an insistence that all divine dealings with humankind, and indeed the entire universe, flowed from the axiomatic truth that God is Love.[53] Erskine therefore probably derived the concept of 'spiritual order' from Law's *Spirit of Prayer*. Alexander Ewing, in his book based on Erskine's teaching, specifically attributed the idea of divine government to

---

[48] Letter to Miss Rachel Erskine, May 2 1827, *Letters-I*, 114-15

[49] *Sp.Order*, 258.

[50] Spencer (ed.), *Prayer*, 127 (footnote).

[51] Stephen, *History*, II, 345-6.

[52] Spencer (ed.), *Prayer* 115.

[53] J.H. Overton, *William Law, Nonjuror and Mystic* (London: Longmans, Green, and Co., 1881), 250-1.

Law.[54] Julia Wedgwood could have equally been describing Erskine when she observed that "the Incarnation, the Atonement, the Crucifixion, were to Law no doubt events in history…but in their essence they were not events in time, they were the laws of the eternal holiness".[55]

Many of Erskine's key themes, such as the inward life, divine love, knowledge and life, the universal inner light and seed of Christ as the inward life in the soul, the inward spiritual Word, punishment and its relationship to God's love, and the 'larger hope', as well as his teaching concerning the fall, election, universal pardon, and incarnational soteriology can be traced back to Law's *Spirit of Prayer* (1749/1750) and *Spirit of Love* (1752/1754). From 1827 they were amongst his most treasured reading.[56] It remains likely that recognisably patristic elements of his thought were also mediated through Law who 'owed a considerable debt' to the Fathers, including Athanasius, and Irenaeus, in particular regarding the recapitulatory atoning work of Christ.[57]

Archibald Robertson, Minister of Greenock, directly accused Erskine in 1830 of perpetuating similar heresies to Law, perceptively summarising their evident points of agreement and forecasting their tendency:

> [Law] supposed that in consequence of the death of Christ, all men have in them the first spark or seed of the divine life, as a treasure hid in the centre of the soul, to bring forth by degrees, a new birth of that life which was lost in paradise; and that no man can be lost, except by turning away from this Saviour within him. You suppose that in consequence of the death of Christ, all men enjoy pardon which, if embraced, is sufficient to restore them to the image of God which they have lost by sin, and that no man can be condemned, except by rejecting this pardon which has been procured for them. Mr. Law, in his writings, always represents the Deity as a God of universal love, who never can have any will towards his creatures but to communicate good. He asserts that there is no wrath standing between God and us, but that which is awakened in our own fallen nature, and that to quench this wrath, and not his own, God gave his only begotten Son to be made man. In these sentiments you exactly coincide with him, and the parallel is so exact, that it entitles you to rank high among the modern Mystics. Finally, Mr. Law believed in a final restoration of all mankind, after long periods of suffering; and to this doctrine your system has a direct and necessary tendency…[58]

---

[54] The Right Revd Alexander Ewing, Bishop of Argyll and the Isles, *Revelation Considered as Light* [2nd edition] (W. Isbister, 1874), vii.

[55] Julia Wedgwood, "William Law, the English Mystic of the Eighteenth Century", *Contemporary Review*, XXXI (December, 1877), 98.

[56] Letters to Miss Rachel Erskine, 2 May 1827, and 10 November 1827, *Letters-I*, 114, 123-4.

[57] Hobhouse, *Mystical Writings*, 252, 254, 299-301, 363.

[58] Robertson, *Vindication*, 128.

Erskine's Sources

Robertson's observations suggesting creative appropriation were perceptive and prophetic. Law's incarnational soteriology understood Christ as redeeming/ regenerating fallen human nature,[59] and emphasised that salvation consisted of imitating Christ through all the events of life "by wholly giving up [ourselves] to *That*, which He was, *viz*., to Patience, Meekness, Humility, and Resignation to God". He emphasised that the entire sanctifying objective of Christ's redemption was to deliver human nature from the effects of the fall, and to restore 'its first heavenly state', pouring God's love into us "to show us that Meekness, Suffering, and Dying to our own Fallen Nature, is the *one, only possible* Way, for fallen Man to be alive again in God".[60] Platonic and Quaker concepts of the universal divine inner light, merged with the Holy Spirit, were fundamental to Law's soteriology:

> See here in short, the State of Man as redeemed. He has a *Spark* of the Light and Spirit of God, as a *Supernatural Gift* of God given into the Birth of his Soul, to bring forth by Degrees a *New Birth* of that Life which was Lost in Paradise. This Holy Spark of the Divine Nature within Him, has a natural, strong and almost infinite Tendency, or Reaching after that eternal Light and Spirit of God, from whence it came forth. It came forth from God, it came *out* of God, it *partaketh* of the Divine Nature, and therefore it is always in a State of Tendency and Return to God. And all this is called the *Breathing*, the *Moving*, the *Quickening* of the Holy Spirit within us, which are so many Operations of this Spark of Life tending towards God.[61]

In Law's hands the inner light became supremely the incarnational revelation of the historic Jesus and the regenerative power of the divine within humanity:

> all that is said of an inward Christ, inwardly formed, and generated in the root of the soul, is only so much said of an inward life, brought forth by the power and efficacy of that blessed Christ, that was born of the Virgin Mary.[62]

So too in Erskine we find that "*every man…is a little world*, where Jesus, the true Light, the quickening Spirit, is though unknown".[63]

At one level, it is possible to view this emphasis in Erskine as an apologetic carry-over from eighteenth-century Enlightenment stress on 'the universal law of God written on the heart', which was a watchword of Deists and Unitarians.[64] The organic theory of 'innate ideas' derived initially from

---

[59] Spencer (ed.), *Prayer*, 20-1.
[60] Spencer (ed.), *Prayer*, 138, cf., Spencer (ed.), *Love*, 172, 287.
[61] Spencer (ed.), *Prayer*, 47.
[62] Spencer (ed.), *Prayer*, 38.
[63] *Election*, 58.
[64] Grenz and Olson, *20th Century Theology*, 20-1; Young, *Maurice and Unitarianism*, 41.

Plato was widely accepted in the eighteenth century, despite Locke's denial of it. But Erskine added to this concept a distinctive spiritual dimension which bore many of the hallmarks of Plato and Law and were also concurrently the subject of Romantic rediscovery. Law rejected Locke's emphasis on empirical knowledge. He insisted, in terms strongly reminiscent of Erskine,

> The *ten commandments*, when written by God on Tables of Stone, and given to Man, did not then first begin to belong to Man; they had their *Existence* in man, were *born* with him, they lay as a *Seed* and *Power* of Goodness, *hidden* in the Form and Make of his Soul, and altogether inseparable from it, before they were shown to Man on *Tables of Stone*. And when they were shown to Man on Tables of Stone, they were only an *outward Imitation* of that which was inwardly in Man...[65]

In addressing the question of spiritual illumination, Erskine tended to follow Law's analogy relating to the 'new birth of Christ in the soul' from the universally implanted 'seed', rather than Law's mentor, Boehme, who spoke more in terms of a dramatic 'flash' of divine light which suddenly breaks through the darkness of the soul.[66] Erskine regularly used Law as a metaphorical source, employing in particular his organic imagery of Jesus as the root or sap in the tree or vine to represent the universal saving humanity of Christ.[67] The borrowing of imagery was coupled with direct quotation when Erskine came to his fundamental concept of universal pardon, which itself may have been stimulated by *The Spirit of Prayer* and *The Spirit of Love* where 'universal love', universal mercy', and 'universal redemption' are prominent. Though Erskine had embraced the concept of universal pardon before reading Law's mystical works in 1827, the publication of *The Unconditional Freeness of the Gospel* immediately followed in which a new and confident dimension appeared, suggesting Erskine had discovered a source for strong, authoritative reinforcement of his own prior convictions. The universality of the gospel, together with the universal purpose of divine love devoted to the "restoration of the ruined race" in which "individual drops are...merged in the ocean", were notions Erskine drew directly from Law, citing approvingly word for word (albeit unacknowledged) Law's description of the "liberty, the universality, the impartiality of heaven".[68]

---

[65] Spencer (ed.), *Love*, 209-10.

[66] Hobhouse, *Mystical Writings*, 335-7; David Walsh, *The Mysticism of Innerworldly Fulfillment: A Study of Jacob Boehme* (Gainesville: University Presses of Florida, 1983), 52.

[67] E.g., Spencer (ed.), *Prayer*, 36-8.

[68] *Freeness*, 110-12, (taken from Spencer [ed.], *Prayer*, 125).

Like Erskine, Law was a determined opponent of Calvinist dogma, regarding *imputation, election, reprobation, satisfaction,* and the *wrath of God*, as "detestable" doctrines and the "grossest of all Fictions".[69] It is likely that Erskine derived his innovatory doctrine of election, with its ultimate logical conclusion, universal salvation, from Law, who clearly taught the possibility of post-mortem sanctification and universal restoration or *apokatastasis*.[70] In *The Spirit of Love*, Law set out the concept, which Erskine was to follow closely, of the two natures, darkness and light, residing simultaneously within humanity as two 'seeds'. The divine seed was 'elected' for salvation; the "fallen evil nature", from which we were to be redeemed, was designated for 'reprobation'. These two natures corresponded to 'Adam' and 'Christ', so that

> the whole *unalterable* Ground of Divine *Election* and *Reprobation*...relates not to any particular Number of People, or Division of Mankind, but solely to the two Natures that are, both of them, without Exception, in every Individual of Mankind...Election therefore and Reprobation, as respecting Salvation, equally relate to every Man in the World; because every Man, as such, has *That* in him which *only* is elected, and that in him which only is reprobated...[71]

Erskine likewise described the corporate nature of humanity in terms of

> the two heads, Adam and Christ, – each being the head of all men, and therefore all men having a part in each; Adam being the corrupt fountain, and therefore rejected, Christ being the renewed fountain, and therefore elected.[72]

Within Erskine's understanding of election, several major ideas combined. His version of entire sanctification, where "sanctification and salvation are all one",[73] and the qualities of spiritual excellence, sanctity of life and holiness were based on reproducing the life of Christ and partaking of the character of God as the necessary salvific outcome of true faith, were predicated on the understanding that Christ came to redeem, restore and perfect corrupt human nature through assuming our fallen flesh and saving us by his new human nature. As with Law, this owed much to an understanding of the fall which was more figurative than historical, consisting essentially of humanity's loss of belief in the love of God and its bleak consequence of selfish independence, but involving the overriding divine goal of ultimate

---

[69] Spencer (ed.), *Prayer*, 108, cf., 138; Spencer (ed.), *Love*, 233.
[70] Spencer (ed.), *Love*, 238-9.
[71] Spencer (ed.), *Love*, 262-4.
[72] *Election*, 305.
[73] *Freeness* 212.

restoration.[74] It is no surprise, therefore, that the idea of salvation as an ongoing process of sanctification by "unerring Conformity to the Life and Spirit of Christ" was a key theme in Law.[75] The focus of Erskine's salvific thought on the idea of "an immanent Christ mediating salvation to us through His humanity, into which we are taken", was strongly developed in the incarnational theology movement of the later nineteenth century, where, significantly, one of its foremost proponents, Charles Gore, cited William Law as a primary source.[76]

It is likely, too, that Erskine's subjective understanding of atonement and suffering was influenced by Law who dealt with it at length in *The Spirit of Love*.[77] Erskine's understanding of 'Hell' as a state of mind or 'disease of the soul',[78] evidently mirrored Law's assertion that Jesus "hung and expired, bleeding on the Cross, not to atone [God's] *own* Wrath against us, but to extinguish our *own Hell* within us, to pour his heavenly Love into us...".[79] Further anticipating Erskine, Law had insisted that the atonement of Christ was representative rather than substitutionary: "He did not suffer in *our Place or Stead*, but only *on our Account*, which is a quite different Matter".[80] Erskine's conviction that the sufferings of Christ were not 'sacrificial' or 'propitiatory' in the traditional sense, and his determination to confront Calvinism by insisting on an understanding of the cross as a manifestation of divine love instead of the appeasement of divine wrath also seems to have been inspired by Law, who had declared that

> the infinite Love, Mercy, and Compassion of God towards fallen Man, are not *purchased*, or *procured* for us by the Death of Christ, but the Incarnation and Sufferings of Christ come from, and are given to us by the infinite *antecedent* Love of God for us, and are the gracious Effects of his own Love and Goodness towards us.[81]

---

[74] See *Election* 257 (footnote); *Sp.Order*, 245. For Law, see Spencer (ed.), *Prayer*, 20-2, 35, 37, 58; Spencer (ed.), *Love*, 253.

[75] Spencer (ed.), *Prayer*, 127.

[76] Charles Gore, "Our Lord's Human Example", *Church Quarterly Review*, XVI, XXXII (1883), 298-300.

[77] Spencer (ed.), *Love*, 231-59.

[78] *Freeness*, 9.

[79] Spencer (ed.), *Prayer*, 138, cf., Spencer (ed.), *Love*, 233.

[80] Spencer (ed.), *Love*, 246.

[81] Spencer (ed.), *Love*, 234.

William Law and the Influence of Edward Irving

We have established that in 1827 Erskine was thoroughly immersed in the mystical writings of William Law, and that Law probably exercised strong formative influence on him. Nevertheless, controversy remains concerning the extent to which Erskine derived his innovatory christology from Law as opposed to Edward Irving, given its close resemblance to Irving's equally innovatory teaching regarding the fallen humanity of Christ.

Law had stated his position concerning the nature of redeemed corporate humanity:

> It is God's unlimited, universal Mercy to all Mankind; and every human Creature, as sure as he is born of *Adam*, has a Birth of the Bruiser of the Serpent within him, and so is infallibly in Covenant with God through Jesus Christ.[82]

Erskine had already adopted the organic concept of the Headship of Christ in *Remarks on the Internal Evidence for the Truth of Revealed Religion*,[83] and he now eagerly developed the federal redemptive concept of Jesus as

> the New Head of the human nature…the second Adam, the real unfigurative Head of the human body. He had suffered death as a partaker of that tainted life which was under the curse; and then He rose again with a new life infused into Him.[84]

This mirrored Law's own assertion that

> Because, by what Christ was in Himself, by what He was in us, by his whole *State*, *Character*, and the Divine *Appointment*, we all had that *natural Union* with Him, and *Dependence* upon Him, as our Head in the Way of Redemption, as we had with *Adam* as our Head in the Way of our natural Birth. So that as it must be said, that because *Adam* fell, we must of all Necessity be Heirs of his fallen State, so with the same Truth and from the same Necessity of the Thing, it must be said, that because Christ our Head is risen victorious out of our fallen State, we as his Members, and having his Seed within us, must be and are made Heirs of all his Glory.[85]

The first intimation of Erskine's distinctive christological views, however, appeared to coincide with publication of Irving's controversial incarna-

---

[82] Spencer (ed.), *Prayer*, 43.
[83] E.g., *Evidence*, 102.
[84] Letter to Rachel Erskine, July 1829, *Letters-I*, 156.
[85] Spencer (ed.), *Love*, 257-8.

tional christology relating to the fallen humanity of Christ.[86] Irving set out his christological ideas in his 1828 sermons on "The Doctrine of the Incarnation Opened",[87] in the magazine, *The Morning Watch*, from March 1829, and in subsequent 1830 publications.[88] Erskine's announcement of the "great secret", specifying that Christ was "a partaker of [our] tainted life", and "was in our fallen nature", initially appeared in private correspondence dating from July 1829.[89] He proceeded to publish his soteriologically motivated views concerning "that great truth of the fallen humanity of Jesus" in 1831 in *The Brazen Serpent,* when he questioned

> why was this suffering of our nature in the person of Jesus needful? It was a *fallen nature;* a nature which had fallen by sin, and which, in consequence of this, lay under condemnation. He came into it as a new head, that he might take it out of the fall, and redeem it from sin, and lift it up to God.[90]

The chronological coincidence might seem to favour assumptions that some transference of ideas took place from Irving to Erskine. However, Erskine, though well aware of the huge controversy concerning the humanity of Christ, as far as we know never formally acknowledged any debt to Irving in this connection. Consequently, Law must arguably remain a potential alternative source for Erskine's christology. We know that Law made such an impression on Erskine that *The Unconditional Freeness of the Gospel*, published early in 1827, reflected his new-found enthusiasm, though as the fallen humanity of Christ was not addressed in *The Unconditional Freeness of the Gospel*, we may assume that Erskine decided to avoid such additional potentially offensive controversy at that time. Conceivably, the Irving controversy served as catalyst and pretext for subsequent open statement of his already forming convictions.

Though Harry Johnson and Nicholas Needham continue to regard Irving as the most likely source for Erskine's christology,[91] we prefer to regard any influential role he may have played in terms of pioneer and model, rather than mentor. Erskine may possibly have had Irving in mind when in

---

[86] For useful summaries of Irving's christology see Thomas Weinandy, *In the Likeness of Sinful Flesh* (Edinburgh: T.&T. Clark, 1993), 56-61; Strachan, *Pentecostal Theology*, 25-52.

[87] See *The Collected Writings of Edward Irving*, in 5 volumes, G. Carlyle [ed.] (London: Alexander Strahan, 1865), Volume V.

[88] Edward Irving, *The Orthodox and Catholic Doctrine of Our Lord's Human Nature* (London: Baldwin and Cradock, 1830); *The Opinions Circulating Concerning Our Lord's Human Nature* (Edinburgh: John Lindsay, 1830).

[89] Letters to Rachel Erskine, July 1829, and unknown correspondent, 15 January 1830, *Letters-I,* 156, 287.

[90] *Serpent,* [2nd edition], 33-4.

[91] Harry Johnson, *The Humanity of the Saviour* (London: Epworth Press, 1962), 182; Needham, *Thomas Erskine,* 241-2, 474-7.

1830 he applauded the 'revival' in his day of the 'glorious truth' concerning the incarnation.[92] But no dependence is implied. Once again, it seems conceivable that we may be dealing with what we have come to regard as the semi-spontaneous development of doctrine among like-minded individuals. Even Irving's former assistant, David Brown, in denouncing Irving, McLeod Campbell, and Erskine for their christological teaching, assumed a common approach rather than an individual source.[93] Erskine's engrossment in Law and divine-human union dated from before the onset of the Irving christological controversy. By contrast, his knowledge of Irving's christological teaching appears to have been relatively second-hand. Though Erskine had been reading a *prophetical* work of Irving's in Rome in April 1827, it was with mixed feelings, and he particularly remarked that he much preferred reading Law to Irving.[94] No direct evidence supports Needham's conviction that Erskine must have read, and been influenced by, Irving's works relating to the humanity of Christ. No specific acknowledgement to Irving is ever admitted, not even in private correspondence, although he regarded Irving's memory highly. Furthermore, in later life Erskine expressly stated under inquiry that he never read Irving's lectures, and he diverged sharply from Irving on matters relating to spiritual authority.[95] He demurred from assisting Mrs Oliphant in her biography of Irving on the basis that his knowledge of Irving was slight.[96] We also know that John McLeod Campbell shared similar sentiments concerning Irving.[97]

We cannot discount the possibility that Irving himself might have been influenced by reading William Law, perhaps at the suggestion of his close friend Samuel Taylor Coleridge, who was a known admirer of Law.[98] F.D. Maurice certainly thought Coleridge was a major influence on Irving.[99]

---

[92] *Serpent*, 129-30.

[93] David Brown, "Letter to a Friend Entangled in Error", *ECI*, II (February and March, 1833), 73-86, 144-53. Brown singled out *The Brazen Serpent* and a sermon of Campbell's for specific criticism. John McLeod Campbell had emphasised how Christ "*took sinful flesh*", (Sermon XIV, *Sermons and Lectures*, in 2 volumes, (3rd edition) [Greenock: R.B. Lusk, 1832], I, 339).

[94] Letters to Miss C. Erskine, 12 April 1827, Thomas Chalmers, 19 April 1827, Miss Rachel Erskine, 10 November 1827, *Letters-I*, 109, 110, 123-4.

[95] See Letter to Thomas Chalmers, 19 April 1827, *NCE CHA* 4. 73. 16; Letter to Mrs Schwabe, 26 July 1854, *NLS MS* 9747-49; cf., Letters to Miss C. Erskine, 12 April 1827, Miss Rachel Erskine, 2 May and 10 November 1827, Edward Irving, probably 16 October 1834, Miss Stuart, 13 December 1834, *Letters-I*, 109, 116, 124, 230-2, 232; Letter to F.D. Maurice, 15 November 1860, *Letters-II*, 134-5.

[96] Letter to F.D. Maurice, 15 November 1860, *Letters-II*, 134-5.

[97] George M. Tuttle, *So Rich A Soil: John McLeod Campbell on Christian Atonement* (Edinburgh: The Handsel Press, 1986), 147 (note 18).

[98] See Coleridge, *Biographia Literaria*, 75.

[99] Maurice, *Sacrifice*, xiv. Edward Irving's main theological mentors were Richard Hooker and John Owen, with Owen in particular influencing his pneumatology, (*DHT*,

And Law taught an incarnational atonement clearly based on a divine-human union:

> Christ given *for us*, is neither more nor less, than Christ given *into us*. And he is in no other Sense, our full, perfect, and sufficient Atonement, than as his Nature and Spirit are born, and formed in us, which so purge us from our Sins, that we are thereby in Him, and by Him dwelling in us, become new Creatures...[100]

Law, through his idea of the divine birth of Christ in the soul, affirmed the universal, organic presence of the Spirit as a divine "inward Seed" affording union between God and humanity from before the fall. Expounding a novel prototypical spiritual incarnation, and an organic universalism which Erskine was to appropriate as his own, Law affirmed that

> the eternal *Word*, or Son of God, did not then first begin to be the Saviour of the World, when He was Born in *Bethlehem* of *Judea*; but that Word which became Man in the Virgin *Mary*, did, from the Beginning of the World, enter as a *Word* of Life, a *Seed* of Salvation, into the first Father of Mankind...Hence it is, that...the Divine Nature is within you, given unto your first Father, into the Light of his Life, and from him, rising up in the life of every Son of *Adam*.[101]

Law taught distinctly that Christ assumed fallen humanity so that the actual incarnation of the Son of God realised a complete restoration to "that *first State* of Holiness" in human nature of that life of Christ which Adam had lost, and was the necessary "Cause of the Renewal of the Divine Life in the human Nature" which is 'efficacious' in effecting our salvation:

> God became Man, took upon him a Birth from the fallen Nature...the Son, the Word of God, entered by a Birth into this fallen Nature, that by this mysterious Incarnation all the fallen Nature might be *born again* of him according to the *Spirit*, in the *same Reality*, as they were born of *Adam* according to the *Flesh*.[102]

Again, God sent Jesus

> to take the human Nature upon Him, in its fallen State, that by this mysterious Union of God and Man...every human Creature might have a Power of

---

275-6). The origins of Irving's innovatory christology, however, remain highly controversial. For surveys of possible antecedents see Johnson, *Humanity*, 178-89; Needham, *Thomas Erskine*, 474-477.

[100] Spencer (ed.), *Love*, 168, 235-6. Sidney Spenser believes Law's source was Boehme, Spencer (ed.), *Prayer*, 35 (footnote 9).

[101] Spencer (ed.), *Prayer*, 42-3.

[102] Spencer (ed.), *Prayer*, 35; Spencer (ed.), *Love*, 167, 253.

being born again according to that Image of God, in which he was first created.[103]

The probability that Erskine creatively appropriated and forged into an innovative and cohesive system a package of connected incarnational soteriological ideas from Law seems more convincing than the suggestion that he adopted an isolated concept from Irving alone. It offers a coherent account of how Erskine developed and combined concepts of christology, prototypical spiritual incarnation, sanctification, self-sacrifice, suffering, and election to produce an innovative, comprehensive scheme of universal incarnational redemption. Thomas Torrance's assertion that Erskine merely taught that Christ 'redeemed' and 'sanctified' fallen human flesh in the act of assumption *through the virgin birth*,[104] omits the novel, broader, prototypical dimension that for Erskine "as Christ was really given to men immediately after the Fall, all are elect in Him, He being in them all".[105] This appeared to derive from Law's singular idea that "the Incarnation…was not limited to the historical manifestation of God in Jesus…his conception, derived from Boehme, [was] of the 'inspoken Word' which entered into Adam after his Fall, and so into all his descendants, and which made it possible for man to be born of God".[106] Therefore,

> from the Moment of Man's Redemption, which began at the Fall, when the *incorruptible Seed of the Word* was given into *Adam*, every Son of *Adam*, to the End of the World, must come into it under one and the same Election and Reprobation with Regard to God.[107]

Accordingly, Erskine was to complete his universal incarnational salvific scheme by demonstrating that "the Spirit of the Word…came into the [human] nature after the fall, as a seed of regeneration, and as an anticipated fruit of the sacrifice of Christ…being in fact the very presence in him of the light and life of Jesus…".[108] He was

> the Word made flesh, who though not personally manifested for four thousand years, yet entered into the nature immediately after the fall, and commenced his great work of the new creation, by bringing his Spirit close to all the individuals of the nature, striving in their consciences, and enabling them to join themselves to him, and in his strength to accept their punishment, and to sacrifice their self-will to the will of God. Wherever this is done, the work of Christ is accomplished, that is, the new nature is formed – for the new na-

---

[103] Spencer (ed.), *Prayer*, 47.
[104] Torrance, *Scottish Theology*, 270.
[105] Letter to Madame Forel, 19 November 1838, *Letters-I*, 337.
[106] Spencer (ed.), *Prayer*, 35 (footnote).
[107] Spencer (ed.), *Love*, 263.
[108] *Election*, 567.

ture, or the new creation, is nothing else than the old nature purged of the corrupt life-blood of self-will, and filled with the will of God instead.[109]

Law's theme of redeemed human nature, and his declaration that all mortals possess the seed of divinity within them which only requires release through revelation, therefore became transmuted by Erskine into a significant innovatory scheme of soteriological thought. For our redemption now was accomplished by the Christ already latent in humanity coming to birth within us, rather than the Christ given for us on the cross as a vicarious substitutionary sacrifice for sin. This meant that, with Law, he understood the incarnation, not as limited to the historical revelation of God in Jesus Christ, but in terms of the 'inspoken Word' (or what Erskine called the indwelling 'seed' or 'inward word') which was implanted into Adam and his descendants immediately after the fall, thus enabling all humanity to be born of God.

Accordingly, we conclude that the weight of evidence suggests Erskine's primary christological dependence was on Law rather than Irving. Law was not only his prime christological source, however, but arguably offered Erskine a substantive framework for harmonising the various elements of his soteriological system. To what extent Erskine, rather than Irving, influenced John McLeod Campbell in his own doctrine of fallen human nature remains open.

Summary

Chapter 8 reviewed the credibility of Erskine's main sources in seeking to understand the inspiration for his innovative, apologetic, soteriological agenda. Rejecting any idea that Erskine's eclectic ideas developed in a vacuum, we highlighted the general influence of the Enlightenment and Romantic movements, which incorporated elements of patristic, Platonic, and mystic thought. Such common elements probably largely account for the strong parallels with developments in Germany (especially in connection with Schleiermacher), and with Unitarian thinking. We questioned the widely assumed link between Erskine and Edward Irving, preferring the hypothesis that William Law was the key formative influence in Erskine's developing incarnational soteriology. More than appropriating selected ideas, he saw in Law the basis for constructing a self-consistent theological scheme which countered the problems posed by Calvinism whilst meeting nineteenth-century sensitivities and arguably maintaining evangelical credentials. The nature of Christ's humanity was conceivably already a formative plank of Erskine's wider apologetic scheme derived from Law, apart

---

[109] *Election*, 279-80.

from Irving's separate, corroborative treatment of it. Though subsequent raising of the issue to controversial heights might lead us to assume that Erskine merely followed Irving, we believe the evidence suggests otherwise.

CHAPTER 9

Erskine in a Reconstructive Victorian Context

Introduction

The 1830s not only saw the accession of Queen Victoria and the inauguration of a new age, but by general consensus the ending of the great age of evangelicalism.[1] Though linked firmly to the evangelical tradition, in many ways Erskine concurrently symbolised the new inquiring spirit of the Victorian age. Otto Pfleiderer suggested the publication of Coleridge's *Aids to Reflection* in 1825 marked the beginning of the revolutionary Romantic reconstructive philosophical/ theological movement in Britain.[2] However, as we have noted, Erskine predated Coleridge in theological publication terms. Whilst acknowledging the key significance of Coleridge, John Tulloch's review of nineteenth-century religious thought nevertheless recognises Erskine as its earliest starting point.[3] David Bebbington regards Erskine's early contribution to the reformulation of doctrine as of "landmark" significance, and notes that only Erskine and John McLeod Campbell from the evangelical tradition achieved any kind of serious theological impact during the century.[4] As Julia Wedgwood recognised, Erskine may arguably be considered alongside Coleridge in terms of his pioneering significance for the theological direction of the century.[5] Bernard Reardon points out the importance of the fact that Erskine's published work actually preceded that of Coleridge by five years, and that his contribution was sufficiently innovatory not only to provoke establishment antagonism, but to inspire pivotal religious leaders.[6]

---

[1] Doreen Rosman, *Evangelicals and Culture* (London: Croom Helm, 1984), 34-7.
[2] Pfleiderer, *Theology*, 355.
[3] Tulloch, *Movements*, 254.
[4] Bebbington, *Evangelicalism*, 92, 139.
[5] Wedgwood, *Teachers*, 74.
[6] Reardon, *Religious Thought*, 294-5, 299.

We are concerned in this chapter to connect Erskine more closely with his context, and consider factors which fuelled his eclectic tendency to reflect a wider nineteenth-century British and American innovative theological milieu, rather than the more confined, conservative, religious outlook of his native Scotland. We note some of the more important ways in which Erskine anticipated, mirrored and influenced major theological, ethical, and social trends of the Victorian age, drawing illustrative comparison with selected key nineteenth-century figures alongside whom Erskine stands as representative of the tendencies which were transforming salvific religion.

The Divine Purpose

The mission of removing incrustations of tradition which obscured eternal universal truths and the original divine order was essentially a Romantic and Platonic one.[7] Erskine's novel vision of an ordered, righteous, spiritual society tended to replace a developed ecclesiology in his thinking, and anticipated mid-nineteenth century Christian Socialist ideas. The expression 'spiritual order' was, in effect, an 'ethico-politico-spiritual' concept standing for a soteriological vision of authentic freedom in which all people realised their true status in a relationship of 'brotherhood' under the divine government and eternal loving Fatherhood of God. It anticipated Ritschl's ethical 'kingdom of God', and von Harnack's "nation of brothers".[8]

Erskine understood God's 'Fatherhood' in a personal, dynamic, world-engaging, universal sense, in which society's order and unity was to be located in restored relationship with God. Reacting to the indifferent Deist divinity of the previous century, the 'humanisation' of God into more 'comfortable' categories also represented the rediscovery of aspects of the divine nature marginalised by Calvinist sovereignty, and reflected an underlying anxiety to find ways of coping with the challenges posed by nineteenth-century scientific, historical, and philosophical developments. By the end of the century, the conservative, evangelical, Glasgow theologian, James Orr, lamented concerning the 'new theology' (of which Erskine was seen as a pioneer), "that God is now regarded as universal Father, whereas formerly this relation of Fatherhood was limited to believers", and that now the 'essence' of the gospel was that "God is the Father of all men; and the relationship of Fatherhood and sonship is held to exhaust the relation subsisting between God and Mankind".[9] The Free Church leader, J.S. Can-

---

[7] Newsome, *Two Classes*, 111-14.

[8] Albrecht Ritschl, "Instruction in the Christian Religion" [1875], in *Three Essays*, (Philip Hefner, ed.) (Philadelphia: Fortress Press, 1972), 222-32; Harnack, *What is Christianity?*, 59-61, 79-81, 87.

[9] James Orr, *The Progress of Dogma* (London: Hodder and Stoughton, 1901), 325, 339.

dlish, approved the emphasis on God's Fatherhood, but agreed that "the difference between us and the school of Erskine is, that while they make that fatherhood and its blessed consequences natural and universal, we regard it as special and gracious". He warned that 'Universal Fatherhood' teaching involved neo-platonic, mystic, and semi-pantheistic tendencies, and resulted in what he regarded as characteristic 'Broad Church' minimising of the 'judicial' doctrines of judgment, condemnation, law, and justification.[10] Notwithstanding later tendencies, for Erskine, it was a soteriological bedrock, the "living union of God with humanity, and not an historical matter, but an eternal spiritual order", an existential 'life in the Spirit', in which humanity rediscovered its rightful relationship of divine order and sonship: "To live in the Spirit is the right condition of man, his normal condition, out of which he is out of order; and to live in the Spirit is to live with God – hearing Him, and knowing Him, and loving Him, and delighting to do His will".[11]

His was a dependent, total, lived-out Christianity, one which, by all accounts, Erskine embodied in his personal saintly life. It bore comparison especially with Schleiermacher's concept of the 'Christian consciousness' in which an experiential sense of redemption through participation and union with Christ was construed in terms of the harmony of the soul with the governing laws and principles of the universe.[12] A major nineteenth-century concern related to whether 'righteousness' was a *legal* or *ethical* quality, a question of *position* or *character*. For Erskine, it was impossible that ethics could conceivably be separated from theology.[13] He redefined 'salvation' as ethical spiritual life lived in a higher consciousness – a "real substantial righteousness...not a mere forgiving of past sin"[14]; not escape from punishment, but deliverance from sin. This necessarily involved both "filial trust", which was the powerful salvific "root-principle" for producing inward righteousness, and "the highest and deepest morality" within the context of a disordered world of sin and suffering.[15] Erskine considered the latter to be God's necessary training school, for "Salvation is true order in the moral world. It means a deliverance from disorder, not a deliverance from punishment, for punishment is desirable when it corrects disorder".[16]

---

[10] Candlish, "Thomas Erskine", 126-7.

[11] Letters to Mrs Schwabe, 9 September 1857 and F.D. Maurice, 28 June 1859, *Letters-II*, 119, 133.

[12] See Schleiermacher, *Christian Faith* §100, 425-31, and Anon., "The Church and Theology of Germany During the Nineteenth Century", *National Review*, XVIII (January-April, 1864), 210-11.

[13] *Sp.Order*, 236.

[14] *Sp.Order*, 149.

[15] *Sp.Order*, 119-20, 149.

[16] Letter to Madame Forel, 24 April 1862, *Letters-II*, 236.

For Erskine, as we have noted, the gospel itself (or more particularly the Christ of the gospel) contained the revelatory power – the "divine dynamics" – not only to deliver from the impact of sin, but to set people free from sin itself into a life of positive righteousness.[17] Mirroring the tendency of his age to reject penal, retributory or deterrent theories of punishment, he presented the issue of human-divine accountability in such a way as to minimise the judicial aspect and emphasise instead a free-will obedience emanating from a relationship of love in which the threat of eternal punishment was not a factor influencing response and behaviour.

Erskine developed a friendship with F.D. Maurice (1805-72) who visited him at Linlathen, and became, in many ways, a natural successor to Erskine, acknowledging significant debt to him.[18] Both men were primarily 'modernists' or 'mediators', concerned to reconcile those watchwords of the Enlightenment, 'reason' and 'conscience', to the Christian faith. They recognised this involved a more contemporary re-statement of orthodox doctrines like the atonement within the context of a universal relational theology of God's 'Fatherhood' and Christian 'brotherhood' in terms which did not offend post-Enlightenment moral sensitivity and distrust of external authority, credal doctrine, and tradition. Both Erskine and Maurice were transitional and reconstructive figures in the sense that, in a generation which acutely experienced deep spiritual uncertainties and anxieties concerning the divine purpose, they were prepared to criticise and reformulate what they considered to be defective or obsolete forms of theological expression, whilst nevertheless retaining a strong determination that nothing of enduring spiritual worth should be lost. Both men made the universal fatherhood of God, participatory atonement, collective inaugurated eschatology, and universal salvation key features of their teaching, before they became hallmarks of the century. Both were described as "Christian optimists", and both held the concept of post-mortem divine education.[19]

The anxiety caused by Victorian uncertainty partly accounts for Erskine's preoccupation with the necessity for *certain* knowledge of the pur-

---

[17] *Sp.Order*, 119, cf., 131, 200, 243.

[18] See Frederick Denison Maurice, *The Prophets and Kings of the Old Testament* (London: Macmillan and Co., 1886). The original 1852 edition incorporated a dedication to Erskine in recognition of his influence upon him, especially through *The Brazen Serpent*. A further fulsome tribute to Erskine was added to the third edition published in 1871, shortly after Erskine's death. In a letter written concurrently to Erskine in 1852, Maurice explained, "I wished to tell others how much I believe they, as well as I, owe to your books; how they seem to me to mark a crisis in theological movements of this time", (Maurice [ed.], *Life*, II, 150). Maurice described Erskine as "so gentle and truthful and loving; the best man I think I ever knew...", (Maurice [ed.], *Life*, I, 533).

[19] J.H. Leckie, *The World to Come and Final Destiny*, [2nd edition] (Edinburgh: T.&T. Clark, 1922), 265; Frederick Denison Maurice, *The Gospel of the Kingdom of Heaven* [1864] (London: Macmillan and Co., 1888), 262.

pose of God for humanity, a purpose which he radically reconstructed in terms of the loving pre- and post-mortem reformatory (as opposed to *retributory*) education of a loving Father, and which came overwhelmingly to dominate his thought. Erskine was well aware of the *angst* of his age, but Bishop Ewing suggested that "the view of life as an education was a deliverance to him from the Atheism which the aspects of this life without that conception [of an Almighty and Beneficent Creator] would involve".[20] Erskine's concerns were similar to those of historic Roman Catholicism in connection with post-baptismal/ justification sin, though he avoided any doctrine of purificatory purgatorial redemption. His post-mortem hopes followed as a logical inference from his initial commitment to universal pardon, culminating in full universalism.

Maurice was 'naturally drawn' to Erskine because of his elevated view of humanity and his convictions concerning life as the divine education of a loving Father, which accorded with his Unitarian background, though unlike Erskine he tended to hold back from express universalism.[21] Maurice offered an illuminating perspective concerning the contemporary importance of the question of God's character and purpose which Erskine had so emphasised. He posed as one of the great concerns of nineteenth-century moral theology, the question how could God be "absolutely good and righteous" and "the source of all good and righteousness to men"? He saw the vital need of addressing the "doubts and difficulties that arose in human hearts respecting their views of the character of God and of His relation to His creatures...there were doubts whether what was preached was a Gospel at all, whether it was not a message of curses rather than blessings". The issue for Maurice was not how many apologists had 'justified God', but rather had God "justified Himself?". Had God himself "made His own righteousness clear?". This was the crucial question which had to be answered, and Maurice regarded Erskine as a creative pioneer in addressing it:

> I do confess my obligations to that...Scotchman...for making me see, as I had never seen before, that the death of Christ was the answer, given once in the end of the world, to that demand; that in it God did fully manifest His own character; that when a man accepts that death as the revelation of God, he owns Him as altogether righteous, as altogether hating sin; sees that His will is that all should be saved from sin...But it is evident from Mr. Erskine's book on Election, that he has perceived more to be involved in this belief than he, perhaps at first, was aware of. 'God', it is said, 'was in Christ reconciling the world to Himself'. 'It pleased God', says St. Paul, 'to reveal His Son *in me*, that I might preach Him among the Gentiles'. Was man, then, according to his original constitution related to Christ? Was the reconciliation of the world to God, the restoration of it to its proper condition in the well-

---

[20] *Ewing-II*, 10, cf., Letter to Bishop Ewing, 10 December 1864, *Ewing-I*, 56.
[21] Young, *Maurice*, 132; Rowell, *Hell*, 88.

beloved Son? Was that Son really in Saul of Tarsus, and did he only become Paul the converted when that Son was *revealed* in him? Could he preach to the Gentiles, who were bowing to gods of wood and stone, Christ is in you? So, 'Barclay and the Friends' had said. It was very shocking to agree with Barclay and the Friends; but I saw no help for it. They said what I found St. Paul and St. John were saying…they said what enabled me, when I grasped it and believed it, to feel that I was in union with every man, however he might differ from me; and that I had nothing good in me but what belongs equally to him.[22]

Erskine, we are reminded, had shown in Christianised Platonic terms that 'to know the good is to do the good'. The relationship between human and divine character was that

the character of man depends on that which is his confidence…The thing in which I put my confidence for happiness has necessarily a directing influence over my whole being; it communicates its own nature to me…Confidence in God makes me one with God…My confidence rests upon what I know of God's character…[23]

It was in his later work, as Maurice noted, that Erskine extensively developed the idea that the recognition and production of God's character in human beings was the logical outworking of Christ's organic presence within the whole of redeemed humanity itself. John McLeod Campbell asserted the same thing.[24] As Maurice acknowledged, it was Erskine's 'Quaker' ideas which initially fuelled Maurice's own salvific principle "*that Christ is in every man*", and that recognition and belief of God's loving Fatherhood in and of itself reconciles humanity to God.[25]

In theological parallel with the Romantic movement, Erskine did much in his century to boost understanding of an elevated human role within the overall purposes of God, and his views were largely adopted by the Broad Church grouping in which Erskine occupied venerable founding status, alongside Coleridge. Nevertheless, by 1868 he still felt that the lessons of the Row affair had not been learnt. Referring to a new generation of Church of Scotland leaders who seemed repentant for its past actions, Erskine affirmed

All that class of men condemn the deposition of Mr. Campbell. And yet I believe that neither in the Church of Scotland nor in the Church of England is the root of the question then agitated understood to this day. Is a man to be-

---

[22] Maurice, *Sacrifice*, xix-xx.
[23] Letter to Madame de Broglie, 14 June 1838, *Letters-I,* 314-5.
[24] Campbell, Sermon XIII, in *Notes of Sermons*, II, 3-5.
[25] Maurice, *Sacrifice*, xxii and 191-3. Maurice engaged in dialogue with the Quakers, calling them back to historic principles.

come a child of God, or is a man already a child of God in virtue of his being a man?[26]

The implications for soteriology were far-reaching. J.S. Candlish felt it was important to recognise the implications of what Erskine, Coleridge and other Broad Church representatives like F.D. Maurice and Charles Kingsley, had actually accomplished:

> When they speak of Christ in every man, they are not using a mere vague unmeaning phrase; and when they speak of all men being sons of God, they are not employing a figurative expression, which raises a mere question of words as to the propriety of its application. It is utterly vain to attempt to meet their position by nicely drawn distinctions, admitting that all men are sons of God by nature in one sense, but holding that there is another sonship with higher privileges peculiar to believers. Any kind of sonship which can be thus had in various ways and degrees, is utterly foreign to their theories. They hold a real and proper sonship, founded on the doctrine that mankind has been created in the Son of God, and that he really dwells in every one of the race, whether they know it or not. No advantage is gained in controversy with them, by admitting a universal sonship of man founded merely on creation in God's image, for that as compared with their idea of sonship is a mere figure of speech, and it tends to make all sonship seem purely figurative.[27]

Erskine's favourite supporting text was Colossians 1.27: "Christ in you, the hope of glory", and he interpreted this as "describing the condition of every man", and as "parallel to" 'man being made in God's image':

> We are members of the Head, whether living members or not; *but this high condition* of our creation is to us the assurance of our Father's loving purpose towards us, and is also the capacity in us of being really and spiritually partakers of the Divine nature, and fellow-workers with God in working out His gracious purpose.[28]

We may recognise here essential innovative elements of Erskine's soteriology: the need to recognise our origins and calling within the 'spiritual order' so that we may actualise our salvation; the incarnational and participative emphasis in sharing or 'recapitulating' Christ's life, with clear pietistic overtones of human sanctification; the semi-Pelagian strand of co-operating with God in working out our own salvation through the events of life, which represents Erskine's theodicy of suffering sanctification. But Erskine always denied he was advocating salvation by works. He opposed any idea of "mere effort to produce that condition which was demanded by the conscience", because it implied doing something to change God's feelings to-

---

[26] Letter to Bishop Ewing, 26 May [no year], *Ewing-II*, 40.
[27] Candlish, "Thomas Erskine", 124-5.
[28] Letter to Rev. David Russell, 13 June 1865, *Letters-II*, 175.

wards us. Rather, human beings should produce works based on their harmony with and knowledge of "the laws of the unseen world".[29] Our capacity to follow Christ was therefore dependent on our choosing by our free will to actualise Christ's incarnate presence within us, something which is universally possible because he is actually already organically 'in' all members of the human race. His potentially full, motivating, presence and power can therefore be experienced by all who choose to appropriate it, resulting necessarily in ethical outworking.

It was a major difficulty for Erskine's organic soteriology that, whilst Christ lived and died for all, not everyone would actually be saved. He was obliged to hold an unsatisfactory transitional position between limited salvation and universalism until the publication of *The Doctrine of Election*. The theological dilemma then became that of advocating universal restoration without infringing human freedom. His response involved his innovatory concept of educationary 'punishment' and 'recapitulatory atonement' to subdue the rebellious will. Erskine's repeated stress on the importance of existentially comprehending God's purpose for humanity becomes comprehensible when we recognise that to embrace that purpose, acceptance of the Father's remedial 'punishment' is, for him, "always therapeutic and didactic", and therefore salvific in itself.[30] We may concur with Connop Thirlwall, then Bishop of St. David's, that such an idea seems both naïve and patently contrary to reality.[31] Nevertheless, Erskine struck the chord of 'human progress' which was manifestly in tune with the spirit of his age. He developed the concept into his revolutionary 'great idea' of life as a divine 'spiritual education' programme for all, to be "continued through all stages of their being until the righteousness of God is fulfilled in them".[32] God's supreme Fatherly plan is thus revealed to be that all of humanity will eventually be fitted, by means of an individually-tailored "suitable course of education" into "the great organized body of the humanity of which Christ is the Head", by means of a gradual process of growth in righteousness towards perfect holiness.[33]

Erskine is often criticised for his peculiar ideas of entire post-mortem sanctification and universal restoration. Ultimately it was the logic of his search for a satisfactory theodicy which forced him to embrace that pioneering and controversial step for an evangelical, that the salvific process

---

[29] Wedgwood, *Teachers*, 72; Letter to Madame de Staël, 4 September 1829, *Letters-I*, 160.

[30] Hart, *Teaching Father*, 42.

[31] Letter to Bishop Ewing, [probably in 1871], *Ewing-II*, 9-10.

[32] *Sp.Order*, 221, cf., 64-5.

[33] Letter to Bishop Ewing, 16 September 1865, *Ewing-I*, 61, cf., Letter to Mrs Blackwell, 23 June 1862, *Letters-II*, 263.

must continue, if necessary, even after death.[34] John McLeod Campbell, who strongly diverged from Erskine's universalism, accepted that "that great distinguishing element in his thoughts, viz., his expectation as to 'the restitution of all things'", actually "had a place in him before I knew him". Campbell felt, however, that it was only in later life that it began totally to dominate his thinking, becoming almost the very "Gospel itself". Nevertheless, he considered that Erskine's strong condemnation of sin distinguished him from standard universalist positions. Whilst regretting that Erskine's focus on the issue in the posthumous *The Spiritual Order* distorted and misrepresented his overall thought, Campbell consoled himself that Erskine's idea of "final restitution" was infinitely preferable to the increasingly fashionable "annihilation".[35]

It was apparently Erskine's life-long wrestling with the Kantian struggle of 'good versus evil' which eventually led him logically to a universalistic solution.[36] The 'larger hope' was apparent in Erskine's thought from an early date,[37] and was probably influenced by his reading of John Foster and William Law, both of whom were instrumental in popularising universalism in Britain. Coleridge had also not excluded the possibility of universal salvation.[38] Whilst he believed that evil would necessarily ultimately be overcome by good, Erskine could not accept the "destruction" and "annihilation" of evil human beings: "that is not the victory of good over evil, but the victory of strength over weakness. The victory of good over evil is the conversion of all evil beings into good beings".[39] The belief in the possibility of moral progress after death, as espoused by Erskine, was in the later nineteenth century boosted by evolutionary thought which found it comforting to understand the concept of hell in quasi-purgatorial terms. In this

---

[34] *Faith*, 91. Erskine admitted that, because from everyday observation the divine process of education into righteousness was not generally evident, it was logically necessary for him to extend the process for an infinite period into post-mortem experience, (*Sp.Order*, 69-70, 75).

[35] John McLeod Campbell, Letters to Mrs MacNabb, 4 March 1868, his eldest son, 17 December 1870, and his third son, 7 July 1871, *Memorials*, II, 198-9, 294-5, 317. J.H. Leckie viewed Erskine as an "evangelical" universalist (as distinct from e.g., 'Unitarian universalists') because his 'larger hope' remained based on the cross. He considered that those who followed him in his belief, apart from the obvious examples of Maurice, Stanley, and the poets Tennyson and Browning, included George MacDonald, Andrew Jukes, and Samuel Cox, (*World to Come*, 269-72).

[36] For Kant, see Reardon, *Kant*, 123-44.

[37] The first unambiguous statement is in a letter to his cousin, Miss Rachel Erskine, 2 January 1827, *Letters-I*, 92.

[38] Leckie, *World to Come*, 266-7; Rowell, *Hell*, 67, 73.

[39] Letter to an unknown correspondent [no date], *Letters-II*, 237.

way, Erskine's concept of suffering and pain in this life as a necessary corollary to spiritual progress was simply extended to the next world.[40]

The certainty Erskine felt concerning "the final salvation of the whole human race" was therefore the logical outcome of his fundamental convictions regarding the eternal righteous character and purpose of God. In about 1863, he declared, with pointed topical reference to the popular writings of contemporary geologist Hugh Miller, that God's purpose for humanity

> cannot be a purpose confined to any one stage of our being, but must extend over all the stages, and the whole duration of our being. It is surely most unreasonable to suppose that God should change His manner of dealing with us, as soon as we quit this world, and that if we have resisted, up to that moment, His gracious endeavours to teach us righteousness, He should at once abandon the purpose for which He created us and redeemed us, and give us up to the everlasting bondage of sin...it is really contrary to sound criticism to hold, that...any ground is allowed or given for a doubt as to the final salvation of the whole human race...No; He who waited so long for the formation of a piece of old red sandstone will surely wait with much long-suffering for the perfecting of a human spirit.[41]

Erskine and Nineteenth-Century Incarnational Soteriology

Though Erskine developed the concept of eternal sonship pre-eminently in *The Doctrine of Election*, it was in about 1830/1831, from *The Brazen Serpent*, that F.D. Maurice began to recognise the revolutionary truth that the central doctrine of Christianity was the incarnation rather than the atonement, and that the true gospel for humanity could not be based merely on traditional views of human sinfulness and the fall.[42]

In *The Brazen Serpent*, Erskine developed his radical soteriological notion of the presence and headship of Christ in every person resulting from his sanctifying human flesh. He brought together concepts of the fullness of the gospel as a revelation of God's nature and character, the universality of love, and the knowledge of God in a new theology of spiritual rebirth. The full character of God as love, rather than as Creator, was not revealed until the fall which "drew forth that full manifestation of his character". Because

> that manifestation is made *in* a *man*, who is the root of the nature, and so connected with every individual of the nature, the character so declared is

---

[40] See Richard J. Bauckham, "Universalism: a historical survey", *Themelios* 4, 2 (January, 1979), 51. Joseph John Murphy was one who acknowledged significant debt to Erskine in disseminating the 'larger hope', in his popular *The Scientific Bases of Faith* (London: Macmillan and Co., 1873).

[41] Letter to Mr Craig, (probably 1863), *Letters-II*, 238-42.

[42] Elliott-Binns, *Religion*, 282.

more than a manifestation; it becomes an infusion; it is a new sap. It is laid up *in that man,* as in a fountain, that it may flow through the rest of the members, just as they open their mouths to receive it. In this way whatever is manifested of God in his dealings with us, when *known,* enters into us, and becomes *life.* And thus it is that life eternal consists in the *knowledge* of the only true God, and Jesus Christ whom he hath sent. And thus also it is that we become partakers of the divine nature, even now, through the knowledge of those promises, which declare the character of God.[43]

Revelatory 'spiritual apprehension' was necessary to release the salvific, self-evidencing, universally implanted divine nature from its latent state within the individual. Erskine here appeared to share with Maurice something akin to a supralapsarian view of the fall as ultimately beneficial and in accord with the ultimate purposes of God.[44] Erskine's developed thinking with regard to the generic humanity of Christ within what has widely been perceived to be an Irvingite incarnational christology[45] was crucial for the operation of Erskine's revolutionary soteriological dynamics:

Unless Christ was truly a man, there was no revelation of the Father through Him to us. My human consciousness enables me to participate in the consciousness of Christ, and the human consciousness is capable of receiving the Divine consciousness.[46]

Erskine asserted that Jesus's "whole life, from the manger to the tomb, was a sacrifice for sin".[47] His commitment to the organic foundational principle of Christ incarnate as the Head of the human nature fuelled his convictions regarding innate human capacity to apprehend and participate in the divine. He was convinced that salvation was effectively incarnational, consisting of the revelation and recognition through the universal divine/ human faculty of conscience, that Christ was already indwelling humanity. Along with Schleiermacher, Erskine has been criticised for elevating the role of human beings in a "private theology of mystical self-consciousness", marginalising the Holy Spirit in realising the presence of God.[48] As we have noted, Erskine preferred the innovative idea of ascribing spiritual capacity to an inward operation of the Spirit which actualised the self-denying presence of Christ within humanity as the true (spiritual) Eucharist.[49] The new humanity was inaugurated through Jesus immediately after the fall, though actually manifested at his incarnation, remaining real and actual irrespec-

---

[43] *Serpent*, 245-6.

[44] Flesseman-Van Leer, *Grace Abounding*, 32-3.

[45] E.g., Needham, *Thomas Erskine*, 241.

[46] Letter to Bishop Ewing, 15 January 1861, *Ewing-I,* 28.

[47] *Serpent*, 54.

[48] Demarest, *General Revelation*, 97.

[49] *Election,* 107-9; Letter to Bishop Ewing, [no date], *Ewing-II,* 61-2.

tive of awareness. The key issue, therefore, became spiritual apprehension and actualisation by identification with the humanity of the risen and ascended Jesus.[50]

Erskine's pioneering incarnational emphasis was taken up enthusiastically in the second half of the nineteenth century. Though marking something of a departure from the traditional evangelical emphasis on the cross, which tended to stress the *distinction* between God and humanity, its immanental stress on the potential of the new humanity inaugurated by Jesus, resonated with the evolutionary, progressive, human-centred atmosphere of the later century and has produced an enduring legacy. In the twentieth century, Thomas Torrance has endorsed and developed the same concept of incarnational reconciliation:

> We are to think of the whole life and activity of Jesus from the cradle to the grave as constituting the vicarious human response to himself which God has freely and unconditionally provided for us. That is not an answer to God which he has given to us through some kind of transaction external to us or over our heads, as it were, but rather one which he has made to issue out of the depths of our human being and life as our own. Nor is it an answer in word only but in deed, not by way of an exemplary event which we may follow but which has no more than symbolical significance, but by way of a final answer to God actualized in the flesh and blood of our human existence and behaviour and which remains eternally valid. Jesus Christ *is* our human response to God. Thus we appear before God and are accepted by him as those who are inseparably united to Jesus Christ our great High Priest in his eternal self-presentation to the Father.[51]

R.H. Hutton

Erskine was aware of the perceived peculiarities of the innovative theological system he had constructed, especially the essential relationship between Christ's divine/ human incarnation and its fitness to meet the needs of humankind, and he feared its rejection.[52] He sensed suspicion and relative isolation, especially in Scotland, in response to his intended apologetic attempts to speak reassuringly into the prevailing climate of human uncertainty regarding the involvement, sympathy, knowability, and trustworthiness of an eternal divine figure in relation to the human condition. Erskine's repeated message had been that we must necessarily know God's loving, righteous, nature and fatherly purpose towards humanity as part of

---

[50] *Election*, 279-80; Letter to Rev. Paton J. Gloag, D.D., March 1858, *Letters-II*, 204-5; Smail, *Once and For All*, 153.

[51] Torrance, *Mediation*, 80.

[52] Wedgwood, *Teachers*; Letter to Mrs Stirling, 23 June 1837, *Letters-I*, 254-5.

our spiritual 'education'. He still considered it axiomatic that God communicates this knowledge directly by divine *revelation*, but to be received by means of capacities divinely built in to the human constitution enabling us to apprehend it. The 'spiritual order' for Erskine was consequently not so much a human philosophical system based on dogmas and abstract ideas, as a 'religion' which 'dominates his spirit'.[53]

Accordingly, in 1862, Erskine was relieved and delighted to discover a new publication which substantially and independently confirmed and reproduced his own views. This was an essay on the incarnation by former Unitarian, and editor of the *National Review* and the *Spectator*, Richard Holt Hutton, published as one of a series of tracts edited by F.D. Maurice.[54] Aimed at providing a reassuring response to the controversy produced by the publication of *Essays and Reviews* in 1860 [55] (widely perceived as a subversive challenge to accepted Christian views), the series adopted a determined middle position between dogmatic tradition at one extreme and liberalism at the other. Erskine welcomed Hutton's essay, hailing it as "one of the most important contributions to theological science which had been made in our day". He suggested that "if I may judge of its author's feelings by my own, I believe that he will be gratified by finding that any other person had independently been led to the same conclusions".[56] It is therefore illuminating to examine the essay more closely for those vital elements considered by Erskine to corroborate his own much earlier innovatory ideas.

Hutton wrote as a recently convinced Anglican and believer in incarnational Christianity amidst a hostile and sceptical milieu.[57] Though he was adamant there could be no return to the old dogmatic orthodoxy, he believed religion needed reconstructing rather than demolishing. He was equally scathing about "the idealising school of religious doubters" who were reducing all divine revelation to human "abstract idealities", and turning theology into "morbid psychology". *Inspiration* regrettably was replacing *revelation* in reference to religious truth.[58]

---

[53] *Sp.Order*, 28-31.

[54] Richard H. Hutton, "The Incarnation and Principles of Evidence, with a Letter to the Writer, by the Rev. F.D. Maurice", in *Tracts for Priests and People,* F.D. Maurice (ed.), No. XIV (Cambridge and London: Macmillan and Co., 1862). For background to the tracts see Brose, *Maurice,* 264-72.

[55] Frederick Temple, et. al., *Essays and Reviews,* [2nd edition] (London: John W. Parker and Son, 1860).

[56] *Sp.Order*, 31 (footnote).

[57] Hutton had been first introduced to belief in the incarnation by F.W. Robertson in 1846/7, though it was F.D. Maurice who helped develop his incarnational thinking in the later 1850s, (Robert H. Tener and Malcolm Woodfield, (eds.), *A Victorian Spectator: Uncollected Writings of R.H. Hutton* [Bristol: The Bristol Press, 1991], 2-3).

[58] Hutton, "Incarnation", 2.

It is not difficult to appreciate why Erskine was delighted with the appearance of Hutton's essay. In an age which increasingly questioned the whole basis for received truth, he had seemed to himself to have ploughed a lone, pioneering furrow for many years, seeking to establish a foundation for Christian assurance based, not on external categories such as Bible and dogma, but on internal divine authorities which provided revealed, self-evidencing, subjective correspondence to objective and historic evidences. The self-revealing ability of God was crucially in question. The means by which human beings were supposed to grasp divine truth had become a critical issue. And despite the somewhat oblique support of men like Campbell and Maurice, for years Erskine had felt himself relatively alone in a hostile environment in advocating incarnational christology as a basis for Christian certainty. Now *Essays and Reviews* had motivated Hutton independently to produce what Erskine regarded as a welcome and vital vindication for his views.

Significantly, incarnational thinking was to dominate the latter decades of the nineteenth century, culminating in the publication in 1889 and 1891 of *Lux Mundi,* edited by Charles Gore, and Gore's own Bampton Lectures on the incarnation.[59] In this regard, had Erskine been less self-effacing, he might have recognised his own innovative role. Though not directly acknowledging Erskine in his essay, it is inconceivable that, as an admirer of F.D. Maurice, Hutton was unaware of Erskine's formative influence on him, and the *Spectator*, under Hutton's editorship, was to pay extended fulsome tribute to Erskine's achievements.

Like Erskine, Hutton argued that divine revelation was not only possible (because God had himself placed within humanity the capacity for knowing him), but essential. Crucially, he regarded the incarnation as "the central truth of the Christian Revelation" which contained within itself the power to "take a strong hold of the human conscience and intellect without aid from the mere external authority of either Church or Bible". Without the incarnation, Hutton believed Christianity was reduced to "a vague idealism"[60] His elevation of conscience as the principal medium by which we apprehend God's love and righteousness, and his stress on the fact that God has placed within humanity the "hopes and yearnings" which correspond perfectly with divine revelation and character so as to match human needs and faith with external and historic testimony, closely replicate Erskine's earliest formulating published thoughts. The existence within humanity of the "highest human virtues", like humility, purity, and self-sacrifice, con-

---

[59] Charles Gore (ed.), *Lux Mundi: A Series of Studies in the Religion of the Incarnation* [12th edition] (London: John Murray, 1891; Charles Gore, *The Incarnation of the Son of God: Being The Bampton Lectures for the Year 1891* [2nd edition] (London: John Murray, 1896).

[60] Hutton, "Incarnation", 9, 57.

firmed for Hutton, as for Erskine, an intuitive conviction that they derived from divine rather than human origin.[61]

Hutton also adopted Erskine's conviction that the incarnation, and especially the concept of *eternal Sonship*, in which the character and mission of Christ were implied within the divine nature itself, provided the main source for salvific apprehension of God. Once humanity became convinced, firstly, of the *historic* claims of Christ to be the eternal Son of God bringing new life for his followers (thereby satisfying *reason*), and secondly, of Christ as the *spiritual* answer to humanity's need for divine aid and illumination (which satisfied *conscience*), then

> the two coalesce into an historical faith, which is something far more than an assent to historical testimony – namely, assent to testimony concerning facts whose roots of causation we discern running deep into the very constitution of man and the character of God.[62]

Hutton affirmed that divine revelation through the incarnation must be "the first truth of our life, the deepest fountain of our being", the "universal fountain of Divine Life within us", which alone could offer us self-understanding.[63] With Erskine, he argued that the incarnation revealed through the eternal Son the essential character of God as a knowable Father, with the necessary moral attributes of righteousness and accessible, purposeful love, evoking corresponding filial relationality and dependent trust in the creature.

Erskine had argued that there are two opposing spirits striving in everyone – the 'spirit of the world' and the 'Spirit of the Father', between which choice must continually be made.[64] Hutton appropriated this idea, together with Erskine's theme of conformity to Christ, to show that it is through the power of the incarnation that 'man's double nature' can be reconciled, because of the "Eternal Son and Word, whose filial Light and Life can stream into and take possession of us, with power to make us like himself". For Hutton, though St. Paul had evidently recognised that Christ was the organic Head of the Christian Church, he had signally 'failed' to extend that reality to "the whole world of heathen humanity" as St. John had done, by showing that Christ was the 'Light which illuminates every man who comes into the world'. Reinforcing Erskine's organic understanding of human constitution in Christ, Hutton asserted

> it *is* our true 'nature' to live in and through the Eternal Word" – we become sons of God by virtue of the "Divine Life" being "engrafted" upon our "per-

---

[61] *Ibid.*, 11, 17-18, 30, 52, 56.
[62] *Ibid.*, 18.
[63] *Ibid.*, 17, 27.
[64] *Election*, 91.

sonality or individuality", so that "the eternal nature of the Son" is the "source of human life and light."[65]

Echoing Erskine's concept of 'spiritual order', Hutton recognised in the freely-willed, filial, dependent trust of the Son of God the same exemplary and representative organic headship functions as Erskine, so that to attain the desired object of goodness and righteousness, and become true sons of God ourselves, we must appropriate the "law of Christ's nature...by a voluntary submission to His life...by admitting *Him* into our hearts".[66] However, like Erskine, the example of Christ was not so much to be *imitated*, as the source of his very divine life was to be *incarnated* within us, so that Christ's life became our life, and the key to the power which released the divine light within human beings remained the sympathetic free-will choice of the individual. Reflecting in this way a new contemporary soteriological emphasis, Hutton was able to present the incarnation as in itself "a new power, a new fountain of life and hope to man".[67]

F.D. Maurice

Hutton's crucial essay not only provoked Erskine into reaction. Erskine had probably received a copy of the essay through F.D. Maurice, and it was Maurice himself who felt strongly motivated to compose a lengthy reply to Hutton, forming a qualificatory postscript to the publication itself. His letter offers retrospective insight into the origins of earlier nineteenth-century controversies which had confronted Erskine, and casts fascinating light upon both historical and contemporary aspects of the debate in which Erskine pioneeringly participated. The relative influence of Edward Irving and Erskine emerges, and it is suggested that both Irving and Erskine rediscovered an *orthodox* incarnational christology in contrast to prevailing Scottish *un*orthodoxy – at least according to Maurice's interpretation of Anglican theology!

Maurice was a classic nineteenth-century reformist, exploratory reinterpreter, and reconstructor of Christian thought, who also attracted the ascription of 'eclecticism'.[68] Maurice regarded Hutton's essay as an opportunity to expound the christological question concerning the theology of the incarnation as a demonstration of the real relation between Christ and humanity, in opposition to purely human-centred systems of religion and eth-

---

[65] Hutton, "Incarnation", 28-29, 44.
[66] *Ibid.*, 33, 40.
[67] *Ibid.*, 35-6.
[68] Reardon, *Religious Thought*, 120.

ics.[69] This, to Maurice, seemed the crux of Hutton's essay, and he felt Hutton had insufficiently addressed the true soteriological issue, namely, how the Son of God really became man, the implications for humanity of the nature he adopted, and above all, that Christ was not "a merely individual Christ" but the "Head of Humanity". Maurice described how he had been brought to the conviction that "the perfect image of God cannot be merely *a* man. He must be *the* man; the Head of the Race; the Person in whom the race is created; by whom it stands".[70] Almost certainly Maurice had in this area of incarnational thinking, as in others, been influenced by Erskine:

> it was from Thomas Erskine…that Maurice derived his doctrine that Christ is the head of the whole human race, and that all are in some sense members of the Church, whether or not they recognize themselves to be such…[71]

Apparently, however, it was Edward Irving who had initially convinced Maurice of the crucial point that

> the basis of human experience and faith must be in theology, or the revelation of God; that human experience and faith can never be its basis. He took his starting point from old Calvinistical ground. He affirmed the will of God to be at the root of all will, being, life, in man…The Eternal Will…must become flesh and dwell among men, if the Will, full of grace and truth, was to make itself fully known to men.[72]

It was in 1830 that

> The Old Theology which Mr. Irving had grafted upon his Scotch Confession showed me the way. According to *that* confession, the race stood in Adam, and had fallen in Adam; then a scheme of salvation, of which the Incarnation formed a step, was necessary to rescue certain persons from the consequences of the fall. Mr. Irving had begun to regard the Incarnation not merely as a means to an end, in which some men were interested, but as the very manifestation of God to men – as the link between the creature and the Creator. But what could the Incarnation on his previous hypothesis be but the descent into a radically *evil* nature? Some of Mr. Irving's Scotch opponents perceived the difficulty, and resorted to the hypothesis of our Lord's taking the unfallen nature of Adam. He regarded the suggestion as a miserable subterfuge, which made the relation between Christ and actual men an utterly unreal one…Old Theology taught quite a different doctrine. Our own Articles[73] set forth Christ very God and very man – not Adam – as now and al-

---

[69] F.D. Maurice, Letter to R.H. Hutton, *Tracts for Priests and People*, XIV, 59-60.
[70] *Ibid.*, 62, 67.
[71] Dennis G. Wigmore-Beddoes, *Yesterday's Radicals* (Cambridge: James Clarke, 1971), 92.
[72] Maurice, Letter to R.H. Hutton, 60.
[73] Here Maurice asserted his own Church of England orthodoxy.

ways the head of the race. They teach us of an infection of nature which exists in every son of Adam. They call them a radical departure from original righteousness. This original righteousness stands, and has always stood, in Christ the Son of God, and in Him only. Here, it seemed to me, was the true practical solution of the difficulty. I could believe that the Head of Man had entered fully into the condition of every man; had suffered the temptations of every man; had wrestled with the enemy of every man; and that He had brought *our* humanity untainted and perfect through that struggle. And this because He had never lost His trust in His Father, His obedience to His Father, had never asserted independence, as Adam did, as each one of us is continually doing...no man has a right to say, 'My race is a sinful, fallen race'...he is bound to contemplate his race in the Son of God, and to claim, by faith in Him, his share in its redemption and its glory.[74]

It would seem, therefore, that chronologically Edward Irving initially inspired Maurice's incarnationalism, which a virtually concurrent reading of Erskine reinforced and developed. The separate question regarding whether Irving was the common source for both Maurice and Erskine remains controversial. However, it would appear that though Irving sowed the seed, it was Erskine's *The Brazen Serpent* that was responsible for the application of Maurice's incarnational thinking, especially in light of the fulsome tributes in Maurice's *Prophets and Kings of the Old Testament*.[75]

Maurice's references to the "Old Theology" are interesting, as he appeared to perpetuate the impression members of the Broad School sought to convey (as indeed did the Oxford Movement) in classic Romantic fashion, that their innovative ideas were actually a rediscovery of original truth as transmitted by the Church Fathers, the Reformers, and other key historical figures. John McLeod Campbell, in *The Nature of the Atonement*, purported to render a 'true' understanding of Luther, Calvin, and Edwards. Erskine also interacted with Luther and Edwards, whilst an entire chapter devoted to extracts from the work of the influential James Fraser of Brea (1638-98), the illustrious precursor of the Marrow men, was appended to *Extracts of Letters to a Christian Friend, by a Lady*, to lend supposed weight to Erskine's introductory remarks.

Moral Idealism

For Erskine, Hutton and Maurice, the orthodox theology of the incarnation was foundational to their ethical outlook. But at the same time they were concerned to emphasise the theology of the indwelling Christ over and against increasing trends to regard Christ as mere human moral example

---

[74] Maurice, Letter to R.H. Hutton, 64-6.
[75] Maurice, *Prophets and Kings*, v-xii, xv-xx. See Maurice (ed.), *Life*, I, 108, 121, 183. See p.197, note 18 above.

and inspiration, rather than a divine, supernatural figure. In this mission, however, Erskine and Maurice especially were frequently misunderstood, being linked with supposedly misguided 'philosophical' attempts to 'rehabilitate' Jesus, and were accused by traditional evangelicals of actually advocating the dangerous tendencies they in fact opposed.

Erskine's incarnational exemplarist approach to soteriological thought placed him within the Abelardian 'moral influence' tradition, in which the love of God, manifested through the atonement of Christ, was deemed to awaken a subjective response of love and faith in the hearts of human beings, which then becomes the ground of their justification. 'Redemption' was therefore understood in more subjective and dynamic terms as increased 'God-consciousness' mediated through the internal sense of Christ's presence or Spirit, generating the ethical impulse to imitate Christ and fulfil God's will in a morally effective way. In *The Brazen Serpent*, Erskine clearly set out his convictions regarding the moral influence of the atonement, where as a result of Christ manifesting the love and righteousness of God

> those who understand this manifestation do indeed become partakers of the same spirit...for the sight of that love is the very spirit of Jesus, and will, in those who see it, work even as it did in Jesus...here then is the simple connexion between the atonement of Christ and the sanctification of his members. The atonement consisted in Christ's accepting the punishment of sin as the head of the nature; and the sanctification of his members consists in their accepting it also in the power of his spirit dwelling in them.[76]

Erskine's particular emphasis was on the intrinsic salvific effect of free subjective response and personal appropriation of the revelation of the loving Fatherly character and purpose of God in Christ. The effects of the fall, on an Abelardian understanding, were not total, therefore through natural reason humanity still had the capacity to choose righteousness, hence the potential of the moral example of Christ to evoke ethical response.[77] Erskine emphasised the loving benevolence of a God who has already acted to counter the effects of the fall, and the psychological and moral impact of Christ's work which impacts the conscience and affections of the individual. Motivated by anxiety lest "even the spiritual understanding may be satisfied without effecting that living change, which is the one thing needful",[78] foundational to Erskine's salvific scheme was the assumption of the 'law of love' within the 'spiritual order' in which through the indwelling Christ love begets love, and necessarily motivates a new ethical lifestyle

---

[76] *Serpent*, [2nd edition], 47-49.

[77] Ted Peters, *God – the World's Future: Systematic Theology for a Postmodern Era* (Minneapolis: Fortress Press, 1992), 209.

[78] Letter to Bishop Ewing, 17 July 1868, *Ewing-II*, 43.

based on the principle of self-sacrifice and conformity to the character of the Redeemer. This stood in contrast to some human-centred, moral, psychological, motivation to duty, or quest to discover "some power which shall enforce the decrees and maxims of morality" which Maurice had feared.[79]

Nineteenth- and early twentieth-century liberal theologians were keen exponents of Abelardian atonement. John McLeod Campbell, Horace Bushnell, and Hastings Rashdall have been described as "modern-" or "neo-Abelardians".[80] Campbell, whilst perceived, like Erskine, to be a precursor of liberal views, was in fact a classic nineteenth-century exponent of incarnational atonement. Bushnell spoke of the atonement as "a transaction moving on character in souls; a regenerative, saving, truth-subjecting, all-restoring, inward change of the life…".[81] Rashdall referred to Abelard as producing "a theory of the atonement which thoroughly appeals to reason and to conscience". He further explained:

> if He who so lays down His life is taken as representing and revealing the character of God, then no other way of ending the earthly life of Him in whom God made this supreme self-revelation could so fully embody and symbolize the fundamental thought of Christianity that God is love, nor is any event in the history of the world so calculated to awaken and stimulate that repentance for sin upon which the possibility of forgiveness depends.[82]

Erskine became increasingly aware, as the century progressed, of the liberal direction in which some of his teaching was being developed by others, and it caused him concern. William Hanna found in *The Brazen Serpent*

> the seeds of many of those ideas as to the moral character of the atonement, and the manner of its operation in the formation of Christian character, which, transplanted to other soil and subject to other treatment, germinated after fashions not altogether such as the first sower relished.[83]

But the relation between Erskine's christological and soteriological thought nevertheless reflected an increasing nineteenth-century 'Abelardian' char-

---

[79] Dillistone, *Christian Understanding*, 325; Maurice, Letter to R.H. Hutton, 59.
[80] Robert S. Paul, *The Atonement and the Sacraments: The Relation of the Atonement to the Sacraments of Baptism and the Lord's Supper* (New York: Abingdon Press, 1960) 186, 188.
[81] Horace Bushnell, *The Vicarious Sacrifice Grounded in Principles of Universal Obligation* (New York: Charles Scribner, 1866), 132.
[82] Hastings Rashdall, *The Idea of Atonement in Christian Theology, Being The Bampton Lectures For 1915* (London: Macmillan and Co., 1919), 360-1.
[83] *Letters-I*, 183.

acteristic to link the *person* with the *work* of Christ.[84] Kant had emphasised that knowledge was restricted to perception, apprehension and impression. Accordingly, Jesus could be known only through his impact upon us, which meant through his *work*. This prompted awareness that Christ's salvific work bears directly on who he *is*, so that *ontological* and *functional* christologies were increasingly seen as interdependent. It was Charles Gore who, writing in 1883 concerning Christ "being an example of what man can do", asserted that "the Nestorian Christ is the fitting Saviour of the Pelagian man",[85] indicating that a *Nestorian* christology, with its emphasis on the humanity of Christ, and a *Pelagian* soteriology, with its stress on the freedom of the will, combined to produce a moral exemplarist understanding of Christianity. An exemplarist soteriology emphasising the moral example of Christ, when associated with an elevated anthropology which highlighted the capacities of human beings and reduced the catastrophic impact of the fall, naturally tended to minimise the ontological dissociation between Christ and humanity. In turn, it was a short step towards a reductionist inspirational or adoptionist 'degree christology', viewing Christ as different in *degree* rather than *nature* from human beings, and the supreme example of authentic humanity who it was now possible to emulate.[86]

Imitation of the ideal moral example of God as revealed in Christ, allied to insistence that the ultimate purpose of God extended to the effective deification of humanity, was certainly fundamental to Erskine's innovative soteriological thought. However, "Christ did all that he did…for us, that we might do it also; not instead of us, or to save us from doing it. He is our Head, and his appearance on earth was an epitome of the right life of man".[87] Crucially, Erskine sought to maintain a clear distinction from mere imitative duty by emphasising God's incarnational purpose in terms of

> an actual participation in His righteousness, not by imputation, but in substance and in reality, as is the participation of Jesus with the Father. This is the full sonship – the participation of the Divine nature, through union with the Son of God.[88]

Platonic ideas are prominent in Erskine's thought, and concepts of *imitatio Dei* and Christ as 'ideal man' were prevalent in the eighteenth century, having already been enthusiastically embraced, amongst others, by Unitari-

---

[84] For aspects of the following I am indebted to Alister E. McGrath, *Christian Theology: An Introduction,* [3rd edition] (Oxford: Blackwell, 2001), 346-7, 426.

[85] Gore, "Our Lord's Human Example", *Church Quarterly Review,* 298.

[86] See Thomas G. Weinandy, *The Father's Spirit of Sonship* (Edinburgh: T.&T. Clark, 1995), 114.

[87] Letter to the Bishop of Argyll, [probably July 1867], in Ewing, "Relation", *Present-Day Papers,* 32-3.

[88] *Election,* 410-11.

ans.[89] Platonism and Kantianism were strong companions in the emergent 'idealist' climate.[90] 'Idealist' concepts were extensively developed within nineteenth-century theology, notably by neo-Kantians such as Schleiermacher, who also acknowledged significant debt to Plato in his presentation of Christ as the ideal form for humanity. Kant was initially responsible for broadening the idea, increasingly adopted by more liberal theologians in the nineteenth century, of Jesus as the human 'prototype' and moral ideal, and many of his typical modes of expression bear remarkable correspondence to Erskine.[91]

Schleiermacher was criticised for presenting an ethical ideal rather than a historical Christ. For many, it was "difficult to believe that he did not include under that title a simple embodiment of the divine in our collective humanity".[92] The 'human potential' tendencies which bothered both Maurice and Erskine, were nevertheless germinal in Erskine. Though he regarded the life of Jesus as something more than historical event, Erskine would certainly not have agreed with implications of Kant or Schleiermacher of a human-centred, *figurative* incarnation, or of the *idea* of Christ as a spiritual experience rather than a historical and present revealed reality.[93] Nonetheless, correspondences appear to be extensive. Erskine's mature themes of life as moral education and character; the imitation of Jesus as God's ideal for humanity; the faith and trust; the self-sacrifice; the freewill embrace of suffering; the innate power and reasonableness of the *idea* itself to motivate transformation; all may be seen as representing, at least in embryonic form, aspects of Kant's effective reduction of the traditional Christian message. Erskine expressed views remarkably similar to Kant in private correspondence:

> Jesus Christ is I believe God's ideal for man, – the full expression of the purpose which He had in making man – God desired to make men His children, and the full expression of this desire is the Divine Son, containing in Himself the Spirit of sonship for all men…Every man who thinks at all, has some *ideal* for himself, some image which he would wish to realize in his own life. One man would wish to be a Shakespeare, another a Plato, another an Alexander the great etc., etc., seeking distinction or self-gratification of some kind. But *God's ideal* for us, is One who tasted death for every man, who bore the sins and sorrows and burdens of all men and who came not to do His

---

[89] William Ellery Channing declared in 1828 that "true religion consists in proposing, as our great end, a growing likeness to the Supreme Being. Its noblest influence consists in making us more and more partakers in the Divinity", ("Likeness to God", in Bartlett (ed.), *Unitarian Christianity*, 86).

[90] Reardon, *Religious Thought*, 50.

[91] See Appendix 1.

[92] Anon., "The Church and Theology of Germany During the Nineteenth Century", in *National Review*, XVIII (January-April, 1864), 211.

[93] For Schleiermacher see *Christian Faith*, e.g., §89, 366-9.

own will, but the will of the Father, making Himself of no reputation, and doing the work which was given Him to do. As this is God's ideal for us, so He desires that we should adopt it as our ideal for ourselves.[94]

Notably with Reimarus, Strauss and Renan, the nineteenth century was distinguished for its studies seeking to reconstruct the life of Jesus. In his 1883 article, Charles Gore remarked on the endless examples of recent literature representing Christ as the human 'ideal' of 'manliness'. The century was conspicuous for a conscious process of 'bringing God down to man', though, if possible, in a way which could nevertheless be made to reconcile with orthodox truth. In effect, 'orthodoxy' became more flexible, as the various ecclesiastical trials relating to key figures, which included F.D. Maurice and the authors of *Essays and Reviews*, were to demonstrate. Erskine certainly did not consider himself as 'unorthodox' in this sense, and Gore probably did not directly include him in that category of men who,

> though they are believers in Christ and speak as such, they yet with more or less of emphasis regard the full Catholic doctrine of Christ's Person as an encumbrance in the presentation of Christ's human example to their contemporaries. They are not in violent revolt from it…they are not in violent revolt from orthodoxy, some of them perhaps not in *revolt* at all: but they regard doctrinal orthodoxy as an encumbrance, as a weight which hangs about a man's neck and prevents him from presenting with freedom what we may call the case for Christ. If we can rid the presentation of Christ, as the Master of human life, of the shackles of dogma, we shall obtain for it (they feel) a readier hearing, a readier acceptance. More men will be Christians, and Christianity will be as powerful as ever.[95]

Nevertheless, the same apologetic motivation, the same desire to reconstruct outmoded dogma, the same wish to preserve orthodox truth which characterised these representatives of Gore's "present generation", were strong motivating factors in Erskine's own drive to make Jesus 'acceptable' to modern humanity. He would have agreed with Gore that by his day things had gone too far in the general "craving to 'bring Christ down'…to our natural fallen level" and to present him as "nothing more than a perfect natural Man". Most likely he would have concurred with Gore's suggestion that "these writers, we believe, who profess to remove encumbrance and bring Christ's example closer to men…are really sapping the foundations of the power of Christ to reconstruct and renovate human life at all".[96] Ironically, Erskine actually found himself in 1865 defending Christian dogma, and needing to issue a reminder that the gospel was "THE POWER

---

[94] Letter to Mrs Schwabe, 1 July 1858, *NLS MS* 9747–76.
[95] Gore, "Our Lord's Human Example", *Church Quarterly Review,* 282-3.
[96] *Ibid.,* 306, 303, 282, 283.

of God unto salvation". In seeking to marginalise Christian dogmas as "encumbrances" when it came to imitating the 'morality' of the Sermon on the Mount, he asserted that Renan, for example, failed to consider

> whether it would be possible to obey those precepts by mere effort, and without knowing what the dogmas teach of the spiritual relations in which we stand both to God and man.

For Erskine, Renan was missing the crucial point by not 'enforcing' the vital necessity of a living awareness of, and relationship with, God to 'produce spontaneously the very life of the precepts within the human soul'.[97]

The Notion of Sacrifice

> Then was the truth received into my heart,
> That under heaviest sorrow earth can bring,
> Griefs bitterest of ourselves or of our kind,
> If from the affliction somewhere do not grow
> Honour which could not else have been, a faith,
> An elevation, and a sanctity,
> If new strength be not given, or old restored
> The blame is ours not Nature's.[98]

Wordsworth reflected increasing Romantic and Victorian apprehensions about suffering and sacrifice in *The Prelude*, highlighting growing recognition of the idea of spiritual progress through a responsible attitude to the trials and storms of life. Erskine's own quest for a satisfactory theodicy directly linked him with the concerns of his age, and his approach to the concept of sacrifice, with new emphasis on God's passibility, prefigured crucial theological and social attitudes of the later nineteenth century.

We noted Erskine's evangelical preoccupation with appropriate human response in the face of suffering, and throughout his own life he stressed the need for personal sacrifice and for living and dying 'well'. The subject of suffering, death and sacrificial living features constantly in Erskine's private correspondence, and opportunity was frequently afforded by repeated tragic experiences amongst his own family and close friends for the exercise of his highly valued pastoral gift of death-bed ministry. In an age of growing uncertainty, comfort, hope, and reassurance were becoming

---

[97] Letter to Lady Augusta Stanley, 11 February 1865, *Letters-II*, 151. See Appendix 3.
[98] William Wordsworth, *The Prelude* [1805], Book X, lines 423-30 (London: Oxford University Press, 1960), 188-9.

increasingly precious commodities.[99] Within this context, the century was conducive to the development of a theology of the 'eternal sacrifice' of God himself, together with associated ideas of *kenosis*, socialism and service. Dominating all Erskine's thought was his novel understanding of God as a loving Father who was training us for 'participation in his own character', and who shared our feelings of sorrow and suffering. He stated bluntly

> The idea of a sorrowing God shocks the minds of many. It does not shock mine; I cannot conceive love being without sorrow...I cannot believe that man can give me a sympathy which does not flow into him from God...God desires the joy of seeing His creatures choose to be good...such a joy is always accompanied with the risk of a great sorrow, which sorrow, I believe, God knows and feels...[this view of God] sets Jesus Christ before us sympathising with and participating in every form of human suffering in order that He might draw men up to love and righteousness".[100]

Erskine believed the universal concept of sacrifice proceeded from an 'eternal Spirit' of 'life-outpouring'. Christ himself offered up his self-sacrifice in this spirit. Erskine spoke of "God, as it were, sacrificing Himself that man might learn to sacrifice himself". Christ's sacrifice was "the very type of what must be done by the spirit of Christ in every human being".[101]

During the century, the 'power of sacrifice' began seriously to be regarded as "a universal principle emanating from God and animating the whole of his creation".[102] Such new sacrificial theology complemented a growing social and political radicalism, becoming closely associated with the birth of Christian Socialism.[103] It involved, firstly, radical reconsideration of the accepted concept of divine impassibility, especially in connection with the implications for God in responding to the condition of a fallen world. Accordingly, the atonement needed to be seen less in forensic and transactional terms, whilst elements of the distinctive twentieth-century notion of a 'suffering God' began to emerge. Secondly, there arose a general ethical and moral unease about *propitiation*, which led to a rediscovery

---

[99] "When the fervour and piety of Evangelicalism began to wane in the last quarter of the nineteenth century, traditional assurances about death and immortality declined with it", Pat Jalland, *Death in the Victorian Family* (Oxford: Oxford University Press, 1996), 2-3.

[100] Letter to Mrs Schwabe, 27 April 1856, *Letters-II*, 268-70.

[101] Letters to Mrs Schwabe, 27 April 1856 and Bishop Ewing, 9 January 1861, *Letters-II*, 270, 220, cf., *Election*, 110-11; Letter to the Bishop of Argyll [no date] in Ewing, "Relation", *Present-Day Papers*, 32-3.

[102] Ian Bradley, *The Power of Sacrifice* (London: Darton, Longman & Todd, 1995), 161, to which I am indebted for aspects of the following.

[103] F.D. Maurice and Charles Kingsley, both well known to Erskine, were early Broad Church proponents of Christian Socialism.

of the biblical concept of Christ's atonement as a sacrifice made by God for humanity, rather than vice versa. This led in due course to the notion of *kenosis,* involving 'continual' and 'eternal' aspects of divine sacrifice. Thirdly, evolutionary considerations introduced a new understanding of how all life on earth depended on struggle, surrender and self-limitation. This amounted to a cosmic application of the principle of sacrifice and recognition of the law of life out of death, encouraging the Victorian sense that death involved a meaning and purpose within the wider scheme of creation and redemption. The idea of suffering, dying, and rising with Christ was also increasingly spiritualised and adopted by liberal theologians to demonstrate "the intimacy of the faith-union of the believer with Christ, enabling him to be taken into Christ's sufferings and death in such a way that his own afflictions are virtually an extension of those of the Lord Himself".[104]

Horace Bushnell

Several eminent nineteenth-century theologians followed Erskine in enunciating similar 'sacrificial' themes. Supremely, John McLeod Campbell redefined the notion of propitiatory suffering in *The Nature of the Atonement*. However, Erskine's American New Haven contemporary, Horace Bushnell (1802-76), increasingly well known in Britain, and sometimes described as the 'American Schleiermacher'[105], was the first American explicitly to articulate modernist themes such as the essential goodness of humanity and the gospel of self-improvement. In a series of 1848 discourses entitled *God in Christ*, Bushnell rejected penal, propitiatory, and substitutionary notions of atonement, emphasising that suffering contained no "interior reality". Rather than "appeasing" God, it "expresses Divine feeling" and "the unconquerable love of God's heart".[106] In *The Vicarious Sacrifice*, like Erskine, he anticipated later nineteenth- and early twentieth-century emphasis on divine suffering with his celebrated "cross in God before the wood is seen upon Calvary".[107] Embracing moral exemplarist ideas concerning Christ and his sacrificial life awakening the human conscience,

---

[104] G.W.H. Lampe, *Reconciliation in Christ* (London: Longmans, Green and Co., 1956), 59-61.
[105] Michael Horton, *In the Face of God: The Dangers and Delights of Spiritual Intimacy* (Dallas: Word Publishing, 1996), 27. Bushnell was deeply influenced by both Schleiermacher and Coleridge. Probably Erskine knew of him through Ewing. See Ross, *Ewing*, 370.
[106] Horace Bushnell, *God in Christ, Three Discourses delivered at New Haven, Cambridge, and Andover* [1848] (New York: Charles Scribner's Sons, 1887), 215-6.
[107] Horace Bushnell, *The Vicarious Sacrifice Grounded in Principles of Universal Obligation* (New York: Charles Scribner, 1866), 73.

Bushnell abandoned forensic substitutionary concepts of sacrifice. Instead, he regarded the inherently salvific principle of experiential 'vicarious sacrifice' or 'power of sacrifice' as fundamental to 'good' living, in which the process of growth towards perfection was demonstrated in ethical behaviour motivated by love inspired by Christ's example.[108]

F.W. Robertson

Frederick William Robertson of Brighton (1816-1853), was a highly influential Victorian theologian, despite death at the early age of 37. Though acknowledging William Ellery Channing's influence, he was an independent-minded Anglican minister, revered by the Broad School, and a contemporary of Erskine, who almost certainly knew of him.[109]

Like Erskine, with whom he was compared,[110] Robertson was particularly associated with the doctrine of the Fatherhood of God. Significantly, in 1858, he translated Lessing's *Education of the Human Race* [1780], with its suggestion that God operated immanently in the processes of human social development to prepare the race for its ultimate destiny of a voluntary 'brotherhood of man' in a universal kingdom of peace.[111] Remarkably reminiscent of Erskine, Robertson held to the revolutionary idea of a type of "remedial not penal" 'purgatorial' process, both in this life and the next, because "the law of the universe is progress". Whilst not an overt universalist, he nevertheless rejected the doctrine of eternal punishment.[112] With Erskine and Bushnell, Robertson asserted the passibility of God. Christ's divine act of sacrifice was, in fact, "the act of humanity – that which all humanity is bound to do". It was thus an eternal law that "we are perfected through suffering", and Christ's sacrifice was the direct cause of "the intro-

---

[108] Bushnell, *Vicarious Sacrifice*, 53-4, 105-6, 155. Robert Bruce Mullin has recently published a biography of Horace Bushnell in which he portrays Bushnell, remarkably like Erskine, as an innovative figure with his roots in two centuries, and in reality a theological liberal and 'defender of the faith' rather than the inaugurator of American liberalism. Like Erskine, Bushnell also toured Europe where he encountered in 1845-6 followers of Schleiermacher. See *The Puritan as Yankee: A Life of Horace Bushnell* (Grand Rapids: Eerdmans, 2002), 1-5.

[109] John McLeod Campbell was suspicious of Robertson, feeling he had 'depreciated' evangelicalism in seeking God by another path and giving up the 'roots', (*Memorials*, II, 108-10). Erskine probably knew of Robertson through Campbell and Ewing. See Ross, *Ewing*, 423-4.

[110] See p.258 below, (footnote 11).

[111] G.E. Lessing, *The Education of the Human Race,* [trans. by F.W. Robertson] (London: Smith, Elder, and Co., 1858).

[112] Stopford A. Brooke (ed.), *Life and Letters of Fred. W. Robertson*, [new edition], in 2 volumes (London: Kegan Paul, Trench, 1882), II, 155-6.

duction of the principle of self-sacrifice into [man's] nature".[113] Robertson also spoke of sacrifice in universal and cosmic terms reminiscent of Erskine's 'spiritual order'. Sacrifice for the life of others was "the grand law of the universe", and "The Power of Sorrow" was a principle for developing spiritual life.[114] Echoing Erskine's 'law of love', Robertson preached in 1849 that the principle of "vicarious sacrifice" was "the Law of Being", fundamental to the laws of the universe and Nature, with its evidence visible in the evolution of the entire creation, and spoke of the necessity for humanity to be redeemed only through the same law of 'vicarious suffering'.[115]

Robertson was influential in ensuring that suffering for the sake of others became a dominant theme in British theology in the second half of the nineteenth century. He closely followed Erskine in interpreting and appropriating the cross inwardly as supremely revealing the eternal righteous character of God. The only way for humanity to be redeemed was by participating with Christ in the death of the cross since life proceeds only out of death: "only the appropriation of the spirit of the cross redeems. Love transmutes all".[116] Accordingly, loving sacrifice must become an existential normative way of life for the Christian in suffering and self-denial, inspired by continuous *imitatio Christi*: "real human life is a perpetual completion and repetition of the sacrifice of Christ…The sacrifice of Christ is done over again in every life which is lived, not to self but, to God".[117]

F.D. Maurice and R.S. Candlish

Erskine provoked wide controversy as the nineteenth century advanced and his revolutionary ideas were perceived to underlie new theological developments. F.D. Maurice found himself the focus of one such debate. He exerted huge influence and controversy. Converted from Unitarianism to Anglicanism in 1831, though continuing to be strongly influenced by Unitarian and Platonic thought,[118] he was eventually ejected from King's College

---

[113] Brooke (ed.), *Life and Letters*, I, 95, 351-2; F.W. Robertson, "The Sacrifice of Christ", *Sermons Preached at Trinity Chapel, Brighton,* Third Series, [9th edition] (London: Smith, Elder and Co., 1864), 105, 113.

[114] Robertson, *Sermons*, Third Series, 117; citation by Dillistone, *Christian Understanding,* 249.

[115] F.W. Robertson, "Caiaphas' View of Vicarious Sacrifice", *Sermons Preached at Brighton,* First Series, [6th edition] (London: Smith, Elder and Co., 1859), 157-9.

[116] Brooke (ed.), *Life and Letters*, I, 304.

[117] Robertson, "The Sacrifice of Christ", *Sermons,* Third Series, 114-5.

[118] Young, *Maurice,* 1, 124-30.

in 1853 for appearing to question the doctrine of everlasting punishment in his *Theological Essays*.[119]

Sacrifice, for Maurice, was a major soteriological theme of liberation. In 1854, he published a series of sermons entitled *The Doctrine of Sacrifice* in which, like Erskine, Bushnell and Robertson, he saw the basic moral principle of self-sacrifice ("the giving up of ourselves") as integral to the Trinity in both immanental and economic terms. Maurice believed the principle of sacrifice "manifests the mind of God", "proceeds from God", "accomplishes the purposes of God in the redemption and reconciliation of his creatures", and "enables those creatures to become like their Father in Heaven by offering up themselves".[120] Like Erskine, Maurice closely identified sacrifice with the total self-surrender of the individual to God in complete trust and dependence.[121] He also rejected traditional concepts of propitiatory sacrifice which dwelt on the need to appease God to secure deliverance from punishment as

> a dead formula of the schools...a dark superstition; a scheme for persuading God to be at peace with that evil against which He has declared eternal war; a scheme for proving that He is still at enmity with a great majority of that race with which he has made peace in the blood of His Son.[122]

In contrast, true sacrifice, as a revelation of the essential character of God, flowed from God to humanity, not the reverse. That principle of sacrifice, which "is the ground of the universe and the ground of our humanity", though pre-eminently revealed in the Cross, was manifested in the incarnate life of Christ as a whole, lived out in our human nature.[123] In his sermon entitled "Christ's Sacrifice a Power to Form us after his Likeness", Maurice affirmed that it was only in participating in the life of Christ as Head of the body of corporate humanity, in having the mind of Christ, namely "obedience, humiliation, sacrifice", we might discover that "mighty conquering power" of the universe.[124]

Like Erskine and Schleiermacher, Maurice regarded sin more in terms of self-centredness and independence from God. He used his central theme of "Conquering by Sacrifice"[125] to promote a self-denying vision of Christianity which emphasised the Fatherhood of God, the Headship of Christ, and the relational, ethical, and corporate nature of redeemed humanity. This

---

[119] Frederick Denison Maurice, *Theological Essays,* [2nd Edition] (Cambridge: Macmillan, 1853).
[120] Maurice, *Sacrifice,* xli, xliii, xxiv.
[121] *Ibid.,* 18, 28.
[122] *Ibid.,* 207.
[123] *Ibid.,* 108.
[124] *Ibid.,* 219.
[125] *Ibid.,* 294-315.

vision of 'spiritual order', which owed so much to Erskine, was immensely influential, and inspired not only movements like 'Christian Socialism', but also classic Victorian leitmotifs such as 'human potential', 'the brotherhood of man', 'Christian manliness' and 'strenuous Christianity', associated with figures such as Thomas Arnold and Charles Kingsley. In effect, anthropology derived from christology. The "heroic ideal of strenuous self-sacrifice, exemplified by moral and physical temperance and self-control and the subordination of the individual will to the cause of the common good" inspired the Victorian ideal of a society modelled on the righteous principle of self-sacrifice, which in turn led to an ethos of moral obligation, responsibility and duty.[126] Erskine had also highlighted aspects like 'truth', 'honesty', 'unselfish love and kindness', and 'manliness' within his concept of "righteousness in man".[127]

Such 'liberal' developments provoked concern and were strongly resisted, especially in Scotland, where the new views took longer to gain a foothold. One leading traditional theologian who opposed the Broad School, and those whom he considered influenced them (singling out Thomas Erskine and Edward Irving), was Robert Smith Candlish (1806-73). Candlish succeeded Thomas Chalmers as leader of the Free Church, becoming Principal of New College, Edinburgh. In a series of lectures published in 1854, Candlish alleged Maurice was obligated to Erskine and Irving for his ideas on the incarnation and atonement, and to the Quakers for his beliefs concerning the universal divine internal light. Resurrecting old charges Erskine faced, Candlish particularly complained that Maurice taught that, as a result of the incarnation and atonement of Christ, "universal humanity is already redeemed, regenerated, glorified". He further objected to Maurice teaching that through the universal influence of the Spirit and through the general leavening effect of Christianity, society was becoming pervaded with a deeper sense of its innate moral righteousness. Describing the new system of thought attributable to Maurice as really initiated by Erskine, Candlish explained:

> Through the influence of that presence men are brought to know and feel, not what they need to be and may be, but what they already are – sons, justified, regenerate. And as this process, not of conversion, but, as it were, of self-recognition, goes on, the Church is in course of being formed. In short, the Church is the world acknowledging its position in Christ; – it is mankind become alive to the apprehension and realisation of the actual and universal redemption of humanity.

Candlish concluded once again that the real problem about this 'symmetrical' system is that "throughout there is a careful and consistent disavowal

---

[126] Bradley, *Power*, 174-5, 179.

[127] *Sp.Order*, 235.

of anything really being done by God". It was all about a process of human 'discovery'.[128]

Maurice used the dedicatory letter to *The Doctrine of Sacrifice* specifically to respond to Candlish's criticisms. He acknowledged that Thomas Erskine had played a vital role in emphasising the relation of humanity to Christ "according to his original constitution", and highlighted the importance of Erskine's *The Doctrine of Election*.[129]

It is apparent, therefore, through comparisons with contemporary theological writings, that Erskine was perceived, either directly or indirectly, as inspiring key revolutionary Victorian religious themes, including incarnational relationality and salvation through sacrifice. Some, however, were alarmed at the spectre of a human-centred soteriology towards which his ideas were deemed to tend.

Summary

Chapter 9 demonstrated how Erskine's pioneering soteriological distinctives resonated within both British and American Victorian contexts, acting as catalysts in the development of changing theological understandings and social attitudes. We noted that his representative, eclectic ideas concerning the nature of God, divine order, revelation and inward authority, universal Fatherhood and sonship, progressive reformatory (as opposed to retributive) education, human dignity in the *imago Dei*, free-will, incarnational soteriology, moral influence and idealism, and sacrifice, were all embraced or developed by key theological figures during the nineteenth century, helping them become part of society and culture. Later observers acknowledged Erskine's influential role in pioneering crucial soteriological issues of the century. We noted how Erskine provoked debate, inevitably prefiguring liberal tendencies consequent on his efforts to make Christ and Christianity acceptable to a new generation. Whilst inseparable from his context, Erskine himself, however, consciously sought to guard against trends which reduced Christianity to a mere human-centred religion of morals and duty.

---

[128] Robert S. Candlish, *Examination of Mr Maurice's Theological Essays* (London: James Nisbet and Co., 1854), 46, 478, 34-5.

[129] Maurice, *Sacrifice*, vi-xli, especially xix.

CHAPTER 10

Erskine in a Reconstructive Continental Context

Introduction

We have sought to demonstrate how the evolution of Erskine's eclectic and innovatory thinking mirrored his intellectual and philosophical context, anticipating soteriological developments during transition from Enlightenment to Victorian Romanticism. This chapter examines the extent to which Erskine's theological development not only reflected wider developments specifically in Britain, but also paralleled similar movements in continental, and particularly German, philosophical and theological thought. We review in detail Erskine's networking activities and the nature of his contacts during the 1820s and 1830s, to suggest that the scope of his eclectic assimilation and appropriation of contemporary currents of thinking extended much wider, and involved greater sophistication, than has hitherto been acknowledged. We consider that Erskine's ability to appropriate, interpret and reinterpret his European intellectual milieu, creatively applying it to his own soteriological system, has been seriously underestimated. Rather, he has tended to be relegated to the relative status of a mere amateur, isolated, liberal, freethinker within a narrow Scottish setting. However, it is suggested that Erskine was cognizant of, and dynamically interacted with, a much larger philosophical and theological picture than has previously been recognised. We believe that his contribution and role deserves greater recognition (not least in a Scottish context, where his legacy is arguably commensurate with Coleridge in England), than it has received. In this sense we argue that Erskine may unashamedly be placed alongside more obvious and illustrious figures who have been credited for helping introduce new German thought into British theology, which, at least until the latter part of the nineteenth century, was regarded as relatively conservative, and desperately in need of the innovatory stimulus which Erskine supplied.

The Extent of German and Romantic Influence

Bernard Reardon suggests that Kant's influence, as the archetypal philosophical/ theological reconstructor, was weak in Britain until the end of the nineteenth century. Britain, and particularly Scotland, were suspicious and slow to consider seriously the work of German historians, philosophers and theologians.[1]

However, at the beginning of the century, the spreading Romantic movement was a catalyst for changing attitudes amongst the educated. From about 1813, Madame de Staël's *De l'Allemagne* was hugely influential in introducing men like Henry Crabb Robinson, Wordsworth and Coleridge, Sir Walter Scott, Thomas de Quincey, Byron, and Shelley to German Romantic thought, and to German thinkers like Kant, Goethe, Schlegel and Schelling.[2] Though Walter Scott was already translating German literature by the end of the eighteenth century,[3] interest in German intellectuals in Scotland did not seriously take off until about 1834.[4] Erskine's initial introduction to German ideas probably derived from the same source, whilst his recorded love of Wordsworth, and frequent lyrical passages in his private correspondence, confirmed close familiarity with the Romantics.[5]

Thomas Erskine was travelling in Germany, Switzerland and France as early as 1822-1823, and from at least 1826, he had become an intimate friend and correspondent of Madame de Staël's daughter-in-law and family. It is inconceivable that he did not know *De l'Allemagne* and like F.D. Maurice had not been influenced by that powerful introduction to a Romantic world view, necessarily including the thought of Kant, Schlegel and Schelling.[6] It is also probable that his close formative relationship with his paternalistic mentor, Dr. Charles Stuart of Dunearn, inspired Erskine's interest in new continental ideas. Stuart was renowned as a liberal scholar who 'loved novelty' and constantly studied theological commentators, "many of them German Socinians, &c".[7]

---

[1] Reardon, *Religious Thought*, 8-9.
[2] Madame de Staël (1766-1817), *De l'Allemagne,* [1813] (Paris: Librairie de Firmin Didot frères, 1850). See Ian Jack, *English Literature 1815-1832* (Oxford: Clarendon Press, 1963), 384-6; Emma Gertrude Jaeck, *Madame de Staël and the Spread of German Literature* (New York: Oxford University Press, 1915), *passim*.
[3] Jack, *English Literature*, 389-90.
[4] Apparently Neander and Tholuck then began to be most sought after, (Fleming, *History*, 15).
[5] For Erskine and Wordsworth, see Machar, "Thomas Erskine", *Andover Review*, 597.
[6] See Young, *Maurice*, 118-19.
[7] Alexander Haldane, *Lives of Robert & James Haldane* [1852] (Edinburgh: Banner of Truth, 1990), 593, cf., Needham, *Thomas Erskine*, 110-16.

Knowledge of Kant's work began slowly to gain ground in the 1820s. By the end of the decade his name was widely known through the work of Coleridge, De Quincey, and Thomas Carlyle (1795-1881).[8] The *Oriel School* and its associates at Oxford began to be aware of the new German historical criticism through contact with the German diplomat and scholar, the Chevalier Bunsen, in the 1820s. Connop Thirlwall and Julius Hare, who were at the time probably the only Englishmen who had seriously studied German literature, translated Schleiermacher's *Essay on Luke* in 1825, and the immensely influential *History of Rome* by B.G. Niebuhr in 1827.[9] Knowledge of Schleiermacher developed only gradually between 1828, when he visited Britain, and 1860, by which time he had become well known.[10]

There is no direct evidence to show that Erskine knew of Kant or Schleiermacher before the 1820s. However, during his university studies, as well as receiving an eclectic education in moral philosophy and the empirical tradition, he may well have come into contact with German literature and philosophy through fashionable intellectual circles in Edinburgh.[11] Edinburgh was a focus in Britain from the end of the eighteenth century for the early dissemination of German literature and the ideas of Kant. Kant played a key role in the decline of Scottish Philosophy, and his first translator into English was the Scotsman, John Richardson, in 1797. Kant was strongly promoted in Edinburgh in the late eighteenth century by German students, and a philosophical circle was meeting there to discuss Kant where he was "already well known" in 1799. The Professor of Moral Theology at Edinburgh University, Dugald Stewart, was aware of Kant by 1810 and finding him difficult to understand (though he offered a detailed analysis of his views in 1821). It was Stewart's successor, Thomas Brown, who in the early nineteenth century paid the first really serious professional attention to Kant.[12]

---

[8] Young, *Maurice,* 113. Coleridge was profoundly influenced by Kant's *Critique of Practical Reason*, and in 1806 had already known Kant's work for several years, (Barth, *Coleridge*, 14-16). Coleridge's *Biographia Literaria* [1817] itself was "a potent, though indirect, factor in the interpretation of German philosophy to England", (Bayard Quincy Morgan and A.R. Hohlfield (eds.), *German Literature in British Magazines 1750-1860* [Madison: University of Wisconsin Press, 1949], 50-52).

[9] See Tulloch, *Movements*, 41-85; Alan P.F. Sell, "The Rise and Reception of Modern Biblical Criticism: A Retrospect", *Evangelical Quarterly*, LII, III (1980), 136; John H. Overton, *The English Church in the Nineteenth Century (1800-1833)* (London: Longmans, Green, 1894), 183.

[10] Ieuan Ellis, "Schleiermacher in Britain", *SJT,* 33, 5 (1980), 417-19.

[11] See Appendix 5, pp.292-93 below.

[12] See Jack, *English Literature,* 384; René Wellek, *Immanuel Kant in England 1793-1838* (Princeton: Princeton University Press, 1931), v, 4, 15, 28-30, 32, 40-2.

Otto Pfleiderer saw German philosophy being mediated in Britain mainly by Coleridge, and also Carlyle who early became attracted to Kant and German literature and did most to spread interest in it.[13] Erskine apparently came into serious contact with neither Coleridge nor Carlyle until the late 1830s. Then he became close friends with Carlyle who was drawn to Erskine through his steadfast belief in the invisible in a mechanistic age, and their shared conviction concerning the independence of inward revelation.[14] It was 1838-39 before Erskine began seriously to inquire about Coleridge's *Aids to Reflection*.[15]

There are many acknowledged areas of similarity between Erskine and Coleridge. Steve Gowler believes there is no evidence that Erskine and Coleridge were in any way interdependent, but were simply "independent minds shaped by common concerns and sharing a common context".[16] James Boulger suggests because of the common influences of "German philosophy", "Romanticism", and "eighteenth-century tradition",

> we should not wonder at [Erskine's] anticipations of Coleridge's views, or feel the need to discover a direct relationship between the two. Once given the similarities of their mentalities and interests and the identical influences under which each fell, the general tendency of their writings to assume the same tone, and sometimes attitude, follows without difficulty.[17]

Thomas Carlyle and Edward Irving were intimate members of the Highgate circle surrounding Coleridge, and A.J. Scott remained close to both, together with Julius Hare. Erskine's and Campbell's deeply influential relationship with A.J. Scott dated from 1826 and 1827 respectively. Indeed, it was Scott who introduced Erskine and Campbell in 1827 or 1828.[18] It is therefore entirely possible that Scott was the common catalyst for further-

---

[13] Pfleiderer, *Theology*, 308-17.

[14] Kenneth J. Fielding, "A Carlylean Elegy in Auchtertool Kirkyard", in *Scottish Christianity in the Modern World*, Stewart J. Brown and George Newlands (eds.) (Edinburgh: T.&T. Clark, 2000), 48.

[15] See Letters to A.J. Scott, 11 July and 2 August, 1838, *Letters-I*, 318, 320, and to Jane Stirling, 8 April 1837, *NLS MS* Acc.11388/120 495a. By July 1839, Erskine was sending books by Coleridge to his friend Alexandre Vinet in Lausanne, (Bovet [ed.], *Lettres*, III, 132, 183). In a letter to Chalmers from Geneva dated 24 October 1839, Erskine was citing approvingly Coleridge's *Aids to Reflection*, especially his views on the necessity for reason and conscience to cohere with Christian doctrines, (*NCLE MS CHA* 7.2.12). In 1840 Erskine was clearly deriving much benefit from Coleridge's *Literary Remains*, (Letters to Madame Forel, 14 October, and Thomas Carlyle, 24 November, *Letters-II*, 8 and 21).

[16] Gowler, *No Second-hand Religion*, 205.

[17] James D. Boulger, *Coleridge as Religious Thinker* (New Haven: Yale University Press, 1961), 43.

[18] Needham, "Thomas Erskine", 210.

ing not only the mutual influence between Irving, Erskine, and Campbell, but also a wider interest in continental thought. All three regarded Scott as "the dominant intellect of the group", the one who could articulate clearly "the radically new and universal theology towards which they had all been independently moving". Philip Newell believes, with some justification, that it may have been the influence of Scott, who "first offered a more clearly articulated Christ-centred theology of incarnation", who was responsible for Erskine's developing incarnational and pneumatological thought, closely associated with the concept of the divine character being reproduced in humanity.[19] Nevertheless, significantly, Erskine was the first of the group to travel in Europe in 1822 (Carlyle did not visit Germany until 1852), and some sixteen years later introduced Campbell and Scott to the experience. It was apparently quite independently, on his own initiative (though conceivably inspired by Charles Stuart), that Erskine set out on journeys of religious exploration and inquiry, coming to know directly leading continental thinkers, taking an inquiring and intelligent interest in their views, even though his surviving personal correspondence modestly tends to minimise, or sometimes even omit entirely, highly significant encounters. For example, whilst in Carlsbad in 1846, almost as an aside, Erskine remarked:

> Schelling is here – I know him and like him very well, but cannot get much out of him – he says that he is here to drink the waters, and not to make out propositions, and that he must avoid everything that would trouble his head…I spoke to Schelling about Carlyle – he said that he could not tolerate his style…he thought a great deal of Coleridge, he spoke of him as a great genius…[20]

Erskine was referring to Friedrich Schelling, Coleridge's mentor, who was seen by many as providing an intellectual and philosophical foundation for the Romantic movement. The context suggests previous mutual acquaintance, and perhaps Erskine may have found his concept of the divine incarnate within humanity helpfully enunciated by Schelling who famously

---

[19] J. Philip Newell, *A.J. Scott and his Circle*, unpublished PhD (University of Edinburgh, 1981), 38-9, 49-50, 67-8, 431, 442, 444, and "Unworthy of the Dignity of the Assembly", *RSCHS*, XXI (1983), 250. See also Erskine's letters to Miss Rachel Erskine, 6 September 1828, and A.J. Scott, 11 February 1864, *Letters-I*, 143, *Letters-II*, 146-7, and Erskine's letter supporting Scott in *The Daily News*, (Saturday, 7 June 1862), 3. Scott became Irving's assistant in London in 1828, and exercised a significant influence upon Irving's own developing thought, especially in the areas of pneumatology and incarnational principles. Erskine had met Scott probably in 1826, and certainly heard him preach in 1828 (though looking back in 1862, Erskine said he 'knew' Scott from 1829), and subsequently attributed significant debt to him (though Scott was indebted himself to Erskine, e.g., for the idea of spiritual consciousness).

[20] Letter to Jane Stirling, 31 August 1846, *NLS MSS* Acc.11388/120.

promoted the key Romantic concept of *pantheism*. Significantly, Schelling was amongst those Romantics who, like William Law in the eighteenth century, had found inspiration in Jacob Boehme to counter prevalent Enlightenment rationalism. As Erskine's note hints, in 1846 Schelling was in the unproductive period of his life, reluctant to engage in discussion, still bitter that Hegel had supposedly stolen some of his main ideas. Nevertheless, he was at that time occupying Hegel's chair of philosophy at Berlin.[21]

Erskine and the Continent

British theological isolation only really began to break down after about 1860. But Thomas Erskine has received little credit for innovation in the sense of being recognised as one of the first to break the mould, with any serious significance attaching to his ground-breaking journeys to the continent having been generally discounted. He has tended to be dismissed as an independent amateur thinker who, though he may in various ways somehow have mirrored theological developments abroad, nevertheless operated in relative isolation, having in reality little or no direct or interactive contact with the revolutionary continental, and especially German, thought which most resembled his own.

Vernon Storr has fittingly remarked concerning parallels between nineteenth-century Scotland and Germany that

> in both countries a reconstruction of Christian doctrine was in process, the keynote of which was the appeal to religious experience and to the ethical significance of dogma, to the inwardness of Christian truth, rather than to the historical forms in which that truth had been handed down from the past. The result of the movement showed itself in a general broadening of theological belief, in a desire to be quit of sectarianism and to find some more comprehensive basis for union, and in a determination to assert the rights of the individual consciousness in face of the claims of authority.[22]

In this context, Otto Pfleiderer singled out Thomas Erskine and John McLeod Campbell for virtually unique accordance in Scotland with fundamental trends in German theology. Their soteriological work was "manifestly the same reconstruction of the Christian doctrine of salvation which was effected by Kant and Schleiermacher in Germany, whereby it is converted from forensic externality into ethical inwardness and a truth of direct religious experience." However, Pfleiderer seemed unaware of any suggestion of direct influence. He concluded that they appeared "to have reached their convictions in entire independence of German theology, by their own

---

[21] See Reardon, *Romanticism*, 88, 112; Wilkens and Padgett, *Christianity*, 71, 76.
[22] Storr, *English Theology*, 356.

absorbing study of the Bible".[23] Bernard Reardon appears to have taken his cue from Pfleiderer by asserting (besides repeating the strange remark, based on the *Spectator*, that Erskine "was not a particularly learned man") that it is "pretty certain" Erskine "was quite unaware of contemporary developments in German theology".[24] Other Erskine commentators have adopted a similar line. Steve Gowler regards Erskine from the outset as "a theological 'outsider'". Noting what he considers to be the absence of references in his writings to other thinkers, he concludes that he was "for the most part, untouched by the critical winds drifting westward from Germany".[25] John Tulloch acknowledges Erskine's contemporaneity with Schleiermacher and Coleridge, but affirms he was "without any indebtedness" to either.[26] Needham likewise largely underplays the significance of the 'European tour' at this crucial period of the early nineteenth century, tending to regard Erskine in the style of a theological dilettante, whose visits to the continent were little more than personal indulgences.[27]

On the other hand, the American abolitionist and London-based pastor, Moncure Daniel Conway, gave the impression that Erskine was somewhat notorious for his German 'credentials'. In 1866, he recorded a conversation with Thomas Carlyle (who should have been an authoritative source[28]), in which Carlyle told him

> Erskine began life as a lawyer, but left that for religion. He wrote much on this subject, but lost his Calvinism by going to study in Germany. He was now not in public favour because of his scepticism, but Carlyle held him in high esteem.[29]

---

[23] Pfleiderer, *Theology*, 382.

[24] Reardon, *Religious Thought*, 294, cf., the *Spectator*, 2 April 1870, 431.

[25] Gowler, *No Second-hand Religion*, 203.

[26] Tulloch, *Movements*, 138.

[27] See Needham, *Thomas Erskine*, e.g., 87, 366, 373. In her section on Erskine's continental 'friends', Marian Foster completely ignores the possibility of any theological significance in Erskine's travels, (*Representation and Substitution*, 54-57). Timothy Stunt recognises somewhat more of the real significance in *From Awakening to Secession*, (Edinburgh: T.&T. Clark, 2000), to which I am indebted for aspects of the following.

[28] Despite their obvious personal dissimilarity, Erskine admired those characteristics in Carlyle which he himself espoused. Carlyle emphasised passionately that life and religion cannot be divorced, and elevated human activity to the realm of the divine. Dismissive of dogma and tradition, he asserted the active presence of God in the world, with religion less a creed than a continual dynamic growth in the human heart. A religious Romantic, he was impressed by vital and active Christianity, and was influenced early by German thought and literature. By 1829 he was lamenting the loss of human belief in the invisible, (Porter, *Enlightenment* [2000], 297).

[29] Moncure Daniel Conway, *Autobiography Memories and Experiences of Moncure Daniel Conway*, in 2 volumes (London: Cassell and Company, 1904), II, 95.

Whilst the mere existence of parallels does not prove assumptions of influence, it is suggested that the extent to which Erskine was affected by exposure to contemporary continental ideas has nevertheless been seriously underestimated. He was certainly prompted initially by his own pietistic study of the Bible, and the general milieu of predominantly eighteenth-century religious knowledge, conversation, and discussion in which he lived and moved (not forgetting that Erskine was a trained lawyer who numbered amongst eminent fellow students and close friends in Edinburgh the Lords Cockburn and Jeffrey). But we adduce that Erskine subsequently received strong corroborative impetus for his developing ideas through his continental journeys of religious discovery in Europe. The first two journeys took place for extended periods, between 1822 and 1825, and 1826 and 1827, when he included in his tours visits to Herrnhut, Berlin, Hamburg, Paris, Milan, Venice, Rome, Basle, and Geneva. Erskine set off to tour Europe again between 1837 and 1839, this time accompanied for two months by John McLeod Campbell, and he was found yet again revisiting Paris, Switzerland, Rome, Dresden and Carlsbad in 1845 and 1846.

At one level, Erskine was engaged in what he considered to be 'quasi-missionary' visits to observe the efforts of Protestants to spread the gospel in the difficult conditions in Europe, supporting their work with books, personal encouragement, and finance for evangelistic and educational efforts. He apparently "exerted widespread influence" at Lausanne in the context of the Swiss evangelical *Réveil*, with which the Haldanes had been prominently involved.[30] On return to Scotland after his first journey in 1825, he joined the Continental Society in Dundee.[31] But more significantly, Erskine was one of the earliest British participants in what became a novel but increasingly 'fashionable' pursuit for inquiring theologians (or 'neologians' as the instigators of fresh doctrines were sometimes rather pejoratively described in the early nineteenth century[32]) during the early to mid-1820s. Coleridge was actually in Germany with Wordsworth before the turn of the century, but following the period of enforced travel restrictions due to the Napoleonic wars, Julius Hare, Connop Thirlwall, Edward Pusey and Charles Hodge were amongst those who first travelled in Germany and elsewhere in Europe during the 1820s with the motivation to become further acquainted with German philosophy and the new movement in German

---

[30] Drummond, *Kirk*, 191.

[31] The Continental Society for the Diffusion of Religious Knowledge was founded by Henry Drummond (host of the 1826-30 Albury prophetical conferences) in 1819. It "played a vital role in promoting relations between English and Genevan evangelicals", and in encouraging evangelism and the revival of vital evangelical Christianity in Europe, especially in France and Switzerland, (Stunt, *Awakening*, 62, 111).

[32] Fuhrmann, *Extraordinary Christianity*, 42.

theology inaugurated by Schleiermacher.[33] Such journeys, whilst apparently considered crucial for others, have generally not been regarded as particularly significant for the development of Erskine's thought. Some reassessment is perhaps therefore necessary, especially in the light of the critically important figures Erskine encountered and befriended, both in the 1820s and later in the 1830s. Many of these became a closely interlinked network of correspondents who were particularly interested in the discussion and propagation of new theological and philosophical ideas. Some of them were aware of Erskine's own writings. They presented him with works in German. He in turn held lengthy theological debates with them, being by nature exceptionally interested in and motivated by philosophical and theological discussion, as the many and varied visitors to his home at Linlathen universally testified.

In line with growing nineteenth-century evangelical missionary fervour, Timothy Stunt has recently shown the importance to British evangelical observers of the *Réveil* in Geneva, which has come to be especially associated with Robert Haldane's visit in 1816. Stunt has noted the key role played there by Thomas Erskine, along with Gerard Noel, Henry Drummond and others. The ending of the Napoleonic Wars presented British evangelicals with the opportunity to set out on the continental tour with a view to aiding and supporting European evangelical dissidents like César Malan and Paul Ami Bost in Geneva, who were suffering in their struggle for a free and pure church community against repressive secular authorities: "Geneva was, therefore, a favoured stopping place for evangelicals visiting the Continent".[34] And for Scottish evangelicals like Robert Haldane, Geneva in particular afforded an obvious outlet for a more vital and fervent evangelicalism, given the close parallel with their own social, political, and religious situation, where an atmosphere of change and general uncertainty, coupled with an entrenched rigid and dogmatic establishment conservatism, prevailed.[35] Though a 'high Calvinist', César Malan became close friends with Erskine, and it may be that Malan's commitment to the 'un-Calvinistic' ideas that 'salvation was already granted and obtained' and that 'assurance of faith was necessary to salvation', initially drew them to each other.[36] Certainly, the evangelical experiential character of the *Réveil* appealed to Erskine who "felt that among such folk in Geneva he was in

---

[33] Young, *Maurice*, 111. For American interest in Germany, notably Charles Hodge, see Walter H. Conser, Jr., *God and the Natural World: Religion and Science in Antebellum America* (Columbia: University of South Carolina Press, 1993), 66-70.

[34] Stunt, *Awakening*, 105.

[35] Cf., Drummond and Bulloch, *Scottish Church, 1688-1843*, 152-3, 213-19; Stunt, *Awakening*, 222.

[36] See Timothy Stunt, "Geneva and British Evangelicals in the Early Nineteenth Century", *Journal of Ecclesiastical History*, 32, 1 (January, 1981), 35-46.

touch with experimental Christianity rather than a theoretical set of beliefs".[37] Erskine observed that the Calvinism of the French and Swiss Reformed Church was of a more 'lively' type than in Scotland. Nevertheless, he insisted, "Men require something now which will commend itself to the conscience and the reason…".[38] However, the interesting ambiguity of Erskine's fervent, radical, evangelical spirit combined with his apparent doctrinal unorthodoxy was somewhat disconcerting to his Calvinist Swiss friends like Malan and Louis Gaussen with whom he enjoyed sharp disagreements.[39] Bishop Samuel Gobat (1799-1879), who trained in Basel, was an observer of these early days in Geneva in 1823 and made the discerning observation that

> Dr. Gaussen's [house] was the centre around which a circle of the *élite*, not only as regards religious excellence, but also intellectual culture, used to meet for mutual improvement and edification, to my great mental and spiritual benefit. About twice a week we used to read together the Epistle to the Romans in the original, when my mind was enriched with many critical and practical views through the comments of Messrs. Gaussen, Gerard Noel, T. Erskine, and others. I did not fully agree with the two latter gentlemen, especially with Mr. Erskine; but as they were thoroughly acquainted with the Greek classics and the Ecclesiastical Fathers, their observations were most interesting and beneficial, especially as Dr. Gaussen always subjected such observations to acute logical criticism.[40]

On his first tour in 1822 Erskine had written excitedly to Thomas Chalmers from Herrnhut concerning the German evangelicals' dislike of Calvinism, and had expressed to Chalmers his own inability to reconcile in his mind what he still accepted as the Calvinist doctrine of predestination and the equally strong reality of moral responsibility. In a particularly telling comment, he informed Chalmers that he then felt able to coexist quite happily with apparently contradictory concepts in a philosophical reflection which seems to have been assimilated almost directly from Kant: "We know things, not absolutely as they are in themselves, but relatively as they are to us and to our practical necessities".[41]

It seems likely that Erskine was inclined to absorb such radical ideas early on in his travels as the result of direct contact with what he perceived as fitting contemporary philosophical concepts, being topical subjects of discussion on the continent in the early 1820s. During Erskine's second European tour, *The Unconditional Freeness of the Gospel* was developed

---

[37] Stunt, *Awakening*, 107.

[38] Letter to Mrs Stirling, 14 September 1838, *Letters-I*, 327.

[39] See, e.g., letters to Mrs Montagu, 13 July 1826, Miss Rachel Erskine, 2 October 1826, and Monsieur Gaussen, 7 December 1832, *Letters-I*, 75, 84, 288-97.

[40] Gobat, *Samuel Gobat*, 42-3.

[41] 12 December 1822, *Letters-I*, 44. See also Appendix 5, p.292.

and written at a time of intense, personal, theological reassessment. Erskine's private correspondence during this period confirms the book's impression that 1826-28 was a passionate, formative, spiritually and intellectually stimulating, almost prophetic, period in Erskine's life. It resulted in a more stirring and polemic edge to his writing than had been previously seen. In Hamburg in 1822, Erskine announced enthusiastically that he had begun to learn German.[42] By 1827, he needed to *re*learn German to read Boehme in the original, and was reading and studying German and Dante on his travels, expressing a strong liking for the German language and preference for "the German mind better than the mind of any other nation, our own not excepted".[43]

Erskine's Relation to German Theology

John Henry Newman categorised Erskine and Schleiermacher together as "arch-exponents" of "an idiosyncratic philosophical development of the eighteenth-century revival of religious feeling".[44] Erskine has also been referred to as "the Scottish Schleiermacher"[45] in view of the correspondence of some of his revolutionary thinking to the ideas of the great German theologian. We have from time to time noted the existence of clear parallels, especially notions of the consciousness of God founded in the feeling of absolute dependence. However, no connection has seriously been established to show that Erskine even knew of Schleiermacher or had exposure to his writings and theology.

It is surprising that Erskine never directly mentions Schleiermacher in any of his surviving writings. However, he certainly knew about him, and apparently asked F.D. Maurice in 1848 whether he existed in translation.[46] Had Erskine tried reading Schleiermacher in German? We have previously observed that he rarely attributed his sources. Nevertheless, it might be expected that if, as must surely have been the case, Schleiermacher had featured in Erskine's extensive continental theological discussions, some mention of him would have been made in his correspondence.[47] Despite the absence of any direct surviving reference, some speculative clues may be gleaned, however. It remains inconceivable that, given the evident concor-

---

[42] Letter to Dr. Charles Stuart, 2 November 1822, *Letters-I,* 42.

[43] Letters to Miss Rachel Erskine, 2 May 1827, Mrs Paterson, 26 July 1827, and Mrs Stirling, 31 July 1827, *Letters-I,* 115, 121, 122; Machar, "Thomas Erskine", *Andover Review,* 475.

[44] Newman, (Tract No. 73), 54.

[45] E.g., Needham, "Thomas Erskine", 457.

[46] Maurice (ed.), *Life,* I, 453.

[47] Though only a fraction of Erskine's continental correspondence remains extant.

dance of much of their thinking, and Erskine's extended sojourns in Germany and Europe, which included lengthy meetings with Schleiermacher's followers, Erskine was not at least made aware of the great theologian and his sympathetic concepts. He may even have attempted to read him but found his style hard going or the print difficult for his poor eyesight, hence the later request for a translation. Just a few years later, in 1854, Mrs Schwabe, a highly intelligent German friend of Erskine's, who knew A.J. Scott, attended J.J. Tayler's Unitarian church in Manchester, and who, being sympathetically drawn to Erskine through the similarity of their views, repeatedly endeavoured to 'convince' him by persuading him to study Tayler's writings, presented Erskine with a notable book which had recently been translated from the German. Significantly, Erskine already possessed the book. He commented:

> Rothe was chaplain at Rome I think when I was there in 1826 – and he gave me the book in German, but my eyes were very weak then and the type was small and indistinct, and I was not a good German scholar – so that I read very little of it, but what little I did read, impressed me with the conviction that the writer was a holy man acquainted with God, and acquainted with the depths of man's heart. And now that it is in good print and good English and my eyes somewhat better, I hope to learn more from it, and get nourishment for my spirit out of it.[48]

It would be fascinating to identify the book presented to Erskine by the celebrated German theologian, Richard Rothe, and some speculative educated guesswork may perhaps be permitted in this respect. Mrs Schwabe was enthusiastic about J.J. Tayler, and he undoubtedly from time to time recommended important works. Tayler was very familiar with German theology, having visited the continent himself as early as 1824, and actually studied in Germany in 1834-5. He conducted services in German at his Manchester church for the many local German merchants and their families, including Mrs Schwabe. He had made a special study of Schleiermacher and the historians Neander and Niebuhr.[49] Whilst a number of Neander's and Niebuhr's works were translated into English from about 1850, and Niebuhr was extensively reviewed in the 1849 *North British Review*, Erskine's comments suggest he was probably not reading history. Rothe had not published anything himself by 1824/1826. Some unknown devotional writer could have been the author of the mystery volume. However, Erskine clearly found it challenging, and Mrs Schwabe's mutual correspondence with Erskine was maintained at a relatively high theological

---

[48] 14 July 1854, *NLS MS* 9747–42.

[49] See Young, *Maurice*, 111-2, and John Hamilton Thom (ed.), *Letters Embracing his Life of John James Tayler,* in 2 volumes (London: Williams and Norgate, 1872), I, 127-9, 137-9, 161-3.

Erskine in a Reconstructive Continental Context 237

level. It is tempting, therefore, to speculate that Rothe had given Erskine one of the few obvious noteworthy theological books available in German in 1824/1826 but not translated into English until the 1850s – namely, a copy of *Kurze Darstellung des theologischen Studiums* [1811] by Rothe's mentor Schleiermacher, which was first translated into English as *Brief Outline of the Study of Theology* by William Farrer, and published by T. & T. Clark in Edinburgh in 1850.[50]

This all sounds highly speculative. However, clear evidence exists that, in fact, Erskine was becoming well acquainted with German theology in the early 1820s. Crucially, Erskine met the widely influential Pietist and revivalist, Augustus Tholuck (1799-1877), professor of theology in Berlin, in 1822 on his first continental tour,[51] whilst on his second journey in 1824, he met in Rome the Lutheran Pietist, Richard Rothe (1799-1867), then chaplain to the Prussian embassy. Both Tholuck and Rothe were distinguished post-Kantian mediating theologians who played critical roles in the regeneration and development of German nineteenth-century evangelical theology, and like Erskine were renowned for their vital personal piety. Both became prominent in Britain, and both developed the ideas of Schleiermacher. Tholock studied under Schleiermacher in Berlin, whilst Rothe was influenced not only by Schleiermacher (under whom he also studied) and the prominent Romantic religious poets Goethe and Novalis, but studied under Tholuck himself, becoming a professor at Heidelberg. Albrecht Ritschl (1822-1889) was another of Tholuck's students, who also studied under Rothe at Heidelberg.[52] In addition, Erskine met and developed a longstanding, warm friendship with the well known and influential German ambassador at Rome and the English court, the Chevalier Bunsen (1791-1860), who became "the most distinguished representative of German Protestantism in Britain",[53] and who was a prominent liberal theological and historical scholar with multiple contacts in the theological world. These key figures were amongst those with whom not only Erskine, but Coleridge, Edward Pusey and Charles Hodge developed highly influential relationships, and Pfleiderer's later apparent ignorance of such contacts (apart from Coleridge) probably owes much to their relative informality and the passage of time.

---

[50] John McLeod Campbell first read Schleiermacher in 1868, (Letter to his eldest son, March, 1868, *Memorials*, II, 201).

[51] Letter to Dr. Charles Stuart, 2 November 1822, *Letters-I*, 41-2.

[52] Tholuck, Novalis, Rothe and Ritschl all feature prominently as key theological figures in Karl Barth's *Protestant Theology in the Nineteenth Century* (London: SCM Press, 1972).

[53] R. William Franklin, "The Impact of Germany on the Anglican Catholic Revival in Nineteenth-Century Britain", *Anglican and Episcopal History*, LXI, 4 (December, 1992), 444. See Erskine's Letter to Chevalier Bunsen, 8 August 1854, *Letters-II*, 87-8.

Augustus Tholuck

When Erskine met Augustus Tholuck in Berlin in 1822 he was very impressed, believing he would make a significant impact in Germany. He expressed (significantly, to his inspirer, Dr. Charles Stuart) the desire to study under him.[54]

Tholuck, who was the protégé of the great German church historian Neander (1789-1850), was also Director of the German Bible Society, later forging connections with the emergent Evangelical Alliance in Britain in the 1840s. He evidenced many similarities to Erskine. Essentially an apologist for Christianity in opposition to rationalism, he was the main source of the neo-Pietist revival which influenced the university of Erlangen and which, like Tholuck, was renowned for its emphasis on subjective experiential regeneration.[55] Referring to the impact of Schleiermacher and the 'subjective school' on the influential Neander, George Smeaton commented

> In his system all the great doctrines connected with God as an authoritative lawgiver, fall into the background. But great and glowing prominence is given to all the views which stand connected with the person of Christ as a fountain of spiritual influences. The centre around which his whole theology moved, was, to use his own expression, the communion of life with the Redeemer, or the fellowship of Christ's life, – a precious truth, of which the importance cannot be overestimated, and which has been breathed in great part through him into the whole theology of Germany, as well as of other lands. That the person of Christ is the true life-source of humanity, was his principle amid all the struggles of modern theology…the essence of Christianity is always represented by Neander as consisting in…the communication of a new divine life, with which man's nature must be imbued from its inmost centre, by which it is raised and ennobled in all its powers, and from which a new tendency of human thought and action will proceed in every direction.[56]

There is evident correspondence here with Erskine's essential developing thought. Tholuck himself exercised a profound influence on many, particularly Edward Pusey, with whom he formed a long-lasting friendship.[57] A progressive evangelical, who, with Erskine, apparently believed in univer-

---

[54] Letter of 2 November 1822, *Letters-I*, 41-2.

[55] Claude Welch, *Protestant Thought in the Nineteenth Century*, in 2 volumes (New Haven and London: Yale University Press, 1972), I, 218-19.

[56] George Smeaton, "August Neander, his Influence, System, and various Writings", in *The British and Foreign Evangelical Review and Quarterly Record of Christian Literature*, VI (1853), 711-12, 714.

[57] Albrecht Geck, "The Concept of History in E.B. Pusey's First Enquiry into German Theology and Its German Background", *Journal of Theological Studies,* 38, 2 (October, 1987), 394-5.

sal restitution, he was notable for resisting the tide of Idealist philosophical influences associated with Hegel by means of a 'corrective' emphasis on the Christian experience of sin and regeneration, accompanied by renewed doctrines of the fall and original sin. Like Erskine, Tholuck identified the heart, rather than mere reason, as the crucial point of contact between God and humanity, which he believed would fulfil the spiritual needs of the age. In this he embraced a theology of personal experience and 'encounter' between humankind and God which, according to Karl Barth,[58] paralleled Schleiermacher, and appeared to teach that the life of God is already within humanity waiting to be 'illuminated' – a conviction strongly adopted by Erskine.

Tholuck has been described, in terms similar to Erskine, as "an eclectic, with a touch of romanticism". Like Erskine, Tholuck saw Christianity as above all "a new principle of life, and that life is demonstrated by itself. To love Christ is better than to be learned; for it is to enter into direct contact with the very source of truth".[59] Barth, citing Tholuck, brings out the close resemblance between him and Erskine in their view of the appropriation of salvific truth:

> He...finds that the New Testament teaches a 'disposition of the inner nature towards Christian truth which consists in the life of the original ἀλήθεια in man'. That man understands the Christian truth shows that he was originally related to it. 'Now that in man which God wants, when it feels itself attracted by its kindred spirit, which comes to it from the Christian revelation, will be filled with self-surrendering love towards that to which it is akin, the more the consciousness of this affinity increases'.[60]

Richard Rothe

As "a compendium of all the religious and theological tendencies of the time", Richard Rothe was a highly significant contact for Erskine.[61] Many of those associated with *Essays and Reviews*, including Mark Pattison, Benjamin Jowett, Rowland Williams, and H.B. Wilson, were later to attribute direct or indirect influence to Rothe. Dean Stanley made a special visit to see him in Germany.[62] Though Erskine has left little record concerning Richard Rothe, this notable German theologian nevertheless him-

---

[58] Barth, *Protestant Theology*, 512.
[59] F. Lichtenberger, *History of German Theology in the Nineteenth Century* (Edinburgh: T.&T. Clark, 1889), 474.
[60] Barth, *Protestant Theology*, 512.
[61] Barth, (citing Heckel), *Protestant Theology*, 598.
[62] Ieuan Ellis, *Seven Against Christ: A Study of 'Essays and Reviews'* (Leiden: E.J. Brill, 1980), 284-5.

self recorded at length extended personal meetings with Erskine in 1824 in his journal published in 1873. Rothe, though regarded as a follower of Schleiermacher and Hegel, nevertheless was independently-minded, and in some respects reserved judgment concerning Schleiermacher.[63] When Erskine met him in Rome, Rothe was immensely impressed by Erskine's practical care and compassion for a dying French painter. In his journal entry recording the event, Rothe makes the crucially significant observation that

> this Mr. Erskine (who, by the way, knows and loves our Heubner) is a spiritual man who engenders love, in fellowship with whom I have passed many happy and instructive hours. In the academic world he is known as the author of several very deeply thought-out treatises...upon Christianity.[64]

As with Samuel Gobat's observations noted previously, here Erskine suggests a quite different picture to the 'unlearned amateur' several commentators have proposed.[65] Though palpably more of a serious theological *thinker* than *scholar*, evidently Erskine was known and seriously respected by continental academics as a competent, articulate, theologian in his own right, capable of dialoguing comfortably with prominent German theologians in a way which inspired and impressed them, and especially was recognised as knowledgeable concerning German theology. The Lutheran H.L. Heubner (1780-1853), was Rothe's mentor and Director at Wittenburg theological seminary, and later became his brother-in-law. Though noted for his piety, he remained a relatively minor theologian. That Erskine should already know him in the early 1820s is remarkable for someone considered to possess little awareness of German thought. It is inconceivable that given such extensive knowledge of comparatively minor German

---

[63] Lichtenberger, *German Theology*, 495-6; Barth, *Protestant Theology*, 597.

[64] Friedrich Nippold, (ed.), *Richard Rothe: Ein Christliches Lebensbild*, in 2 volumes (Wittenberg: Verlag von Hermann Koelling, 1873, 1874), I, 371-2. My rendering of the German original; cf., William Hanna's version in *Letters-I*, 373.

[65] E.g., Anon., *British Critic, Quarterly Theological Review and Ecclesiastical Record*, 23, XLVI (April, 1838), 323. Views differ in this regard. Principal Shairp portrays Erskine as a man with a thirst for learning, who would have been genuinely recognised as learned, but for the hindrance of weak eyesight, ("Reminiscences", *Letters-II*, 367, 372). William Knight, Professor of Philosophy at St. Andrews, commented that Erskine "was a great reader and an unceasing thinker. He had as extensive an acquaintance with theological and general Literature as perhaps any man of his time, although his secluded habits hid his many accomplishments from public view". Linlathen contained "one of the most extensive libraries in Forfarshire", (*Some Nineteenth Century Scotsmen*, [Edinburgh and London: Oliphant, Anderson & Ferrier, 1903], 187, 190). Even Andrew Thomson knew of Erskine's reputation as a Greek scholar, (*Universal Pardon*, 426). In contrast, Julia Wedgwood thought "he was not a very wide reader", though she knew Erskine only during the years of seriously failing eyesight, (*Teachers*, 73).

theological figures and evident exposure to contemporary German theology, Erskine remained unaware of the teaching and influence of major personages like Schleiermacher. It is more credible that Erskine had somehow already been introduced to the ideas of leading nineteenth-century continental thinkers, and took an enduring inquiring interest in their views, comparing them with his own formative thoughts, even though like Schelling and Rothe they receive relatively little specific mention in his few surviving continental writings.

R.S. Franks described Richard Rothe as a 'disciple' of Kant and Schleiermacher; a 'mediating theologian', seeking to accommodate rationalism to orthodoxy.[66] Franks saw him as leading on naturally to the classic 'mediator', Isaac Dorner (1809-1884), who himself shared many of Erskine's leading themes, though he was more specifically compared with F.D. Maurice who went to Germany to meet him in 1850.[67] 'Mediating theology' was a diverse, eclectic, contextual, continental apologetic movement, whose objectives compared remarkably with Erskine's:

> The nineteenth century saw the birth of a great many theological proposals which mediated between Christ and culture, spoke of Christianity as incentive towards human potentiality and in more or less qualified terms reckoned with man's goodness. One of these movements was 'mediating theology' which rose to an apogee through Schleiermacher and whose later exponents were Dorner, Rothe, Neander and Martensen, among others. Ritschl belongs in part to this school.[68]

Rothe evidenced close kinship with Erskine and Tholuck, especially as an advocate of Christian consciousness. A dedicated Bible student, and proponent of "immediate contact and of personal intercourse with the living God", he had been repelled by "the dry preaching of the Rationalists…Christianity appeared to him as an immense spiritual power in the world, a fact which in its greatness and richness greatly surpassed his reason, and was consequently a mystery. At a time when everybody was a rationalist, Rothe preserved his faith in the supernatural", believing that the Christian revelation at the same time "contained nothing which was contrary to our reason". Rothe regarded faith as "the key to the most elevated

---

[66] On the German mediating school see Conser, *God and the Natural World*, 48-54.

[67] Franks, *Work of Christ*, 561-78 *passim*; Welch, *Protestant Thought*, I, 273-82; Pfleiderer, *Theology*, 373; Young, *Maurice*, 112. See also the introductory essay by John MacPherson to Richard Rothe's *Still Hours*, [trans. Jane T. Stoddart] (London: Hodder and Stoughton, 1886), 21-2. Erskine anticipated especially Dorner's objective/ subjective approach to salvific knowledge emanating from awareness of a new redeemed humanity; see Isaac August Dorner, *A System of Christian Doctrine*, in 4 volumes, [trans. Alfred Cave and J.S. Banks] (Edinburgh: T.& T. Clark, 1896), IV, 117-9.

[68] Hoffman, *Luther and the Mystics*, 239; cf., Fisher, *Christian Doctrine*, 512-28.

knowledge", and the person of Christ the true object of faith and understanding.[69]

He was "a man of the deepest piety and devoted to the cause of genuine Christianity", and was also, like Erskine, "quite conscious of himself as being in conflict with both the theological liberals and the orthodox". This was because of his concern on the one hand for the rediscovery of the element of the transcendent and supernatural, whilst on the other, remaining opposed to traditional interpretations of Christian truth, typically through dogma, doctrinal formulations and biblicism.[70] Like Tholuck, Rothe was convinced that Christ came not to bring new doctrine, but to instil in us "a new principle of divine life".[71] Like Erskine, he believed in Christ's representative atonement, and divine/ human union in the incarnation, so that "potentially in [Christ] the old sinful race were regenerated", with the objective of removing sin and instilling holiness.[72] Many of those influenced by Idealist philosophy and Pietism on the continent in the nineteenth century espoused universalist views, but interestingly, Rothe held to a type of conditional immortality which implied that all humanity could be saved provided that they 'converted themselves'. This echoed Erskine's insistence on human responsibility to co-operate with God in the matter of salvation, starting from the universal light God had given to everyone, and leading ultimately to acceptance of universalism itself as the eventual outcome of God's 'school of life'.[73]

Initially Rothe was not overly impressed by Schleiermacher, disliking his critical approach. However, he followed Schleiermacher in teaching absolute dependence and Christ's vicarious suffering of sympathetic identification with humanity. This was developed by his belief that God's purpose in creating humanity was to conform them to his own likeness. God's plan of redemption had made this possible because through Christ's incarnation he inaugurated a new humanity of which Christ was its archetypal head.[74] Erskine himself was an early advocate of absolute filial dependence, and was holding developed views concerning the universal Headship of Christ by 1829. Significantly, the Ritschlian critic, James Orr, linked together Erskine, Maurice and Rothe as holding identical ideas concerning Christ's headship, and sharing the belief that, in offering atonement by way of self-sacrifice and surrender of the will, Christ effectively represented all

---

[69] Lichtenberger, *German Theology*, 493-5.
[70] Welch, *Protestant Thought*, I, 282-3.
[71] Lichtenberger, *German Theology*, 495.
[72] Fisher, *Christian Doctrine*, 518-21.
[73] See Rowell, *Hell*, 208.
[74] See Grensted, *Atonement*, 332; Franks, *Work of Christ*, 573.

humanity.[75] Like Erskine, Rothe also developed a strong ethical theology based on the inward consciousness of God, emphasising the inseparable link between religion, doctrine, and morality, where life was seen in evolutionary terms as an education process towards the moral perfection of humanity, whether in this life or the next. He further saw the ongoing task of Protestantism as "the transformation of Christianity from a churchly to an 'ethically-human form'.[76] Like Erskine, Rothe struggled with the final fate of the wicked, though unlike Erskine, who turned to universalism, Rothe apparently adopted annihilationist views.[77]

Rothe was a strong proponent of revelation as personal encounter, which was to dominate the theological thought of subsequent generations, though with Erskine, he held both a natural and supernatural view of its origin, since it represented divine activity within an overarching world process. George Smeaton particularly identified Rothe as a proponent of views similar to Erskine regarding the universal inward illumination of the Spirit.[78] Revelation for Rothe was self-authenticating: "an utterly moral, personal event that takes place through human functioning", with God as an active person entering into natural history and placing himself "'in such nearness to men that he can be evident even to man whose eyes are darkened by sin.'"[79] By the total surrender of oneself to God in a life characterised by moral commitment, "love for God proves itself in our collaboration with the moral purpose of the world, an activity for which man is free and towards which he is in a position to direct himself."[80] The process of revelation for Rothe was

> the setting in motion of natural psychical powers of the human consciousness of God by God himself, in a way that is to be compared with the playing of the organ. This happens on the one hand through evident events of history (manifestation), and on the other through corresponding inner illumination (inspiration). Both elements coincide in Christ as the Revealer. He is redeemer in that he communicates his being to an increasing number of men. He is reconciler in that because of him God can forgive sin even before it has been completely sublimated, since the achievement of the divinely appointed goal is guaranteed in him.[81]

---

[75] James Orr, *The Christian View of God and The World* [1893] (Grand Rapids: Kregel Publications, 1989), 308-9.

[76] Welch, *Protestant Thought*, I, 284-7, 291.

[77] See Orr, *Christian View,* 337; Herman Bavinck, *The Last Things* (Carlisle: Paternoster, 1996), 147.

[78] Smeaton, *Holy Spirit,* 151.

[79] Welch, *Protestant Thought,* I, 288-9. For Rothe's teaching concerning the self-authentication of divine-truth within the human spirit see Barth, *Protestant Theology,* 599.

[80] Barth, *Protestant Theology,* 601.

[81] Barth, *Protestant Theology,* 602.

The young Erskine would have readily appreciated the synergy between Rothe and his own early convictions concerning universal pardon and incarnational redemption. After their meeting in 1824, Rothe became a theological professor at Wittenberg seminary, and later Director at Heidelberg. Rothe remained deeply impressed with Erskine's combination of a 'rationalistic world view' with his 'warm personal Christian piety'. We know they were still in close mutual contact in 1827.[82] Erskine was to make regular use of the Greek lexical work of Rothe's senior colleague at Wittenberg, J.F. Schleusner (1759-1831), in his commentary on Romans in *The Doctrine of Election*.[83]

Erskine's Assimilation of German Thought

Whilst Richard Rothe developed a highly sophisticated speculative theological/ philosophical system, in essence it encompassed much of the substance of Erskine's own comparatively unsystematic thinking. This suggests that it might not be far-fetched to reconsider Erskine as a Scottish version of speculative theology in his own right, paralleling or reflecting something of the evangelical, post-Kantian, 'neo-Schleiermacherian' thought world evolving in the Germany of his day. Erskine himself was aware, like some of his friends, of his predilection for "trains of speculative thought".[84]

Erskine's thinking was still highly formative when he met Tholuck and Rothe. We have previously suggested ways in which his thought processes were influenced and directed. This did not occur in a vacuum. That Coleridge and others were also thinking independently on similar lines, with similar inputs, suggests that Erskine read widely and assimilated a measure of radical, philosophical, speculative thought, at least considerably more than has generally been supposed. Erskine found a readier reception for his ideas abroad, and his incipient thoughts were more than confirmed and reinforced by his continental experiences. His affinity with neo-Kantian and neo-Schleiermacherian ideas is remarkable, and the quality of his foreign contacts affords an evidential base adequate to suggest that Erskine imbibed continental views to a greater extent than has been acknowledged hitherto. Certainly, there would appear to be little room for the suggestion that Erskine was relatively ignorant and untutored about wider contemporary theological matters.

Tholuck and Rothe were regarded as prominent leaders of the post-Kantian, 'neo-Schleiermacherian' 'mediating' or 'conciliating' school'

---

[82] Nippold (ed.), *Rothe*, 479 (including footnote).

[83] See introduction by John MacPherson to Rothe's *Still Hours*, 33.

[84] Letter to Bishop Ewing, 20 June 1865, *Ewing-I*, 58.

which included Neander, Bunsen, and later, Dorner, and those of the 'Erlangen school'. It is remarkable to compare how closely the eclectic mediating theology corresponded with Erskine, especially concerning the tension between established dogma and the perceived necessity for its reconstruction. In a highly illuminating article on Augustus Neander, George Smeaton captured its essence:

> It belonged to the peculiarity of his system, as it does to all subjective schools, rather to lay accent on the character of faith as living faith, than on that imputed righteousness which this faith should believe. Rising up in a time of prevailing spiritual death, he very illogically, but by no means unnaturally, discovered far more anxiety to remove the death than to re-animate orthodoxy. Introverting his regards to an undue extent, he occupied his thoughts more with the personal Redeemer, and with the restoration of light, and life, and holiness through him, than with the more distinct appreciation of the specially meritorious ground of our acceptance before the Judge of all the earth.[85]

John Tulloch perceptively noted of Erskine that "in many points he anticipates the German Erlangen school",[86] which according to Karl Barth "represented a mild yet powerful union of Schleiermacher, Revival theology, confessionalism and biblicism".[87] George Smeaton was strongly critical of this 'non-forensic' "spiritual life" and "moral redemption" school, which he saw as furthering the ideas of Schleiermacher, especially of redemption consisting of "the fellowship of life with Christ". Smeaton categorically regarded this as a type of

> mysticism, where all the great doctrines connected with God as a Lawgiver and Judge are ignored, and where the restoration of life, absolutely considered – nay, such as it was in the person of Christ Himself – is supposed to be repeated in every Christian, without any appreciation of the specially meritorious ground of our acceptance before the Judge of all the earth, or any provision made for the expiation of sin.[88]

Erskine was strongly to develop the same concept of following in Christ's footsteps in *The Brazen Serpent* and *The Doctrine of Election*. Smeaton furthermore saw the Erlangen school as emphasising the idea of the atonement as supremely manifesting 'holy love' in the sufferings of Christ, a theme explored and developed by Erskine in *The Brazen Serpent*. Highly significantly, Smeaton suggested that this "mystic theory of the atonement in Germany" was specifically influenced by William Law's *Spirit of Love*

---

[85] Smeaton, "August Neander", *British and Foreign Evangelical Review*, VI, (1853), 711.
[86] Tulloch, *Movements*, 662.
[87] Barth, *Protestant Theology*, 607.
[88] Smeaton, *Christ's Doctrine*, 486-7, cf., 482-3.

and *Spirit of Prayer*, which we have established were highly influential for Erskine. In describing the salient representative of the Erlangen school, J.C.K. von Hofmann (1810-1877), Smeaton could well have substituted Erskine:

> he apprehends the whole history of Jesus, from His incarnation to His death, as the carrying out of the plan to which the three-one God resorted to change or alter the *relation of man* to Him. He regards the Church doctrine as not having equal claims to recognition, because it leads to an arithmetical reckoning and counter-reckoning between the divine claims and Christ's performance. He thinks, too, that it does not put the divine grace in its proper light, to say that sin must be expiated before God can be gracious.
> The whole theory of this able man, who in many points follows Menken and Schleiermacher, proceeds on the supposition that the atonement makes no change on God's relation, but simply on man's. He allows no wrath as a principle of action in God, and acknowledges only love in God. The whole effect of Christ's death, according to him, is to initiate a new humanity, or a new starting-point which shall renovate the nature. Agreeably to this representation, justification is, with him, not a forensic act, and complete at once: it grows and is never perfect. All that he says of the mystic union is good. But as to reconciliation, it is not THROUGH Christ's finished work, but IN him. The objective is thus merged in the subjective.[89]

Writing in the 1860s, when Erskine had become less well-known, Smeaton saw the principal British representatives of this school as F.D. Maurice and F.W. Robertson.[90] However, undoubtedly the above summary broadly reflects the thrust of Erskine's soteriology, especially in *The Brazen Serpent*. As John Tulloch implied, Erskine was in his own way a 'mediator', leading the way in Scotland, and also in England, in seeking a 'mediating' path between the 'formal orthodoxy' and 'formal rationalism' of the eighteenth century.[91] Erskine shared with Schleiermacher the label of 'mysticism'. Andrew Thomson accused Erskine of "raving mysticism",[92] and Schleiermacher regarded his own religious conception as 'mystical' or a via media between 'magic' and 'empiricism'.[93] Significantly, B.B. Warfield referred to incarnational atonement theology of the type propounded by Erskine, as 'mystical', claiming it was a neo-platonic idea descending in a line including Pseudo-Dionysius, Schwenckfeld, Boehme, Swedenborg, Schleiermacher, Rothe, Hofmann, Irving and Maurice.[94] Now, in the nineteenth century, "it was axiomatic that all men possessed a faculty by which they

---

[89] Smeaton, *Christ's Doctrine*, 490, cf., 487 (footnote).

[90] Smeaton, *Christ's Doctrine*, 491-2.

[91] Tulloch, *Movements*, 138-9.

[92] Thomson, *Universal Pardon*, 485.

[93] Schleiermacher, *Christian Faith*, §100, 428-9.

[94] Benjamin Breckinridge Warfield, *Studies in Theology*, [1932] (Edinburgh: Banner of Truth, 1988), 267-9.

could attain direct communion with God, provided they reached out to him and let him impart it". Theologians and philosophers were engaged in the task of pushing the door Kant had left open, to investigate how God gave humanity the direct knowledge of himself "which the Pure Reason could not obtain according to Kant, because it was limited to regulative or constitutive ideas which had only an empirical use and could not be extended to objects which transcended experience, like God."[95]

Though Kant rejected the possibility of apprehending God phenomenally through reason, he had suggested that the noumenal sphere might be apprehended through a 'higher faculty' which he did not define, though he called it 'practical reason'. Kant preferred to locate God in practical experience and in moral expression rather than in mystical experience. His followers, however, who were influenced by the powerful Romantic movement, considered the challenge legitimate, and indeed imperative, to seek to discover the nature of that 'higher human faculty' or knowledge of the absolute truth within human beings themselves. They inevitably turned inward to the feelings, will, intuition, 'higher' reason, and mystical experience.[96] Kant's followers included Schleiermacher, who located this 'higher faculty' in the feeling of absolute dependence. Total dependence on God was essentially a Romantic conception of faith which exercised a profound impact on experiential theology as the nineteenth century wore on.[97] Erskine had claimed as early as 1824 that

> The perfection of a creature does not consist in its own self-possessed powers, but in the maintenance of its proper place in relation to its Creator; and the name of that place is Constant Dependence. This place can only be held by affectionate confidence; and this requires a constant sense of the favourable presence and protection of God.[98]

This parallels Schleiermacher's concept of 'God-consciousness' which he too developed within an apologetic context. Taking the form of an immediate and intuitive certainty of God, the feeling of dependence was equivalent to universal divine immanence:

> This feeling of absolute dependence, in which our self-consciousness represents the finitude of our being…is a universal element of life; and the recog-

---

[95] Kent, *End of the Line?*, 49.

[96] Peter Hicks, *Evangelicals & Truth* (Leicester: Apollos, 1998), 61-2.

[97] Bebbington, *Holiness*, 88.

[98] *Baxter*, 269. Erskine, as we have seen, regarded a spirit of dependence as equivalent to possessing the spirit of sonship, and hence to salvific blessing, (*Sp.Order*, 233-4).

nition of this fact entirely takes the place, for the system of doctrine, of all the so-called proofs for the existence of God.[99]

In a similar context, and employing a similar approach, in seeking to explain how we salvifically apprehend God Erskine suggested that all we need do is become 'sympathetically aware' of our universal, innate, latent sense of the divine. Once we recognise this, the importance of evidences or doctrines becomes relativised: "the inward test of truth, moral and intellectual...the intuitive perception of truth...I have perfect sympathy with all such things".[100] Fundamental to 'knowing God' was Erskine's concept of 'sympathy' with God. By this he meant entering fully into the mind, heart, character, and purposes of God with all the affections and will of humanity, including suffering:

> The loving purpose of our Father in it is to be known and felt as love. Our Father Himself is to be met in it, and known in it, and sympathised with in it. Love seeks sympathy, and can be satisfied with nothing else; sympathy with God is partaking in the mind and blessedness of God.[101]

'Sympathy' was a watchword of the Enlightenment. Adam Smith, deriving inspiration from David Hume, formulated an innovative idea of 'sympathy' which encompassed theories of conscience, moral judgment and the virtues.[102] Christ's 'sympathy' with the human condition became a basic Schleiermacherian concept, and both Erskine in *The Brazen Serpent* and John McLeod Campbell in *The Nature of the Atonement* were to adopt it. 'Sympathy' was derivative for Erskine, and Christ's assumption of humanity introduced a new power of total sympathetic filial relationship into the race which was itself salvific in the same way that Schleiermacher asserted that "The Redeemer assumes believers into the power of His God-consciousness, and this is His redemptive activity".[103] Schleiermacher made little distinction between the Spirit of God and the spirit of humanity since 'God-consciousness' was identical with "immediate self-consciousness".[104] Schleiermacher's followers were careful to open up a greater distinction, as indeed Erskine did, but it is significant in this context

---

[99] Schleiermacher, *Christian Faith*, §33, 133-4. This work was well known in Britain by 1860, though not in translation until 1928. It remains a matter of speculation whether Erskine knew of it.
[100] Letter to Madame de Broglie, 21 July [probably 1838], *Letters-I*, 319.
[101] Letter to Lady Augusta Stanley, 6 July 1862, *Letters-II*, 141.
[102] Adam Smith, *The Theory of Moral Sentiments* [1759] (New York: Prometheus Books, 2000), 3-26, 60-69. Erskine read both Adam Smith and David Hume; see *Evidence*, 2, 56.
[103] Schleiermacher, *Christian Faith*, §100, 425.
[104] Schleiermacher, *Christian Faith*, §3, 5.

that Erskine was frequently criticised for reducing or confusing the role of the Holy Spirit.

By 1828 Erskine had developed his own version of 'dependence' theology. In emphasising the importance of what he termed 'sympathising' with God, rather than just 'knowing' and 'believing', he affirmed that

> this full sympathy...is the full receiving of the revealed will, and thoughts, and purposes of God; it is the casting out of self to make room for God; it is the being cut off from our own root, and the being grafted on the root of God; it is the spirit of affectionate dependence.

Erskine could now proceed to redefine what 'eternal life' really was for us, not just future promise but present gift: "it is a living principle then, and not a mere notion; it is a participation of the life of God; it is an indwelling of the Spirit of God".[105] Light enters our darkness when we recognise the 'Fountain of universal life' loves us and died for us, but a man "must sell all that he has in order to possess this pearl. Nothing less than all will serve"; "The pearl of great price is eternal life – it is the love of God reigning in the heart, – it is the being grafted on the true vine."[106] This concept of 'total surrender' or 'yielding' of the self to God in contrast to 'independence', was at heart an innovative version of Schleiermacher's pietistic concept, though simultaneously enhanced by evangelical Wesleyan holiness overtones. What we have to do to possess the 'pearl' is to deny or 'sell' the 'self' which occupies our heart. Erskine was adamant: we cannot be Christians without God reigning fully within. Note especially the flexibility of metaphor which retains a strong degree of orthodox terminology.

Eventually Erskine was able to bring his existential, self-denying redefinition of 'eternal life' into complete conformity with his fully-fledged convictions concerning universal salvation, divorced from associations with "finality", where (probably influenced by the work of F.D. Maurice on the subject of the meaning of αἰώνιος) he committed himself to the novel concept of eternity as relating to quality rather than time, and to "man's essential or spiritual state". Accordingly, "eternal life is living in the love of God; eternal death is living in self".[107]

---

[105] *Freeness*, 201.

[106] *Freeness*, 203-4.

[107] Letter to Mr Craig, [probably 1863], *Letters-II*, 240. Debate concerning the meaning of the word 'eternal' focused much nineteenth-century controversy concerning the fate of the lost. John McLeod Campbell disagreed with Maurice's and Erskine's interpretation of it, (*Memorials*, I, 256).

Charles Hodge

To illustrate further the contemporary genius of German thought to draw foreign interest and inform theological development elsewhere, it is instructive to compare briefly the formative impact of Erskine's eclectic continental experience with that of an evangelical contemporary who also travelled to the continent to broaden his theological understanding.

The Princeton theologian, Charles Hodge (1797-1878), was one of the first American theologians to visit Germany in 1827, where he studied for fifteen months with Tholuck and Neander at Hallé. Here he encountered Pietism, post-Kantian philosophy, the speculative theology of Schleiermacher, and the mediating theology of Tholuck's circle.[108] He was particularly impressed with the vital moral and pious lives of men like Tholuck, who appeared successfully to work out immanental truth in practical morality. Hodge tried to combine a balance of head and heart religion, emphasising, like Erskine, the *internal* work of God in illuminating revealed truth to the mind of the believer, which, however, he unambiguously emphasised was the work of the Spirit. Hodge believed that, because ultimate justification is to be found in God rather than in reason, and that God is the foundation for knowledge, our experience of God revealing himself to the whole person, intellect and feeling, is self-authenticating, or more accurately, God himself provides his own authentication.

Hodge described this non-rational experience and knowledge of God in various ways, which reflect the influence of Schleiermacher's school and the Scottish Common Sense philosophy of Thomas Reid, and remarkably paralleled Erskine's own thought, suggesting the influence of common sources. Hodge affirmed:

> the soul is so constituted that it sees certain things to be true immediately in their own light. They need no proof. Men need not be told or taught that the things thus perceived are true. These immediate perceptions are called intuitions, primary truths, laws of belief, innate knowledge, or ideas.

So for Hodge knowledge of God was an innate universal awareness or intuition, a "sense of dependence, our consciousness of responsibility, our aspirations after fellowship with some Being higher than ourselves…",[109] though he was also concurrently able to describe it in terms of "a supernatural intervention of God by the Spirit".[110] Peter Hicks makes the point that "it is this self-authenticating experience of God that formed the foun-

---

[108] Peter Hicks, *The Philosophy of Charles Hodge* (Lewiston: Edwin Mellen Press, 1997), 37-45.
[109] Hodge, *Systematic Theology*, I, 191, 200.
[110] Hodge, *Systematic Theology*, II, 666.

dation for Hodge's theology, which in turn provided the base for his confidence in reason and our ability to know the truth".[111] Once again we find a similarly inquisitive early nineteenth-century theologian seeking to discover in German thought a key to interpret and process his own developing theological system.

Epistemologically, Hodge bears strong similarities to Erskine, especially regarding his endorsement of human intuition, with the consequent inner 'knowledge' and 'feeling' that "[men] are by very nature bound to believe in God; that they cannot emancipate themselves from that belief without derationalizing and demoralizing their whole being".[112] Together with his desire to harmonise academic and scientific learning with historic Protestant theological commitments, Hodge illustrates the nature of contemporary forces for theological integrative innovation which were similarly driving Erskine. Where he differed from Erskine was most evident in the latter's dislike of systematising doctrine. He was perceive more clearly than Erskine the tendency of the 'new immanentist philosophy' to undermine eternal doctrinal truths and biblical revelation. Hodge therefore sought to emphasise the sovereign God, Creator and Governor of a world in which he was not bound by 'processes of development' or 'fixed laws', and religion was not reduced to 'individual consciousness' and 'intuitive feeling'.[113]

Summary

Chapter 10 investigated Erskine's direct links with German Romantic mediating theology, discovering that many of the emphases found in the neo-Schleiermacherian school were paralleled in Erskine's own soteriological interpretation, suggesting not only common apologetic, reconstructive, motivation, but significant mutual inspiration, transfer or reinforcement of ideas and influence. We emphasise, contrary to accounts which prefer to regard Erskine as an isolated, idiosyncratic phenomenon, the real stimulative significance for Erskine's innovatory and eclectic soteriological scheme of his European journeys and relationship network. We suggest Erskine effectively became a 'mediator' of German eclectic mediating theology in Britain and especially Scotland, anticipating later direct Scottish interest.[114]

---

[111] Hicks, *Evangelicals*, 63-4.

[112] Hodge, *Systematic Theology*, I, 200-1.

[113] James Turner, "Charles Hodge in the Intellectual Weather of the Nineteenth Century", in John W. Stewart and James H. Moorhead, (eds.), *Charles Hodge Revisited: A Critical Appraisal of his Life and Work* (Grand Rapids: Eerdmans, 2002), 56-7.

[114] See Franks, *Work of Christ*, 662, cf., Pfleiderer, *Theology*, 382.

Part 2 adopted a wider view of Erskine's theological context, examining not only alleged direct sources of influence, in which the pivotal role of William Law was highlighted, but also parallel soteriological developments both in Britain and on the continent. In this way, we have sought to show, contrary to understandings of Erskine which tend to reduce him to an insular figure who merely coincidentally corresponded with revolutionary theological developments occurring elsewhere, that he reflected the mood, and formed an innovatory and influential part, of a much larger and powerful creative theological drama played out on a comparatively bigger stage. He was, in fact, a product of his wider European intellectual environment, with roots in both eighteenth and nineteenth centuries, incorporating elements of both Enlightenment and Romantic world views. Though essentially an eclectic, transitional, figure who reformulated soteriological thought through the creative, religious, application of new ideas already in circulation, he retained a strongly independent mindset, whilst nevertheless evidencing the impact particularly of mystical and German philosophical speculative thought. We have also demonstrated that Erskine's innovatory ideas and pious personality signally influenced greater thinkers than himself, anticipating and paralleling theological developments in Victorian Britain, Europe and America. It was Alexandre Vinet, speaking for many, who illustrated the impact Thomas Erskine made in his resounding declaration:

> Si je ne haïssais par principe ces expressions: je suis d'Apollos ou de Céphas', je me laisserais aller volontiers à dire: je suis d' Erskine.[115]

---

[115] Vinet, Letter to Charles Monnard, 5 November 1823, *Lettres*, Pierre Bovet (ed.), I, 170.

Chapter 11

Concluding Comments

We have examined not only how Thomas Erskine was perceived in the nineteenth century as a soteriological innovator, but we have analysed the nature and extent of his so-called innovation. This has been considered both in terms of its motivation and inner cohesion, and of its place within the wider setting of a theologically reconstructive period, characterised by the tension of uncertainty, the undermining of tradition, and a background of immense socio-economic groundshifts. Our study has challenged some common assumptions that Erskine was a minor, eccentric, amateur, theologian, now largely forgotten, who tended to play a relatively isolated and idiosyncratic 'bit part' in a much bigger drama which he did not fully comprehend, valiantly supporting other more momentous lead characters. Instead, we conclude that Erskine was a significant, innovatory, transitionary theologian in his own right, who was supremely conscious of the need to preserve meaningful understanding of the central doctrine of salvation against an Enlightenment background destructive of historic atonement models. He set out with the laudable apologetic motivation of making the gospel relevant to his rapidly changing era. In this task he played a significant part in the theological reconstructive activity of his generation. A somewhat different portrait thus emerges, suggesting that Erskine has been significantly underestimated.

The nineteenth century was characterised by new eclectic currents of thought and rapidly expanding horizons of knowledge. Theology was evolving equally fast. We have demonstrated that Erskine was pre-eminently a product of his transforming context, in which he innovatively tapped into many of those eclectic currents. He exercised a unique theological role spanning periods in which society was changing from agrarian to industrial, and in which received belief was giving way to scientific discovery as accepted authority. His era was one in which the whole basis of authority was open for reconsideration. Erskine wrestled with the hesitant mood of the age, anticipated its direction, injected notes of hope and security, and though himself, as a relative layman, not possessing the skills of a systematic theologian, nevertheless, with remarkable insight, innovation, and lawyer's reasoning, laid a basis which paved the way for others who provided more lasting monuments to the reformulation of soteriological understanding.

We conclude that, to a significant extent, especially in Scotland, but also in Britain as a whole, Erskine helped set the soteriological agenda for the nineteenth and twentieth centuries. He rediscovered neglected aspects of the divine character and enduring life-giving principles, in contrast to stern, legalistic, worn out, stultifying doctrine, and encouraged movement away from narrow concentration on doctrinal minutiae. Internal debate between theologians was of no use if it did not touch peoples' lives. Erskine's understanding of truth was pre-eminently Johannine, incarnational, and paraenetic, founded on the principle of love and the practical ethical implications of conformity to Christ. This effectively made him an applied theologian, bridging the relevancy gap between academy and church, theologians and people. He deserves greater recognition than he has received. In particular, we have shown that Erskine was not afraid to challenge and reinterpret traditional assumptions, whilst remaining largely within the bounds of acceptable orthodoxy. We have concluded evidence suggests his influence and impact, both in Britain and Europe, was considerably more significant than has been generally appreciated. Temperamentally opposed to narrow exclusiveness, his pioneering eclectic role in assimilating at first hand new theological, philosophical and scientific concepts both from Britain and from the continent, which served as a catalyst for introducing his own innovatory ideas, merits proper acknowledgement.

We have consequently cast doubt over narrower theories regarding the origin of some key aspects of Erskine's novel soteriological ideas. Rather, we suggest a wider context for the development of his doctrines, and have indicated ways in which his ideas were taken up and developed by others. At the same time, we have argued that the single direct influence which may be regarded as highly significant was William Law, concluding, perhaps somewhat controversially, that Edward Irving played a comparatively minor role in Erskine's soteriological development. Of course, as a theological innovator and reconstructor, Erskine was a controversial figure, not least in his native Scotland, and we have illustrated and assessed reaction and opposition, some of which appeared to be justified by fears of the potential undermining of orthodox evangelical theology.

Erskine wrestled with a milieu in which philosophical and theological thinking were vying with each other for supremacy. Unsurprisingly, elements of both feature widely in his synthesising approach. He was inevitably involved in a much broader contemporary quest, in which conclusions often varied widely, to express in subjective terms (whilst yet retaining transcendent and objective categories) the nature and meaning of the moral 'power' which was believed somehow to be released in the Christian life as a result of encounter with divine truth. The starting point inescapably involved adaptation of eighteenth-century ideas of self-evidencing natural religion, according to which Christianity, as a religion of nature, was the highest expression, operating in accordance with natural laws from which Erskine deduced the necessary existence of parallel 'spiritual laws'. Revelation became not so much a supernatural, special, heavenly, soteric communication, as an autonomous dimension of knowledge within the natural world expressed by such immanent divine/ human self-validating faculties as conscience, insight, intuition, consciousness and discovery. The Romantic movement, which embodied a panentheistic 'natural supernaturalism' involving the capacity to discern mystery and spiritual significance in the everyday world, profoundly inspired many who were seeking for deeper spiritual answers to life's ultimate questions. We have suggested that such an overall transitional setting provided the backdrop for many of the remarkable correspondences between Erskine and his forward-looking contemporaries.

Controversial questions inevitably remain. To what extent was Erskine a genuine innovator and how much was he merely an interpreter of his time? How successful was he in reformulating a viable soteriology? Did he preserve evangelical truth in his apologetic mission, or did he subvert orthodoxy and initiate a subsequent drift to liberalism? Both opponents and followers described him as a theological 'speculator'.[1] Speculation may be both positive and negative. We have argued that Erskine was a positive 'speculator', an innovator who was not afraid to challenge and transcend the narrow confines of Scottish dogmatic Calvinism by adopting new and inquiring modes of thought, whilst at the same time remarkably holding in balance the received evangelical outlook which informed his deepest religious instincts. But we have insisted it is impossible to separate him from his broader cultural setting. Whilst we have maintained Erskine's primacy as a pioneer in nineteenth-century British soteriological thought, we have examined important subsequent and parallel developments to his thinking to illuminate the power of the context in which he formulated his ideas. Rather than forming any narrow sectarian attachment, Erskine combined his Enlightenment-educated, Scottish, legal temper with an essentially open and eclectic outlook. Accordingly, he derived from a combination of eighteenth- and nineteenth-century intellectual, philosophical, and spiritual movements (including Rationalism, Empiricism, Idealism and Romanticism), those interpretative tools which allowed him to present a convincing apologetic case for serious Christian faith and practice within a sceptical age. His success may be measured not only by those who, like John McLeod Campbell, F.D. Maurice, Alexander Ewing, and others of the Broad School, found inspiration in his creative thinking and godly personality, but by the many who adopted aspects of his reconstructive approach to maintain the viability of Christian soteriology.

---

[1] Eg., Dean Stanley. See pp.257-58 below.

Whilst some inevitably looked to him as the father of more liberal ideas, including universalism, others drew inspiration from his deeper thinking about the nature of God and revelation, spirituality, election, forgiveness, and sanctification, which were important elements in later nineteenth-century emphasis on holiness. If we accept that the defined objective of a 'liberal' is to "reconstruct Christian belief in the light of modern knowledge",[2] and that 'liberalism' "affirms continuity and similarity between God and humanity",[3] then Erskine would appear to fit such descriptions. But we consider it is as inaccurate to attach the label of 'liberalism' in the mould of the great late nineteenth- and early twentieth-century liberal theologians to Thomas Erskine, as Julia Wedgwood considered it was in 1884 similarly to categorise F.D. Maurice.[4] It is probably more fair and appropriate to understand Erskine as 'liberating' a freer understanding of the gospel, rather than inaugurating a liberal trend. He achieved this not merely by accommodating his views to the current intellectual and social context, but by propounding and embodying a radical inward, experimental, practical and evangelical faith, whilst maintaining belief in transcendent Christianity. If Erskine is to be regarded by some as a precursor of liberal theology, equally arguably his vision may be (and was) regarded as taken up by the late nineteenth-century evangelical revival and holiness movements. Responding to nineteenth-century challenges for theology to reconcile classic dogmatic dilemmas of judgment versus salvation, wrath versus love, and moral responsibility versus divine initiative, Erskine's genius lay in evolving a reconstructive approach to soteriological thinking which sought gently to redress the balance from emphasis on concepts of judgment towards those of grace. The aim of Christ's work was not so much to enable humanity to avert punishment, as to lead them to live holy lives. In this, Erskine may be considered to have left an enduring heritage.

Whilst his hermeneutical approach sometimes appears today as relatively subjective and naïve (though he anticipated later exegetical developments, for example, in his method of calling on latest scientific philology in his exegesis of Romans), we have argued that much of Erskine's genius was to be both contemporary and innovative, whilst at the same time remaining substantially orthodox. The extent to which he succeeded remains arguable, depending on one's theological standpoint. Nevertheless, we maintain that, whilst clearly venturing beyond certain evangelical boundaries, Erskine remained at heart a conservative and evangelical apologist, despite being linked with tendencies which were subsequently pressed by

---

[2] L. Miller and Stanley J. Grenz (eds.), *Introduction to Contemporary Theologies* (Minneapolis: Fortress Press, 1998), 202.

[3] Linda Woodhead, (ed.), *Reinventing Christianity: Nineteenth-Century Contexts* (Aldershot: Ashgate, 2001), 6.

[4] Wedgwood, *Teachers*, 50.

Concluding Comments 257

others in distinctly liberal directions. The eventual embrace of universalism, which to him was the logical conclusion of his thought, has been perceived as perhaps the most obvious of a number of problematic aspects in Erskine, having received much more attention from critics than Erskine publicly devoted to it. He restricted his personal beliefs concerning the 'larger hope' mainly to private conversations and correspondence. It is consequently unfair to characterise Erskine's entire theological contribution as heterodox based on this aspect alone. Perceptions of orthodoxy remain largely relative. The *Spectator* of June 24 1871 reflected a popular view that Thomas Erskine had rendered a major service to his era since, due largely to him, "orthodoxy no longer demands of us that we believe in an endless Hell...", and a hearty welcome was accorded his convictions regarding "ultimate blessedness for every human soul".[5] Whether we agree with this assessment or not, almost certainly the fact that Erskine helped to inaugurate a trend, welcomed by many in Scotland, which resulted in the widespread moderation of Calvinist soteriological orthodoxy, remains largely beyond dispute.

Recognition of Erskine has been patchy, and needs to be updated. Compared to John McLeod Campbell, Erskine has remained comparatively unacknowledged by his country.[6] It took English churchmen like Dean Stanley and the Dean of Salisbury first to recognise the extent of his influence in Scotland.[7] In 1865 and 1872, Stanley surveyed the most notable achievements of nineteenth-century theology. He acknowledged Erskine's

---

[5] The *Spectator*, June 24 1871, 769.

[6] In May 1868, Glasgow University conferred an honorary doctorate on Campbell. The *Glasgow Herald* called it "a leisurely repentance of a hasty deed", (*Memorials*, II, 208). It has not generally been highlighted that Thomas Erskine was awarded an honorary LL.D. in person by Edinburgh University in April 1866, *before* Campbell, at the same time as his friend Thomas Carlyle was installed as Rector. There is a reference regarding 'this matter of Thomas Erskine Esqr. and a few others' in the Senatus Minutes dated 27 March 1866, (Edinburgh University Library ref. Da 31, cf., *Alphabetical List of Graduates of the University of Edinburgh from 1859 to 1888*, published by the Senatus Academicus, S.R. Ref. 378 (41445) Edi., [Edinburgh: James Thin, 1889], 117). Apparently it was hardly the sign of establishment reconciliation Campbell's degree was taken to symbolise. Erskine remarked with characteristic humour and modesty in a letter to the Rev. Thomas Wright Mathews dated 16 April 1866, "I believe that the fact of Carlyle being my guest whilst he was in Edinburgh for the purpose of being installed Lord Rector of the University was the chief reason of my being honoured with the LL.D. degree. Of course nobody calls me Dr., except for fun", (Letter to Rev. Thomas Wright Mathews, 16 April 1866, *Letters-II*, 187).

[7] Dean Stanley highlighted the 'gift' of Erskine to the Scottish Church in his 1872 *Lectures on the History of the Church of Scotland* (London: John Murray), 159-61. The Dean of Salisbury referred to "the wonderful old man who exercised so much influence in Scotland, Thomas Erskine of Linlathen", (*The Recollections of the Very Rev. G.D. Boyle Dean of Salisbury* [London: Edward Arnold, 1895], 81).

important contribution to Scottish theology, describing him as "always on the highest summits at once of intellectual cultivation and of religious speculation". Referring to the theology of Erskine's era, Stanley singled out for special mention recovery of "the importance which it attaches to the moral and spiritual aspect of religion", and welcomed the fact that "the value of Internal Evidence has now been recognised in theory as well as practice, in theology as well as in philosophy". In Britain, and certainly in Scotland, Thomas Erskine was accordingly to be acknowledged amongst those who first recognised and enunciated "the moral attributes of God, and the moral duties of man, as the point from which all theology starts and to which it must return".[8]

Though well before the end of the nineteenth century Scotland was seriously beginning to reassess its treatment of Erskine, Campbell, Scott and Irving, recognition of Erskine's contribution has nevertheless seemed generally grudging. By the time of his death, Alexander Ewing felt bold enough to affirm, in reference to Erskine and the doctrines of the Row movement, that they "are now all but universally accepted"[9], whilst the great Scottish Congregationalist theologian, A.M. Fairbairn, having singled out Erskine's pioneering, influential spirit, concluded in 1872 that "a new and sweeter conception of God had come, which rendered a return to the old, however subtly conducted, impossible".[10] But full establishment rehabilitation never came, although writing in 1899, his biographer, Henry Henderson, considered that Erskine nevertheless

> exercised a great influence both at home and in America. The progress and increasing prominence of religious thought that this century has witnessed, the liberation of the mind from the hard, unhappy views of Divine truth, the widening and enrichment of the idea of God and of the redemptive purpose of God, the awakening of a new interest in Religion, and the reconciliation of the ethical with the doctrinal contents of the gospel have been perhaps more directly due to the teaching and personal character of Thomas Erskine than to any other single source of influence that can be named.[11]

---

[8] Arthur Penrhyn Stanley, "Theology of the Nineteenth Century", in *Essays Chiefly on Questions of Church and State from 1850 to 1870* (London: John Murray, 1870), 468-9, and *Lectures*, 159.

[9] *Ewing-I*, 9. In the charge to his clergy delivered in 1860, Bishop Ewing declared that Erskine's major tenet had now become the Episcopalians' "special mission in Scotland being the declaration of the Universal Redemption of man in Christ", (*A Charge Delivered to the Clergy of Argyll & The Isles, 12th September, 1860* [Edinburgh: Messrs. Grant, 1860], 15).

[10] A.M. Fairbairn, "The Westminster Confession of Faith and Scotch Theology", in *Contemporary Review*, XXI (December 1872 – May 1873), 80, 82.

[11] Henderson acknowledged that F.W. Robertson of Brighton had been recognized as exercising even greater influence on the Christian Church. However, he suggested that "as a thinker, as well as a personal force, Erskine was of larger account, while as a

In 1877, the *Spectator* affirmed, in a fulsome review of Erskine's posthumously published *Letters* that

> The Church of Scotland, if it has not perished, has been rent in twain...the old order in Scotland is rapidly changing, and perhaps no more unmistakable proof of the change could be supplied than is furnished by the fact that the biographer of Thomas Chalmers is now the editor of the *Letters of Thomas Erskine, of Linlathen*, – editor, and if we mistake not, by no means an unsympathising one...the Confessional formulae no longer represent the beliefs of the prominent teachers of the Kirk. The views of Thomas Erskine, who is undoubtedly the father of all the faithful who within the last half-century have been insurgent against the dismal Calvinistic decrees, are proclaimed in many Scotch pulpits, are published in the Press by one or two eminent Scotch clergymen, but no ecclesiastical inquisition has been set in motion against any one of them...it is now more than half a century since Thomas Erskine...published the first of those Essays which, as we believe, are revolutionising the whole theology of the North; and not of the North only...this is his claim to our affection and lasting gratitude that, in an age which had substituted 'seriousness of mind in the place of the Gospel of Christ,' and had converted God into a 'bundle of attributes,' he tore away the veils of tradition, and enabled us once more to see God manifesting himself in human nature, in order to penetrate it with his own love and make it partaker of his own blessedness...Dr. Hanna has only felt too profoundly that he had to edit the letters of one of the most remarkable men of our times.[12]

But such assessments and tributes mainly emanated from England. And sadly today, both there and in his native Scotland, Erskine's status and achievement in British theology has passed relatively unacknowledged.[13]

What seemed innovative in the 1820s appears commonplace today, and in rehabilitating Thomas Erskine we are concerned not to go to the other extreme by portraying him as a more significant and original contributor to soteriological development than he actually was. John Tulloch referred to his apparent ignorance of historical theology in noting Erskine's 'astonishment' at the hostile reception he received in Scotland, and suggested that "a good deal of his distinctive teaching was not new in the thought of the Church,... [though] it touched so very different a pole of thought from that of the theology of the Westminster Divines...".[14] We have presented Erskine as a creative facilitator of change rather than an original thinker, al-

---

product of the stiff Calvinistic soil of Scotland, he was a more extraordinary phenomenon", (*Erskine,* ix-x).

[12] *The Spectator*, 23 June 1877), 793-4. See also Drummond and Bulloch, *Church in Victorian Scotland*, 301-2.

[13] Trevor A. Hart, "Erskine, Thomas" in *DHT*, 192. However, the picture may be changing, as Erskine begins to occupy a serious place in recent surveys and reference works on Scottish and Historical Theology.

[14] Tulloch, *Movements*, 143-4.

though (we consider he may legitimately be regarded as exercising a unique and timely innovative influence in inspiring a shift towards more enlightened evangelical soteriological thought.) He selected what he regarded as the most appropriate contemporary concepts, dared to think differently and creatively, and risked his thoughts in the public arena, though his concerns were always passionately altruistic, never merely polemical. Showing little interest in public controversy, he shied away from the limelight, spending the larger part of his career persuading through private debate and exemplary personal piety. The sense of holiness perceived to pervade his household was proverbial. His priority remained always the preservation of meaningful ethical Christian religion amidst the twin opposing forces of reaction and progress. Of course, the inherent relativism of orthodoxy implies that Erskine will always have his supporters and detractors, and as evangelicals of his day were offended by him, some remain so. Erskine was well ahead of the nineteenth-century evangelical mood then, but many of his ideas have unobtrusively been integrated into present-day evangelical orthodoxy. Few evangelicals now think twice about unconditional love, universal pardon, the universal Fatherhood of God, salvation by incarnation, and the figurative nature of hell. Even the corporate salvation of humanity, universalism, and post-mortem evangelism now find their place in twentieth-century evangelical thought.[15] So Erskine continues to speak to us today as old issues and ideas re-surface under new guises.

We acknowledge that in places the absence of firm surviving evidence has involved us in reasoned speculation, notably concerning Erskine's activities on the continent, and we have largely surmised, in the light of remarkably coincident parallel developments, to what extent he was actually influenced by German thought. Nevertheless, the evidence supports the probability of greater exposure to continental influence than has generally been accepted, and is certainly preferable to presentations of Erskine which tend to portray him as little more than a cloistered, eccentric, philanthropic, religious commentator, engaged on pious private missions. Further research in this area, and especially comparative studies of Erskine with the German mediating school and Alexandre Vinet would be valuable, as would examination of Erskine's legacy in the late nineteenth, and early twentieth centuries.

We believe that some potentially fruitful lines of research in this direction have been raised by our study. In particular, there is scope for serious study of Erskine's relationship to John McLeod Campbell, who appeared to develop many of Erskine's soteriological ideas. It would also be valuable to investigate Erskine's relationship with liberal theology, not least in the

---

[15] See e.g., Clark H. Pinnock "Salvation By Resurrection", in *Ex Auditu* 9 (1993), 3-8; Smail, *Once and for All*, 100-19, 148-53, 163-81; Robin A. Parry and Christopher H. Partridge, *Universal Salvation? The Current Debate* (Carlisle: Paternoster, 2003).

form of the social gospel, where Walter Rauschenbusch especially developed many of the principles close to Erskine's heart. These included rejection of metaphysical theology in favour of praxis within the ethical kingdom of God, rejection of forensic concepts of atonement, an organic view of human moral- and God-consciousness, the power of the 'law of love' to motivate the transformation of society, the 'democratising' of the Fatherhood of God, and the moral ideal of Jesus Christ as representing the unity of the divine and the human in a new type of humanity.[16]

Investigation of Erskine's heritage in connection with the late nineteenth-century holiness movement represents a potentially fascinating study. Already earlier in the century, Erskine could be seen as theologically anticipating Finney's concept of entire sanctification, together with his abandonment of Calvinism, and movement towards Arminian soteriological concepts, especially the universal gospel appeal. But it is with the beginnings of the British holiness movement that Thomas Erskine appeared to carry significant influence. David Bebbington has shown that "the Enlightenment and Romanticism...generated ways of thinking that helped shape nineteenth-century patterns of holiness".[17] Erskine can be viewed as a transitional figure between Wesleyan eighteenth- and holiness nineteenth-century entire sanctification movements, and, combined with his remarkably prophetic openness to the gifts of the Spirit, anticipating the latter's merger into twentieth-century Pentecostalism. Erskine's particular brand of spirituality was, in fact, evident and influential at the pre-Keswick Broadlands conferences which started in 1874, just after his death. Chaired by Quakers Robert and Hannah Pearsall Smith,[18] speakers included Theodore

---

[16] See Walter Rauschenbusch, *A Theology for the Social Gospel* [1917] (Louisville, Kentucky: Westminster John Knox Press), 1997.

[17] Bebbington, *Holiness*, 92-3.

[18] Hannah Pearsall Smith's posthumously published dialogues and private correspondence indicate that she was sympathetic to the idea of universal salvation, refusing to believe that a loving God could consign any of his creatures to eternal torture. Her views were openly shared by Lady Mount-Temple (formerly Mrs Cowper-Temple) of Broadlands, close friend of Emelia Russell Gurney, and who knew Thomas Erskine; see Logan Pearsall Smith (ed.), *A Religious Rebel: The Letters of "H.W.S."* (London: Nisbet , 1949), 27-28; Erskine's Letter to Mrs Gurney, 14 May 1862, *Letters-II*, 253-4. Of further interest is the fact that John Ruskin, whom Erskine heard and liked, was a close friend of Lord and Lady Mount-Temple. Ruskin's return to Christianity (though distinctly not of the evangelical variety and involving rejection of eternal damnation) came via a spiritualist séance held at Broadlands in 1875. The apparently close links between Broadlands evangelicalism and late nineteenth-century spiritualism (though Mrs Pearsall Smith reputedly frowned on the latter) represents a potentially fascinating subject for further investigation. See Erskine's Letter to Mrs Burnett, 9 November 1853, *Letters-II*, 82; Van Akin Burd, *Ruskin, Lady Mount-Temple and the Spiritualists: An Episode in Broadlands History* (London: Brentham Press: 1982); Tim Hilton, *John Ruskin: The Later Years* (New Haven and London: Yale University Press, 2000), 67-9, 325-32.

Monod (nephew of Erskine's friend, Adolphe Monod), Asa Mahan from Oberlin, Erskine's fellow universalist, George MacDonald,[19] and Andrew Jukes, whose book, *The Restitution of All Things,* published in 1867, caused controversy on account of its avowed universalism, citing Thomas Erskine, William Law and Augustus Tholuck as authorities.[20]

Key themes at Broadlands emphasised holiness and moral transformation, entire surrender and sanctification, 'the spiritual law of love' and the 'higher life' – subjects close to Erskine's heart.[21] Erskine's advocacy of the deeper and higher spiritual life, especially through suffering, and his appeal to inward experience, surrender of the will, and the crucified life, merged easily into the Holiness/ Keswick type of 'evangelical mysticism', in which William Law was acknowledged as a direct progenitor.[22] Coleridge was also quoted authoritatively at Broadlands.[23] But there were actual direct links between Erskine and Broadlands via Emelia Russell Gurney who had been strongly influenced by years of devoted contact with Erskine, and who was closely related to the owners of the Broadlands estate, knowing personally and corresponding directly with many of the conference speakers, including Hannah Pearsall Smith, McDonald, and Jukes. She was also a close friend of Dean Stanley. The spiritual atmosphere of Broadlands profoundly reminded Mrs Gurney, together with her intimate friend, Julia Wedgwood, of Linlathen's haunting spiritual power. For Mrs Gurney, Linlathen evoked enduring mystical, romantic and spiritual associations, as "the home of my soul", and "a gate of heaven", leaving her agonising how to 'take up its torch and walk in its light'.[24] She reminisced in 1891 that, "Before Broadlands it was my most sacred spot. Broadlands opened just as the door of Linlathen was closing".[25] Envious that a friend was making a pilgrimage to "Saint Erskine's Linlathen, my Linlathen" she plaintively expressed the prayer, "Well, may some of his spirit come upon you".[26]

---

[19] George MacDonald travelled to Linlathen specially to meet Erskine. See letters from Erskine to MacDonald (undated) in Beinecke Rare Book and Manuscript Library, Yale University: General *MSS* 103, Box No.2, Folder No.68.

[20] Andrew Jukes, *The Second Death and the Restitution of All Things* (W. Knochaven, California: Scripture Studies Concern and Concordant Publishing Concern, 1976), 190.

[21] See Edna V. Jackson, *The Life That is Life Indeed: Reminiscences of the Broadlands Conferences* (London: James Nisbet, 1910), *passim,* cf., Edward Clifford, "Broadlands as it was" (including selected letters of Andrew Jukes), in *A Green Pasture* (London: The Church Army Bookroom, no date – probably 1901).

[22] J.I. Packer, "'Keswick' and the Reformed Doctrine of Sanctification", in *Evangelical Quarterly,* XXVII (1955), 153, footnote 3.

[23] Melvin E. Dieter, *The Holiness Revival of the Nineteenth Century,* [2nd edition] (Lanham, Maryland: Scarecrow Press Inc., 1996), 151.

[24] *Gurney,* 11, 37, 73, 219.

[25] Letter to Edward Clifford, 15 October 1891, *Gurney,* 220, cf., 139, 142-3.

[26] Letters to Edward Clifford, 15 and 17 October 1891, *Gurney,* 219-20.

The twentieth century offers further varied avenues for comparative investigation. In particular, P.T. Forsyth was to develop many of Thomas Erskine's themes, including divine Fatherhood and the role of the conscience in spiritual matters. Leslie McCurdy has recently highlighted interest in exploring sources for Erskine's apparently original theme of the 'holy love of God', so closely associated later with Forsyth.[27]

Further potential study involves comparison of Erskine with Karl Barth, and their respective approaches to restating the historic Christian faith. Both Erskine and Barth were influenced by Platonism. Like the Romantics, and Kant and Schleiermacher, both reacted against, and sought to come to terms with, the Enlightenment, whilst concurrently appropriating some of its ideas and concerns, and admitting, whilst criticising, "the intrusion of philosophy into theology".[28] We have noted how, in a variety of ways, Erskine remarkably anticipated Barth, notably in his Christocentrism, understanding of redemption and atonement, emphasis on God's love and human freedom, concepts of justification and election, and the importance of the humanity of Christ. Like Erskine, "Barth was engaging in a terrific struggle with theological and philosophical language".[29] For Barth, as for Erskine, soteriology flowed from christology, and Barth shared other close correspondences with Erskine, notably an implied universalism.

Last but not least, there is scope for further research on the variations between the different editions of Erskine's works which reflect development in Erskine's thinking even within relatively short timescales. For example, in 1828 *The Unconditional Freeness of the Gospel* went through two editions in which minor changes are evident, whilst other works show significant variations, notably *The Brazen Serpent,* where at least two editions appeared in 1831.

In any study which seeks to assess the influences exerted upon and by particular historical figures, there remains always the danger either of minimising or of exaggerating certain aspects. In attempting to demonstrate that Erskine has been insufficiently appreciated for his pivotal transitionary role, we are mindful that it is easy to overstate his importance as a primary nineteenth-century theologian. Nevertheless, we believe it is undeniable to affirm that

> theology was harder, sterner, less genial, and the Church of Scotland less merciful and tolerant, before Erskine seized and held fast the simple truth

---

[27] Leslie McCurdy, *Attributes and Atonement: The Holy Love of God in the Theology of P.T. Forsyth* (Carlisle: Paternoster, 1999), 11-12. The present author has reason to believe that likely sources for the phrase lie within the mystical tradition.

[28] Donald G. Bloesch, *Jesus is Victor! Karl Barth's Doctrine of Salvation* (Nashville: Abingdon, 1976), 72-3, 100-1.

[29] Thomas F. Torrance, *Karl Barth: An Introduction to His Early Theology, 1910-1931* (London: SCM, 1962), 88.

that the Father in heaven was...infinitely more patient, tender and kind, than a good father on earth, and that life was his way of educating his children...[30]

Eventually, by the last quarter of the nineteenth century, Thomas Erskine, with his friend John McLeod Campbell, were recognised by a rapidly changing Scotland, to be "original thinkers, founders, and pioneers who had brought in influential "new revelation" and "new thought" to shake the bastions of Calvinistic orthodoxy.[31] Whilst he helped replace the 'old orthodoxy' of the sovereignty of God with the 'new theology' of divine Fatherhood, Erskine's eclectic synthesising genius, and largely orthodox but innovative soteriological consciousness, meant that in his hands soteriology nevertheless remained robust and doctrinally and ethically viable, offering broader understandings, deeper insights, and inspirational gains, rather than losses of historic truth. Perhaps the abiding achievement of his innovative blend of old and new was that it "made religion seem sweeter and less harsh than it too often did of old, more human though equally still divine, less loaded with unnecessary dogma, less of a system and more of a spirit".[32]

---

[30] Lees, "Ewing", 387.
[31] Lees, "Ewing", 369-70.
[32] Lees, "Ewing", 388, 369-70.

APPENDIX 1

Thomas Erskine and Kant in the Nineteenth Century

Kant's demolition of Enlightenment assumptions regarding the prime role of reason in interpreting the external world was largely responsible for increasing nineteenth-century emphasis on exploring the world of inner experience, where the natural autonomous reason, conscience, and will of the individual became the norm for beginning theological reflection and judging truth and rightness. Kant initiated a seminal philosophical and analytical approach to the study of human consciousness and the ultimate grounds for belief, stressing the supremacy of conscience in relation to the universal innate sense of moral obligation and absolutes, whilst still retaining transcendental categories. In effect, he established that the essential truths of religion were based on the supposed fundamental structure of human nature, Christianity being its highest expression.

However, the nineteenth century also saw the full flowering of neo-Kantian reaction, and the Romantic movement emphasised and developed Kantian themes, whilst simultaneously rejecting the stale rationality of the previous century. Subjectivity, feeling, imagination, and the need for unity and universality dominated the Romantic quest for truth. The Romantic individual 'inward turn' was accompanied by a rejection of 'supernaturalism' and the theistic transcendence of the Deist eighteenth century, as new conceptions of God's relation to the world took an immanental and panentheistic direction. Platonism was again in vogue, becoming the "lifeblood of Romanticism" which reflected reaction against reason and empiricism, as well as offering a refuge for those seeking "to transcend the bounds of understanding by exploring the realms of the infinite". The start of the nineteenth century was therefore marked by the emergence of "a common philosophical vocabulary, as attempts were made to articulate or to define such concepts as the relationship between thought and reason, the limits of human understanding, the sources of moral convictions and the intercommunion (or lack of it) between the finite and the infinite".[1]

Platonic ideas and idealist concepts were prominent in Thomas Erskine's moral thought, both co-existing comfortably within a neo-Kantian framework in the nineteenth century. As we have seen, Kant inaugurated the increasingly popular idea of Jesus as human 'prototype' and moral ideal. Though Erskine was bothered by the tendencies of this way of viewing Jesus, Kantian echoes in Erskine are nevertheless unmistakable. Writing of what he termed "*Humanity…in its full moral perfection*", Kant seemed to combine philosophical concepts with virtually evangelical language in affirming

> that a human being should become not merely *legally* good, but *morally* good (pleasing to God) i.e. virtuous according to the intelligible character of virtue and thus in need of no other incentive to recognize a duty except the representation of duty itself – that, so long as the foundation of the maxims of the human being remains impure, cannot be effected through gradual *reform* but must rather be effected through a *revolution* in the disposition of the human being (a transition to the maxim of holiness of disposition). And so a 'new man' can come about only through a kind of rebirth, as it were a new creation…and a change of heart…it follows that a human being's moral education must begin, not with an improvement of mores, but with the transformation of his attitude of mind and the establishment of a character…[2]

Kant continued to appropriate the evangelical theme by seeking to discover the key to moral power which so bothered F.D. Maurice. Pressing the human possibility of self-sacrifice, imitation of, and union with, Christ and his sufferings consequent on his *supposed* incarnation, and suggesting that recognition of the very concept contained within itself an ethical, transforming, salvific power, he affirmed,

> only in him [Jesus] and through his dispositions can we hope 'to become children of God', etc. Now it is our universal human duty to *elevate* ourselves to this ideal of moral perfection, i.e. to the prototype of moral disposition in its entire purity, and for this the very idea, which is presented to us by reason for emulation, can give us force [or 'power']. But, precisely because we are not its authors but the idea has rather established itself in the human being without our comprehending how human nature could have been receptive of it, it is better to say that that *prototype* has *come down* to us from heaven, that it has taken up humanity…this union with us may therefore be regarded as a state of *abasement* of the son of God if we represent to ourselves this God-like human being, our prototype, in such a way that, though himself holy and hence not bound to submit to sufferings, he nonetheless

---

[1] Newsome, *Two Classes*, 12, 13.
[2] Immanuel Kant, *Religion Within the Bounds of Mere Reason* [1793], translated and edited by Allen Wood and George Di Giovanni (Cambridge: Cambridge University Press, 1998), 67-68, 79.

takes these upon himself in the fullest measure for the sake of promoting the world's greatest good…we cannot think the ideal of a humanity pleasing to God…except in the idea of a human being willing not only to execute in person all human duties, and at the same time to spread goodness about him as far wide as possible through teaching and example, but also, though tempted by the greatest temptation, to take upon himself all sufferings, up to the most ignominious death, for the good of the world and even for his enemies…in the *practical faith in this Son of God* (so far as he is represented as having taken up human nature) the human being can thus hope to become pleasing to God (and thereby blessed [or 'saved']); that is, only a human being conscious of such a moral disposition in himself as enables him to *believe* and self-assuredly trust that he, under similar temptations and afflictions…would steadfastly cling to the prototype of humanity and follow this prototype's example in loyal emulation, only such a human being, and he alone, is entitled to consider himself not an unworthy object of divine pleasure.[3]

Once again, distinctive themes developed by Erskine and others in the nineteenth century appear to have roots in Kantian concepts from the previous century, although Erskine sought to maintain a balance between moral idealism and living religion based on a personal, experiential filial relationship with God, which, contrary to Kant, Erskine believed to be not only possible, but essential.

---

[3] Kant, *Religion Within the Bounds*, 80-1.

APPENDIX 2

Thomas Erskine, William Ellery Channing and the Unitarians

There were many points of comparison between Thomas Erskine and the Unitarians, though he retained a strong dislike of their anti-trinitarianism. His difficulties with traditional Calvinism were closely mirrored by the Unitarians, as voiced by their most eloquent spokesman and Erskine's contemporary, William Ellery Channing:

> the principal argument against Calvinism…is the moral argument, or that which is drawn from the inconsistency of the system with the divine perfections. It is plain that a doctrine which contradicts our best ideas of goodness and justice cannot come from the just and good God or be a true representation of his character.[1]

Although there is no evidence of direct association with the Unitarians until the 1850s, Erskine was well aware of the Unitarian school of thought. Both Channing and the Unitarians were enormously influential in late eighteenth- and early nineteenth-century Britain, and had already highlighted most of the theological issues which were later to exercise thinking Christians.[2] Channing, who offered a credible alternative to Calvinism, was hugely influential in nineteenth-century Britain, being himself influenced by Scottish philosophy, and probably having received an introduction to Kant and German thought in similar fashion to Erskine.[3] Channing was seen as a direct precursor of Ralph Waldo Emerson and American Transcendentalism, that American manifestation of the European Romantic

---

[1] William Ellery Channing, "The Moral Argument Against Calvinism", in Bartlett (ed.), *Unitarian Christianity*, 43.

[2] Rowell, *Hell*, 32; Wigmore-Beddoes, *Yesterday's Radicals*, 99-101.

[3] See Irving H. Bartlett, "Introduction" to Channing, Bartlett (ed.), *Unitarian Christianity*, xxiv; Rowell, *Hell*, 51-2; Wigmore-Beddoes, *Yesterday's Radicals*, 99-101.

movement.[4] Erskine was directly compared with Channing.[5] Both Channing and Erskine were influential in the development of New England theology from about 1820. Erskine's work was well known to the Andover Theological Seminary professors, Moses Stuart and Leonard Woods, who corresponded constructively with Channing, as well as engaging with him in robust public dialogue. The perception that Channing and Erskine also had much in common, would therefore seem to be well grounded, though there is no direct evidence that Erskine actually read Channing or vice versa.[6]

Channing adopted the same approach as Erskine in seeing the chief evidence for the truth of Christianity as residing in the 'cause and effect' principle – that is, that 'God' could be the only real explanation for a human nature which corresponded perfectly with the universally accepted revelation of the divine character, as mediated supremely through the person of Christ. Employing virtually identical perception and even metaphorical expression to Erskine, Channing explained his view that 'internal evidence' was one of the chief evidences of Christianity:

> I refer to that conviction of the divine original of our religion which springs up and continually gains strength in those who apply it habitually to their tempers and lives, and who imbibe its spirit and hopes. In such men there is a consciousness of the adaptation of Christianity to their noblest faculties – a consciousness of its exalting and consoling influences, of its power to confer the true happiness of human nature, to give that peace which the world cannot give – which assures them that it is not of earthly origin but a ray from the Everlasting Light, a stream from the Fountain of heavenly wisdom and love.[7]

Erskine and Channing shared a common Enlightenment inheritance. The emphasis on the inward consciousness, so fundamental to Erskine, was prominent in Channing, who concurred that human beings had the capacity to discover and understand the moral perfection of God by searching into their own minds. Channing was adjudged to have helped transform the concept of revelation:

---

[4] Bartlett, "Introduction" to Channing, Bartlett (ed.), *Unitarian Christianity*, xxv.

[5] Anon., "Mysticism-Erskine on Election", in *The Presbyterian Review* X, III (February, 1838), 488-9.

[6] See Letter to Thomas Erskine from Professor Noah Porter, 1866, *Letters-I*, 364-5; Earle Morse Wilbur, *A History of Unitarianism* (Cambridge, Mass: Harvard University Press, 1952), 428-30; Bennet Tyler and Andrew A. Bonar, *Nettleton and His Labours* [1854] (Edinburgh: Banner of Truth, 1975), 380-3.

[7] William Ellery Channing, "The Evidences of Revealed Religion", in Bartlett (ed.), *Unitarian Christianity*, 84.

from the communication of objective truths by a heaven-accredited messenger, the function of Christ came to be interpreted as the manifestation of the divine character under the limits of humanity, which received its attestation from the witness of the soul within.[8]

Also in the area of revelation and authority, the Unitarians had already begun to explore the sphere of conscience. Channing remarkably anticipated Erskine in the overriding importance he attributed to the vital role of conscience and the power of inward witness:

> Conscience, the sense of right, the power of perceiving moral distinctions, the power of discerning between justice and injustice, excellence and baseness, is the highest faculty given us by God, the whole foundation of our responsibility, and our sole capacity for religion. Now we are forbidden by this faculty to love a being, who wants, or who fails to discover, moral excellence. God, in giving us conscience, has implanted a principle within us, which forbids us to prostrate ourselves before mere power, or to offer praise where we do not discover worth – a principle, which challenges our supreme homage for supreme goodness, and which absolves us from guilt, when we abhor a severe and unjust administration. Our Creator has consequently waived his own claims on our veneration and obedience any farther than he discovers himself to us in characters of benevolence, equity, and righteousness. He rests his authority on the perfect coincidence of his will and government with those great and fundamental principles of morality written on our souls. He desires no worship, but that which springs from the exercise of our moral faculties upon his character, from our discernment and persuasion of his rectitude and goodness. He asks, he accepts, no love or admiration but from those, who can understand the nature and the proofs of moral excellence.[9]

Another perspective which Erskine shared with the Unitarians was belief in the providential design of the journey of life and even sin itself as a learning experience for eternity. Channing stated that

> We look upon this world as a place of education in which [God] is training men by prosperity and adversity, by aids and obstructions, by conflicts of reason and passion, by motives to duty and temptations to sin, by a various discipline suited to free and moral beings for union with himself and for a sublime and ever-growing virtue in heaven.[10]

The revelatory and transformatory power of the character of God, and emphasis on his loving Fatherliness, were Unitarian convictions dating from the eighteenth century, which both Thomas Erskine and F.D. Maurice

---

[8] J. Estlin Carpenter, *James Martineau, Theologian and Teacher* (London: Philip Green, 1905), 175.
[9] Channing, "The Moral Argument Against Calvinism", in Bartlett (ed.), *Unitarian Christianity*, 52.
[10] Channing, "Unitarian Christianity", in Bartlett (ed.), *Unitarian Christianity*, 23.

adopted. In terms reminiscent of Erskine, Channing employed the benevolent, paternal image of God as a principal method of repudiating Calvinist concepts of natural depravity and election:

> We believe in the *moral perfection of God*. We consider no part of theology so important as that which treats of God's moral character; and we value our views of Christianity chiefly as they assert his amiable and venerable attributes…God is infinitely good, kind, benevolent…good not to a few, but to all…[11]

Channing was also accused, like Erskine, of emphasising the natural (higher) faculties of "understanding, conscience, love, and the moral will" in approaching God, at the expense of the Holy Spirit. Channing nevertheless denied any heterodox variance concerning the role of the Spirit, affirming, in terms similar to Erskine, that

> by the Holy Spirit, we are to understand a divine assistance adapted to our moral freedom and accordant with the fundamental truth that virtue is the mind's own work. By the Holy Spirit, I understand an aid which must be gained and made effectual by our own activity; an aid which no more interferes with our faculties than the assistance which we receive from our fellow beings.[12]

Yet again we may observe that, without any acknowledged reliance, and indeed with differing religious outlooks, two independently-minded theologians reflected the dual power of the Enlightenment and the new Romantic mood to inform their apologetic interpretation of Christianity for their generation, resulting in a remarkable coincidence of views.

---

[11] Channing, "Unitarian Christianity", in Bartlett (ed.), *Unitarian Christianity*, 21-2.
[12] William Ellery Channing, "Likeness to God", in Bartlett (ed.), *Unitarian Christianity*, 99-100.

APPENDIX 3

Thomas Erskine and Biblical Criticism

Whilst Thomas Erskine's innovative approach to external authority stood him in good stead in the face of severe theological pressures later in the century, he experienced a certain hesitancy when he perceived the tendencies to which some of his ideas were leading.

When Scripture came under intense historical and scientific critical attack, notably during the 1860s, Erskine was frequently pressed for his views regarding the Bible's supposed infallibility. His response was characteristically relaxed, contentedly reliant on his own developed position. He suggested that undue concern for the possible undermining of faith consequent on such criticism involved misapprehension regarding the nature of salvation, divine inspiration and the proper location of authority. The universal apprehension of the "necessary truth" of "principle" was, for him, more important than the strict verbal and historical accuracy of Scripture. Inward conviction or faith concerning divine truth should afford ample protection against any attempts to 'demolish' outward authority.[1] Erskine used the opportunity provided by the rise of biblical criticism to reinforce his conviction that belief in the intrinsic truth of the Bible was more important than adhering to doctrines of biblical infallibility:

> the object of the Bible is not to teach us to receive things as truths, but to teach us to apprehend the truth of truths…we are not to be led away either by miracles or prophecies – we are to know the truth of things for ourselves. Confidence in an infallible authority has just the other tendency. It comes as a substitute for the perception of truth.[2]

His emphasis on *internal* as opposed to *external* evidence, revealed that Erskine's view of the Bible was influenced by a Romantic prophetic anticipation of contemporary critical currents. The 'inward turn' offered a means

---

[1] *Sp.Order*, 77-81.
[2] Letter to Bishop Ewing, 5 October 1864, *Ewing-I*, 52.

of placing the Scriptures' salvific authority beyond the reach of a rising tide of destructive criticism, which in the mid-nineteenth century manifested itself notably in the work of David Strauss, Bishop John Colenso, Ernest Renan, and the authors of *Essays and Reviews*. However, for Erskine, "The records are the vehicle of principles which are true independently of the records, and which criticism cannot touch".[3]

Whilst John Henry Newman as early as 1835 detected dangerous novel tendencies in Erskine's well-meaning apologetics, in fact, Erskine was well aware of other potential dangers which he believed he had largely avoided. He was undoubtedly concerned that others might misunderstand and develop his ideas in liberal directions he in fact disclaimed, but he nevertheless remained confident in his self-constructed theological position. However, as a product of his era, though only partly conscious of it, he was actually an integral part of a relentless theological paradigm shift. Erskine knew and disapproved of Strauss, and he almost certainly knew of George Eliot's 1846 translation of *Das Leben Jesu*.[4] He displayed a rather more ambivalent attitude to *Essays and Reviews*, Colenso's *The Pentateuch and Book of Joshua Critically Examined*, and Renan's, *La Vie de Jésus*, published in 1860, 1862, and 1863 respectively.[5] Having found his own solution to the uncertainties posed by the undermining of biblical truth by retreating into the private truth world of his inward consciousness which could not be disturbed by exterior storms, Erskine manifested a superior, calm, and detached approach to the relative havoc around him.[6] He deplored the way such authors had popularised their speculations, with the consequent deleterious effect on the faith of the common people, and in particular the 'spiritual blindness' and 'misleading' nature of *La Vie de Jésus* (which, according to Principal Shairp, was the catalyst for causing Erskine to take up his pen once again).

But Erskine nevertheless felt that they were raising issues which thinking people needed to consider and which required answers, actually affording Christianity a unique apologetic opportunity.[7] *La Vie de Jésus* did more

---

[3] 'Julia Wedgwood's Journal', *Letters-II*, 161.

[4] Strauss, David Friedrich, *The Life of Jesus, Critically Examined*, translated from the fourth German edition by Marian Evans, afterwards Cross, [i.e. George Eliot] (London: Chapman Brothers, 1846). See Erskine's Letter to Mrs Scott, 20 February 1839, *Letters-I*, 350, and Letter to Miss Wedgwood, 5 November 1866, *Letters-II*, 191.

[5] Frederick Temple, et. al., *Essays and Reviews* [2nd edition] (London: John W. Parker and Son, 1860); John William Colenso, *The Pentateuch and Book of Joshua Critically Examined* (London: Longman, 1862-79); Joseph Ernest Renan, *Histoire des Origines du Christianisme*, in 8 volumes, [volume 1, *Vie de Jésus*] (Paris: 1863-83).

[6] *Sp.Order*, 76-99.

[7] See *Sp.Order*, 77-99; Shairp, "Reminiscences", *Letters-II*, 375; Letters to John McLeod Campbell, 21 November 1862, Dean Stanley, 4 April 1864, Mrs A.J. Scott, 18 April 1864, *Letters-II*, 146, 147-8, 149; Letter to Principal Shairp, 24 December 1863,

than any contemporary work "to dissolve orthodox faith among the public, as contrasted with the learned".[8] However, although Erskine especially deprecated what he saw as Renan's separation of faith and morality, it appears he was simultaneously intrigued by Renan, who sometimes evidently pursued Erskine's favourite themes, for example, by portraying a Jesus who advocated "a pure worship, a religion without priests and external observances, resting entirely on the feelings of the heart, on the imitation of God, on the direct relation of the conscience with the heavenly Father...".[9]

Although he disliked it, remarkably *Essays and Reviews* raised numerous issues dear to Erskine's heart which had interested him much earlier, particularly education of the human race, the biblical work of Chevalier Bunsen, evidences of Christianity, the Genevan church, biblical interpretation, and eighteenth-century rationalistic thought.

So far as Bishop Colenso was concerned, Erskine decided to write to him personally, expressing his dismay that the Bishop had been insufficiently considerate to preserve confidence in the Bible for those who needed Scripture as a guide to Christianity addressed to their reason and conscience.[10] Though Erskine remained personally unperturbed by the tide of destructive historical criticism, his own approach had nevertheless caused him trouble even with some of his closest evangelical friends and admirers. Madame de Broglie was one of several who 'misunderstood' *The Doctrine of Election* as apparently suggesting that belief was possible through conscience alone without the need for the Bible.[11] Erskine's concern, however, had been with internalising and incarnating the truth of the Bible within an authentic personal existential framework, which meant that the traditional evangelical emphasis on plenary biblical inspiration was not a primary issue for him. Indeed, he saw that, particularly in Scotland, "where a belief in the Bible is often substituted for faith in God, and a man is considered religious, not because he walks with God in his spirit, but because he acknowledges and maintains the verbal inspiration of the sacred canon", it could be harmful. Nevertheless, he strongly opposed the brutal way in which the Bible was being undermined by critics like Colenso who he believed undermined spiritual truth and the faith of the ordinary people:

> I believe that ninety-nine out of a hundred of the religious people of Scotland believe in the verbal inspiration of the Bible, and would have their faith shaken to pieces...I should like to see them disabused, but I should like this

---

Knight, *Shairp*, 212; Letters to Bishop Ewing, 5 October 1864, 3 December 1864, 10 December 1864, *Ewing-I*, 52-6.

[8] S.C. Carpenter, *Church and People, 1789-1889: A History of the Church of England from William Wilberforce to "Lux Mundi"* (London: SPCK, 1933), 503.

[9] Ernest Renan, *The Life of Jesus* (New York: Prometheus Books, 1991), 64-5.

[10] Erskine, Letter to Bishop Colenso [no date – probably 1862], *Letters-II*, 211-12.

[11] Letter to Madame de Broglie, 13 August [probably 1838], *Letters-I*, 322-4

Appendix 3 275

to be done in a way that would transfer their faith from the letter to the spirit, and not destroy their faith altogether".[12]

Instead, Erskine insisted

> until a man apprehends and knows the inward word...he never can rightly appreciate the outward word...When once I discover the identity of the word in me, the Christ in me, the hope of glory, with the word I find in the Bible, and with the Christ whose history is given there, I have got the only perfectly satisfactory evidence that the book is really the Revelation of God's purposes towards men...[13]

The distinction Erskine wished to make was rather that the Bible *contained* inspired spiritual truth. Its salvific 'value' consisted in the truth to be found in it, "not in the manner in which it was composed". Its 'authority' consisted of witnessing to, authenticating and releasing the universal divine light already within humanity, addressing "a reality within us, which is its business and duty to develop into maturity. When this is done, we know the thing that has been taught us, and not till then. When I believe a thing [it is] because the Bible has helped me to see its truth, and not because the Bible has said that it is true...".[14] In particular, the Bible illuminated individuals and pointed them to the saving character of God himself as "a teaching Father who eternally desires and seeks the holiness of His reasonable creatures"[15]. This was further to be apprehended, internalised and appropriated through "that in man which is of the nature of inspiration", i.e., conscience, or the "true light lightening every man", so that everything which God speaks to us through *external* means "is intended to make us better apprehend what He is speaking to each of us in the secret of our own being".[16] The principal object of the Bible, therefore, was to lead people to know God himself rather than merely know *about* him. Erskine acknowledged a supernatural element in this process which he allowed conferred unique status on the Bible.[17] It was pre-eminently a book of introduction, comparative to the education of a child: "the principles received at first on the authority of Scripture, ought gradually to be transferred to the higher sphere, the authority, not of a book, but of God Himself, in the reason and conscience".[18]

---

[12] Letter to Professor Lorimer, 14 July 1858, *Letters-II*, 212-3.
[13] Letter to Bishop of London, 11 July 1863, *Ewing-II*, 54-5.
[14] Letter to Bishop of London, 11 July 1863, *Ewing-II*, 55, cf., Letter to Bishop Colenso [no date-probably 1862], *Letters-II*, 210.
[15] Letter to Professor Lorimer, 5 August 1858, *Letters-II*, 216.
[16] Letter to Professor Lorimer, 5 August 1858, *Letters-II*, 213-4.
[17] Letter to Bishop of London, 11 July 1863, *Ewing-II*, 56.
[18] Letter to Bishop Ewing, 27 March 1860, *Ewing-I*, 20.

It was in such an existential context, therefore, that Erskine felt justified in declaring concerning the Bible, "I am prepared to hear any criticisms on the book; they do not trouble me in the least. I have found a medicine which heals me". "Textual emendations", "improved translations", were all to be welcomed, as long as they commended and clarified what he regarded as the central revelation of the Bible, the character of God. Too often, however, Erskine complained, the zealous critics were men who were "cold" towards this truth, so that their critical "processes are mere matters of philology".[19] When the Colenso controversy questioning the supposed historicity of the book of Exodus dominated the religious headlines in 1862, Erskine responded significantly that it was

> a remarkable fact, which may shake much of that faith which does not rest on God alone. I grieve for it, and yet I believe the man to be an earnest and good man. I have myself always been seeking for a self-evidencing light in divine truth not resting on any authority whatever, but children must begin by trusting to authority, and throughout this land 999 out of every 1000 are children.[20]

The more liberal approach to Scripture, creed, and doctrine which Erskine had unconsciously pioneered whilst fearing its less constructive outcome, anticipated subsequent developments in Scotland which duly arrived in the 1870s. Though later than in England, they involved the sensational controversy surrounding Free Church minister and biblical scholar, William Robertson Smith, who himself was deeply influenced by German theologians like Richard Rothe and Albrecht Ritschl, and contemporary biblical criticism.[21] Furthermore, shortly after his death, Erskine's prophecy concerning the fate of the Westminster Confession[22] was realised when the broad Scottish theologian A.M. Fairbairn (1838-1912), who studied under Isaac Dorner and Augustus Tholuck in Germany, advised his fellow countrymen to accept the passing of its place of authority: "Modern tendencies in Scotland, as elsewhere, [were] modifying, even in the most unexpected quarters, the old faith and its characteristic dogmas...the general mind of the country [had] grown into what is equal to a new faith...". And to whom did Fairbairn attribute the "modifying influences" which had brought about the changing climate?:

> A few earnest spiritual men [who] could not rest in the arid metaphysics of Westminster. Thomas Erskine of Linlathen began to write, and his books carried sweet and needed truths to many a wearied spirit, though the best thing

---

[19] Letter to Professor Lorimer, 5 August 1858, *Letters-II,* 216-7.
[20] Letter to Rev. Thomas Wright Mathews, 4 November 1862, *Letters-II,* 145.
[21] *DSCHT,* 782.
[22] Letter to Bishop Ewing, 8 March 1866, *Ewing-II,* 29.

Sir Henry Moncrieff could say of one of the mildest was, 'It ought to be burned by the common hangman'.[23]

Thomas Erskine was therefore perceived to have directly contributed to theological change in late Victorian Scotland. In 1864, Erskine advised that classic representative of the English Broad Church, Arthur Penryhn Stanley, Dean of Westminster, in connection with the furore over *Essays and Reviews*, that the value of any revelation, inspired or uninspired, depended on its remaining true independently of the revelation itself.[24] His innovative views concerning biblical criticism were directly taken up by Stanley and addressed appropriately to Erskine's native land. Invited to give an inaugural address in 1875 to the University of St. Andrew's by Principal Shairp, Stanley acknowledged the rapid changes in Scotland, commended the recently deceased Thomas Erskine, and as if sensing the time had finally arrived to transmit Erskine's very sentiments, boldly appealed for students to embrace the 'new criticism':

> We shall welcome without fear the keenest dissection and freest handling of the form, construction, and derivation of the letter, whether of the Scripture or of the Confessions of Faith, if we are convinced that the true 'supernatural' is the inner spiritual life, which remains after criticism has done its best and its worst…".[25]

---

[23] A.M. Fairbairn, "The Westminster Confession of Faith and Scotch Theology", in *Contemporary Review*, XXI (December, 1872 – May, 1873), 63, 65, 80. Sir Henry Moncrieff (1809-83) was the well-known conservative Free Church leader.

[24] Letter to Dean Stanley, 4 April 1864, *Letters-II*, 147, cf., Letter to Bishop Ewing, 18 May 1864, *Ewing-I*, 42.

[25] Arthur Penrhyn Stanley, "The Study of Greatness", in *Addresses and Sermons Delivered in St. Andrew's in 1872, 1875 and 1877* (London: Macmillan and Co., 1877), 38.

APPENDIX 4

Thomas Erskine and the Implications of Sandemanianism

Associated with concerns relating to Thomas Erskine's pneumatology, Nicholas Needham has recently resurrected a particular nineteenth-century critique. Convinced that Erskine's supposed adoption of the 'Sandemanian' concept of faith offers the key to understanding the aetiology of what he regards as Erskine's 'psychologising' approach to saving belief, he reproves Erskine's idea that belief contains within itself a dynamic ability to engender love and conformity to Christ:

> The crucial role attributed here to belief may be related to Erskine's Sandemanian concept of saving faith as mental assent...it is a concept which easily lends itself to a highly psychological approach to salvation, and indeed Erskine's tendency throughout...is to regard individual salvation in natural, psychological terms.[1]

The assumption made is that "Erskine basically takes that view of faith which is usually labelled 'Sandemanian'", and that he actually "held Sandemanian views".[2] Erskine's supposed 'Sandemanian' view of faith, which Needham summarises as 'essentially an intellectual act of assent', is linked to what he regards as Erskine's 'psychological' version of belief, and to his ambiguity concerning the role of the Spirit in regeneration. What in effect is presented as a heretical or unorthodox reduction of 'conversion' to a "human emotional mechanism" within "the realm of natural psychology", is deplored.[3] However, we believe the narrow linking of Erskine with 'Sandemanianism' actually confuses the picture. The reality is likely to be more complex and significant than one of mere 'Sandemanian' influence or dependence. There is therefore need for further analysis in an endeavour to

---

[1] Needham, *Thomas Erskine*, 61.
[2] *Ibid.*, 82, 13. See also 73, 309, 343, 496, etc.
[3] *Ibid.*, 83-4.

Appendix 4

ascertain what Erskine's contemporaries really feared in the novelty of Erskine's system to provoke such accusations.

'Sandemanianism' was the name given to the ecclesiological and theological system of an elder of the Scottish *Glasite* movement, Robert Sandeman (1718-71), who developed and promoted the views of John Glas (1695-1773). Whilst the underlying theology of the group was solidly Calvinist, recovery of what he saw as 'New Testament' ecclesiology was the most prominent aspect of Sandeman's system. However, amongst his radical beliefs was Sandeman's insistence that faith must not be confused with its effects. Faith was a "bare cold assent, or rather perception of the truth, in which, he even suggested that the mind did not act at all". This gave rise to the reputation of Sandemanianism as a cold, mechanical expression of religion:

> saving faith was reduced to a mere intellectual reception of the truth and nothing more – and as to emotion or holy feeling, or approbation, or obedience, it was all delusion and nonsense – faith he decided to mean assent or credence, and nothing more nor less.[4]

Needham appears to follow J.S. Candlish, whose 1873 critique of Erskine associated 'Sandemanianism' with his tendency to link faith in those Christian truths which especially exhibited the love and holiness of God with their natural impartation of salvation to the soul:

> There begins to appear the ill effect of viewing the work of Christ as merely or chiefly an exhibition of the character of God. Saving faith is regarded as a purely intellectual act, the perception and belief of the truth, and that without any of those cautions and qualifications with which that opinion has sometimes been held by the most evangelical divines. The intellectual view of faith was, indeed, prevalent at that time and earlier in Scotland; and no other idea of it seems ever to have occurred to Thomas Erskine. Not to speak of the Sandemanians, it was maintained by his uncle, the celebrated Dr John Erskine, and by Dr Chalmers.[5]

Now crucially, Candlish does not classify Erskine as 'Sandemanian'. Neither did most of Erskine's Methodist and subsequent critics. The accusation was comparatively rare with very few critics actually making a specific connection. Rather, Candlish suggested *comparison* with a range of others, *including* Sandemanians, who held similar 'intellectual' views of faith, but

---

[4] Anon., "Sandemanian Theology", *Eclectic Review*, IV (November, 1838), 521. Sandeman's views were influential in Scotland (especially in Dundee, where Erskine lived from 1816), England and New England. For background see Derek B. Murray, "The Influence of John Glas", in *RSCH*, XXII (1986), 45-56; Andrew Gunton Fuller, "Strictures on Sandemanianism", in *The Complete Works of the Rev. Andrew Fuller*, in 5 volumes (London: William Ball, 1837), II, 333-451.

[5] Candlish, "Thomas Erskine", 114-5.

who, he implies, were somehow more 'cautious' and able to retain their essential Calvinist 'orthodoxy' in a way Erskine perhaps did not. Nevertheless, a wider view was in prospect. Erskine was linked with general trends of his age, and his views, though *associated* with Sandemanianism, despite some dangerous additional tendencies peculiar to Erskine, were apparently more or less shared by orthodox Calvinists in general.

In *An Essay on Faith* and elsewhere, as we have noted, Erskine often appeared to reduce faith and belief to a kind of free intellectual act, authentication, or assent to revelatory truth, which then persuaded through its own power and influence. But, as both Needham and Candlish admit, this was not necessarily of itself an unusual or unorthodox concept.[6] Mainstream 'enlightened' evangelical thought in eighteenth-century Scotland regarded faith as signifying intellectual persuasion or assent,[7] and Sandeman's 'intellectual' view of faith was shared by Calvinist men of repute like Thomas Chalmers, James Haldane, Ralph Wardlaw, and his own uncle, Dr John Erskine, in addition to many others such as Erskine's own Congregational minister in Dundee, David Russell. It is therefore difficult not to conclude that most orthodox theologians in Erskine's Scotland were considered to have been substantially influenced by Sandemanian ideas to a greater or lesser extent.[8]

It seems remarkable that Candlish attributed Erskine's 'going astray' to his apparent advocacy of mere intellectual assent to truth without insistence on 'the consent of heart and will'. This cannot seriously be substantiated in Erskine's life and work as a whole, and even in *An Essay on Faith* which Candlish highlighted, Erskine clearly affirmed that all the highest faculties and affections were involved in the process of faith.[9] So it is pertinent to inquire why Erskine was associated specifically with Sandemanianism.

Candlish was echoing an earlier accusation. It was that 'organ of Scottish Calvinist orthodoxy', the *Edinburgh Christian Instructor*, which in

---

[6] Needham, *Thomas Erskine*, 82-3.

[7] John R. McIntosh, *Church and Theology in Enlightenment Scotland* (East Lothian: Tuckwell Press, 1998), 167.

[8] "Like most of the Congregational preachers of his day, [Russell] owed something also to the writings of Glass and Sandeman, though from the chilling coldness of many of their peculiar views he heartily recoiled", (William Lindsay Alexander, *The Good Man's Grave: A Discourse Occasioned by the Lamented Death of David Russell, D.D., Pastor of the Congregational Church Assembling in Ward Chapel, Dundee* [Glasgow: James Maclehose, 1848], 24-25, cf., Smeaton, *Holy Spirit*, 345). John Calvin declared (though with the necessary corrective pneumatological balance) "we shall possess a right definition of faith if we call it a firm and certain knowledge of God's benevolence towards us, founded upon the truth of the freely given promise in Christ, both revealed to our minds and sealed upon our hearts through the Holy Spirit", (*Institutes,* III. ii. 2 and 7).

[9] *Faith*, 50-1.

1830 apparently first associated those involved in "the Row Heresy" with Sandemanianism.[10] The context suggests that the intention was to condemn through guilt by association. By Erskine's day the epithet 'Sandemanian' had apparently (at least in England, and probably also in Scotland) acquired the status virtually of a 'catch-all' theological term of abuse, the precise definition of which remained comparatively irrelevant. It was the fact that dangerous associations were involved that counted, and the more discerning critics were aware of them. James Haldane declared "the name of Sandemanianism has long been employed in England as a bugbear, in order to excite prejudice against whatever was viewed with disapprobation".[11] But what was the nature of the underlying 'dangerous associations'? In a separate reference to the dangers of Sandemanianism, Haldane pinpointed a crucial aspect:

> Sandeman may be said to set aside the work of the Spirit, for he discourages all concern about salvation in the unconverted; but he carries the doctrine of Divine sovereignty so high, that it would appear the sinner has nothing to do but to wait till God reveal his Son in him.[12]

George Smeaton confirmed that Sandeman "allowed no work of the Spirit in the effectual application of redemption", repudiating all inward grace as counterfeit. Effectively, Sandeman "identified the influence of the truth and the influence of the Spirit".[13]

Though this strikes certain chords, in other ways it sounds so directly contrary to Erskine's fundamental approach that it remains important to understand why Erskine could have been associated with this divisive issue, which in fact dated back to 1729. Though Haldane disapproved of Erskine, he himself never actually associated him with Sandemanianism. Indeed, this would have been most unlikely since ironically he associated a defective salvific pneumatology with Sandemanian ultra-Calvinism, and Erskine was perceived as a threat to Calvinism itself. But extreme Calvinism was equally frowned upon in Erskine's day following the influence especially of Andrew Fuller.[14] Hyper-Calvinism placed excessive emphasis on the doctrine of irresistible grace, "with the tendency to state that an elect man is not only passive in regeneration but also in conversion...[leading]

---

[10] *ECI*, XXIX, V (May, 1830), 332. The article actually targeted John McLeod Campbell as the movement's "high priest".

[11] J.A. Haldane, *The Doctrine of the Atonement; with Strictures on Recent Publications*, [1845], [3rd edition] (Edinburgh: William P. Kennedy, 1862), 290.

[12] Letter of the Rev. James Haldane to the Editor concerning Sandemanianism, *Evangelical Magazine*, XXIV (May, 1846), 250.

[13] Smeaton, *Holy Spirit*, 345-7.

[14] *DSCHT*, 342.

its adherents to hold that evangelism was not necessary...". [15] Sandeman, as a type of extreme Calvinist, discouraged evangelism or any doctrine of prevenient grace on the basis that God saved designated individuals through sovereign election alone. There was no room, or indeed, necessity, for the Spirit's agency. If, therefore, Erskine was to be validly linked with Sandemanianism it could only be because specific aspects of that movement, namely an intellectual reception of faith combined with a relativising of the Spirit, were deemed to be identifiable elements within Erskine's soteriological system. Erskine could in certain respects be compared with some of the worst aspects of extreme Calvinism, but there any serious comparison ended.

However, Erskine was also cited in connection with "ultra Sandemanianism" in an anonymous letter to the editor of the *Christian Examiner* in 1831. This criticised his introductory essay in *Extracts of Letters to a Christian Friend, by a Lady*, though it acknowledged that Erskine's 'Sandemanianism' was limited to one particular aspect, i.e., faith. Ironically, Erskine was simultaneously accused of "ultra Arminianism". The issue of complaint involved Erskine's apparent understanding of *faith* and *universal pardon*, with the writer regarding Erskine's views as virtually synonymous with John Wesley's understanding of *justification,* i.e., that "the personal state of all human beings is supposed to be changed in consequence of the death of Christ, independent of the belief of any truth, or even the knowledge of any".[16] To maintain the concept that pardon was universal and free, faith could not be necessary to pardon; however, to enjoy pardon it must be known and believed. Hence the relevance of the charge of 'Sandemanianism' in respect of *faith.* Erskine was perceived to prescribe a passive, self-generated, intellectual reception of a pardon which was deemed already to exist, thereby condemning believers of the orthodox doctrine that pardon becomes effective only as a result of faith. This was tantamount to admitting the ability and freedom of human beings, by the operation of their own wills, to believe and exercise salvific faith apart from the working of the Holy Spirit. John Smyth appeared to confirm this general perception in 1830, declaring that Erskine's doctrine of universal pardon

> dishonours the grace of the Holy Spirit. The scheme unavoidably presupposes, that man has power to believe and obey the gospel, independently of any superadded strength from on high. It is, therefore, a system not of free

---

[15] Peter Toon, *The Emergence of Hyper-Calvinism in English Nonconformity 1689-1765* (London: Olive Tree, 1967), 145.

[16] Anon., *Christian Examiner*, XI, LXXIV (August, 1831), 586. John Wesley, who was regarded with suspicion in Scotland, came to regard *justification* quite simply as meaning 'pardon or the forgiveness of past sins', (Kenneth J. Collins, *The Scripture Way of Salvation: The Heart of John Wesley's Theology* [Nashville: Abingdon Press, 1997], 90).

Appendix 4 283

grace, but of free will, in the most exceptionable and dangerous sense of the word.

Though significantly he did not mention 'Sandemanianism', Smyth lamented the failure of Erskine and his followers "to reconcile their notions with the doctrine of the Christian's entire dependence on the renovating grace of the Holy Spirit", and complained that "he is thus necessarily led to look inward for the ground of his confidence". By contrast, Calvinist orthodoxy affirmed that the Spirit was the author of belief and that "man has neither the ability nor inclination to generate it in his own heart".[17]

Whilst Sandeman's concept of election dispensed with the need for the Spirit in conversion, Erskine, for different reasons, was nevertheless similarly perceived to minimise it, or just as objectionable, to acknowledge the Spirit's operation only *following* belief. In other words, the evoking of the despised association was a pretext for a wider complaint. The crucial point for his more discerning critics was that, like Sandeman, Erskine allowed little role for the Spirit in the human heart *prior to* belief, and consequently relegated faith to a human work instead of the grace of God by the Spirit. This in turn raised the dreaded spectre of 'Arminianism'. Whilst most of the established ministers who had been influenced by Sandemanian views managed to avoid the extremes of ultra-Calvinism and Arminianism, Erskine was perceived to have fallen into the Arminian camp. Arminianism was identified with semi-Pelagianism or synergism, emphasising the role of the human will in salvation, and thereby reducing the divine role in what amounted to a co-operative effort of belief. This explains the regular reactive reproach of 'Arminianism' against the 'new system' or 'neology' of Erskine and his followers,[18] because they were understood to teach universal atonement, and assurance as being of the essence of saving faith.[19] The concept of universal pardon and its implication that "no man is a believer who does not know that his sins are forgiven" was anathema to Erskine's Calvinist contemporaries dwarfing all other antagonistic reactions.[20] The association was clearly made by James Haldane who cited Erskine directly:

> The advocates of universal pardon ascribe salvation to faith. This is also a doctrine of the word of God, but faith is there represented as a grace flowing to believers through the death of Christ. According to the new system, it is the exercise of the power which every man has of 'coming to God if he chooses', and does not flow to us from the death of Christ. Faith is thus made

---

[17] Smyth, *Treatise*, 112, 114, 116.

[18] E.g., Anon., *ECI*, XXVII, VI (June, 1828), 414, 424.

[19] E.g., Thomson, *Universal Pardon*, 309-12, 328-33, 386-7.

[20] David Davidson, *A Sermon on Acts, x.43; in which the doctrine of Universal Pardon is considered and refuted* (Dundee: James Chalmers, 1830), 11.

the condition of salvation, which every man 'who chooses' has the power to fulfil.[21]

We have seen that Erskine was perceived to emphasise the Spirit's ministry of sanctification in the human heart *following* saving belief, and to minimise its role in conversion, resulting also in the charge of 'Pelagianism'. But Erskine clearly understood the Spirit to be operative throughout the entire salvific process, even though his concept of the nature of the Spirit remained somewhat ambiguous and reductionist. There is, however, no evidence that he denied a role for the Spirit in the formation of belief. Indeed, as early as 1820, in an unremarkably orthodox exposition, Erskine had made his understanding of the comprehensive work of the Spirit in the salvific apprehension of truth readily apparent, concluding unremarkably that the Spirit's special role was to convince the mind, complementary to, and in association with, the innate power of the truth itself, so that "the doctrine of the Spirit is connected…simply with a belief of his accompanying and giving weight and authority to revealed truth".[22] Erskine therefore cannot properly be said to have 'adopted' Sandemanian views, since so much of what Sandeman denied Erskine accepted. Rather, the perceived implications of his teaching were sometimes deemed to merit the association since it seemed a suitable pejorative label to attach to certain elements of it. Other such labels were regularly applied to the 'Erskineites', with Robert Burns describing the Erskine – Campbell system as comprising the 'worst parts' of 'the Bereans, the Sandemanians, the Moravians, and the Antinomians'.[23] Erskine's teaching was also repeatedly derisively compared to that of the 'classic heretics', Joanna Southcott and Antoinette Bourignon.[24] So the 'Sandemanian' ascription implied detected heterodoxy, not necessarily the actual adoption of Sandemanian views. Nevertheless, it is important to understand Erskine's position regarding the work of the Spirit in salvation.

Though his tendency to ambiguity caused confusion, Erskine presented a muted, complementary, but nevertheless largely orthodox role for the Holy Spirit, though certainly not afforded the prominence many would have preferred. Such an approach, though unsatisfactory to traditionalists, seemed to owe much to the apologetic reconstructive context in which Erskine worked. In this endeavour he was unlikely to have made recourse to an

---

[21] J.A. Haldane, *Observations on Universal Pardon, the Extent of the Atonement, and Personal Assurance of Salvation* (Edinburgh: W. Whyte, 1831), 56; (Haldane is objecting to a comment in *Freeness*, 61). See also Thomson, *Universal Pardon*, 317-27.

[22] *Evidence*, 147-50.

[23] Robert Burns, *The Gairloch Heresy Tried; in a letter to the Rev. John M. Campbell, of Row; and a Sermon preached at Helensburgh, and at Port-Glasgow* [3rd edition] (Paisley: Alex. Gardner, 1830), 54.

[24] E.g., Robertson, *Vindication*, 127, 246, 248, 299.

ultra-Calvinist sect. We have established that Candlish's concern about Erskine was manifestly not with 'Sandemanianism' as such. His concerns involved Erskine's supposed appropriation of what were considered to be Sandemanian concepts. Effectively Candlish was acknowledging that "Erskine stood in the midst of the Popular tradition of thought on the nature of faith". Consequently, any underlying concerns were more to do with Erskine's perceived synthesising, reconstructive activity and what it might lead to. As John McIntosh confirms, Erskine's primary aim was once again to accommodate traditional ideas to current thought:

> the Popular perception of faith as involving fundamentally intellectual assent to the truths of the gospel allowed a faith which might not be 'saving faith'. The significance of [Erskine was] that he provided an analysis of faith which made it possible to retain the mainstream, orthodox Calvinist perception of faith as 'saving knowledge' and yet assimilate contemporary insights relating to the operation of the understanding, the will, and the senses.[25]

Comparisons with Edwards, Hervey, and Marshall

Enthusiastic popular acclaim following publication of *Remarks on the Internal Evidence for the Truth of Revealed Religion* confirmed that Erskine was initially considered to be in line with orthodox Calvinism. Significantly, it was not until the onset of the controversies towards the end of the 1820s that there was any serious Calvinist opposition to Erskine's apparent novelty, especially relegation of the Spirit's role, when such suspicions were voiced in connection with his interpretation of how a saving knowledge of Christ was acquired.

The delay may perhaps have owed something to the fact that in 1820s Scotland, Jonathan Edwards remained a strong theological force, especially in connection with the doctrine of the Spirit,[26] and he was also known to hold the view that "faith is itself a form of knowledge and that it implies a direct and cognitive relationship to God".[27] Though he placed greater stress on the role of the Spirit, Edwards was nevertheless not dissimilar from Erskine in understanding the workings of divine activity within natural humanity:

> Many other ways might be mentioned wherein the Spirit acts upon, assists, and moves natural principles; but after all it is no more than nature moved, acted and improved.

---

[25] McIntosh, *Church and Theology*, 167.
[26] Smeaton, *Holy Spirit*, 342, 347.
[27] Michael J. McClymond, *Encounters with God: An Approach to the Theology of Jonathan Edwards* (New York and Oxford: Oxford University Press, 1998), 23.

Edwards stressed the importance of the 'affections of the mind', which he defined as "the more vigorous and sensible exercises of the inclination and will of the soul". He affirmed that "those affections that are truly holy, are primarily founded on the loveliness of the moral excellency of divine things", and "arise from the mind being enlightened, rightly and spiritually to understand or apprehend divine things". He believed that "knowledge is the key that first opens the hard heart, and enlarges the affections, and so opens the way for men into the kingdom of heaven".[28] Though George Smeaton later regarded Edwards' "distinction between NATURAL and MORAL ABILITY...[as] a capital mistake" which fuelled later speculation in both England and America concerning the "*natural* power to believe in Christ and repent",[29] Erskine's early Scottish readers would almost certainly have recognised echoes of Jonathan Edwards, which perhaps partly explains his initial popularity. However, they would also readily have sensed reminders of what began as a major eighteenth-century Calvinist controversy involving Edwards' views on the Spirit as interpreted by Walter Marshall, James Hervey, Joseph Bellamy, the Marrow men, and continued by others.

The underlying issue concerned the operation of the Spirit in connection with saving faith and regeneration, "whether the Holy Spirit acts on the mind MEDIATELY or IMMEDIATELY", and whether the Spirit's agency preceded or followed "the action of the human mind in conversion".[30] Association with Sandemanian pneumatological defects was close, and doubts about Erskine's understanding of the role of the Spirit would therefore also be linked to remaining sensitivities concerning this historical yet still controversial subject. This is precisely what occurred. Thomas Erskine aroused controversy concerning the extent to which he could be compared with Hervey and Marshall in his understanding of faith as affording universal unconditional pardon "a moral influence, by which it may heal the spiritual disease of the soul".[31]

Conclusions

That Erskine believed he was not advocating anything contrary to orthodox belief was confirmed by his concluding statement in *Remarks on the Internal Evidence for the Truth of Revealed Religion*, that "there is nothing new

---

[28] Jonathan Edwards, *The Religious Affections* [1746] (Edinburgh: Banner of Truth, 1961), 24, 135, 179, 192.

[29] Smeaton, *Holy Spirit*, 342-3.

[30] Smeaton, *Holy Spirit*, 347-9.

[31] Tyler, and Bonar, *Nettleton*, 380-5. Significantly, Nettleton associated Erskine's views with universalism.

Appendix 4 287

in this cursory sketch of Christian doctrines". Furthermore, he was cautiously anxious not to create a wrong impression, being concerned lest he

> should be doing a real injury to the cause which I wish to advocate, were I to be the means of conducting any one to the conclusion that Christianity is nothing more than a beautiful piece of moral mechanism, or that its doctrines are mere typical emblems of the moral principles in the Divine mind, well adapted to the understandings and feelings of men.[32]

It is therefore surprising to find Erskine accused of propounding a merely 'cold', 'intellectual' understanding of faith. In reply to what he deemed to be the discredited propagators of 'external evidence', understandably Erskine was concerned to emphasise that the truth and the power of Christianity were best attested by *subjective* means, which for Erskine implied that authoritative revelation will show itself to correspond with humankind's moral nature. The actual experience, emotion, or inner sense of moral congruity which flowed from the appeal to and regeneration of the moral will through the gospel, was what for him provided the most convincing proof of the authenticity of Christianity. Accordingly, "it is not surprising to find in *The Essay on Faith* a general derogation of the reasoning process in the establishment of faith and an insistence that real assent or faith is moral assent, accompanied by very definite emotions and an active compliance of the will".[33] Trevor Hart accurately summarises Erskine's understanding of faith in *existential* rather than intellectual terms:

> Faith is not a currency with which starving men are able to purchase the bread of salvation; rather it is the very act of receiving and eating that bread which is freely offered. Nor is this faith, which the Gospel properly 'demands' of us, to be understood in terms of intellectual 'belief' alone; rather it is the casting in desperation of the sinner's very self upon the one who has given all to save him. Faith is thus an existential orientation, a relationship with God, and not merely a correct rational assent to some body of facts or truths, although, as Erskine often notes, it is nonetheless faith *in something*, which must therefore be known and understood.[34]

Rather than adopting particular dogmatic viewpoints, primarily therefore, Erskine was once again eclectically appropriating the "intellectual environment of the Scottish Enlightenment" within an apologetic context.[35] J.S. Candlish was intent on defending orthodox Calvinism against what he saw as dangerous and powerful trends to undermine it. His concerns about Erskine were, like John Henry Newman, to do with the dangerous tendencies

---

[32] *Evidence*, 204, 144.
[33] Boulger, *Coleridge*, 44.
[34] Hart, *Teaching Father*, 26.
[35] McIntosh, *Church and Theology*, 167.

towards which his innovatory ideas might lead if taken to extremes. Needham perhaps tends to overstate and over-simplify the parallels between Erskine and Sandemanianism, underestimating the context in which comparisons were made and precedents drawn upon in attempts to delineate and classify Erskine's novel and alarming ideas. Without noting that Sandeman specifically relativised the Spirit, Needham's evident underlying concern is that Erskine's 'Sandemanian' understanding of faith led him to 'naturalise' or 'psychologise' what should be the Spirit's function. It is easy now to read back liberal tendencies into Erskine following a century of liberal pneumatology. But as we have argued throughout, Erskine was ahead of his time in creatively taking account of his context as he sought to make Christian dogma accessible and intelligible to his generation.

However Erskine may have anticipated later liberal trends, it is apparent he owed little to Sandemanianism as such. In some incidental ways, Sandemanian views of faith and the role of the Spirit corresponded with Enlightenment assumptions concerning revelation, but they proceeded from a quite different premise. Erskine owed no known allegiance to Sandemanianism, even though he may have been aware of its teachings. What is of real importance is that the contemporary objections to Erskine involved perception of soteriological innovation which at root implied a defective theology of regeneration and salvific pneumatology, as measured by a supposed traditional orthodoxy, but that in fact Erskine believed he was merely accommodating orthodox pneumatology to the new intellectual milieu.

APPENDIX 5

Thomas Erskine and Moral Government

Nicholas Needham directly connects Thomas Erskine's "highly psychological approach to salvation" with what he regards as his "strongly moral government understanding of the atonement as a public display of God's disapprobation of sin, aimed at preventing His mercy being misinterpreted as bland indulgence".[1]

This suggestion takes up John Henry Newman's observation that Erskine's idea of Christ's work on the cross necessarily producing "ascertainable moral effects on the character" owes much to rationalistic concepts of benevolent divine governance where God's justice becomes connected with "the well-being of His creation, as *a final end*". Accordingly, through the atonement of Christ

> God's justice was satisfied...inasmuch as He could then pardon man consistently with the good of His creation; consistently with their salutary terror of His power and strictness; consistently with the due order of His Government.

Because Newman considered that Erskine connected moral religious doctrines with the facts and principles of revealed divine governance, what becomes especially important concerning Christ's death is its meaning, which "illustrates" and "quickens" the historical fact, and "adapts it for influencing the soul".[2]

The moral government theory of atonement associated with a modified 'softer' form of Calvinism had been popularised in early nineteenth-century Scotland mainly by Jonathan Edwards and Andrew Fuller through the medium of the Haldanes and Congregationalism, and was taken up enthusiastically by the 1843 Seceders.[3] Prominent moral government theologians

---

[1] Needham, *Thomas Erskine*, 61.

[2] Newman, (Tract No. 73), 30, 31.

[3] Fairbairn, "Westminster Confession", *Contemporary Review*, XXI (December 1872 – May 1873), 79. Erskine may well have come into contact with Andrew Fuller through

included Ralph Wardlaw, George Payne, John Pye Smith, and Thomas Jenkyn. They sought to retain God's hatred of sin and lawlessness whilst simultaneously stressing his benevolence and desire for universal order. Whilst God punished sin and upheld his moral law through the death of Christ, nevertheless it was an essentially non-retributory presentation of divine justice, which moderated and attempted to mitigate the apparent harshness of Calvinist 'satisfaction' theory. Congruent with the more moderate evangelical Calvinism introduced by Edwards and adopted in Scotland by, for example, Thomas Chalmers, it was a system which incorporated a commitment to universal atonement. A.A. Hodge summarised the governmental theory as follows:

1. All moral excellence is ultimately reducible to benevolence. 'The attributes of God are not so many distinct qualities, but one perfection of excellence, diversified in our conceptions by the diversity of the objects towards which it is manifested.' This is a felicitous statement of the truth, provided that LOVE OR BENEVOLENCE be that 'one perfection of excellence'...
2. God is a wise and benevolent ruler. The *origin* and *end* of the moral law lie in the divine purpose to promote by means of it the good of the universe. The ultimate ground of the divine government...is to be found in the benevolence of God...
3. 'The sufferings of Christ (the atonement) were not...the penalty of the law, but a *substitute for it,* and *an equivalent*; that is, *had the same efficacy in respect to the divine law and government* that the penalty was designed to have...'
4. The atonement renders the salvation of all men possible...the principles which secure its actual application to individual men...have no place in the atonement itself...the only thing Christ purchases for mankind is pardon on condition of faith, and that after we believe we are rewarded for our own goodness...[4]

Often associated with moral government theology was the related concept of 'moral influence', the idea that a doctrine like the atonement, which displayed the excellent moral character of God, the 'Supreme Governor', derived its importance from the moral influence it brought to bear on the subject, so that contrary to traditional interpretation, it was individuals rather than God who were changed by the death of Christ.

Erskine's belief in the moral power of truth to reproduce its likeness was evidently fundamental to his soteriological outlook, and he also adopted strong moral influence views of the atonement. Similarities with Hodge's summary are immediately apparent. Needham unhesitatingly considers

---

his early formative friendship with Charles Stuart of Dunearn, who was a close confidant of Fuller, (*DSCHT*, 803).

[4] A.A. Hodge, *The Atonement* [1867] (London: Evangelical Press, 1974), 328-30.

Erskine a moral government theologian, though he insists its source is a matter of speculation: "The reason for Erskine's adherence to this theology...remains a mystery...".[5] By contrast, however, Henry Henderson appears to subvert Needham's view, concluding that "Erskine did not believe in this pseudo-liberalism any more than in the harsh Calvinism it displaced. To him there was nothing to choose between the two".[6] Once again, the controversial question of alleged influence requires closer examination.

As the nineteenth century advanced, the Enlightenment/ Kantian concept of a benevolent 'moral Governor' or 'moral Ruler' who was the originator of the universal moral law by which humanity would progress gained greatly in popularity, fostered notably by the Unitarians, who in turn acknowledged a debt to the Cambridge Platonists.[7] For the purposes of Christian apologetics in a sensitive age, it was quickly realised that the concept of the universal benevolent government of a God recognisably immanent within humanity afforded a useful device. Reliance on the relationship of religion to virtue as a primary argument for the reality of God became increasingly dominant. The existence of a moral Governor was effectively 'proved' by the universal sense of moral obligation, as intimated by conscience. Because the moral perfection of God was comprehended through our corresponding moral nature, religion was increasingly construed as a question of unconditional obedience and duty to God and humanity.

However, though he may have accorded with the concept of the benevolent government of God, the existence of similarities does not necessarily imply that Erskine adhered to, or was directly influenced by, a specifically 'moral government' theology. Erskine, as we have seen, was eclectically inclined, being instinctively unattracted to dogmatic systems of any kind. In any case, the introduction of moral government theology into Scotland occurred *in parallel to* and did not precede Erskine's own theological development, albeit motivated by the same concerns which had already prompted Erskine. It seems more probable, therefore, that Erskine was once again innovatively inspired more generally by eclectic Kantian concepts and analogies, rather than by attachment to a particular dogmatic form of atonement theory, especially since in Scotland it was adopted in the main by stalwart, if 'modified', Calvinists.

Erskine's first extended 'government' analogy appeared in his introductory essay to the *Letters of the Rev. Samuel Rutherford*, composed as early as 1816, and adopted an overtly apologetic, analogical tone, divorced

---

[5] Needham, *Thomas Erskine*, 42-4.
[6] Henderson, *Erskine*, 55.
[7] Young, *Maurice*, 39, 43, cf., Hugh Ross Mackintosh, *Types of Modern Theology* (London: Nisbet, 1937), 22.

from systematic theory.[8] Erskine believed that the very existence of goodness, truth and righteousness involved "eternal realities" which necessarily implied "a living personal will, a good, loving, righteous God...", with the 'inward demand of righteousness' counting as corroborating evidence. The very capacity of human beings for love and apprehension of God Erskine regarded as confirmation of God's saving purposes.[9] His view that practical, moral and spiritual benefit could only be gained from correct apprehension of the inner truth and meaning of historical facts, and that once the excellence of the divine character was truly perceived it self-generated free response of love and obedience, may be considered as applied development of Kantian thought.[10] There are distinct epistemological similarities between Erskine and Kant in relation to Kant's denial that we can know 'things in themselves', but that our knowledge may take a more morally practical, intuitional, and self-evidencing form. Erskine may possibly have been thinking of Kant and the creative potential of using him for apologetic purposes when stating his belief concerning the "principle of the self-evidencing nature of light", that "no argument outside of the thing itself can be of much use. We require to see *light in the thing...*".[11] Bishop Ewing, who considered Erskine reached his own views mainly by intuition, commented that, for Erskine, the very "fact of the existence of morals involved to him the necessity of a Personal and Living Source. It was here that he came upon a personal God, and the unanswerable proof of His existence and character".[12]

It is entirely likely that during his law studies at Edinburgh University between about 1805 and 1811, Erskine came into contact, not only with the empirical philosophical tradition, but with the prevalent *Scottish Common Sense* philosophy of Thomas Reid (1710-96), as promoted by Enlightenment professor Dugald Stewart (1753-1828), who then held the chair of moral philosophy. Both men were considered heroic champions of common sense and true religion, arguing contrary to David Hume's scepticism that the human mind directly apprehends the natural world and the fundamental truths of Christianity. Reid saw the first principles of morality as self-evident to anybody who acknowledged a conscience. Conscience itself was the law of God written in the heart which it was unnatural to disobey. This effectively implied the necessity of moral duty. Moral government theology, especially in America, where Nathaniel Taylor and William Ellery Channing were major influences behind its expression in New Haven

---

[8] *Salvation*, 289-96.
[9] Letters to Miss Wedgwood, 18 May and 12 June 1865, *Letters-II*, 154-7.
[10] See Pelikan, *Christian Doctrine*, 185-6.
[11] Letters to Bishop Ewing, December 1865 and 10 December 1864, *Ewing-II*, 25, *Ewing-I*, 55.
[12] *Ewing-II*, 11-14.

theology and Unitarianism, was strongly influenced by Scottish philosophy, with its "profound reliance on moral principles as self-evident intuitions...a demand for 'ethical' formulations in theology...insistence upon the freedom of man and the universality of sin".[13]

In Erskine's student days, Edinburgh University was "a school, not so much of philosophy as of philosophically directed education adapted to the needs of the time". Dugald Stewart included in his renowned *Outlines of Moral Philosophy* course psychological investigation 'of the active and of the moral powers of man' including 'the duties which respect the Deity' based on a 'preliminary inquiry into the principles of natural religion', together with 'the duties which respect our fellow-creatures' and ourselves.[14] Thomas Chalmers knew Stewart well, and largely accepted the Scottish philosophy of Reid. Sir Walter Scott and Erskine's companions and fellow law students, Lords Cockburn and Jeffrey, studied under Stewart, and it is reasonable to suppose that Erskine did so too.[15] Few distinctions were to be drawn between English and Scottish Enlightenment traditions, with much common ground subsisting in philosophy and moral and natural science. Stewart, who was passionately committed to the unity of logic, moral and political philosophy, and psychology, together with the integration of "natural philosophical views within rational religion", was likely a prime source of inspiration for Erskine's eclectic moral philosophy education.[16] Erskine may accordingly have been appropriating widely held understandings about God from the broader context of compulsory moral philosophy studies for the purposes of formulating an innovative Christian apologetic, a task for which his legal training, stylistically evident throughout his work, equipped him well.

Significantly, the organ of American moral government theology, the New Haven *Quarterly Christian Spectator*, enthusiastically reviewed Erskine's *The Unconditional Freeness of the Gospel*, warmly commending his moral arguments whilst simultaneously dissociating itself from his views on pardon, which it regarded as actually inconsistent with moral government soteriology. However, the periodical appeared to endorse Erskine's salvific ideas concerning the moral adaptability of Christianity for the restoration of humankind, highlighting

---

[13] Welch, *Protestant Thought*, 128, 135, cf., Holmes, *Fact, Value, and God*, 115; Hicks, *Evangelicals & Truth*, 59.

[14] W.L. Renwick, *English Literature 1789-1815* (Oxford: Clarendon Press, 1963), 198-9.

[15] See Daniel F. Rice, "Natural Theology and the Scottish Philosophy in the thought of Thomas Chalmers", *SJT* 24 (1971), 23, 27; "Stewart, Dugald", in *Encyclopaedia Britannica* [11th edition], XXV, 913-4.

[16] Porter, *Enlightenment*, [2000], 243, 256-7.

the universality of that moral influence which, in consequence, it exerts upon sinners to subdue them to the love of God and actual reconciliation. Now this influence of motive arises...from the affecting exhibition of the benevolent compassion of God made in the provision of such an atonement...Every heart is plied by the atonement, because...this lays on every heart the burning motives of the divine character – deep compassion to excite hope, rich benefit to excite gratitude, unexampled goodness to excite confidence, unbending holiness to excite esteem and veneration.[17]

Whilst he exhibited theological and philosophical features common to the moral government scheme, it is noteworthy, however, that Erskine was not considered to belong to the moderate Calvinist theological grouping, and was actually rejected by them. Ralph Wardlaw, the prominent moral government theologian, despite his personal friendship and admiration for Erskine, distanced himself from his views and informed his fellow theologian, Leonard Woods, of Andover Theological Seminary, who was inquiring about Erskine, of his grief and pain at the publication of *The Unconditional Freeness of the Gospel*, principally on account of Erskine's interpretation of universal pardon as an accomplished fact.[18] In contrast, as a moral government theologian and moderate Calvinist, Wardlaw understood the gospel in terms of a universal *offer* of pardon. Neither did J.S. Candlish specifically connect Erskine with moral government theology, widespread in Scotland by the time of Erskine's death. Instead, he noted the importance of moral influence to his soteriological scheme as a whole, incidentally highlighting Erskine's and John McLeod Campbell's innovatory role:

> what Erskine and Campbell had embraced was in reality at bottom a form of the theology that has become so prevalent in modern times...The atonement of Christ and the forgiveness of sins...being quite universal and actually accomplished facts, they had only an historical importance as things to be believed, and the practical concern for men now was made to be entirely the moral influence of these beliefs in the renewal of their character.[19]

Candlish could have linked Erskine and Campbell with the moral government group, but clearly did not make the association in view of the general prevalence of moral influence theories apart from moral government theology itself, and their evidently dissonant convictions concerning universal pardon. Candlish was also aware of the mutual opposition, and that Campbell had actually opposed the 'rectoral or public justice' theologians by name as 'modified Calvinists' in *The Nature of the Atonement*, claiming

---

[17] Anon., Review of Thomas Erskine's 'The Unconditional Freeness of the Gospel', in *Quarterly Christian Spectator*, I, II (June, 1829), 305.
[18] William Lindsay Alexander, *Memoirs of the Life and Writings of Ralph Wardlaw* (Edinburgh: Adam and Charles Black, 1856), 275.
[19] Candlish, "Thomas Erskine", 116-7.

Appendix 5

that their moral scheme did not adequately account for the purpose of atonement, and that the limited concept of God as a moral Governor was not in keeping with the "full-orbed revelation of God" as an Eternal Father.[20]

Accordingly, once again we are obliged to reject any attempt to pin Erskine down to any specific theological category or grouping. Despite overlapping with convictions of moral government theologians in a number of areas to the extent of debate regarding allegiance, Erskine resists any such neat classification. Quite simply, as an independent theological eclectic, owning no associations, in his own idiosyncratic way he inevitably mirrored selected aspects of the theological and philosophical currents of his era, of which moral government theology was one expression.

↳ originality was a key characteristic of the Romantics

---

[20] Campbell, *NOTA*, e.g., 65, Chapter IV, 81-104.

BIBLIOGRAPHY

Principal Manuscript Collections Consulted

Beinecke Rare Book and Manuscript Library, Yale University Library. Letters from Thomas Erskine to George MacDonald (undated) regarding MacDonald's visit to Linlathen. General *MSS* 103, Box No.2, Folder No.68.

British Museum. Letter from Thomas Erskine dated 15 May (1838?) and Saturday (1838?) from the Hotel Wampam, Paris, to The Lady Olivia Bernard Sparrow. *MS* Ref. Eg. 1966 ff. 41, 43.

Cambridge, Ridley Hall. Hopkins Collection, *MS* No. 462. Letter from Thomas Erskine to Charles Simeon dated 14 December, 1821.

National Library of Scotland. *MS* 10459, 10949. Letters written by Thomas Erskine of Linlathen in 1814 and 1816 to his uncle, Thomas Graham Stirling.

National Library of Scotland. *MS* 9747. Letters written by Thomas Erskine of Linlathen between 1851 and 1868 to Mrs Schwabe.

National Library of Scotland. Various *MSS* Collections containing letters written by Thomas Erskine of Linlathen to Thomas Carlyle, Jane Stirling, Jane Welsh Carlyle, Lady Ashburton, David Dundas, and others. Microfilm Repayment Order *MS*/874/99.

New College, Edinburgh. Various letters from the Chalmers *MS* Collection, principally between Thomas Chalmers and Thomas Erskine of Linlathen.

Works by Thomas Erskine and Published Correspondence

- *Remarks on the Internal Evidence for the Truth of Revealed Religion* [10th combined edition] (Edinburgh: David Douglas, 1878), (first published 1820), including Introductory Essays:
    1. To Gambold's Works (*The Works of the Rev. John Gambold* with an introductory essay, by Thomas Erskine, Glasgow: Chalmers and Collins, 1822).
    2. To Baxter's Saints' Rest (Richard Baxter, *The Saints' Everlasting Rest*, abridged by Benjamin Fawcett with an introductory essay by Thomas Erskine, Glasgow: Chalmers & Collins, 1824).
    3. To Rutherford's Letters (*Letters of the Rev. Samuel Rutherford* with an introductory essay, by Thomas Erskine, Glasgow: Chalmers & Collins, 1825). [Originally an essay entitled *Salvation*, written in 1816].

    Citations are from the 1878 combined volume.
- *An Essay on Faith* [5th edition] (Edinburgh: Waugh and Innes, 1829), (first published in 1822).
- *The Unconditional Freeness of the Gospel: in Three Essays* (Edinburgh: Waugh & Innes, 1828).
- *The Unconditional Freeness of the Gospel: in Three Essays* [2nd edition] (Edinburgh: Waugh & Innes, 1828).
- *The Unconditional Freeness of the Gospel*, [new edition] (Edinburgh: David Douglas, 1879), [this edition first published in 1870].

    Citations are from the 2nd edition except where indicated.
- *Extracts of Letters to a Christian Friend, by a Lady. With An Introductory Essay by Thomas Erskine, Esq., Advocate* (Greenock: R.B. Lusk, 1830).
- *The Gifts of the Spirit* (Greenock: R.B. Lusk, 1830).
- *The Brazen Serpent; or Life Coming Through Death*, (Edinburgh: Waugh and Innes, 1831).
- *The Brazen Serpent; or Life Coming Through Death* [special 1st edition including an extract, later to be inserted in the 2nd edition, entitled "That Christ Suffered as our Head, to lead us through Suffering to Glory, – and not as our Substitute to dispense with our Suffering"] (Edinburgh: Waugh and Innes, 1831).
- *The Brazen Serpent; or, Life Coming Through Death*, [2nd edition] (Edinburgh:Waugh and Innes, 1831).

    Citations are from the 1st edition except where indicated.

- *The Doctrine of Election and its Connection with the General Tenor of Christianity, illustrated from Many Parts of Scripture, and especially from the Epistle to the Romans* (London: James Duncan, 1837).
- *The Spiritual Order and Other Papers Selected from the Manuscripts of the late Thomas Erskine of Linlathen* [3rd edition] (Edinburgh: David Douglas,1884), [first published 1871].
- *The Purpose of God in the Creation of Man* (Edinburgh: Edmonston and Douglas, 1870), [being the third chapter of *The Spiritual Order*, published separately as a tract in accordance with Erskine's dying instructions].
- *True and False Religion* (London: Hamilton, Adams, and Co., 1874), [being Erskine's introductory essay to *Extracts of Letters to a Christian Friend from a Lady,* re-published in a slightly shorter version].
- *The Supernatural Gifts of the Spirit: with Remarkable Cases of Modern Miracles, by "Sir.* (sic.) *Thomas Erskine",* R. Kelso Carter (ed.), (Philadelphia: Office of 'Words of Faith', 1883), [being Chapter V, "Christ the King" of *The Brazen Serpent*].
- *Letters of Thomas Erskine of Linlathen*, in 2 volumes; Vol. 1 from 1800 till 1840; Vol. 2 from 1840 till 1870, Hanna, William, [ed.], (Edinburgh: David Douglas, 1877).
- Various letters of Thomas Erskine, in Knight, William, *Principal Shairp and his Friends* (London: John Murray, 1888).
- "Professor Scott and Mrs Oliphant's Life of Edward Irving". Letter to the Editor. *The Daily News* (Saturday, 7 June 1862), p.3.
- Letter to Dean Ramsay, 19 October 1869, in E. B. Ramsay, *Reminiscences of Scottish Life and Character* [1858], [27th edition] (London: Gall and Inglis, 1875), pp. lxxxvii – lxxxviii.
- Various letters of Thomas Erskine in *Present-Day Papers on Prominent Questions in Theology,* Third Series, Ewing, The Right Revd Alexander, Bishop of Argyll and the Isles, (ed.); including: Part 1: "Some Letters of Thomas Erskine of Linlathen". Part 4: "Some Further Letters of Thomas Erskine of Linlathen". Part 6: "The Relation of Knowledge to Salvation, and the place of Knowledge in Relation to the Christian Sacraments", by the editor, with Letters from the Archbishop of Canterbury, Bishop Thirwall, the Rev. Dr. McLeod Campbell, and Mr. Erskine. Part 7: "Reconciliation", by the Editor. With Letters from the Rev. Dr. McLeod Campbell, the Rev. F.D. Maurice, and Mr. Erskine, [first edition] (London: Strahan & Co., 1871); [supplementary edition] (London: Daldy, Isbister & Co, 1878).
- "The Righteousness of God in the Heart of Man", and "God's Welcome to the Returning Sinner", in *Fragments of Truth: being expositions of passages of scripture chiefly from the teaching of John McLeod Campbell, D.D., with a preface by his son* (Donald Campbell, also editor) [4th edition] (Edinburgh: David Douglas, 1898), [being selected

sermons of Thomas Erskine, together with those of John McLeod Campbell and A.J. Scott, based on shorthand notes taken by Miss Jane Gourlay]. First published in 1843 as *Fragments of Expositions of Scripture*.
- *The Internal Word, or, Light becoming Life: A Short Guide to the Rule of Faith and of Life. Being an Abridgement of the Concluding Portion of Mr. Erskine's Volume on the Doctrine of Election,* The Right Revd Alexander Ewing, Bishop of Argyll and the Isles, (ed.), (Edinburgh: Edmonston and Douglas, 1865).

Primary Works Consulted

'Anglicanus' (probably the Rev. Henry Grey, Minister of St. Mary's, Edinburgh), *Universal Redemption, a Truth according to the Scriptures, defended from the Misrepresentations and Calumnies contained in a late Pamphlet entitled "The Gareloch Heresy Tried" in a Letter addressed to the Rev. Robert Burns, D.D., F.S.A., Minister of St. George's, Paisley, author of the aforesaid pamphlet* (Glasgow: W. Collins, M. Ogle, and G. Gallie, 1830).

A Layman (Henry Drummond), *Candid Examination of the Controversy between Messrs. Irving, A. Thomson, and J. Haldane, respecting the Human Nature of the Lord Jesus Christ* (London: James Nisbet, 1829).

A Priest Evangelist (probably John Craig) *Epistle on the Final Salvation of All Mankind From Sin, to "The Angel" of the "Holy Catholic Apostolic Church in Glasgow", with a letter to the author from Thos. Erskine, Esq., Advocate* [2nd Edition] (Glasgow: George Gallie, 1863).

Abbot, Evelyn and Campbell, Lewis, *The Life and Letters of Benjamin Jowett, M.A., Master of Balliol College, Oxford,* in 2 volumes (London: John Murray, 1897).

Adam, Thomas, *Private Thoughts on Religion and other subjects connected with it, to which is prefixed a short sketch of his life and character* [by James Stillingfleet] (Philadelphia: Presbyterian Board of Publication, n/d), [first published in 1795].

Alexander, William Lindsay, *Memoirs of the Life of and Writings of Ralph Wardlaw, D.D.* (Edinburgh: Adam and Charles Black, 1856).
- *The Good Man's Grave: A Discourse Occasioned by the Lamented Death of David Russell, D.D., Pastor of the Congregational Church Assembling in Ward Chapel, Dundee* (Glasgow: James Maclehose, 1848).

Anon., (probably John Arthur) *An Examination and Refutation of the Unscriptural Principles and Sentiments Advocated by Mr. Erskine in his*

Preface to *"Extracts of Letters to a Christian Friend: by a Lady"* (Edinburgh: J. & D. Collie, 1830).
Anon., (probably Rev. James Russel, Minister of Gairloch), *A Letter to a Friend, on Universal Pardon, as Advanced by Thomas Erskine, Esq, and Others* (Dundee: James Adam, 1830).
Anon., *An Essay on the Extent of Human and Divine Agency in the Production of Saving Faith* (Edinburgh: William Blackwood, London: T. Cadell, 1827).
Anon., *Be Careful for Nothing* (Greenock: R.B. Lusk, 1830).
Anon., by "A Lover of Truth," *Critical Remarks on 'The Everlasting Gospel,' a Sermon preached in the Floating Chapel at Greenock by the Rev. J. M. Campbell* (Glasgow: G. Gallie, W. Collins & M. Ogle, 1830).
Anon., *Candour; or an Impartial Examination of the Row Heresy: with hints to the General Assembly on the Treatment of Controversies* (Glasgow: W.R. M'Phun, 1831).
Anon., *Christianity and Calvinism. The Rev. J. M. Campbell of The Row, The Synod of Glasgow & Ayr, The Confession of Faith, and The Bible* [2nd edition] (Glasgow: J. Hedderwick & Son, 1831).
Anon., *The Condition in which all men are placed through the death of the Son of God; being an examination of the sentiments of Dr Wardlaw, of Glasgow, and Mr Russell, of Dundee, regarding the Atonement, Forgiveness, and Justification by Faith* (Glasgow: James A. Begg, 1834).
Anon., *Notes and Recollections of Some of the Addresses and Conversation at the Broadlands Conference, of August, 1887 with a few additions from a former conference* (Hereford: Jakeman and Carver, undated), (for private circulation).
Anon., *The Port Glasgow Miracles. Strictures on a Publication entitled 'The Gifts of the Spirit' by Thomas Erskine, Esq. Advocate, Author of the 'Unconditional freeness of the Gospel'* (Hamburg: Hartwig & Müller, 1830).
Arndt, Johann, *True Christianity*, translated with an introduction by Peter Erb, The Classics of Western Spirituality (London: SPCK, 1979).
Arnold, Matthew, *Literature and Dogma: An Essay Towards A Better Apprehension of the Bible* (London: Smith, Elder, & Co., 1886).
Athanasius, *Contra Gentiles and De Incarnatione*, edited and translated by Robert W. Thomson (Oxford: Clarendon Press, 1971).
Barclay, George, *Strictures on the "Notes and Recollections of Two Sermons by the Rev. Mr. Campbell; delivered in the Parish Church of Row, on Sunday, 8th September, 1829"* [2nd edition] (Glasgow: Maurice Ogle, 1830).
Barclay, Robert, *Apology for the True Christian Divinity,* [14th edition], (Glasgow: R. Barclay Murdoch, 1886) [first published in 1678].
Barr, James, "Last General Assembly Vindicated", in *Edinburgh Christian Instructor,* Vol. I, No. I, New Series, (January 1832), 18-31.

Baxter, Robert, *Narrative of Facts Characterising the Supernatural Manifestations, in Members of Mr. Irving's Congregation, and Other Individuals in England and Scotland and Formerly in the Writer Himself* (London: James Nisbet, 1833).
Bellamy, Joseph, *Letters and Dialogues, beween Theron, Paulinus, and Aspasio, on the Nature of Love to God, Faith in Christ, and Assurance of Salvation. With an Introductory Essay, by the Rev. Robert Burns, D.D. F.A. S. Minister of St. George's, Paisley* (Glasgow: George Gallie, 1830).
Bovet, Pierre, (ed.), *Alexandre Vinet: Lettres, 1813 – 1847*, in 4 volumes (Lausanne: Librairie Payot, 1947-49).
Boyle, G.D., *The Recollections of the Very Rev. G.D. Boyle Dean of Salisbury* (London: Edward Arnold, 1895).
Brooke, Stopford A., (ed.), *Life and Letters of Fred. W. Robertson, M.A.*, [new edition] in 2 volumes (London: Kegan Paul, Trench, & Co., 1882).
Brotherston, Rev. Peter, *A Brief View of Faith; in which the saving belief of the Gospel is distinguished from Antinomian Confidence* (Edinburgh: William Whyte & Co., 1828).
Brown, David, "Letter to a Friend Entangled in Error", in *Edinburgh Christian Instructor*, Vol. II, No. II, (February 1833), 73-86, and Vol. II, No. III (March 1833), 145-153.
Brown, John and Forrest, D.W., (eds.), *Letters of Dr. John Brown with Letters from Ruskin, Thackeray, and Others* (London: Adam & Charles Black, 1907).
Buchanan, James, *A Letter to Thomas Erskine, Esq., Advocate, Containing Remarks on his Late Work, entitled "The Unconditional Freeness of the Gospel"* (Edinburgh: John Lindsay & Co., 1828).
– *The Doctrine of Justification: An Outline of its History in the Church and of its Exposition from Scripture* (Grand Rapids, Baker Book House, 1977), [first published in 1867].
Burns, Robert, *Reply to the Lay Member of the Church of Scotland; with a note for the Reverend James Russel, Minister of Gairloch* (Paisley: Alex. Gardner, 1830).
– *The Gairloch Heresy Tried; in a letter to the Rev. John M. Campbell, of Row; and a Sermon preached at Helensburgh, and at Port-Glasgow*, [3rd edition] (Paisley: Alex. Gardner, 1830).
Bushnell, Horace, *God in Christ, Three Discourses delivered at New Haven, Cambridge, and Andover* (New York: Charles Scribner's Sons, 1887), [originally delivered in 1848].
– *The Vicarious Sacrifice Grounded in Principles of Universal Obligation* (New York: Charles Scribner & Co., 1866).
Butler, Joseph, *Fifteen Sermons Preached at the Rolls Chapel and a Dissertation upon the Nature of Virtue* (London: G. Bell & Sons Ltd., 1964), [first published in 1726].

Caird, W.R., *A Letter to the Rev. R.H. Story, Rosneath, respecting certain misstatements contained in his memoir of the late Rev. R. Story* (Edinburgh: Thomas Laurie: 1863).

Calvin, John, *Institutes of the Christian Religion*, John T. McNeil (ed.), translated by Ford Lewis Battles, in The Library of Christian Classics, Volumes XX and XXI (Philadelphia: The Westminster Press, 1960), [first published in 1559].

Campbell, Donald, (ed.), *Memorials of John McLeod Campbell, D.D. Being Selections from his Correspondence,* in 2 volumes (London: Macmillan and Co., 1877).

– *Reminiscences and Reflections, Referring to His Early Ministry in the Parish of Row, 1825-1831. By the late John McLeod Campbell, D.D.* (London: Macmillan and Co., 1873).

– *The Whole Proceedings before the Presbytery of Dumbarton, and Synod of Glasgow and Ayr, in the case of the Rev. John McLeod Campbell, Minister of Row. Including the Libel, Answers to the Libel, Evidence, and Speeches* (Greenock: R.B. Lusk, 1831).

– *The Whole Proceedings in the case of the Rev. John McLeod Campbell, Late Minister of Row, before the Presbytery of Dumbarton, the Synod of Glasgow and Ayr, and the General Assembly of the Church of Scotland; including the Libel, Answers to the Libel, Evidence, and Speeches*; together with *A Full Report of the Proceedings in the General Assembly of the Church of Scotland, in the case of the Rev. John McLeod Campbell, Late Minister of Row on the 24th and 25th of May, 1831, taken in short-hand* [2nd edition] (Greenock: R.B. Lusk, 1831).

– *Fragments of Truth: being expositions of passages of scripture chiefly from the teaching of John McLeod Campbell, D.D., with a preface by his son* (Donald Campbell, also editor) [4th edition] (Edinburgh: David Douglas, 1898), [being selected sermons of John McLeod Campbell, together with those of Thomas Erskine and A.J. Scott, based on shorthand notes taken by Miss Jane Gourlay]. First published in 1843 as *Fragments of Expositions of Scripture*.

Campbell, John McLeod, *Sermons and Lectures,* in 2 volumes, taken in shorthand, [3rd edition] (Greenock: R.B. Lusk, 1832).

– *Notes of Sermons by the Rev. J. M^{c}L. Campbell, Minister of Row, Dumbartonshire, taken in shorthand,* in 3 volumes (Paisley: Printed only for the subscribers by John Vallance, Lithographer, 1831-32).

– *The Nature of the Atonement and its Relation to Remission of Sins and Eternal Life,* [new edition] (Edinburgh: The Handsel Press, 1996), [first published in 1856].

– *Thoughts on Revelation, with Special Reference to the Present Time* [2nd edition] (London, Macmillan and Co., 1874) [first published in 1862].

- *Responsibility for the Gift of Eternal Life. Compiled by permission of the late John McLeod Campbell, D.D., from sermons preached chiefly at Row in the years 1829-31* (London: Macmillan & Co.,1873).
Candlish, James S., *The Biblical Doctrine of Sin* (Edinburgh: T.&T. Clark, undated, 1893?).
- "Thomas Erskine of Linlathen", in *British and Foreign Evangelical Review*, Vol. XXII, No. LXXXIII (January, 1873), 105-129.
Candlish, Robert S., *Examination of Mr Maurice's Theological Essays* (London: James Nisbet and Co., 1854).
- *Reason and Revelation* (London: T. Nelson and Sons, 1864).
- *An Inquiry into the Completeness and Extent of the Atonement, with especial reference to the universal offer of the gospel, and the universal obligation to believe* (Edinburgh: John Johnstone, 1845).
- *The Atonement: Its Efficacy and Extent* (Edinburgh: Adam & Charles Black, 1867).
- *The Fatherhood of God*, [5th edition] (Edinburgh: Adam & Charles Black, 1870).
- *The Fatherhood of God: Supplementary volume to fifth edition containing reply to Dr. Crawford, with answers to other objections, and explanatory notes* (Edinburgh: Adam and Charles Black, 1870).
Cardale, John B., "On the Extraordinary Manifestations in Port-Glasgow", in *The Morning Watch or Quarterly Journal on Prophecy, and Theological Review*, Vol. II, No.IV, (March, 1830), 869-873.
Carlyle, Alexander, (ed.), *New Letters of Thomas Carlyle*, in 2 volumes (London and New York: John Lane, The Bodley Head, 1904).
Carlyle, G. (ed.), *The Collected Writings of Edward Irving*, in 5 volumes (London: Alexander Strahan, 1865).
Carlyle, Thomas, *Reminiscences* (Oxford: Oxford University Press, 1997), [first published in 1881].
- *The Life of John Sterling* (London, New York and Toronto: Henry Frowde, Oxford University Press, 1907), [first published in 1851].
Chalmers, Thomas, *The Evidence and Authority of the Christian Revelation*, [5th edition] (Edinburgh: William Blackwood, 1817).
Channing, William Ellery, *Unitarian Christianity and Other Essays*, edited with an introduction by Irving H. Bartlett (New York: The Bobbs-Merrill Company Inc., 1957).
- *William Ellery Channing: Selected Writings*, David Robinson (ed.) (New York: Paulist Press, 1985).
Cockburn, Henry, *Journal of Henry Cockburn being a continuation of the 'Memorials of His Time' 1831-1854,* in 2 volumes (Edinburgh: Edmonston and Douglas, 1874).
- *Memorials of His Time* (Edinburgh: Adam and Charles Black, 1861).
Colenso, John William, Bishop of Natal, *The Pentateuch and Book of Joshua Critically Examined* (London: Longman & Co., 1862-79).

Coleridge, Samuel Taylor, *Aids to Reflection* (Edinburgh: John Grant, 1905), [first published in 1825].
- *Biographia Literaria* (London: J.M. Dent, 1906), [first published in 1817].
- *Confessions of an Inquiring Spirit, to which are added miscellaneous essays from 'The Friend'* (London: Cassell & Company, Limited, 1892), [first published in 1840].
- "Notes on the Book of Common Prayer", in *Confessions of an Inquiring Spirit, to which are added miscellaneous essays from 'The Friend'* (London: Cassell & Company, Limited, 1892), [first published in 1840].
- *Table Talk* (Edinburgh: John Grant, 1905).

Conway, Moncure Daniel, *Autobiography Memories and Experiences of Moncure Daniel Conway*, in 2 volumes (London: Cassell and Company Limited, 1904).

Cox, Samuel, *Salvator Mundi: or, Is Christ the Saviour of All Men?*, [6th Edition] (London: C. Kegan Paul & Co., 1879) [first published in 1877].

Craig, Edward, *A Letter to Thomas Erskine, Esq., In Reply to His Recent Pamphlet in Vindication of The West Country Miracles* (Edinburgh: William Oliphant, 1830).

Crawford, Thomas J., *The Doctrine of Holy Scripture Respecting the Atonement*, [3rd edition] (Edinburgh and London: William Blackwood and Sons, 1880).
- *The Fatherhood of God Considered in its general and special aspects and particularly in relation to the Atonement with a review of recent speculations on the subject, and a reply to the strictures of Dr Candlish* [3rd edition] (Edinburgh and London: William Blackwood and Sons, 1868).

Darby, J.N., "Reflections upon the Prophetic Inquiry, and the Views Advanced in it", in *The Collected Writings of J.N. Darby*, 'Prophetic', Vol. I, William Kelly (ed.) (London: G. Morrish, no date), [first published Dublin, 1829].

Davidson, David, (Minister of the Chapel of Ease, Broughty Ferry), *A Sermon on Acts, x.43; in which the doctrine of Universal Pardon is considered and refuted* (Dundee: James Chalmers, 1830).

Dessain, Charles Stephen, and Gornall, Thomas, S.J., (eds.), *The Letters and Diaries of John Henry Newman*, Vol. XXX, *A Cardinal's Apostolate, October 1881 to December 1884* (Oxford: Clarendon Press, 1976).

Doddridge, Philip, *The Rise and Progress of Religion in the Soul; illustrated in a course of serious and practical addresses; with a devout mediation, or prayer added to each chapter* (London: The Religious Tract Society, 1892), [first published in 1745].

Dods, Marcus, *Early Letters of Marcus Dods,D.D., Late Principal of New College, Edinburgh, 1850-1864* selected and edited by his son (London: Hodder and Stoughton, 1910).
- *On the Incarnation of the Eternal Word* (Edinburgh: John Johnstone, 1848).

Dorner, Isaac August, *History of the Development of the Doctrine of The Person of Christ,* in 5 volumes (Edinburgh: T.& T. Clark, 1863).
- *A System of Christian Doctrine*, in 4 volumes, translated by Alfred Cave and J.S. Banks (Edinburgh: T.& T. Clark, 1896), [various dates].

Douglas, James, *The Truths of Religion* (Edinburgh: Adam Black, 1830).

Drummond, James, and Upton, C.B., *The Life and Letters of James Martineau,* in 2 volumes (London: James Nisbet & Co., Limited, 1902).

Edinburgh University Senatus Academicus, *Alphabetical List of Graduates of the University of Edinburgh from 1859 to 1888*, published by the Senatus Academicus (Edinburgh: James Thin, 1889), [S.R. Ref. 378 (41445) Edi.].

Edwards, Jonathan, *An Inquiry into the Modern Prevailing Notions of that Freedom of the Will which is supposed to be essential to moral agency, virtue and vice, reward and punishment, praise and blame* (Pennsylvania: Soli Deo Gloria Publications, 1996), [first published in 1754].
- *The Religious Affections* (Edinburgh: The Banner of Truth Trust, 1961), [first published in 1746].
- "Christian Knowledge: or, the Importance and Advantage of a Thorough Knowledge of Divine Truth", in *The Works of Jonathan Edwards*, in 2 volumes, revised and corrected by Edward Hickman (Edinburgh: The Banner of Truth Trust, 1974).

Ewing, The Right Revd Alexander, Bishop of Argyll and the Isles, *Revelation Considered as Light: A Series of Discourses*, [2nd edition] (London: W. Isbister & Co., 1874).
- *A Charge Delivered to the Clergy of Argyll & The Isles, 12th September, 1860* (Edinburgh: Messrs. Grant, 1860).
- *An Address to the Younger Clergy and Laity on the Present State of Religion, being some contribution towards a Defence of the Church of England* (London: Longman, Green, Longman, Roberts, & Green, 1865).

Ewing, The Right Revd Alexander, Bishop of Argyll and the Isles, (ed.), *Present-Day Papers on Prominent Questions in Theology,* Third Series, including: Part 1: "Some Letters of Thomas Erskine of Linlathen". Part 4: "Some Further Letters of Thomas Erskine of Linlathen". Part 6: "The Relation of Knowledge to Salvation, and the place of Knowledge in Relation to the Christian Sacraments", by the editor, with Letters from the Archbishop of Canterbury, Bishop Thirwall, the Rev. Dr. McLeod Campbell, and Mr. Erskine. Part 7: "Reconciliation", by the Editor. With Letters from the Rev. Dr. McLeod Campbell, the Rev. F.D. Maurice, and Mr. Erskine, [first edition] (London: Strahan & Co., 1871); [supplementary edition] (London: Daldy, Isbister & Co, 1878).

Fairbairn, A.M., *The Place of Christ in Modern Theology,* [10th edition] (London: Hodder and Stoughton, 1902), [first published in 1893].

- "The Westminster Confession of Faith and Scotch Theology", in *The Contemporary Review,* Vol.XXI (December 1872 – May 1873), 63-84.

Farrar, Frederic W., *Eternal Hope: Five Sermons Preached in Westminster Abbey, November and December, 1877* (New York: E.P. Dutton & Company, 1878).

Finney, Charles G., *Lectures on Systematic Theology* (London: William Tegg and Co., 1851).

Forsyth, Peter Taylor, *God the Holy Father* [1897] (London: Independent Press Ltd, 1957).

- *The Justification of God* (London: Independent Press Ltd, 1948).
- *The Work of Christ* (London: Independent Press Ltd, 1897).

Foster, John, "On a Man's Writing Memoirs of Himself", in *Essays* (London: The Religious Tract Society, undated).

Fraser of Brea, James, *A Treatise on Justifying Faith. Wherein is opened the Grounds of Believing, or the Sinner's sufficient warrant to take hold of what is offered in the everlasting gospel. Together with an appendix concerning the extent of Christ's death, unfolding the dangerous and various pernicious errors that hath been vented about it* (Edinburgh: William Gray, 1749).

Froude, James Anthony, *Thomas Carlyle: A History of his Life in London, 1834-1881,* in 2 volumes (London: Longmans, Green, and Co., 1884).

Fuller, Andrew Gunton, *The Complete Works of the Rev. Andrew Fuller,* in 5 volumes (London: William Ball, 1837).

Gobat, Samuel, *Samuel Gobat, Bishop of Jerusalem. His Life and Work. A Biographical Sketch, drawn chiefly from his own journals* (London: James Nisbet & Co., 1884).

Gore, Charles, (ed.), *Lux Mundi: A Series of Studies in the Religion of the Incarnation,* [12th edition] (London: John Murray, 1891), [first published in 1889].

Gore, Charles, *The Incarnation of the Son of God: Being The Bampton Lectures for the Year 1891,* [2nd edition] (London: John Murray, 1896).

- "Our Lord's Human Example", in *Church Quarterly Review,* Vol. XVI, No.XXXII (July, 1883), 282-313.

Groves, Anthony N., *Journal of a Residence in Bagdad, during the years 1830 and 1831,* edited with an introduction and notes by A.J. Scott (London: James Nisbet, 1832).

Gurney, Ellen Mary, (ed.), *Letters of Emelia Russell Gurney,* (London: James Nisbet & Co., Limited, 1902).

Haldane, Alexander, *The Lives of Robert and James Haldane* (Edinburgh: The Banner of Truth Trust, 1990), [first published in 1852 as *Memoirs of the Lives of Robert Haldane of Airthrey, and of his Brother, James Alexander Haldane*].

Haldane, J.A., *Observations on Universal Pardon, the Extent of the Atonement, and Personal Assurance of Salvation* (Edinburgh: W. Whyte & Co., 1831).

– *Refutation of the Heretical Doctrine Promulgated by the Rev. Edward Irving, respecting the Person and Atonement of the Lord Jesus Christ* (Edinburgh: William Oliphant, 1829).

– *The Doctrine of the Atonement; with Strictures on Recent Publications,* [3rd edition] (Edinburgh: William P. Kennedy, 1862), (first published in 1845).

Hamilton, James, (ed.), *Life and Remains of the Late Rev. William Hamilton, D.D., Minister of Strathblane,* in 2 volumes (Glasgow: Maurice Ogle & Son, 1836).

Hamilton, William, *An Essay on the Assurance of Salvation* (Glasgow: Maurice Ogle, 1830).

– *Remarks on Certain Opinions Recently Propagated, Respecting Universal Redemption and other topics connected with that subject* (Glasgow: Maurice Ogle, 1830).

Hanna, William, (ed.), *Letters of Thomas Erskine of Linlathen,* in 2 volumes; Vol. 1 from 1800 till 1840; Vol. 2 from 1840 till 1870 (Edinburgh: David Douglas, 1877).

– *A Selection from the Correspondence of the Late Thomas Chalmers, D.D. LL. D.* (Edinburgh: Thomas Constable and Co., 1853).

– *Select Works of Thomas Chalmers, D.D. LL. D.,* in 12 volumes (Edinburgh: Thomas Constable and Co., 1856), [various dates].

– *Memoirs of the Life and Writings of Thomas Chalmers, D.D. LL. D.* in 4 volumes (Edinburgh: Sutherland and Knox for Thomas Constable, 1849-51).

Harnack, Adolf, *What Is Christianity?,* [5th edition], with an introduction by Thomas Bailey Saunders (London: Ernest Benn Limited, 1958), [first published in 1900].

Henderson, Henry F., *Erskine of Linlathen:* S*elections and Biography* (Edinburgh and London: Oliphant Anderson & Ferrier, 1899).

Hodge, Archibald Alexander, *The Atonement* (London: Evangelical Press, 1974) [first published in 1867].

– *The Confession of Faith: A Handbook of Christian Doctrine Expounding The Westminster Confession* (London: The Banner of Truth Trust, 1958), [first published 1869].

– *The Atonement* (London: Evangelical Press, 1974), [first published in 1867].

Hodge, Charles, *A Commentary on Romans* (Edinburgh: The Banner of Truth Trust, 1986), [first published in 1835].

- *Systematic Theology,* in 3 volumes (London and Edinburgh: Thomas Nelson and Sons, 1871, 1872, 1880).
- Hooker, Richard, *The Works of that learned and judicious divine, Mr. Richard Hooker, with an account of his life and death,* by Isaac Walton, in 2 volumes (Oxford: Oxford University Press, 1841), [first published 1593-1661].
- Hume, David, *A Treatise of Human Nature* [1737-9], David Fate Norton and Mary J. Norton (eds.) (Oxford: Oxford University Press, 2000).
- Hutton, Richard H., "The Incarnation and Principles of Evidence, with a Letter to the Writer, by the Rev. F.D. Maurice", in *Tracts for Priests and People,* F.D. Maurice (ed.), No. XIV (Cambridge and London: Macmillan and Co., 1862).
- Irenaeus, "Against Heresies", in Alexander Roberts and James Donaldson, (eds.), *Ante-Nicene Christian Library,* Vol. IX (Edinburgh: T. and T. Clark, 1868).
- Irving, Edward, *Facts connected with Recent Manifestations of Spiritual Gifts* [extracted from *Fraser's Magazine* for January, March, and April, 1832] (London: James Fraser, 1832).
- *The Orthodox and Catholic Doctrine of Our Lord's Human Nature* (London: Baldwin and Cradock, 1830).
- *The Opinions Circulating Concerning Our Lord's Human Nature* (Edinburgh: John Lindsay & Co., 1830).
- Jackson, Edna V., *The Life That is Life Indeed: Reminiscences of the Broadlands Conferences* (London: James Nisbet & Co., Limited, 1910).
- Jukes, Andrew, *The Second Death and the Restitution of All Things* (W. Knochaven, California: Scripture Studies Concern and Concordant Publishing Concern, 1976), [first published in 1867].
- Kant, Immanuel, *Critique of Practical Reason* (Indianapolis: Bobbs-Merrill Educational Publishing, 1956), [first published in 1788].
- *Foundations of the Metaphysics of Morals* and *What Is Enlightenment?,* translated by Lewis White Beck, [2nd edition] (New Jersey: Prentice-Hall, Inc., 1997), [first published in 1785].
- *Religion Within the Bounds of Mere Reason and other writings,* translated and edited by Allen Wood and George Di Giovanni (Cambridge: Cambridge University Press, 1998), [first published in 1793].
- Kingsley, Charles, *Charles Kingsley: his Letters and Memories of his Life,* edited by his wife, [2nd edition], in 2 volumes (London: Henry S. King & Co., 1877).
- Knight, William, *Principal Shairp and his Friends* (London: John Murray, 1888).
- Law, William, *The Spirit of Prayer and The Spirit of Love,* Sidney Spencer, (ed.) (Cambridge & London: James Clarke & Co. Ltd, 1969), [first published in 1749/1750 and 1752/1754 respectively].

- *The Works of the Reverend William Law, M.A.*, in 9 volumes (London: J. Richardson, 1762).
Leathes, Stanley and others, *Future Probation: A Symposium on the Question 'Is Salvation Possible After Death?'* (London: James Nisbet & Co., 1886).
Leighton, Robert, *The Whole Works of the Most Reverend Father in God, Robert Leighton, D.D.*, in 2 volumes (London: Henry G. Bohn, 1846).
Leslie, J., *The 'Christian Intructor' Instructed; or, Important Observations on the 'Irving and Row Heresies', Contained in a Letter Addressed to Dr. A. Thomson. Also, a Letter to J.A. Haldane, Esq.* (Edinburgh: Printed for the author, 1830).
Lessing, G.E., *The Education of the Human Race*, [translated by F.W. Robertson] (London: Smith, Elder, and Co., 1858).
Lidgett, J. Scott, *The Spiritual Principle of the Atonement: As a Satisfaction made to God for the Sins of the World*, [4th edition] (London: The Epworth Press, 1907), [first published in 1897].
- *The Fatherhood of God in Christian Truth and Life* (Edinburgh: T. & T. Clark, 1902).
London Evangelical Magazine, (ed.), *Exposure of Certain Errors Put Forth in "Notes and Recollections of Two Sermons by the Rev. Mr. Campbell of Row," being Extracts from a Review of said Sermons in the London Evangelical Magazine. With a Brief Introductory Notice by the Editor* (Greenock: John Hislop, 1830).
MacDonald, George, *The Miracles of Our Lord* (London: Longmans, Green and Co., 1886).
- *Unspoken Sermons*, Series I, II, and III (Whitethorn, California: Johannesen, 1997), [first published in 1867, 1885, and 1889].
- *The Poetical Works of George MacDonald*, in 2 volumes (Whitehorn, California: Johannesen, 1996).
Macleod, Donald, *Memoir of Norman Macleod, D. D.* (London: Charles Burnet & Co., 1891).
Martineau, James, "Mediatorial Religion", in *The National Review* (April, 1856), 478-500.
Matheson, J.J., *A Memoir of Greville Ewing, Minister of the Gospel, Glasgow* (London: John Snow, 1843).
Maurice, Frederick Denison, *Modern Philosophy; or A Treatise on Moral and Metaphysical Philosophy from the fourteenth century to the French Revolution with a glimpse into the nineteenth century* (London: Griffin, Bohn, and Company, 1862).
- *Social Morality* (London and Cambridge: Macmillan and Co., 1869).
- *The Doctrine of Sacrifice Deduced from the Scriptures*, [new edition], (London: Macmillan and Co., 1879), (first published in 1854).
- *The Gospel of the Kingdom of Heaven* (London: Macmillan and Co., 1888), [first published in 1864].

- *The Gospel of St. John: A Series of Discourses,* [2nd edition] (London: Macmillan and Co., 1893).
- *The Kingdom of Christ or Hints to a Quaker Respecting the Principles, Constitution and Ordinances of the Catholic Church,* [new edition], Alec R. Vidler (ed.), in 2 volumes (London: SCM Press, 1958), [first published in 1838].
- *The Prophets and Kings of the Old Testament* (London: Macmillan and Co., 1886), [first published in 1852].
- *The Word "Eternal", and the Punishment of the Wicked: A Letter to the Rev. Dr. Jelf, Canon of Christ Church, and Principal of King's College* [3rd edition] (Cambridge: Macmillan and Co., 1854).
- *Theological Essays,* [2nd Edition] (Cambridge: Macmillan & Co., 1853).
- *What is Revelation? A Series of Sermons on the Epiphany; to which are added Letters to a Student of Theology on the Bampton Lectures of Mr. Mansel* (Cambridge: Macmillan & Co., 1859).

Maurice, Frederick, (ed.), *The Life of Frederick Denison Maurice Chiefly Told in His Own Letters* [2nd Edition], in 2 volumes (London: Macmillan and Co., 1884).

Mitchell, W. Fraser, (ed.), *The Purpose of Life. Selections Mainly from the Correspondence of Erskine of Linlathen* (London: Epworth Press, 1945).

Monod, Adolphe, *Life and Letters of Adolphe Monod, Pastor of the Reformed Church of France,* by one of his daughters (London: James Nisbet & Co., 1885).

Murphy, Joseph John, *The Scientific Bases of Faith* (London: Macmillan and Co., 1873).

Newman, John Henry, "On the Introduction of Rationalistic Principles into Religion", Tract No.73, in *Tracts for the Times* [3rd edition], by Members of the University of Oxford, Vol.III, 1835-6 (London: J.G. & F. Rivington, 1838), 1-56.
- *An Essay in Aid of A Grammar of Assent* (Notre Dame, Indiana: University of Notre Dame Press, 1979), [first published in 1870].
- *Essays Critical and Historical,* [9th edition] in 2 volumes (London: Longmans, Green, and Co., 1890), [first published in 1871].
- *An Essay on the Development of Christian Doctrine* [6th edition] (Indiana: University of Notre Dame Press, 1989), [first published in 1845].
- *Lectures on Justification* (London: J.G. & F. Rivington, 1838).
- *Apologia Pro Vita Sua* [1864] (London: Dent, 1966).

Nippold, Friedrich, (ed.), *Richard Rothe: Ein Christliches Lebensbild,* in 2 volumes (Wittenberg: Verlag von Hermann Koelling, 1873, 1874).

Noel, Gerard T., *Arvendel; or Sketches in Italy and Switzerland* (London: James Nisbet, 1826).

- *Sermons, intended chiefly for the use of families* (London: John Hatchard and Son, Vol. I, 1826, Vol. II, 1827), (Vol. II is entitled *Sermons Delivered in the Parish Church of Richmond*).
Norrie, W., *Dundee Celebrities of the Nineteenth Century: being a series of biographies of distinguished or noted persons connected by birth, residence, official appointment, or otherwise, with the town of Dundee; and who have died during the present century* (Dundee: William Norrie, 1873).
Norton, Robert, *Memoirs of James & George MacDonald, of Port-Glasgow* (London: John F. Shaw, 1840).
Oliphant, Mrs, *The Life of Edward Irving* (New York: Harper and Brothers, 1862).
- *A Memoir of the Life of John Tulloch, D.D., LL.D.* [2nd edition] (Edinburgh and London: William Blackwood and Sons, 1888).
Orr, James, *The Christian View of God and The World* (Grand Rapids: Kregel Publications, 1989), [first published as *The Christian View of God and The World as Centring in the Incarnation: Being the First Series of Kerr Lectures,* in 1893].
- *The Progress of Dogma: Being the Elliott Lectures, Delivered at the Western Theological Seminary Allegheny, Penna., U.S.A.* (London: Hodder and Stoughton, 1901).
Owen, John, *The Works of John Owen, The Works of John Owen,* in 16 volumes, Vol.III, *The Holy Spirit* [1674] (Edinburgh: Banner of Truth, 1965).
Pearsall Smith, Logan (ed.), *A Religious Rebel: The Letters of "H.W.S."(Mrs Pearsall Smith)* [London: Nisbet & Co. Ltd., 1949].
Plato, *The Collected Dialogues of Plato: including the letters,* Edith Hamilton and Huntington Cairns, (eds.) (Princeton: Princeton University Press, 1961).
Plumptre, E. H., *The Spirits in Prison and other studies on the Life after Death,* [3rd edition] (London: Wm. Isbister Limited, 1885).
Prothero, Rowland E., *The Life and Correspondence of Arthur Penrhyn Stanley, D.D., Late Dean of Westminster,* in 2 volumes (London: John Murray, 1893).
Ramsay, E.B., *Reminiscences of Scottish Life & Character* [27th edition], with a Memoir by Cosmo Innes (London: Gall and Inglis, undated, probably 1875), [first published in 1858].
Rashdall, Hastings, *The Idea of Atonement in Christian Theology, Being The Bampton Lectures For 1915* (London: Macmillan and Co., Limited, 1919).
Rauschenbusch, Walter, *A Theology for the Social Gospel*, introduction by Donald W. Shriver, Jr. (Louisville, Kentucky: Westminster John Knox Press, 1997), [first published in 1917].

Reimarus, H.S., *Fragments,* Charles H. Talbert (ed.) (London: SCM, 1971), [first published in 1774-8].

Renan, Joseph Ernest, *Histoire des Origines du Christianisme,* in 8 volumes, [volume 1, *Vie de Jésus*] (Paris: 1863-83).

- *The Life of Jesus* (New York: Prometheus Books, 1991), [first published in 1863].

Ritschl, Albrecht, *Three Essays: Theology and Metaphysics; 'Prologemena' to 'The History of Pietism'; Instruction in the Christian Religion,* edited and translated by Philip Hefner (Philadelphia: Fortress Press, 1972), [first published in 1881, 1877, 1875 respectively].

- *The Christian Doctrine of Justification and Reconciliation: The Positive Development of the Doctrine,* translated by H.R. Mackintosh and A.B. Macaulay (Edinburgh: T.& T. Clark, 1900).

Roberts, Alexander, and Donaldson, James (eds.), *Ante-Nicene Christian Library,* in 23 volumes (Edinburgh: T. and T. Clark, various dates from 1867).

Robertson, A., *A Vindication of "The Religion of the Land" from Misrepresentation; and An Exposure of the Absurd Pretensions of the Gareloch Enthusiasts. In a Letter to Thomas Erskine, Esq., Advocate* (Edinburgh: William Whyte & Co., 1830).

Robertson, Frederick W., *Sermons Preached at Brighton,* First Series, [6th edition] (London: Smith, Elder and Co., 1859).

- *Sermons Preached at Trinity Chapel, Brighton,* Third Series, [9th edition] (London: Smith, Elder and Co., 1864).

- *Sermons Preached at Oxford, Cheltenham & Brighton,* Fifth Series, [people's edition] (London: Kegan Paul, Trench, Trübner & Co. Ltd., 1898).

Ross, Alexander J., *Memoir of Alexander Ewing, D.C.L., Bishop of Argyll and the Isles* (London: Daldy, Isbister & Co., 1877).

Rothe, Richard, *Still Hours,* translated by Jane T. Stoddart, with an introductory essay by John MacPherson (London: Hodder and Stoughton, 1886).

Russell, David, *Letters, Chiefly Practical and Consolatory: Designed to Illustrate the Nature and Tendency of the Gospel,* [3rd Edition], in 2 volumes (Edinburgh: Waugh and Innes, 1825).

- *The Way of Salvation. A Discourse, the Substance of which was preached at a meeting of Sabbath School Scholars in Dundee, on the 22nd April, 1829, with additional Notes and Illustrations, containing Remarks on the Doctrine of Universal Pardon* (Dundee: James Chalmers,1830).

Russell, Francis, (ed.), *The Fatherhood of God Revealed in Christ, the Comfort and Hope of Man. A Lesson From "The Letters" of Thomas Erskine of Linlathen* (Edinburgh: David Douglas, 1888).

Sadler, Glenn Edward, (ed.), *An Expression of Character: The Letters of George MacDonald* (Grand Rapids: Eerdmans, 1994).

Salmond, Stewart D.F., *The Biblical Doctrine of Immortality* (Minneapolis: Klock and Klock, 1984), [first published as *The Christian Doctrine of Immortality* in 1895].

Schleiermacher, Friedrich, *On Religion: Speeches to its Cultured Despisers* (New York: Harper & Row, 1958), [first published in 1799].

– *The Christian Faith* (Edinburgh: T.&T. Clark, 1989), [first published in 1821-22. 2nd revised edition on which this translation is based first published in 1830].

– *The Life of Jesus*, Jack C. Verheyden, (ed.), S. Maclean Gilmour, (translator) (Philadelphia: Fortress Press, 1975).

Scott, Alexander J., *Discourses* (London and Cambridge: Macmillan and Co., 1866).

– *Neglected Truths; No.1: Hints on I Corinthians XIV* (London: L.B. Seeley and Sons, 1830).

– *On the Divine Will* (Greenock: R.B. Lusk, 1830).

Seeley, Sir J.R., *Ecce Homo: A Survey of the Life and Work of Jesus Christ* (London: J.M. Dent & Sons Ltd., 1908), [first published in 1865].

Shairp, John Campbell, *Portraits of Friends* (Boston and New York: Houghton, Mifflin & Company, 1889).

– *Studies in Poetry and Philosophy,* [4th edition] (Edinburgh: David Douglas, 1886), [first published in 1868].

– *Culture and Religion in some of their relations* (Edinburgh: David Douglas, 1878).

Shedd, William G.T., *The Doctrine of Endless Punishment* (Edinburgh: The Banner of Truth Trust, 1986), [first published in 1885].

Simpkinson, John Nassau, *Memoir of the Rev. George Wagner, M.A.* (Cambridge: Macmillan and Co., 1858).

Smeaton, George, "Augustus Neander, his Influence, System, and various Writings", in *The British and Foreign Evangelical Review and Quarterly Record of Christian Literature,* No.VI (1853), 701-739.

– *Christ's Doctrine of the Atonement* (Edinburgh: The Banner of Truth Trust, 1991), [originally published in 1870 as *The Doctrine of the Atonement as Taught by Christ Himself or the Sayings of Jesus Exegetically Expounded and Classified*].

– *The Apostles' Doctrine of the Atonement* (Edinburgh: The Banner of Truth Trust, 1991), [originally published in 1870 as *The Doctrine of the Atonement as Taught by the Apostles; or, the Sayings of the Apostles Exegetically Expounded and Classified. With Historical Appendix*].

– *The Doctrine of the Holy Spirit* (London: The Banner of Truth Trust, 1958), [first published in 1882].

Smith, Adam, *The Theory of Moral Sentiments* [1759] (New York: Prometheus Books, 2000).

Smyth, John, *A Treatise on the Forgiveness of Sins as the Privilege of the Redeemed; in Opposition to the Doctrine of Universal Pardon, founded on Ephesians i. 7* (Glasgow: Thomas Ogilvie, 1830).
Staël, Madame de, *De l'Allemagne*, [1813] (Paris: Librairie de Firmin Didot frères, 1850).
Stanley, Arthur Penrhyn, *Essays Chiefly on Questions of Church and State from 1850 to 1870* (London: John Murray, 1870).
- *Addresses and Sermons Delivered at St. Andrew's in 1872, 1875 and 1877* (London: Macmillan and Co., 1877).
- *Lectures on the History of Scotland delivered in Edinburgh in 1872* (London: John Murray, 1872).
- *The Life and Correspondence of Thomas Arnold, D.D.*, 12th edition, in 2 volumes (London: John Murray, 1881).
- "Theology of the Nineteenth Century", in *Fraser's Magazine,* Vol. LXXI, No.CCCCXXII (February, 1865), 252-268.
- Review of *Essays and Reviews* and related publications, in *Edinburgh Review or Critical Journal,* Vol. CXIII, No.CCXXX (April, 1861), 461-500.
Stephen, Leslie, "The Broad Church", in *Fraser's Magazine,* Vol. I, No.III, New Series (March, 1870), 311-25.
- *History of English Thought in the Eighteenth Century,* [3rd edition] in 2 volumes (London: Harbinger Books, 1962), [first published in 1876].
Story, Robert Herbert, *Memoir of Robert Herbert Story, D.D., LL.D., Principal and Vice-Chancellor of the University of Glasgow, One of His Majesty's Chaplains in Scotland,* by his daughters (Glasgow: James Maclehose and Sons, 1909).
- *Memoir of the Life of the Rev. Robert Story, Late Minister of Rosneath, Dunbartonshire. Including Passages of Scottish Religious and Ecclesiastical History During the Second Quarter of the Present Century* (Cambridge and London: Macmillan and Co., 1862).
- *The Apostolic Ministry in the Scottish Church* (Edinburgh and London: William Blackwood and Sons, 1897).
- *The Risen Christ: A Sermon Preached in Rosneath Church on the Lord's Day After the Death of John McLeod Campbell, D.D.* (Glasgow: James Maclehose, 1872).
Strauss, David Friedrich, *The Life of Jesus, Critically Examined*, translated from the fourth German edition by Marian Evans, afterwards Cross, [i.e., George Eliot] (London: Chapman Brothers, 1846).
Temple, Frederick, et. al., *Essays and Reviews* [2nd edition] (London: John W. Parker and Son, 1860).
Thom, John Hamilton, (ed.), *Letters Embracing his Life of John James Tayler, B.A.,* in 2 volumes (London: Williams and Norgate, 1872).
Thomson, Andrew, *Sermons on Various Subjects* (Edinburgh and London: William Whyte and Co., and Longman and Co., 1829).

- *The Doctrine of Universal Pardon Considered and Refuted in a Series of Sermons, with Notes, Critical and Expository* (Edinburgh: William Whyte and Co., 1830).
Tindal, Matthew, *Christianity as Old as the Creation: Or, the Gospel, a Republication of the Religion of Nature* (London: 1730).
Toland, John, *Christianity Not Mysterious: or, a Treatise shewing, that there is nothing in the Gospel contrary to Reason, nor above it: and that no Christian Doctrine can be properly call'd a Mystery* (Stuttgart-Bad Cannstatt: Friedrich Frommann Verlag, 1964), [first published in 1696].
Trench, Archbishop Richard Chevenix, *Letters and Memorials*, in 2 volumes, Maria Trench (ed.) (London: Kegan Paul, Trench & Co., 1888).
Tulloch, John, *Movements of Religious Thought in Britain During the Nineteenth Century* (Leicester: Leicester University Press, 1971), [first published in 1885].
- *Theism: the witness of Reason and Nature to an All-Wise and Beneficent Creator* (Edinburgh and London, William Blackwood and Sons, 1855).
- *Theological Controversy; or, the function of debate in Theology. An Address delivered to the members of the Theological Society in the University of Edinburgh. With an Appendix on the study of the Confession of Faith,* [4th edition] (Edinburgh and London 1866).
- *Theological Tendencies of the Age: An Inaugural Lecture Delivered at the Opening of St. Mary's College, on Tuesday, the 28th November, 1854,* [2nd Edition] (Edinburgh: Paton and Ritchie, 1855).
- "Progress of Religious Thought in Scotland", in *The Contemporary Review*, Vol. XXIX (March, 1877), 535-551.
Tyler, Bennet and Bonar, Andrew A., *Nettleton and His Labours* (Edinburgh: Banner of Truth Trust, 1975), [first published in 1854].
Urwick, William, *The True Nature of Christ's Person and Atonement stated: in reply to the unscriptural views of the Rev. Edward Irving "On the human nature of Christ."* (Dublin: William Curry, Jun. and Company, 1831).
Various Authors, *The Atonement in Modern Religious Thought: A Theological Symposium* (London: Kames Clarke & Co., 1900).
Vinet, Alexander, *Outlines of Theology,* (London: Strahan and Co., 1872).
- *Vital Christianity: Essays and Discourses on the Religions of Man and the Religion of God,* translated with an introduction by Robert Turnbull (Boston: Gould, Kendall and Lincoln, 1845).
- *Lettres de Alexandre Vinet et de quelques-uns de ses correspondants*, in 2 volumes (Lausanne: Georges Bridel Editeur, 1882).
Walker, Norman L., *Robert Buchanan,D.D. An Ecclesiastical Biography* (London: Thomas Nelson and Sons, 1877).
Wardlaw, Ralph, *Systematic Theology,* in 3 volumes (Edinburgh: Adam & Charles Black, 1861).

- *Two Essays: I. On the Assurance of Faith: II. On the Extent of the Atonement, and Universal Pardon*, [2nd edition] (Glasgow: Archibald Fullarton & Co., 1831).
Watson, Richard, Review of *An Essay on Faith* by Thomas Erskine, in *The Wesleyan-Methodist Magazine*, Vol. VII, Third Series (August, 1828), 531-545.
- *Theological Institutes, or, A View of the Evidences, Doctrines, Morals, and Institutions of Christianity* (New York: J. Emory and B. Waugh, 1831), [first published in 1823].
Watson, Robert A. and Elizabeth S., *George Gilfillan: Letters and Journals, with Memoir* (London: Hodder and Stoughton, 1892).
Wesley, John, *Sermons on Several Occasions*, in 3 volumes (London: Wesleyan Conference Office, 1874).
- *Sermons on Several Occasions*, in 4 volumes (London: J. Kershaw, 1825).
White, Edward, *Life in Christ*, [3rd edition] (London: Elliott Stock, 1878), [first published in 1875].
Wight, Ninian, *Memoir of the Rev. Henry Wight, by his Son* (Edinburgh: Edmonston and Douglas, 1862).
Wordsworth, William, *The Prelude*, Ernest de Selincourt (ed.), [revised impression] (London: Oxford University Press, 1960), [first published in 1805].

Unpublished Theses Consulted

Foster, Marian, 'Representation and Substitution in Thomas Erskine of Linlathen', unpublished Ph.D, King's College, University of London (1992), DX187481.
Logan, John B. 'The Religious Thought of Thomas Erskine of Linlathen', unpublished masters thesis, New York, Union Theological Seminary (1931).
Newell, J. Philip, 'A.J. Scott and his Circle', unpublished PhD, Edinburgh University (1981).
Stevenson, Peter K., 'The Person and Work of Christ in the Preaching and Theology of John McLeod Campbell', unpublished PhD, King's College, London (2001). [Publication forthcoming by Paternoster]
Warren, Zillah Anne, 'Concepts of Judgment and Salvation with Special Reference to the Work of Thomas Erskine of Linlathen, John McLeod Campbell, and F.D. Maurice', unpublished M.A. thesis, Durham (1977).

Other Works Consulted

Abbott, Jacob J., "Boardman's Higher Christian Life", in *Bibliotheca Sacra*, Vol. XVII (July, 1860), 508-535.

Ahlstrom, Sydney E., "The Scottish Philosophy and American Theology", in *Church History*, Vol. XXIV (1955), 257-272.

Allen, Charlotte, *The Human Christ: the Search for the Historical Jesus* (Lion, Oxford, 1998).

Allison, C.F., *The Rise of Moralism: The Proclamation of the Gospel from Hooker to Baxter* (London: SPCK, 1966).

Altholz, Josef L., *Anatomy of a Controversy: the Debate over 'Essays and Reviews' 1860-1864* (Aldershot: Scolar Press, 1994).

– "The Mind of Victorian Orthodoxy: Anglican Responses to 'Essays and Reviews', 1860-1864", in *Church History*, Vol. 51, No.2 (June, 1982), 186-197.

Atherton, John, *Public Theology for Changing Times* (London: SPCK, 2000).

Avis, Paul, (ed.), *The Science of Theology* (Basingstoke, Marshall Pickering, 1986).

Baillie, Donald M., *God Was In Christ* (London: Faber and Faber, 1956).

Baillie, John, *The Interpretation of Religion: An Introductory Study of Theological Principles* (Edinburgh: T. & T. Clark, 1929).

Barth, J. Robert, *Coleridge and Christian Doctrine* (New York: Fordham University Press, 1987).

Barth, Karl, *Church Dogmatics*, G.W. Bromiley and T.F. Torrance (eds.) (Edinburgh: T.&T. Clark, 1956-75).

– "Evangelical Theology in the 19th Century", in *The Humanity of God* (John Knox Press, 1960).

– *Protestant Theology in the Nineteenth Century* (London: SCM Press Ltd, 1972).

– *The Humanity of God* (John Knox Press, 1960).

Bauckham, Richard J., "Universalism: a historical survey", in *Themelios*, Vol. 4, No.2 (January 1979), 48-54.

Bavinck, Herman, *The Last Things: Hope for this world and the Next* (Carlisle: Paternoster, 1996).

Bebbington, D.W., "Evangelical Christianity and Romanticism," in *Crux*: Vol. XXVI, No.1 (March, 1990), 9-15.

– "Evangelical Christianity and the Enlightenment", in *The Gospel in the Modern World*, Martyn Eden and David F. Wells (eds.) (Leicester: IVP, 1991).

– "Evangelicalism in Modern Scotland", in *Scottish Bulletin of Evangelical Theology*, Vol.9, No.1 (Spring, 1991), 4-12.

- "Scottish Cultural Influences on Evangelicalism", in *Scottish Bulletin of Evangelical Theology,* Vol. 14, No.1 (Spring, 1996), 23-36.
- *The Baptists in Scotland: A History* (Glasgow: The Baptist Union of Scotland, 1988).
- *Evangelicalism in Modern Britain: A History from the 1730s to the 1830s* (London and New York: Routlege, 1989).
- "Evangelical Conversion, c. 1740-1850", in *Scottish Bulletin of Evangelical Theology,* Vol.18, No.2 (Autumn, 2000), 102-127.
- *Patterns in History: A Christian perspective on Historical Thought* (Leicester: Apollos, 1990).
- *Holiness in Nineteenth-Century England* (Carlisle: Paternoster, 2000).

Begbie, Jeremy, "Rediscovering and Re-Imagining the Atonement", in *Anvil,* Vol. 11, No.3 (1994), 193-202.

Bell, M. Charles, *Calvin and Scottish Theology: The Doctrine of Assurance* (Edinburgh: The Handsel Press, 1985).

Benn, Alfred William, *The History of English Rationalism in the Nineteenth Century,* in 2 volumes (London: Longmans, Green, and Co., 1906).

Bewkes, Eugene Garrett, *Legacy of a Christian Mind; John McLeod Campbell, eminent contributor to theological thought* (Philadelphia: The Judson Press, 1937).

Bloesch, Donald G., *Jesus Christ, Saviour and Lord* (Carlisle: Paternoster Press, 1997).
- *Jesus is Victor! Karl Barth's Doctrine of Salvation* (Nashville: Abingdon, 1976).

Boardman, W.E., *The Higher Christian Life*, [new edition] (London: Morgan and Chase, no date).

Boer, Harry R., *An Ember Still Glowing: Humankind as the Image of God* (Grand Rapids: Eerdmans, 1990).

Boulger, James D., *Coleridge as Religious Thinker* (New Haven: Yale University Press, 1961).

Bradley, Ian, *The Power of Sacrifice* (London: Darton, Longman and Todd, 1995).

Briggs, Asa, *The Age of Improvement 1783-1867* (London and New York: Longman, 1979).

Broadie, Alexander, *The Scottish Enlightenment* (Edinburgh: Birlinn, 2001).

Brose, Olive J., *Frederick Denison Maurice: Rebellious Conformist, 1805-1872* (Ohio University Press, 1971).

Brown, Colin, *Christianity & Western Thought,* Volume 1, *From the Ancient World to the Age of Enlightenment* (Leicester: Apollos, 1990).

Brown, Stewart J., *Thomas Chalmers and the Godly Commonwealth in Scotland* (Oxford: Oxford University Press, 1982).

Brown, Stewart J., and Newlands, George (eds.), *Scottish Christianity in the Modern World*: [*Essays*] *in Honour of A.C. Cheyne* (Edinburgh: T.&T. Clark, 2000).

Bruce, Alex. B., *The Humiliation of Christ in its Physical, Ethical, and Official Aspects* (Grand Rapids: Eerdmans, 1955), [first published in 1876].

Brunner, Emil, *The Mediator: A Study of the Central Doctrine of the Christian Faith*, translated by Olive Wyon (London: Lutterworth Press, 1934).

Buckle, Henry Thomas, *On Scotland and the Scotch Intellect* (Chicago and London: The University of Chicago Press, 1970).

Burd, Van Akin, *Ruskin, Lady Mount-Temple and the Spiritualists: An Episode in Broadlands History* (London: Brentham Press: 1982).

Burleigh, J. H. S., *A Church History of Scotland* (London: Oxford University Press, 1960).

Butler, D., *John Wesley and George Whitefield in Scotland* (Edinburgh and London: William Blackwood and Sons, 1898).

Butler, Henry Montagu, "Thomas Erskine of Linlathen," in *Ten Great and Good Men* (London: Edward Arnold, 1909).

Byrne, James, *Glory, Jest and Riddle: Religious Thought in the Enlightenment* (London: SCM Press, 1996).

Byrne, Peter, and Houlden, Leslie, (eds.), *Companion Encyclopaedia of Theology* (London: Routledge, 1995).

Cairns, David S., *Life and Times of Alexander Robertson MacEwen, D.D., Professor of Church History, New College, Edinburgh* (London: Hodder & Stoughton, 1925).

Cairns, John, *Unbelief in the Eighteenth Century as contrasted with its earlier and later history*, The Cunningham Lectures for 1880 (Edinburgh: Adam and Charles Black, 1881).

Caldecott, Alfred, *The Philosophy of Religion in England and America* (London: Methuen & Co., 1901).

Cameron, Nigel M. de S., (ed.), *Universalism and the Doctrine of Hell* (Paternoster, Carlisle, 1992).

Cameron, Nigel M. de S., Wright, David F., Lachman, David C., Meek, Donald E., (eds.), *Dictionary of Scottish Church History and Theology* (Downers Grove, Illinois: IVP, 1993).

Cameron, Nigel M. de S., *Biblical Higher Criticism and the Defense of Infallibilism in 19th Century Britain* (Lewiston, New York: The Edwin Mellen Press, 1987).

Campbell, Andrew J., *Two Centuries of the Church of Scotland, 1707-1929* (Paisley: Alexander Gardner Ltd., 1930).

Campbell, Lewis and Garnett, William, *The Life of James Clerk Maxwell With A Selection from his Correspondence and Occasional Writings and a Sketch of his Contributions to Science* (London: Macmillan and Co., 1882).

Carpenter, J. Estlin, *James Martineau Theologian and Teacher: A Study of his Life and Thought* (London: Philip Green, 1905).

Carpenter, S.C., *Church and People, 1789-1889: A History of the Church of England from William Wilberforce to "Lux Mundi"* (London: SPCK, 1933).

Cauthen, Kenneth, *The Impact of American Religious Liberalism* (New York: Harper & Row, 1962).

Cave, Alfred, *The Scriptural Doctrine of Sacrifice* (Edinburgh: T. & T. Clark, 1877).

Chadwick, Owen, *The Secularization of the European Mind in the Nineteenth Century* (Cambridge: Cambridge University Press, 1975).

Chambers, D., "Doctrinal Attitudes in the Church of Scotland in the Pre-Disruption Era: the Age of John McLeod Campbell and Edward Irving", in *Journal of Religious History*, Vol. 8 (1974-75), 159-182.

Channing, William Henry, *The Life of William Ellery Channing, D.D.* (Boston: American Unitarian Association, 1904).

Chavannes, F.L. Fréd., *Alexandre Vinet considéré comme Apologiste et Moraliste Chrétien* (Leyden: E.J. Brill, 1883).

Cheyne, A.C., (ed.), *The Practical and the Pious: Essays on Thomas Chalmers (1780-1847)* (Edinburgh: The Saint Andrew Press, 1985).

Cheyne, A.C., "The Westminster Standards: A Century of Re-appraisal", *Records of the Scottish Church History Society*, Vol. XIV (1962), 199-214.

– *Studies in Scottish Church History* (Edinburgh: T.&T. Clark, 1999).

– *The Transforming of the Kirk: Victorian Scotland's Religious Revolution* (Edinburgh: The Saint Andrew Press, 1983).

Christensen, Torben, *The Divine Order: A Study in F.D. Maurice's Theolog,* (Leiden: E.J. Brill, 1973).

Clark, Kitson, G.R., "The Romantic Element: 1830 to 1850" in *Studies in Social History: A Tribute to G.M. Trevelyan,* J.H. Plumb, (ed.) (London: Longmans, Green and Co., 1955).

Clarkson, George E., *The Mysticism of William Law* (New York: Peter Lang, 1992).

Clements, Keith, *Friedrich Schleiermacher: Pioneer of Modern Theology* (London: Collins, 1987).

Clifford, Edward, "Broadlands as it was" (including selected letters of Andrew Jukes), in *A Green Pasture* (London: The Church Army Bookroom, no date – probably 1901), 400-441.

Coad, F. Roy, *A History of the Brethren Movement* (Exeter: Paternoster Press, 1968).

Cockshut, A.O.J., *Religious Controversies of the Nineteenth Century: Selected Documents* (London: Methuen & Co. Ltd, 1966).

Coffey, David, *Deus Trinitas: The Doctrine of the Triune God* (New York: Oxford University Press, 1999).

Collins, Kenneth J., *The Scripture Way of Salvation: The Heart of John Wesley's Theology* (Nashville: The Abingdon Press, 1997).

Colloms, Brenda, *Charles Kingsley: The Lion of Eversley* (London: Constable, 1975).

Conser, Walter H., Jr., *God and the Natural World: Religion and Science in Antebellum America* (Columbia: University of South Carolina Press, 1993).

Cort, John C., *Christian Socialism: An Informal History* (New York: Orbis Books, 1988).

Cross, F.L., and Livingstone, E.A. (eds.), *The Oxford Dictionary of the Christian Church*, [3rd edition] (Oxford: Oxford University Press, 1997).

Cunliffe, Christopher, (ed.), *Joseph Butler's Moral and Religious Thought: Tercentenary Essays* (Oxford: Clarendon Press, 1992).

Cunningham, William, *Historical Theology: A Review of the Principal Doctrinal Discussions in the Christian Church Since the Apostolic Age*, in 2 volumes (London: The Banner of Truth Trust, 1960), [first published in 1862].

Curle, Richard, (ed.), *Robert Browning and Julia Wedgwood: A Broken Friendship as revealed in their Letters* (London: John Murray and Jonathan Cape, 1937).

Dabney, Robert L., *Discussions: Evangelical and Theological,* in 3 volumes (Edinburgh: The Banner of Truth Trust, 1967), [first published in 1890].

– *Systematic Theology* (Edinburgh: The Banner of Truth Trust, 1985), [first published in 1871].

Dallimore, Arnold, *The Life of Edward Irving* (Edinburgh: The Banner of Truth Trust, 1983).

Daniélou, Jean, *Gospel Message and Helleistic Culture* (London: Darton, Longman and Todd, 1973).

Davies, Horton, *Worship and Theology in England:* Volume III, *From Watts and Wesley to Maurice, 1690-1850;* Volume IV, *From Newman to Martineau, 1850-1900,* [combined edition] (Grand Rapids: Eerdmans, 1996).

Davies, W. Merlin, *An Introduction to F.D. Maurice's Theology* (London: SPCK, 1964).

Deddo, Gary W., and Deddo, Catherine A., *George MacDonald: A Devotional Guide to his Writings* (Edinburgh: Saint Andrew Press, 1996).

Demarest, Bruce A., *General Revelation: Historical Views and Contemporary Issues* (Grand Rapids: Zondervan Publishing House, 1982).

- *The Cross and Salvation* (Wheaton, Illinois: Crossway Books, 1997).
Denney, James, *The Atonement and the Modern Mind* (London: Hodder and Stoughton, 1903).
- *The Christian Doctrine of Reconciliation* (London: James Clarke & Co., Ltd, 1959), [first published in 1917].
Dent, N.J.H., *Rousseau: An Introduction to his Psychological, Social and Political Theory* (Oxford: Basil Blackwell, 1988).
Devenish, Philip E., "Divinity and Dipolarity: Thomas Erskine and Charles Hartshorne on What Makes God 'God'", in *Journal of Religion*, No.62 (1982), 335-58.
Dewar, Daniel, *The Atonement: Its Nature, Reality and Efficacy*, [3rd edition] (London: James Nisbet and Co., 1860).
Dieter, Melvin E., *The Holiness Revival of the Nineteenth Century*, [2nd edition] (Lanham, Maryland: The Scarecrow Press Inc., 1996).
Dieter, Melvin E., Hoekema, Anthony A., Horton, Stanley M., McQuilkin, J. Robertson, Walvoord, John F., *Five Views on Sanctification*, (Grand Rapids: Zondervan, 1987).
Dillistone, F.W., *The Christian Understanding of Atonement* (Welwyn: James Nisbet & Co. Ltd, 1968).
Dorrien, Gary, *The Making of American Liberal Theology: Imagining Progressive Religion 1805-1900* (Louisville: Westminster John Knox Press, 2001).
Dowey Jr., Edward A., *The Knowledge of God in Calvin's Theology* (Grand Rapids: Eerdmans, 1994).
Driver, John, *Understanding the Atonement for the Mission of the Church* (Scottdale, Pennsylvania: Herald Press, 1986).
Drummond, Andrew L. and Bulloch, James, *The Church in Late Victorian Scotland, 1874-1900* (Edinburgh: The Saint Andrew Press, 1978).
- *The Church in Victorian Scotland, 1843-1874* (Edinburgh: The Saint Andrew Press, 1975).
- *The Scottish Church, 1688-1843* (Edinburgh: The Saint Andrew Press, 1973).
Drummond, Andrew Landale, *The Kirk and the Continent* (Edinburgh: The Saint Andrew Press, 1956).
- *Edward Irving and his Circle* (London: James Clarke & Co., Ltd, undated, probably 1934).
Eaton, Michael, *A Theology of Encouragement* (Carlisle: Paternoster, 1995).
Edwards, David L., *Leaders of the Church of England 1828-1944* (London: Oxford University Press, 1971)
Ella, George M., *James Hervey: Preacher of Righteousness* (Eggleston, Co. Durham: Go Publications,1996).
- *Law and Gospel in the Theology of Andrew Fuller* (Eggleston, Co. Durham: Go Publications,1996).

Elliott-Binns, L.E., *English Thought 1860-1900: The Theological Aspect* (London: Longmans, Green and Co., 1956).
- *The Development of English Theology in the Later Nineteenth Century* (London: Longmans, Green and Co., 1952).
- *Religion in the Victorian Era*, [2nd edition] (London: Lutterworth Press, 1946).

Ellis, Ieuan, "Schleiermacher in Britain", in *Scottish Journal of Theology*, Vol. 33, No.5 (1980), 417-452.
- *Seven Against Christ: A Study of 'Essays and Reviews'* (Leiden: E.J. Brill, 1980).

Encyclopedia Britannica [11th edition] (Cambridge: Cambridge University Press, 1910).

Erskine, Claude and Kenneth, *The Erskines of Linlathen* (Linlathen, Harding, Natal: 1960).

Escott, Harry, *A History of Scottish Congregationalism* (Glasgow: The Congregational Union of Scotland, 1960).

Faber, Geoffrey, *Jowett: A Portrait with Background,* (London: Faber & Faber Limited, 1957).

Fergusson, David A.S., "Predestination: A Scottish Perspective", in *Scottish Journal of Theology,* Vol. 46, No.4 (1993), 457-478.

Fiddes, Paul S., *Past Event and Present Salvation: The Christian Idea of Atonement* (London: Darton Longman & Todd, 1989).

Fielding, Kenneth J., "A Carlylean Elegy in Auchtertool Kirkyard", in *Scottish Christianity in the Modern World*: [*Essays*] *in Honour of A.C. Cheyne*, Stewart J. Brown and George Newlands (eds.) (Edinburgh: T.&T. Clark, 2000).

Finlayson, Duncan, "Aspects of the Life and Influence of Thomas Erskine of Linlathen, 1788-1870", in *Scottish Church History Society Records,* Vol. XX (1980), 31-45.

Finlayson, J., "Professor A.J. Scott, M.A.", Part II, in *The Owens College Magazine,* Vol. XXI (1888-1889), 7-13.

Finlayson, R.A., *Reformed Theological Writings* (Fearn, Ross-shire: Mentor/ Christian Focus Publications, 1996).

Fisher, George Park, *History of Christian Doctrine*, [2nd edition] (Edinburgh: T. & T. Clark, 1896)

Fleming, J.R., *A History of the Church in Scotland 1843-1874* (Edinburgh: T. & T. Clark, 1927).

Flesseman-Van Leer, Ellen, *Grace Abounding: A Comparison of Frederick Denison Maurice and Karl Barth* (London: King's College, 1968).

Flew, R. Newton, *The Idea of Perfection in Christian Theology* (London: Oxford University Press, 1934).

Flint, Robert, "Norman Macleod", in *Scottish Divines 1505-1872,* by Various Authors (Edinburgh: MacNiven and Wallace, 1883).

Forsyth, Peter Taylor, "Dr. Martineau", in *London Quarterly or Holborn Review* (April, 1900), 213-250.

Franklin, R. William, "The Impact of Germany on the Anglican Catholic Revival in Nineteenth-Century Britain", in *Anglican and Episcopal History*, Vol. LXI, No.4 (December, 1992), 433-448.

Franks, Robert S., *The Work of Christ: A Historical Study of Christian Doctrine* (London: Thomas Nelson and Sons Ltd., 1962), [originally published as *A History of the Doctrine of the Work of Christ in its Ecclesiastical Development* in 1918].

Froom, Leroy Edward, *The Prophetic Faith of Our Fathers: The Historical Development of Prophetic Interpretation*, in 4 volumes (Washington, D.C.: Review and Herald, 1946).

– *The Conditionalist Faith of Our Fathers: the Conflict of the Ages over the Nature and Destiny of Man*, in 2 volumes (Washington, D.C.: Review and Herald, 1966).

Fuhrmann, Paul T., *Extraordinary Christianity: The Life and Thought of Alexandre Vinet* (Philadelphia: The Westminster Press, 1964).

Fuller, Daniel P., *Easter Faith and History* (London: The Tyndale Press, 1965).

Garnett, Jane, "Bishop Butler and the Zeitgeist", in *Joseph Butler's Moral and Religious Thought: Tercentenary Essays*, Christopher Cunliffe, (ed.) (Oxford: Clarendon Press, 1992).

Garvie, Alfred E., *The Ritschlian Theology, Critical and Constructive: An Exposition and an Estimate*, [2nd Edition] (Edinburgh: T. & T. Clark, 1902).

Gay, Peter, *Deism: An Anthology* (Princeton, New Jersey: D. Van Nostrand Company Inc., 1968).

– *The Enlightenment: An Interpretation. The Science of Freedom* (New York and London: W.W. Norton & Company, 1969).

Geck, Albrecht, "The Concept of History in E.B. Pusey's First Enquiry into German Theology and Its German Background" in *Journal of Theological Studies*, New Series, Vol. 38, Part 2 (October, 1987), 387-408.

Gerrish, B.A., *A Prince of the Church: Schleiermacher and the Beginnings of Modern Theology* (London: SCM, 1984).

– *Tradition and the Modern World; Reformed Theology in the Nineteenth Century* (Chicago: University of Chicago Press, 1978).

Gilley, Sheridan, "Edward Irving: Prophet of the Millennium, in *Revival and Religion Since 1700: Essays for John Walsh*, Jane Garnett and Colin Matthew (eds.) (London: The Hambledon Press, 1993).

Goldingay, John, (ed.), *Atonement Today* (London: SPCK, 1995).

Goodloe, James C. IV, "John McLeod Campbell: Redeeming the Past by Reproducing the Atonement" in *Scottish Journal of Theology*, Vol.45, No.2 (1992), 185-208.

- "John McLeod Campbell: The Extent and Nature of the Atonement", in *Studies in Reformed Theology and History,* New Series, No.3 (1997), 1-74.
- Gowler, Steve, "No Second-hand Religion: Thomas Erskine's Critique of Religious Authorities", *Church History,* No.54 (1985), 202-14.
- Grant, Robert M., *Irenaeus of Lyons* (London: Routledge,1997).
- Grass, Tim, " 'The Taming of the Prophets': Bringing prophecy under control in the Catholic Apostolic Church", in *Journal of the European Pentecostal Theological Association*, Vol.XVI (1996), 58-68.
- Grave, S.A., *The Scottish Philosophy of Common Sense* (London: Oxford Clarendon Press, 1960).
- Green, Joel B., and Baker, Mark D., *Recovering the Scandal of the Cross: Atonement in New Testament and Contemporary Contexts* (Downers Grove, Illinois: IVP, 2000).
- Greene, Colin J.D., *Christology in Cultural Perspective*, (Carlisle: Paternoster, 2003).
- Grensted, L.W., *A Short History of The Doctrine of the Atonement* (Manchester: The University Press, 1920).
- Grensted, L.W., (ed.), *The Atonement in History and in Life* (London: SPCK, 1920).
- Grenz, Stanley J., and Olson, Roger E., *Twentieth Century Theology: God & the World in a Transitional Age* (Carlisle: Paternoster Press, 1992).
- Gunton, Colin E., (ed.), *The Cambridge Companion to Christian Doctrine* (Cambridge: Cambridge University Press, 1997).
- Gunton, Colin E., "An English Systematic Theology?", in *Scottish Journal of Theology,* Vol. 46, No.4 (1993), 479-496.
- *The Actuality of Atonement: A Study of Metaphor, Rationality and the Christian Tradition* (Edinburgh: T.&T. Clark, 1988).
- *Theology Through the Theologians: Selected Essays 1972-1995* (Edinburgh: T.&T. Clark, 1996).
- *The Promise of Trinitarian Theology*, [2nd edition] (Edinburgh: T.&T. Clark, 1997).
- "A Rose By Any Other Name? From 'Christian Doctrine' to 'Systematic Theology'", in *International Journal of Systematic Theology*, Vol.1, No.1 (March, 1999), 4-23.
- Guy, Jeff, *The Heretic: A Study of the Life of John William Colenso 1814-1883* (Johannesburg: Raven Press and Pietermaritzburg: University of Natal Press, 1983).
- Haight, Roger, *Jesus: The Symbol of God* (New York: Orbis Books, 1999).
- Hamilton, Ian, *The Erosion of Calvinist Orthodoxy: Seceders and Subscription in Scottish Presbyterianism* (Edinburgh: Rutherford House, 1990).
- Haroutunian, Joseph, *Piety versus Moralism: the passing of the New England Theology* (New York: Henry Holt and Company, 1932).

Harris, Horton, *David Friedrich Strauss and his Theology* (Cambridge: Cambridge University Press, 1973).

Harrold, Charles Frederick, *Carlyle and German Thought: 1819-1834*, Yale Studies in English LXXXII (New Haven: Yale University Press, 1934).

Hart, Trevor A., and Thimell, Daniel P., (eds.), *Christ In Our Place: The Humanity of God in Christ for the Reconciliation of the World: Essays Presented to Professor James Torrance* (Exeter: Paternoster, 1989).

Hart, Trevor, (ed.), *Justice the True and Only Mercy: Essays on the Life and Theology of Peter Taylor Forsyth* (Edinburgh: T.&T. Clark, 1995).

Hart, Trevor A., (general editor), *The Dictionary of Historical Theology* (Carlisle: Paternoster, 2000).

Hart, Trevor A., "Anselm of Canterbury and John McLeod Campbell: Where Opposites Meet?" in *Evangelical Quarterly* No.62 (1990), 311-33.

- *Regarding Karl Barth: Essays Toward a Reading of his Theology* (Carlisle: Paternoster, 1999).
- *The Teaching Father: An Introduction to the Theology of Thomas Erskine of Linlathen* (Edinburgh: The Saint Andrew Press, 1993).
- "Humankind in Christ and Christ in Humankind: Salvation as Participation in our Substitute in the Theology of John Calvin", in *Scottish Journal of Theology*, Vol.42 (1989), 67-84.

Hastings, James, and others (eds.), *Encyclopedia of Religion and Ethics*, in 12 volumes (Edinburgh: T.&T. Clark, 1918), [various dates].

Hatch, Nathan O., and Stout, Harry, S., (eds.), *Jonathan Edwards and the American Experience* (New York and Oxford: Oxford University Press, 1988).

Hayes, A.J., and Gowland, D.A., (eds.), *Scottish Methodism in the Early Victorian Period: the Scottish Correspondence of the Rev. Jabez Bunting 1800-57* (Edinburgh: Edinburgh University Press, 1981).

Haykin, Michael A.G., *One Heart and One Soul: John Sutcliff of Olney, his friends and his times* (Darlington: Evangelical Press, 1994).

Hein, Rolland, *The Harmony Within: The Spiritual Vision of George MacDonald* (Chicago: Cornerstone Press, 1999).

Helmstadter, Richard J., and Lightman, Bernard, (eds.), *Victorian Faith in Crisis: Essays on Continuity and Change in Nineteenth-Century Religious Belief* (Basingstoke: Macmillan, 1990).

Henderson, G.D., "Arminianism in Scotland", in *London Quarterly or Holborn Review* (October, 1932), 493-504.

- *The Burning Bush: Studies in Scottish Church History* (Edinburgh: The Saint Andrew Press, 1957).
- *The Claims of the Church of Scotland* (London: Hodder and Stoughton. Limited, 1951).

Henderson, Henry F., *The Religious Controversies of Scotland* (Edinburgh: T. & T. Clark, 1905).
Hennell, Michael, *Sons of the Prophets: Evangelical Leaders of the Victorian Church* (London: SPCK, 1979).
Heron, Alasdair I. C., *A Century of Protestant Theology* (Cambridge: Lutterworth Press, 1980).
Hick, John, *Evil and the God of Love* (London: Macmillan, 1985).
– *God and the Universe of Faiths: Essays in the Philosophy of Religion* (London: Macmillan, 1973).
Hicks, Peter, *Evangelicals & Truth* (Leicester: Apollos, 1998).
– *The Philosophy of Charles Hodge: A 19th Century Evangelical Approach to Reason, Knowledge and Truth* (Lewiston: The Edwin Mellen Press, 1997).
Higham, Florence, *Frederick Denison Maurice* (London: SCM, 1947).
Hilborn, David, and Horrocks, Don, "Universalistic Trends in the Evangelical Tradition: A Historical Perspective", in Parry, Robin A., and Partridge, Christopher H., (eds.), *Universal Salvation? The Current Debate* (Carlisle: Paternoster, 2003).
Hilton, Boyd, *The Age Of Atonement:the Influence of Evangelicalism on Social and Economic Thought 1785-1865* (Oxford: Clarendon Press, 1988).
Hilton, Tim, *John Ruskin: The Later Years* (New Haven and London: Yale University Press, 2000).
Hinchliff, Peter, *Benjamin Jowett and the Christian Religion* (Oxford: Clarendon Press, 1987).
– *John William Colenso: Bishop of Natal* (London: Nelson, 1964).
Hobhouse, Stephen, (ed.), *Selected Mystical Writings of William Law* (London: The C.W. Daniel Company Ltd., 1938).
Hobhouse, Stephen, "Sin and Salvation: A Study in William Law", *Theology*, Vol. XVIII, No.104 (February, 1929), 66-77.
– *William Law and Eighteenth Century Quakerism* (London: George Allen & Unwin Ltd., 1927).
Hodgson, Peter C., (ed.), *G.W.F. Hegel: Theologian of the Spirit* (Edinburgh: T.&T. Clark, 1997).
Hoffman, Bengt R., *Luther and the Mystics* (Minneapolis: Augsburg Publishing House, 1976).
Holmes, Arthur F., *Fact, Value, and God* (Leicester: Apollos, 1997).
Hooker, Morna D., *From Adam to Christ: Essays on Paul* (Cambridge: Cambridge University Press, 1990).
Hopkins, J.K., *A Woman to Deliver Her People: Joanna Southcott and English Millenarianism in an Era of Revolution* (Austin: University of Texas Press, 1982).
Hopkinson, Arthur W., *About William Law* (London: SPCK, 1948).

Horton, Michael, *In the Face of God: The Dangers and Delights of Spiritual Intimacy* (Dallas: Word Publishing, 1996).
Hunt, John, *Religious Thought in England in the Nineteenth Century* (London: Gibbings & Co., Limited, 1896).
Hurst, John Fletcher, *Bibliotheca Theologica: a select and classified bibliography of theology and general religious literature* (New York: Charles Scribner's Sons, 1883).
Huxtable, John, (ed.), *Revelation Old and New: Sermons and Addresses by P.T. Forsyth* (London: Independent Press Ltd., 1962).
Inge, William Ralph, *Studies of English Mystics* (London: John Murray, 1921).
— *Vale* (London: Longmans, Green and Co., 1934).
Jack, Ian, *English Literature 1815-1832* (Oxford: Clarendon Press, 1963).
Jackson, Samuel Macauley, and others (eds.), *The New Schaff-Herzog Encyclopedia of Religious Knowledge* in 12 volumes (New York and London: Funk and Wagnalls Company, 1908), [various dates].
Jaeck, Emma Gertrude, *Madame de Staël and the Spread of German Literature* (New York: Oxford University Press, 1915).
Jalland, Pat, *Death in the Victorian Family* (Oxford: Oxford University Press, 1996).
James, William, *The Varieties of Religious Experience: A Study in Human Nature* (London: Longmans, Green and Co., 1928).
Janzen, J. Gerald, "Coleridge and 'Pistis Christou'", in *The Expository Times*, Vol. 107, No.9 (June, 1996), 265-8.
Jasper, David and Wright, T.R., (eds.), *The Critical Spirit and the Will to Believe: Essays in Nineteenth-Century Literature and Religion* (Basingstoke: Macmillan, 1989).
Jasper, David, (ed.), *The Interpretation of Belief: Coleridge, Schleiermacher and Romanticism* (Basingstoke: Macmillan, 1986).
Jasper, David, *Coleridge as a Poet and Religious Thinker, Inspiration and Revelation* (London: Macmillan, 1985).
Jeanes, W.P., "Jonathan Edwards' Conception of Freedom of the Will", in *Scottish Journal of Theology*, Vol. 14 (1961), 1-14.
Jinkins, Michael, *A Comparative Study in the Theology of Atonement in Jonathan Edwards and John McLeod Campbell: Atonement and the Character of God* (San Francisco: Edwin Mellen Research University Press, 1993).
Johnson, Dale A., *The Changing Shape of English Nonconformity, 1825-1925* (Oxford: Oxford University Press, 1999).
Johnson, Harry, *The Humanity of the Saviour* (London, The Epworth Press, 1962).
Jones, R. Tudur, *Congregationalism in England 1662-1962* (London: Independent Press Ltd., 1962).

Kendall, R.T., *Calvin and English Calvinism to 1649* (Carlisle: Paternoster Press, 1997).
Kennedy, Donald, *Alexandre Vinet Liberal Evangelical: Fifty Years of Vinet Study c. 1940-1990* (Private Publication, n/d).
Kent, John H.S., *The End of the Line? The Development of Christian Theology in the Last Two Centuries* (London: SCM Press, 1982).
Kessler, J.B.A., *A Study of the Evangelical Alliance in Great Britain* (Goes, Netherlands: Oosterbaan & Le Cointre N.V., 1968).
Kettler, Christian D., "The Vicarious Repentance of Christ in the Theology of John McLeod Campbell and R.C. Moberly", in *Scottish Journal of Theology*, Vol. 38, No.4 (1986), 529-43.
– *The Vicarious Humanity of Christ and the Reality of Salvation* (Lanham, Maryland: University Press of America, 1991).
Knight, William, *Retrospects,* First Series (London: Smith, Elder, & Co., 1904).
– *Some Nineteenth Century Scotsmen* (Edinburgh and London: Oliphant, Anderson & Ferrier, 1903).
Lachman, David C., *The Marrow Controversy 1718-1723* (Rutherford House, Edinburgh, 1988).
LaCugna, Catherine Mowry, *God For Us: The Trinity and Christian Life* (New York: HarperSanFrancisco, 1973).
Lampe, G.W.H., "The Atonement: Law and Love", in *Soundings: Essays Concerning Christian Understanding*, A.R. Vidler (ed.) (Cambridge: Cambridge University Press, 1962).
– "The Saving Work of Christ", in *Christ for us Today*, Norman Pittenger (ed.) (London: SCM Press, 1968).
– *Reconciliation in Christ* (London: Longmans, Green and Co., 1956).
– "The Holy Spirit and the Person of Christ", in *Christ in Faith and History: Cambridge Studies in Christology*, S.W. Sykes and J.P. Clayton (eds) (Cambridge: Cambridge University Press, 1972).
Lane, Laura M., *The Life and Writings of Alexander Vinet* (Edinburgh: T & T Clark, 1890).
Larrimore, Mark (ed.), *The Problem of Evil: A Reader* (Oxford: Blackwell, 2001).
Leckie, J.H., *The World To Come and Final Destiny,* [2nd edition] (Edinburgh: T. & T. Clark, 1922).
Lees, James Cameron, "Bishop Ewing", St. Giles Lectures, 3rd Series, in *Scottish Divines 1505-1872,* by Various Authors (Edinburgh: MacNiven and Wallace, 1883).
Lehrer, Keith, *Thomas Reid,* (London and New York: Routledge, 1991).
Leighton, C.D.A., "William Law, Behmenism, and Counter Enlightenment", in *Harvard Theological Review*, 91:3 (July, 1998), 301-20.
Letham, Robert, *The Work of Christ* (Leicester: IVP, 1993).

Lewis, Donald M. (ed.), *The Blackwell Dictionary of Evangelical Biography, 1730-1860*, in 2 volumes (Oxford: Blackwell, 1995).

Lichtenberger, F., *History of German Theology in the Nineteenth Century* (Edinburgh: T.&T. Clark, 1889).

Lidgett, J. Scott, *The Victorian Transformation of Theology* (London: Epworth Press, 1934).

Lincoln, Rev. Varnum, "Thomas Erskine of Linlathen, His Life, Writings, and Theology", in *The Universalist Quarterly and General Review*, New Series, Vol. XVII (1880), 149-163.

Livingstone, David N., *Darwin's Forgotten Defenders: The Encounter Between Evangelical Theology and Evolutionary Thought* (Vancouver: Regent College Publishing, 1984).

Loades, Ann, "Coleridge as a Theologian: Some Comments on his Reading of Kant", in *Journal of Theological Studies*, New Series, Vol. XXIX, Part 2 (October, 1978), 410-426.

Loewenich, Walther von, *Luther's Theology of the Cross* (Belfast: Christian Journals Ltd, 1976).

Logan, John B., "Thomas Erskine of Linlathen: Lay Theologian of the 'Inner Light'", in *Scottish Journal of Theology*, No.37 (1984), 202-14.

Lossky, Vladimir, *Orthodox Theology: An Introduction* (Crestwood, New York: St. Vladimir's Seminary Press, 1978).

Louth, Andrew, *The Origins of the Christian Mystical Tradition: From Plato to Denys* (Oxford: Clarendon Press, 1981).

Ludlow, Morwenna, "Universal Salvation and a Soteriology of Divine Punishment", in *Scottish Journal Of Theology*, Vol.53, No.4 (2000), 449-71.

MacEwen, Alex. R., *Antoinette Bourignon, Quietist* (London: Hodder and Stoughton, 1910).

MacGregor, Geddes, "The Row Heresy", in *Harvard Theological Review*, Vol. XLIII, No.4 (October, 1950), 281-301.

Machar, Agnes Maule, "Leaders of Widening Religious Thought and Life. 1. Thomas Erskine of Linlathen" in *The Andover Review*, Vol. XIV, No.LXXXIII (November, 1890), 464-479, and Vol.XIV, No.LXXXIV (December, 1890), 588-609.

MacIntyre, Alasdair, *Whose Justice? Which Rationality?* (Notre Dame, Indiana: University of Notre Dame Press, 1988).

MacIntyre, John, "John McLeod Campbell – Heretic and Saint", *Records of the Scottish Church History Society*, Vol. XIV (1963), 49-66.

Mackintosh, Hugh Ross, *The Doctrine of the Person of Jesus Christ* (Edinburgh: T. & T. Clark, 1912).

– *Types of Modern Theology: Schleiermacher to Barth* (London: Nisbet & Co. Ltd., 1937).

Mackintosh, Robert, "Recent Thoughts on the Doctrine of the Atonement", in *The Expository Times,* Vol. XXXVII, No.5 (February, 1926), 198-203.
- *Historic Theories of Atonement with Comments* (London: Hodder & Stoughton, 1920).
Macleod, Donald, "The Doctrine of the Incarnation in Scottish Theology: Edward Irving", in *Scottish Bulletin of Evangelical Thelogy,* Vol. 9, No.1 (Spring, 1991), 40-50.
- *The Person of Christ* (Leicester, IVP, 1998).
- *Jesus is Lord: Christology Yesterday and Today* (Fearn, Ross-shire: Mentor, 2000).
MacLeod, James Lachlan, *The Second Disruption: The Free Church in Victorian Scotland and the Origins of the Free Presbyterian Church*, Scottish Historical Review Monographs Series (East Linton, East Lothian: Tuckwell Press, 2000).
MacLeod, John, *Scottish Theology in Relation to Church History Since the Reformation* (Edinburgh: The Publications Committee of the Free Church of Scotland, 1943).
MacLeod, Norman, "John MacLeod Campbell", in *Good Words* (May, 1872), 353-360.
Macpherson, John, *A History of the Church in Scotland: From the Earliest Times Down to the Present Day* (London: Alexander Gardner, 1901).
Macrae, David, *George Gilfillan: Anecdotes and Reminiscences,* [2nd edition] (Glasgow: Morison Brothers, 1891).
Macquarrie, John, *Jesus Christ in Modern Thought* (London: SCM, 2003).
MacWhirter, Archibald, "Unitarianism in Scotland", in *Records of the Scottish Church History Society,* Vol. XIII (1959), 101-143.
Malcolm, John, *The Parish of Monifieth in Ancient and Modern Times. With a History of the Landed Estates and Lives of Eminent Men* (Edinburgh and London: William Green & Sons, 1910).
Marrat, Rev. J., "Erskine of Linlathen", in the *Wesleyan Methodist Magazine,* Sixth Series, Vol. II (August and September, 1878), 583-593, and 671-674.
Martin, Hugh, *The Atonement: in its relations to the Covenant, the Priesthood, the Intercession of our Lord* (Edinburgh: Lyon and Gemmell, 1877).
Marwick, William H., "Studies in Scottish Quakerism", in *Records of the Scottish Church History Society,* Vol. XVI (1969), 89-98.
Mayor, J.B., "The Restitution of all Things", in *The Contemporary Review*, Vol.XXV (May, 1875), 927-939.
McClain, Frank Mauldin, *Maurice: Man and Moralist* (London: SPCK, 1972).

McClymond, Michael J., *Encounters with God: An Approach to the Theology of Jonathan Edwards* (New York and Oxford: Oxford University Press, 1998).

McCormack, Bruce L., *Karl Barth's Critically Realistic Dialectical Theology: Its Genesis and Development 1909-1936* (Oxford: Clarendon Press, 1995).

- "Grace and Being: the role of God's gracious election in Karl Barth's theological ontology", in John Webster (ed.), *The Cambridge Companion to Karl Barth* (Cambridge: Cambridge University Press, 2000).

McCurdy, Leslie, *Attributes and Atonement: The Holy Love of God in the Theology of P.T. Forsyth* (Carlisle: Paternoster, 1999).

McDonald, H.D., *The Atonement of the Death of Christ: in Faith, Revelation, and History* (Grand Rapids: Baker Book House, 1985).

- *Ideas of Revelation: An Historical Study, A.D. 1700 to A.D. 1860*, [one volume edition] (Grand Rapids: Baker Book House, 1979).

- *Theories of Revelation: A Historical Study, 1860-1960*, [one volume edition] (Grand Rapids: Baker Book House, 1979).

McFarlane, Graham, *Why Do You Believe What You Believe about the Holy Spirit?* (Carlisle: Paternoster, 1998).

- *Christ and the Spirit: The Doctrine of the Incarnation according to Edward Irving* Carlisle: Paternoster, 1996.

McGonigle, Herbert Boyd, *Sufficient Saving Grace: John Wesley's Evangelical Arminianism*, (Carlisle: Paternoster, 2001).

McGowan, A.T.B., *The Federal Theology of Thomas Boston* (Carlisle: Paternoster, 1997).

McGrath, Alister E., *Christian Theology: An Introduction*, [3rd edition] (Oxford: Blackwell, 2001).

- *Iustitia Dei: A History of the Christian Doctrine of Justification*, [2nd edition] (Cambridge: Cambridge University Press, 1998).

- *The Making of Modern German Christology 1750-1990* (Leicester: Apollos, 1994).

- *Studies in Doctrine* (Grand Rapids: Zondervan, 1997).

- "The Moral Theory of the Atonement: An Historical and Theological Critique" in *Scottish Journal of Theology*, Vol. 38, No.2 (1985), 205-220.

McGrath, Alister E., (ed.), *The Blackwell Encyclopedia of Modern Christian Thought* (Oxford: Blackwell, 1993).

McGrath, Francis, *John Henry Newman: Universal Revelation* (Tunbridge Wells: Burns & Oates, 1997).

McIntosh, John R., *Church and Theology in Enlightenment Scotland: The Popular Party, 1740-1800,* Scottish Historical Review Monographs Series (East Linton, East Lothian: Tuckwell Press, 1998).

McIntyre, John, *The Shape of Soteriology* (Edinburgh: T.&T. Clark, 1992).

Mechie, Stewart, "The Marrow Controversy Reviewed", in *Evangelical Quarterly*, Vol.22 (1950), 20-31.

Members of the Church of England, *Liberal Evangelicalism: An Interpretation* (London: Hodder and Stoughton, undated).

Meynell, Hugo, *Is Christianity True?* (London: Geoffrey Chapman, 1994).

Michalson, Gordon E., *Kant and the Problem of God* (Oxford: Blackwell, 1999).

Mikolaski, Samuel J., "P.T. Forsyth on the Atonement", in *Evangelical Quarterly,* Vol. XXXVI, No.2 (April – June, 1964), 78-91.

– "The Theology of P.T. Forsyth", in *Evangelical Quarterly,* Vol. XXXVI, No.1 (January – March, 1964), 27-41.

Miller, Edward, *The History and Doctrines of Irvingism, or of the So-Called Catholic Apostolic Church,* in 2 volumes (London: C. Kegan Paul & Co., 1878**).**

Miller, Ed. L., and Grenz, Stanley J., *Introduction to Contemporary Theologies* (Minneapolis: Fortress Press, 1998).

Mitchison, Rosalind, *Life in Scotland* (London: B.T. Batsford Ltd, 1978).

Moore, Edward Caldwell, *An Outline of the History of Christian Thought Since Kant* (London: Duckworth & Co., 1912).

Morgan, Bayard Quincy and Hohlfield, A.R., (eds.), *German Literature in British Magazines 1750-1860* (Madison: University of Wisconsin Press, 1949).

Mullin, Bruce, *The Puritan as Yankee: A Life of Horace Bushnell* (Grand Rapids: Eerdmans, 2002).

Murray, Derek B., "The Influence of John Glas", in *Records of the Scottish Church History Society,* Vol. XXII (1986), 45-56.

Murray, John, *Collected Writings of John Murray*, in 4 volumes (Edinburgh: The Banner of Truth Trust, 1976).

Murray, Michael J., (ed.), *Reason for the Hope Within* (Grand Rapids: Eerdmans, 1999).

Needham, Nicholas R., *Thomas Erskine of Linlathen: his Life and Theology, 1788-1837* (Edinburgh: Rutherford House Books, 1990).

Newell, J. Philip, "'Unworthy of the dignity of the Assembly': the deposition of Alexander John Scott in 1831", in *Records of the Scottish Church History Society,* Vol. XXI (1983), 249-262.

– "The Other Christian Socialist: Alexander John Scott", *The Heythrop Journal,* Vol. XXIV, No.3, July (1983), 278-289.

Newman, Francis William, *Phases of Faith; or, Passages from the History of my Creed* (London: John Chapman, 1850).

Newsome, David, "Justification and Sanctification: Newman and the Evangelicals", in *Journal of Theological Studies,* N.S., Vol. XV, Part 1 (April, 1964), 32-53.

– *The Parting of Friends: A Study of the Wilberforces and Henry Manning* (London: John Murray, 1966).

- *Two Classes of Men: Platonism and English Romantic Thought* (New York: St. Martin's Press, 1974).
Noll, Mark A., (ed.), *The Princeton Theology 1812-1921* (Phillipsburg, New Jersey: Presbyterian and Reformed Publishing Company, 1983).
Norman, Edward, *The Victorian Christian Socialists* (Cambridge: Cambridge University Press, 1987).
Norris, Richard A., *God and the World in Early Christian Theology* (London: Adam & Charles Black, 1966).
Norris, Thomas J., *Newman and His Theological Method: A Guide for the Theologian Today* (Leiden: E.J. Brill. 1977).
O'Callaghan, Paul, *Fides Christi: The Justification Debate* (Dublin: Four Courts Press, 1997).
Oliver, Grace A., *Arthur Penrhyn Stanley: His Life, Work, and Teachings* [3rd Edition] (London: Sampson Low, Marston, Searle, & Rivington, 1885).
Olson, Roger E., *The Story of Christian Theology: Twenty Centuries of Tradition & Reform* (Leicester: Apollos, 1999).
Overton, John H., *The English Church in the Nineteenth Century (1800-1833)* (London: Longmans, Green, & Co., 1894).
- *William Law, Nonjuror and Mystic: A Sketch of his Life, Character, and Opinions* (London: Longmans, Green, and Co., 1881).
Packer, James I., " 'Keswick' and the Reformed Doctrine of Sanctification", in *The Evangelical Quarterly,* Vol. XXVII (1955), 153-167.
- "Introductory Essay" to *The Death of Death in the Death of Christ,* by John Owen (Edinburgh: The Banner of Truth Trust, 1959).
- "What Did the Cross Achieve?", *Tyndale Bulletin,* No.25 (1974), 3-45.
- "The Way of Salvation: The Problems of Universalism" in *Bibliotheca Sacra,* Vol. 130, No.517 (January – March, 1973), 3-11.
Pals, Daniel L., *The Victorian 'Lives' of Jesus* (San Antonio: Trinity University Press, 1982).
Park, Edwards A., "John McLeod Campbell's Theory of the Atonement" *in Bibliotheca Sacra,* Vol.XXX, No.118 (April, 1873), 334-360.
Parry, Robin A., and Partridge, Christopher H., (eds.), *Universal Salvation? The Current Debate* (Carlisle: Paternoster, 2003).
Parsons, Gerald, (ed.), *Religion in Victorian Britain:* in 4 volumes (volume 3 also edited by James R. Moore) (Manchester and New York: Manchester University Press and the Open University, 1988).
Paul, Robert S., *The Atonement and the Sacraments: The Relation of the Atonement to the Sacraments of Baptism and the Lord's Supper* (New York and Nashville: Abingdon Press, 1960).
Pelikan, Jaroslav, *Jesus Through the Centuries: His Place in the History of Culture* (New Haven and London: Yale University Press, 1985).

- *Christian Doctrine and Modern Culture (since 1700): The Christian Tradition: A History of the Development of Doctrine:* Volume 5 (Chicago and London: The University of Chicago Press, 1989).
Peters, Ted, *God – the World's Future: Systematic Theology for a Postmodern Era* (Minneapolis; Fortress Press, 1992).
Peterson, David, *Where Wrath and Mercy Meet: Proclaiming the Atonement Today* (Carlisle: Paternoster, 2001).
Peterson, David, (ed.), *The Word Became Flesh: Evangelicals and the Incarnation* (Carlisle: Paternoster, 2003).
Pettingell, John Hancock, *The Unspeakable Gift: The Gift of Eternal Life Through Jesus Christ Our Lord,* with an introduction by Edward White (Yarmouth, M.E: I.C. Wellcome,1884).
Pfleiderer, Otto, *The Development of Theology in Germany since Kant and its Progress in Great Britain since 1825,* [2nd edition] (London: Swan Sonnenschein & Co., 1893).
Phillips, Michael R., (ed.), *George MacDonald: Discovering the Character of God* (Minneapolis: Bethany House Publishers, 1989).
Pinnock, Clark H., *Flame of Love: A Theology of the Holy Spirit* (Downers Grove, Illinois: IVP, 1996).
- "Salvation By Resurrection", in *Ex Auditu*, Vol. 9 (1993), 1-11.
- *Tracking the Maze: Finding Our Way Through Modern Theology from an Evangelical Perspective* (San Francisco: Harper & Row, 1990).
Pinnock, Clark H., (ed.), *The Grace of God and the Will of Man* (Minneapolis: Bethany House Publishers, 1989).
Pollock, J.C., *The Keswick Story* (Chicago: Moody Press, 1964).
Porter, Roy, *Enlightenment: Britain and the Creation of the Modern World* (London: Allen Lane, The Penguin Press, 2000).
- *The Enlightenment* (Basingstoke: Palgrave, 2001).
Powell, Samuel M., *The Trinity in German Thought* (Cambridge: Cambridge University Press, 2001).
Powys, David J., *'Hell': A Hard Look at a Hard Question: The Fate of the Unrighteous in New Testament Thought* (Carlisle: Paternoster Press, 1998).
Prickett, Stephen, *Romanticism and Religion: The Tradition of Coleridge and Wordsworth in the Victorian Church* (Cambridge: Cambridge University Press, 1976).
Pritchard, C.E., "Modern Views of the Atonement". Review of *The Nature of the Atonement*, by John McLeod Campbell; *The Vicarious Sacrifice*, by Horace Bushnell; *The Life and Light of Men*, by John Young; *Cur Deus Homo*, by St. Anselm, in *North British Review,* Vol. XLVI, No. XCII (June, 1867), 343-380.
Rack, Henry D., "Evangelical Endings: Death-Beds in Evangelical Biography" in *Bulletin of the John Rylands University Library of Manchester,* Vol. 74, No.1 (Spring, 1992), 39–56.

—————, *Reasonable Enthusiast: John Wesley and the Rise of Methodism* (London: Epworth Press, 1992).
Rambert, E., *Alexandre Vinet: Histoire de sa vie et de ses ouvrages*, [3rd edition], in 2 volumes (Lausanne: Georges Bridel, 1876).
Ramm, Bernard, *The Evangelical Heritage: A Study in Historical Theology* (Grand Rapids: Baker Books, 1973).
Ramsey, Arthur Michael, *F.D. Maurice and the Conflicts of Modern Theology* (Cambridge: Cambridge University Press, 1951).
Reardon, Bernard M.G., (ed.), *Liberal Protestantism* (London; Adam & Charles Black, 1968).
Reardon, Bernard M.G., *Religion in the Age of Romanticism* (Cambridge University Press, 1985).
— *Religious Thought in the Victorian Age: A Survey from Coleridge to Gore*, [2nd edition] (London: Longman, 1995).
— *Kant as Philosophical Theologian* (Totowa, New Jersey: Barnes & Noble, 1988).
Reeves, Dudley, "Andrew Fuller in Scotland", in *The Banner of Truth Magazine,* No.106 (July/ August, 1972), 33-40.
Reid, Daniel G., Linder, Robert D., Shelley, Bruce L., Stout, Harry S., (eds.), *Dictionary of Christianity in America* (Downers Grove, Illinois: IVP, 1990).
Renwick, W.L., *English Literature 1789-1815* (Oxford: Clarendon Press, 1963).
Rice, Daniel F., "An Attempt at Systematic Reconstruction in the Theology of Thomas Chalmers", in *Church History*, Vol. 48 (1979), 174-188.
— "Natural Theology and the Scottish Philosophy in the Thought of Thomas Chalmers", in *Scottish Journal of Theology*, No.24 (1971), 23-46.
Richardson, C., "Thomas Erskine of Linlathen," in *Friends Quarterly Examiner,* Vol.XII, No.46 (March, 1878), 296-313.
Rilliet, Jean-H., *La Conception du Salut dans L'Oeuvre d' Alexandre Vinet, Apologiste Romantique* (Geneva: Les Éditions Labor, 1939).
Robert, Daniel, *Les Eglises Réformées en France (1800-1830)* (Paris, Presses Universitaires de France, 1961).
Robinson, David, "The Legacy of Channing: Culture as a Religious Category in New England Thought", in *Harvard Theological Review*, 74:2 (April, 1981), 221-239.
Rodgers, John H., *The Theology of P.T. Forsyth* (London: Independent Press, 1965).
Rogerson, John, *Old Testament Criticism in the Nineteenth Century: England and Germany* (London: SPCK, 1984).
Rosman, Doreen, *Evangelicals and Culture* (London and Canberra: Croom Helm, 1984).

Rowell, Geoffrey, "The Origins and History of Universalist Societies in Britain, 1750-1850", in *Journal of Ecclesiastical History,* Vol. XXII, No.1 (January, 1971), 35-56.
- *Hell and the Victorians* (Oxford: Clarendon Press, 1974).
Ruthven, Jon, *On the Cessation of the Charismata: The Protestant Polemic on Postbiblical Miracles* (Sheffield: Sheffield Academic Press, 1993).
Ryle, J.C., *Holiness: its nature, hindrances, difficulties, and roots* (Darlington: Evangelical Press, 1979) [first published 1879].
Sanders, Charles Richard, *Coleridge and the Broad Church Movement: Studies in S.T. Coleridge, Dr. Arnold of Rugby, J.C. Hare, Thomas Carlyle and F.D. Maurice* (New York: Octagon Books, 1972).
Schneider, H.W., "The Developments in Protestantism During the Nineteenth Century Throughout the World", in *Journal of World History,* Vol. VI, No.1 (1960), 97-121.
Schreiner, Thomas R., and Ware, Bruce A., *Still Sovereign: Contemporary Perspectives on Election, Foreknowledge, & Grace* (Grand Rapids: Baker Books, 2000).
Schwöbel, Christoph, and Gunton, Colin E., (eds.), *Persons, Divine and Human: King's College Essays in Theological Anthropology* (Edinburgh: T.&T. Clark, 1991).
Scotland, N.A.D., " 'Essays and Reviews' (1860) and the Reaction of Victorian Churches and Churchmen", in *The Downside Review,* Vol. 108, No.372 (July, 1990), 146-156.
Selby, Thomas G., *The Theology of Modern Fiction* (London: Charles H. Kelly, 1897).
Sell, Alan P.F., *The Spirit our Life* (Shippensburg, Pennsylvania: Ragged Edge Press, 2000).
- "The Rise and Reception of Modern Biblical Criticism: A Retrospect", in *The Evangelical Quarterly,* Vol. LII, No.III (1980), 132-148.
- *Theology in Turmoil: The Roots, Course and Significance of the Conservative-Liberal Debate in Modern Theology* (Eugene, Oregon: WIPF & Stock Publishers, 1998).
- *Commemorations: Studies in Christian Thought and History* (Eugene, Oregon: WIPF & Stock Pulishers, 1998).
- *Defending and Declaring the Faith: Some Scottish Examples 1860-1920,* (Exeter: Paternoster Press, 1987).
Shaw, Robert, *An Exposition of the Westminster Confession of Faith* (Fearn, Ross-shire: Christian Focus Publications, 1992), [first published in 1845].
Sinkinson, Christopher, *The Universe of Faiths: A Critical Study of John Hick's Religious Pluralism* (Carlisle: Paternoster, 2001).
Smail, Tom, *Once and for All: A Confession of the Cross* (London: Darton, Longman & Todd, 1998).

Smart, Ninian, Clayton, John, Katz, Steven, and Sherry, Patrick, *Nineteenth Century Religious Thought in the West,* in 3 volumes (Cambridge: Cambridge University Press, 1985).
Smith, William C., "Thomas Erskine of Linlathen," in *Theological Review,* (London), Vol.XII (July, 1875), [Whitfield, Green & Son], 353-372.
Solomon, Robert C., *Continental Philosophy Since 1750: The Rise and Fall of the Self* (Oxford: Oxford University Press, 1988).
Stackhouse, John G., Jr., (ed.), *What Does it Mean to be Saved?: Broadening Evangelical Horizons of Salvation,* (Grand Rapids: Baker Academic, 2002).
Stephenson, Alan M.G., *The Rise and Decline of English Modernism* (London: SPCK, 1984).
Stevens, George Barker, *The Christian Doctrine of Salvation* (Edinburgh: T. & T. Clark, 1905).
Stewart, Herbert Leslie, *Modernism, Past and Present* (London: John Murray, 1932).
Stewart, John W., and Moorhead, James H., (eds.), *Charles Hodge Revisited: A Critical Appraisal of His Life and Work* (Grand Rapids: Eerdmans, 2002).
Stibbe, Mark, *From Orphans To Heirs: Celebrating Our Spiritual Adoption* (Oxford: The Bible Reading Fellowship, 1999).
Storms, C. Samuel, "Jonathan Edwards on the Freedom of the Will", *Trinity Journal*, Vol. 3, No. 2, New Series (Fall, 1982), 131-169.
Storr, Vernon F., *Development and Divine Purpose* (London: Methuen & Co., 1906).
– *The Development of English Theology in the Nineteenth Century 1800-1860* (London, Longmans, Green and Co., 1913).
Story, Robert Herbert, (ed.), *The Church of Scotland: Past and Present,* in 5 volumes (London: William Mackenzie, 1894).
Story, Robert Herbert, "Edward Irving", in *Scottish Divines 1505-1872,* by various authors (Edinburgh: MacNiven and Wallace, 1883).
Strachan, Gordon, *The Pentecostal Theology of Edward Irving* (Peabody, Mass: Hendrickson, 1973).
Strange, Daniel, *The Possibility of Salvation Among the Unevangelised: An Analysis of Inclusivism in Recent Evangelical Theology* (Carlisle: Paternoster, 2002).
Strange, Roderick, *Newman and the Gospel of Christ* (Oxford: Oxford University Press, 1981).
Stunt, Timothy C.F., *From Awakening to Secession: Radical Evangelicals in Switzerland and Britain 1815-35* (Edinburgh: T.&T. Clark, 2000).
– "Geneva and British Evangelicals in the Early Nineteenth Century", *Journal of Ecclesiastical History*, Vol. 32, No.1 (January, 1981), 35-46.
Swinburne, Richard, *Responsibility and Atonement* (Oxford: Clarendon Press, 1989).

- *Providence and the Problem of Evil* (Oxford: Clarendon Press, 1998).
Sykes, S.W., (ed.), *England and Germany: Studies in Theological Diplomacy* (Frankfurt Am Main: Verlag Peter D. Lang, 1982).
Sykes, Stephen, *Friedrich Schleiermacher* (London: Lutterworth Press, 1971).
- *The Identity of Christianity: theologians and the essence of Christianity from Scheiermacher to Barth* (London: SPCK, 1984).
Symondson, Anthony, (ed.), *The Victorian Crisis of Faith* (London: SPCK, 1970).
Tatum, W. Barnes, *In Quest of Jesus* (Nashville: Abingdon Press, 1999).
Tener, Robert H., and Woodfield, Malcolm, (eds.), *A Victorian Spectator: Uncollected Writings of R.H. Hutton* (Bristol: The Bristol Press, 1991).
Thomas, G. Michael, *The Extent of the Atonement: A Dilemma for Reformed Theology from Calvin to the Consensus (1536-1675)* (Carlisle: Paternoster, 1997).
Thomas, Stephen, *Newman and Heresy: The Anglican Years* (Cambridge: Cambridge University Press, 1991).
Toon, Peter, *Evangelical Theology 1833-1856: A Response to Tractarianism* (London: Marshall, Morgan & Scott, 1979).
- *Justification and Sanctification* (London: Marshall Morgan & Scott, 1983).
- *The Emergence of Hyper-Calvinism in English Nonconformity 1689-1765* (London: The Olive Tree, 1967).
Torrance, James B., "Covenant or Contract? A Study of the Theological Background of Worship in Seventeenth-Century Scotland", in *Scottish Journal of Theology*, Vol.23 (1970), 51-76.
- "The Contribution of McLeod Campbell to Scottish Theology", in *Scottish Journal of Theology*, Vol.26 (1973), 295-311.
- "The Vicarious Humanity of Christ", in T.F. Torrance, (ed.), *The Incarnation* (Edinburgh: The Handsel Press, 1981).
- "The Incarnation and 'Limited Atonement'", in *Evangelical Quarterly*, Vol. 55, No.3 (1984), 83-94.
Torrance, Thomas F., (ed.), *The Incarnation* (Edinburgh: The Handsel Press, 1981).
Torrance, Thomas F., *Scottish Theology: From John Knox to John McLeod Campbell* (Edinburgh: T.&T. Clark, 1996).
- *The Mediation of Christ* [revised edition] (Edinburgh: T.&T. Clark, 1992).
- *The Trinitarian Faith: the Evangelical Theology of the Ancient Catholic Church* (Edinburgh: T.&T. Clark, 1988).
- *Theology in Reconciliation* (London: Geoffrey Chapman, 1975).
- *Karl Barth: An Introduction to His Early Theology, 1910-1931* (London: SCM, 1962).

Trigg, Joseph Wilson, *Origen: The Bible and Philosophy in the Third-Century Church* (Atlanta: John Knox Press, 1983).
Tuell, Anne Kimball, *John Sterling: A Representative Victorian* (New York: The Macmillan Company, 1941).
Tuttle, George M., *So Rich A Soil: John McLeod Campbell on Christian Atonement* (Edinburgh: The Handsel Press, 1986).
Van Dyk, Leanne, *The Desire of Divine Love: John McLeod Campbell's Doctrine of the Atonement* (New York: Peter Lang, 1995).
– "Towards a New Typology of Reformed Doctrines of Atonement", in *Towards The Future of Reformed Theology: Tasks, Topics, Traditions,* David Willis and Michael Welker (eds.) (Grand Rapids and Cambridge: Eerdmans, 1999).
Vaughan, D.J., "Scottish Influence Upon English Theological Thought", in *The Contemporary Review,* Vol. XXXII (June, 1878), 457-473.
Vidler, Alec R., *The Theology of F.D. Maurice* (London: SCM, 1948).
– *F.D. Maurice and Company* (London: SCM Press, 1966).
Vosges, Friedhelm, "Moderate and Evangelical Thinking in the later Eighteenth Century: Differences and Shared Attitudes", in *Records of the Scottish Church History Society,* Vol. XXII (1986), 141-157.
Wainwright, Geoffrey, (ed.), *Keeping the Faith: Essays to Mark the Centenary of Lux Mundi* (London: SPCK, 1989).
Walker, A. Keith, *William Law: His Life and Work* (London: SPCK, 1973).
Walker, D.P., *The Decline of Hell* (Chicago: The University of Chicago Press, 1964).
Walker, James, *The Theology and Theologians of Scotland Chiefly of the Seventeenth and Eighteenth Centuries,* [2nd Revised Edition] (Edinburgh: Knox Press, 1982), [first published in 1888].
Wallace, Robert, "Church Tendencies in Scotland", in *Recess Studies,* Sir Alexander Grant (ed.) (Edinburgh: Edmonston and Douglas, 1870).
Wallace, Ronald S., *The Atoning Death of Christ* (London: Marshall Morgan & Scott, 1981).
Waller, Ralph, "James Martineau: The Development of his Religious Thought", in Barbara Smith, (ed.), *Truth, Liberty, Religion: Essays Celebrating Two Hundred Years of Manchester College* (Oxford: Manchester College, 1986).
Walsh, David, *The Mysticism of Innerworldly Fulfillment: A Study of Jacob Boehme* (Gainesville: University Presses of Florida, 1983).
Walsh, Walter, *George Gilfillan: Twenty Years After* (Dundee: William Kidd, 1898).
Ward, W.R., "Faith and Fallacy: English and German Perspectives in the Nineteenth Century", in *Victorian Faith in Crisis: Essays on Continuity and Change in Nineteenth-Century Religious Belief,* Richard J. Helmstadter and Bernard Lightman (eds.) (Basingstoke: Macmillan, 1990).

- *Religion and Society in England 1790-1850* (London: B.T. Batsford Ltd, 1972).
Warfield, Benjamin Breckinridge, *Counterfeit Miracles* (Edinburgh: The Banner of Truth Trust, 1972).
- *Critical Reviews* (New York: Oxford University Press, 1932).
- *Perfectionism,* Samuel Craig (ed.) (Philadelphia: The Presbyterian and Reformed Publishing Company, 1980).
- *The Person and Work of Christ* (Phillipsburg, New Jersey: The Presbyterian and Reformed Publishing Company, 1950).
- *The Saviour of the World* (Edinburgh: The Banner of Truth Trust, 1991).
- *Studies in Theology* [1932] (Edinburgh: The Banner of Truth Trust, 1991).
Watson, Jean L., *Life of Andrew Thomson, D.D., Minister of St. George's Parish, Edinburgh* (Edinburgh: James Gemmell,1882).
Watson, Philip S., (ed.), *The Message of the Wesleys* (Grand Rapids: Francis Asbury Press, 1984).
Weaver, Rebecca Harden, *Divine Grace and Human Agency: A Study of the Semi-Pelagian Controversy* (Macon, Georgia: Mercer Universtity Press, 1996).
Webb, Clement C.J., *A Study of Religious Thought in England from 1850* (Oxford: The Clarendon Press, 1933).
- *Studies in the History of Natural Theology* (London: Oxford Clarendon Press, 1915).
Webster, John, (ed.), *The Cambridge Companion to Karl Barth* (Cambridge: Cambridge University Press, 2000).
Wedgwood, Julia, *Nineteenth Century Teachers and Other Essays* (London: Hodder & Stoughton, 1909).
- "William Law, the English Mystic of the Eighteenth Century", in *The Contemporary Review,* Vol. XXXI (December, 1877), 82-102.
Weinandy, Thomas G., *In the Likeness of Sinful Flesh: An Essay on the Humanity of Christ* (Edinburgh: T.&T. Clark, 1993).
- *The Father's Spirit of Sonship: Reconceiving the Trinity* (Edinburgh: T.&T. Clark, 1995).
- *Does God Change? The Word's Becoming in the Incarnation* (Still River, Mass: St. Bede's Publications, 1985).
- *Jesus the Christ* (Huntingdon, Indiana: Our Sunday VisitorPublishing Division, 2003).
Weir, David A., *The Origins of the Federal Theology in Sixteenth-Century Reformation Thought* (Oxford: Clarendon Press, 1990).
Welch, Claude, *Protestant Thought in the Nineteenth Century,* Volume I, 1799-1870, Volume II, 1870-1914 (New Haven and London: Yale University Press, 1972 and 1985).

Wellek, René, *Immanuel Kant in England 1793-1838* (Princeton: Princeton University Press, 1931).
White, Vernon, *Atonement and Incarnation: An Essay in Universalism and Particularity* (Cambridge: Cambridge University Press, 1991).
Widdicombe, Peter, *The Fatherhood of God From Origen to Athanasius*, [revised edition] (Oxford: Clarendon Press, 2000).
Wigmore-Beddoes, Dennis G., *Yesterday's Radicals: A Study of the Affinity Between Unitarianism and Broad Church Anglicanism in the Nineteenth Century* (Cambridge and London: James Clarke & Co. Ltd., 1971).
Wilbur, Earle Morse, *A History of Unitarianism* (Cambridge, Mass: Harvard University Press, 1952).
Wilkens, Steve, and Padgett, Alan G., *Christianity & Western Thought, Volume 2, Faith and Reason in the 19th Century* (Illinois: InterVarsity Press, 2000).
Wilkinson, Alan, *Christian Socialism: Scott Holland to Tony Blair* (London: SCM Press, 1998).
Willey, Basil, *More Nineteenth Century Studies: A Group of Honest Doubters* (London: Chatto and Windus, 1956).
– *Nineteenth Century Studies: Coleridge to Matthew Arnold* (London: Chatto and Windus, 1949).
– *Samuel Taylor Coleridge* (London: Chatto and Windus, 1972).
– *The Eighteenth Century Background: Studies in the Idea of Nature in the Thought of the Period* (London and New York: Ark Paperbacks, 1986).
Williams, Garry J., "Was Evangelicalism Created by the Enlightenment?", in *Tyndale Bulletin*, 53.2 (2002), 283-312.
Williams, Robert R., *Schleiermacher the Theologian: The Construction of the Doctrine of God* (Philadelphia, Fortress Press, 1978).
Wilson, Jonathan R., *God So Loved the World: A Christology for Disciples* (Grand Rapids: Baker, 2001).
Winslow, Donald F., *Thomas Erskine: Advocate for the Character of God* (University Press of America, Lanham, Maryland, 1993).
Wood, A. Skevington, *The Inextinguishable Blaze: Spiritual Renewal and Advance in the Eighteenth Century* (Exeter: Paternoster Press, 1960).
Wood, H.G., *Frederick Denison Maurice* (Cambridge: Cambridge University Press, 1950).
Woodhead, Linda, (ed.), *Reinventing Christianity: Nineteenth-Century Contexts* (Aldershot: Ashgate, 2001).
Worrall, B.G., *The Making of the Modern Church: Christianity in England Since 1800* (London: SPCK, 1988).
Wright, D.F. and Badcock, G.D., (eds.), *Disruption to Diversity: Edinburgh Divinity 1846-1996* (Edinburgh: T. & T. Clark, 1996).

Young, B.W., *Religion and Enlightenment in Eighteenth-Century England* (Oxford: Clarendon Press, 1998).
Young, David, "F.D. Maurice and the Unitarians", in *Churchman,* Vol. 98, No.4 (1984), 332-40.
- *F.D. Maurice and Unitarianism* (Oxford: Clarendon Press, 1992).
Zachman, Randall C., *The Assurance of Faith: Conscience in the Theology of Martin Luther and John Calvin* (Minneapolis: Fortress Press, 1993).
Zizioulas, John D., *Being As Communion: Studies in Personhood and the Church* (New York: St. Vladimir's Seminary Press, 1985).

Anonymous Periodical, Newspaper and Journal Articles Consulted

Blackwood's Edinburgh Magazine, Vol.CXXII, No. DCCXLIII (September, 1877). "A School of the Prophets", 283-302.
British and Foreign Evangelical Review, Vol.XVI, No.LX (April, 1867). "Trials of Irving and Campbell of Row", (by 'N.L.W.'), 331-354.
British Critic, Quarterly Theological Review and Ecclesiastical Record, Vol. V, No. IX (January, 1829). Review of *The Unconditional Freeness of the Gospel*, by Thomas Erskine, 54-80.
- Vol. 23, No. XLVI (April, 1838). Review of *The Doctrine of Election,* by Thomas Erskine, and *The Primitive Doctrine of Election,* by G.S. Faber, 320-328.
British Friend, Vol. XLII, Nos.I-XII (12th Month 1st, 1884). Review of *A Reasonable Faith*, 299-300.
Christian Examiner and Church of Ireland Magazine, Vol. XI, No.LXXIV, (August 1831), 586-588, and Vol. I, New Series (1832), 18-21. "Erskine's View of Faith Contrasted with Scripture", (by 'T.K.').
Christian Guardian and Church of England Magazine, (December 1830). Review of *Two Essays*, by Ralph Wardlaw, and *The Doctrine of Universal Pardon*, by Andrew Thomson, 482-491.
- (January 1829). Review of *The Unconditional Freeness of the Gospel,* by Thomas Erskine, 32-34.
- (March 1823). Review of *Remarks on the Internal Evidence for the Truth of Revealed Religion*, by Thomas Erskine, 110-112.
- (November 1831). "Modern Fanaticism – Pretended Miracles". Review of *Modern Fanaticism Unveiled*, and *Remarks on the [supposed] Revival of Miraculous Powers in the Church*, by Baptist W. Noel, 426-436.
Christian Observer, Vol. XIX, No. XI (November, 1820). "On the Comparative Frigidness of Scholastic Divinity", (by 'X.Q.'), 720-724.

- Vol. XXIII, No.VIII (August, 1823). Review of *An Essay on Faith*, by Thomas Erskine, 502-511.
- Vol. XXIX, No.II (February, 1829). Review of *The Unconditional Freeness of the Gospel*, by Thomas Erskine, 107-114.

Dundee Advertiser, Obituary of Thomas Erskine of Linlathen, (Monday and Tuesday, 28 and 29 March 1870).

Eclectic Review, Vol. XVI, New Series (August, 1821). Review of *Remarks on the Internal Evidence of the Truth of Revealed Religion*, by Thomas Erskine, 180-185.

- Vol. XXX (December, 1828). Review of *The Epistle of Paul the Apostle to the Romans*, by C.H. Terrot, and *The Unconditional Freeness of the Gospel*, by Thomas Erskine, 508-526.
- Vol. IV, New Series (July, 1830). Review of various publications relating to "The Row Heresy", including *Extracts of Letters to a Christian Friend*, by a Lady. With an Introductory Essay by Thomas Erskine, 61-77.
- Vol. IV, New Series (November, 1830). "Erskine on Miraculous Gifts": Review of *The Gifts of the Spirit*, by Thomas Erskine and *A View of Inspiration*, by Alexander Macleod, 417-428.
- Vol. IV, New Series (July, 1838). Review of *The Doctrine of Election*, by Thomas Erskine, 100-107.
- Vol. IV, New Series (November, 1838), "Sandemanian Theology": Review of *Essays and Correspondence chiefly on Scriptural Subjects*, by John Walker, 519-531.

Edinburgh Christian Instructor, Vol. XXII, No. IV (April, 1823). Review of *Remarks on the Internal Evidence for the Truth of Revealed Religion*, by Thomas Erskine, 243-256.

- Vol. XXII, No.XII (December, 1823). Review of *The Works of the Rev. John Gambold*. With an Introductory Essay by Thomas Erskine, 839-845.
- Vol. XXVII, No. VI (June, 1828). Review of *The Unconditional Freeness of the Gospel*, by Thomas Erskine, 410-427.
- Vol. XXVII, No. XII (December, 1828). "Review of Thomson's 'Questions Preparatory to the Communion'", 847-849.
- Vol. XXIX, No.II (February, 1830). Review of *The Gairloch Heresy Tried*, by Dr. Robert Burns, 102-117.
- Vol. XXIX, No.V (May, 1830). "Information and Warning to the Erskinites", 316-319.
- Vol. XXIX, No.V (May, 1830). "Review of Publications on the Row Heresy", 331-352.
- Vol. XXIX, No.VI (June, 1830). "Mr. Erskine's Doctrine hailed by the Unitarians", 409-410.
- Vol. XXIX, No.VII (July, 1830). Review of *A Vindication of the "Religion of the Land"*, by A. Robertson, 502-504.

- Vol. XXX, No. II (February, 1831). "Review of 'The Morning Watch', No.VI", 113-128.
- Vol. XXX, No. IX (September, 1831). "Mr. Irving and the General Assembly", (by 'D.D.'), 603-609.
- Vol. XXX, No. IX (September, 1831). "Brainerd versus the Erskineites", (by 'Verus'), 610-616.
- Vol. XXX, No. VI (June, 1831). "Modern Heresies shown to be Old Delusions", (by 'Perthensis'), 402-11.
- Vol. XXX, No. XI (November, 1831). Review of *Observations on Universal Pardon, the Extent of the Atonement, and Personal Assurance of Salvation*, by J.A. Haldane, 798-803.
- Vol. XXX, No.IV (April, 1831). "Religious Intelligence – Synod of Glasgow and Ayr – Row Heresy", 298-300.
- Vol. I, No.III, New Series (March, 1832). "Review of Works on Modern Miracles", 197-209.

Edinburgh Review or Critical Journal, Vol. LIII, No. CVI (June, 1831). "Pretended Miracles – Irving, Scott, and Erskine". Review of various publications including *A Letter on the Gifts of the Spirit* and *The Brazen Serpent,* by Thomas Erskine, 261-305.

- Vol. CXLVII, No. 302 (April, 1878). "Three Scottish Teachers". Review of *Letters of Thomas Erskine of Linlathen, Memorials of John McLeod Campbell,* and *Memoir of Bishop Alexander Ewing,* 386-409.

Evangelical Magazine and Missionary Chronicle, Vol. VI, New Series (November, 1828). Review of *The Unconditional Freeness of the Gospel,* by Thomas Erskine, 481-484.

- Vol. VII, New Series (1829). Supplement for the Year. Review of *Notes and Recollections of Two Sermons by the Rev. Mr. Campbell*; *The Peace of Believing Distinguished from Antinomian Assurance,* by James Barr; *The Way of Salvation,* by David Russell, 582-587.
- Vol. XVI, New Series (1838). Review of *The Doctrine of Election,* by Thomas Erskine, 119.
- Vol. XXIV, New Series (May, 1846). Letter of the Rev. James Haldane to the Editor concerning Sandemanianism, 249-251.

Glasgow Daily Herald, (Tuesday, 13 December 1870). Review of *Present-Day Papers on Prominent Questions in Theology,* by Alexander Ewing, 2.

- (Wednesday, 28 February 1872). Obituary of John McLeod Campbell, 4

Literary Churchman, (8 March 1856). Review of John McLeod Campbell's *The Nature of the Atonement,* 89-90.

Morning Watch or Quarterly Journal on Prophecy, and Theological Review, Vol. I, No.II (March, 1829). "On the Theology of the Periodical Journals of the Present Day", 243-267.

- Vol. II, No.II (March, 1830), "On the Secondary Causes which Influence the Character of Controversial Writings, Illustrated by Recent Examples" (by 'J.T.'), 428-448.
- Vol. IV, No.I (September, 1831). "Messrs. Campbell, Scott, and Maclean, versus the General Assembly of the Church of Scotland", 179-193.

National Review, Vol. XVIII (January-April, 1864). "The Church and Theology of Germany During the Nineteenth Century", 191-230.

Owens College Magazine, Vol. XIII, No.3 (June, 1881). "Professor A.J. Scott, M.A." (by A.W.W.), 105-113.

Presbyterian Review and Religious Journal, Vol. I, No.I (July, 1831). "Proceedings of the General Assembly – The Row Case – Heresy", 111-134.
- Vol. X, No.III (February, 1838). "Mysticism-Erskine on Election", 480-494.

Quarterly Christian Magazine, Vol. IV, No.24 (January, 1838). "Erskine's Doctrine of Election, and its Connexion with the General Tenor of Christianity", (probably by J.A. Haldane), 352-363.

Quarterly Christian Spectator, Vol. I, No.II (June, 1829). Review of *The Unconditional Freeness of the Gospel*, by Thomas Erskine, 289-306.

Scotsman (The), (31 March 1870). Obituary of Erskine (by Principal Shairp).

Scottish Presbyterian, Volume I, New Series (November, 1843). Review of *Discourses on the Nature and Extent of the Atonement of Christ*, by Ralph Wardlaw, 259-287.

Spectator (The), (2 April 1870). "Thomas Erskine of Linlathen", 430-2.
- (24 June 1871). "Mr. Erskine's Posthumous Fragments", 768-70.
- (14 October 1871). "The Bishop of Argyll's Present Day Papers", 1241-3.
- (28 October 1871). "Mr. Erskine's view of Life", (by 'J.W.F.'), 1302.
- (12 July 1873). "Bishop Ewing's Latest Teachings", 896-7.
- (23 June 1877). "The Letters of Thomas Erskine", 793-4.
- (29 December 1877). "The Letters of Thomas Erskine", 1661-1662.

Weekly Review and Presbyterian Record, (12 August 1871). Review of *The Spiritual Order*, by Thomas Erskine, 777-8.

Index of Subjects

Adam and Christ, 34, 58, 105, 127-29, 133, 150, 157-58, 185, 187, 190-92, 210-11
Adoptionism, 83, 158, 214
Albury, 232
Anakephalaiosis, 104, 106-7, 111-13, 158, 182, 200-1
Andover Theological Seminary, 269, 294
Anglican Church, 167, 209, 210, 220, 221
Antinomianism, 100, 160, 284
Apokatastasis, 182, 185-86, 201-3, 238-39
Arminianism, 4, 12, 142, 155, 157, 169, 261, 282-83
Ascension, 107
Assurance, 41, 75, 84, 96-101,
Atonement, 13, 48, 75, 88, 98, 101-10, 124-25, 133, 145-47, 182, 186, 190, 197, 201, 203, 212-13, 218-19, 223, 242, 245, 246, 253, 261, 289-91, 294-95
Augustinianism, 168, 175
Authority, 23, 46-93, 138, 143, 145-46, 167-68, 177, 178, 181, 207, 230, 270, 275
Bereans, The, 284
Berlin, 230, 232, 237, 238
Bible, 48, 53, 71, 79-80, 88-92, 138, 143, 145-46, 168, 169, 170, 242, 272-77
Broad Church/ School, The, 6, 35, 88, 123-24, 196, 199, 200, 211, 218, 220, 223, 255, 277
Broadlands conferences, 261-62
Calvinism, 5, 8, 9-13, 23, 27, 29, 41, 44, 55, 56, 63, 69, 75, 76, 93, 96, 98-100, 104, 108-9, 111, 113, 126, 130, 133, 135, 140-42, 155-57, 167, 185, 186, 192, 233-34, 255, 257, 259, 261, 264, 268, 271, 279-88, 290
Cambridge Platonists, 57, 178-80, 291
Catholic Apostolic Church, The, 13, 76
Christ, blood of, 108-10, 119, 125, 133, 186
  birth in soul, 184, 190, 192
  body of, 36
  confession of sin, 113, 117-18, 125, 133, 135
  cross of, 108, 120, 125, 134, 151, 178, 186, 205, 221, 222, 289
  death of, 103, 105, 107-10, 122, 177-78, 182, 283, 289
  divinity of, 36, 113
  dying with, 107-16, 183
  faith of, 81-2
  fallen flesh of, 39, 82, 103, 105, 108, 113, 116, 118, 132-33, 135, 158, 185, 186-92, 210-11
  headship of, 36, 41-2, 82-3, 94, 97, 103-4, 106-9, 113-15, 118, 127, 133-34, 157-58, 187, 204, 208, 210-11, 222, 242
  identification with, 107-16, 128, 183, 205, 218, 221
  incarnation of, 157, 191, 203, 210-11, 215
  light of, 24, 55-6, 67, 74, 78, 82, 92, 145, 148, 153, 191, 208, 223, 243, 275
  moral ideal, 47, 84, 124-25, 130, 170, 211-17, 261, 266
  union with, 25, 36-7, 40, 82, 107, 110, 114, 116, 125, 261

133, 140, 143, 178, 187, 190, 196, 219, 242, 266
vicarious humanity of, 114, 158, 242
vicarious repentance of, 113, 158
Christian consciousness, 25, 46-7, 50, 53, 71, 82, 85, 87, 91, 93, 122, 124-5, 127, 143-44, 148, 175, 179, 196, 204, 212, 235, 241, 242-43, 247-51, 261, 265
Christian Socialism, 195, 218-19, 223
Christology, 10, 39, 57, 187-92, 106, 113, 174, 187-92, 204, 209-10, 213-15, 223
Church of Scotland, 99-101, 167, 199, 259, 263
Confession of sin, 98, 151
Congregational Church, 167, 280, 289
Conscience, 22, 24, 36, 39, 46, 48-58, 65, 67, 70-1, 74, 76, 77, 78, 80, 90-1, 143, 145-46, 153, 156-57, 168-69, 197, 204, 207, 212, 219, 248, 255, 265, 270, 274-75, 292
Continental Society, The, 232
Conversion, 65-6, 148-59, 178, 283, 286
Death, 121, 217-19
Deism, 8, 52, 68, 138, 168, 183, 195, 265
Dependence, 25, 34, 37, 39, 64-5, 70, 74, 81-4, 108-9, 139, 154-55, 157, 175, 196, 208-9, 222, 242, 247-50
Disruption, The, 13, 289
Divinisation, 24, 33, 37, 39-41, 67, 114, 142, 192, 204, 214
Doctrine, 53, 56-7, 59, 83, 88-92, 94, 108-9, 146-47, 156, 160, 169, 170, 181, 185, 216-17, 230, 231, 242, 248, 254, 287

Eastern Orthodoxy, 40
Ecclesiology, 41-2, 89, 167, 210, 223, 279
Eclecticism, 8, 15, 21, 25, 47, 55, 64, 68, 69, 93, 130, 131, 144, 146, 147, 159, 161, 165-67, 169, 172, 179-80, 192, 195, 209, 224, 225, 227, 239, 241, 245, 250-55, 264, 287, 291, 293, 295
Edinburgh University, 4, 227, 232, 257, 292-93
Education, 23, 56, 63, 82, 95, 96, 111, 117, 121, 124, 125, 129, 152-53, 169, 173-75, 197-98, 201-2, 206, 220, 243
Election, 32, 42, 98, 126-29, 150, 182, 185, 191, 256, 282-83
Empiricism, 50, 70, 93, 184, 227, 246, 255, 265, 292
Enlightenment, 8, 22, 47, 51, 53, 64, 66-7, 84, 85, 87, 93, 122-23, 138-40, 151, 167-69, 172, 178, 179, 183, 225, 248, 252, 253, 261, 263, 269, 271, 287, 288, 291, 292-93
Entire sanctification, 185, 261, 262
Episcopalian Church, 4, 167, 258
Epistemology, 73, 93, 153, 166, 169, 251
Equivalence, doctrine of, 113
Erlangen, 238, 245
Essays and Reviews, 206-7, 216, 239, 273-74, 277
Eternal life, 105, 118, 153, 249
Eternal sonship, 36-7, 41, 203, 208-9
Eternal punishment, 173, 175, 197, 220, 222, 261
Ethics, 22, 23, 26, 51, 53, 55, 57, 64, 67-8, 72, 76, 77, 83, 85, 87, 88-90, 93, 95, 123, 134-35, 139, 160, 167, 170, 196, 201,

Index of Subjects

211-13, 220, 230, 242, 254, 261, 265-66
Eucharist, 41, 204
Evangelical Alliance, 238
Evangelicalism, 8, 29, 50, 65-6, 68, 93, 119, 126, 130, 131-32, 136-37, 146, 148, 150, 151, 153, 171, 192, 194, 201, 205, 212, 217-18, 220, 232-35, 237, 254-57, 260, 280
Evidence, 24, 31, 49-53, 71, 90, 99-100, 135, 145, 168, 170, 173, 248, 258, 269, 272-73
Evil, 25, 60, 116, 121-22, 153, 175, 202
Evolution, 174, 202, 205, 219, 221, 243
Expiation, 103, 124, 245
Faith, 24, 52, 55, 62, 69-88, 97, 106, 109, 119, 129, 136-37, 139, 141, 149, 151, 155, 168, 241-42, 245, 276, 278-88
Fall, The, 79, 85, 104-5, 113-14, 127-28, 133-34, 157, 175, 182, 183, 185-86, 190-91, 202, 203-4, 212, 214, 239
Federalism, 8, 10, 27, 133
Forgiveness, 75, 76, 83, 84, 95, 97, 99, 110, 113, 118, 160, 256
Freedom of the will, 79, 141, 154-55, 168, 173, 214
Geneva, 232, 233-34, 274
Germany, 8, 49, 107, 226-30, 123-24, 130, 143, 166-68, 192, 225, 225-52, 260, 268
Glasgow University, 257
God, as Judge, 22, 27-9, 86, 181, 245
  character of, 22, 27-45, 50, 53, 56, 59-62, 69, 75, 83, 88, 90, 94-5, 98, 111, 114, 120, 122, 145-46, 153, 198-99, 203-4, 208, 213, 229, 254, 256, 269, 270-71, 290-92
  condemnation of, 106-8, 117, 121, 196
  Fatherhood of, 10, 22, 27, 28, 35ff, 43-4, 80, 81-3, 86, 95, 195-97, 199, 208, 218, 220, 222, 260, 261, 263-64, 270-71, 295
  grace of, 81, 97, 103, 114, 128, 141-43, 151, 256
  image of, 28-9, 33, 55, 62, 82, 88, 94-5, 139, 191, 200, 210, 242
  immanence of, 143, 148, 181, 186, 251, 255
  justice of, 28, 56, 144, 152, 289-90
  love of, 22-3, 29-30, 59-60, 96, 103, 109, 114, 122, 150, 160, 181, 186, 245, 246, 263
  passibility of, 217-18, 220
  sovereignty of, 27, 44, 98, 130, 147, 149, 155, 195, 251, 264, 281-82
  wrath of, 117, 119, 123, 125, 152, 185, 186, 246
Gospel, 22, 49, 60-2, 68, 72, 74, 81, 84, 91, 96, 100, 103, 116, 121, 133, 136, 145, 160, 170-71, 178, 195, 197, 202, 203, 216, 253, 256
Hallé, 250
Heaven, 160
Hegelianism, 93
Heidelberg, 237, 244
Hell, 186, 202, 257, 260
Hermeneutics, 79-80, 256
Higher life, 262
Historical criticism, 58-9, 92, 93, 195, 227, 272-77
Holiness, 24, 32, 75, 83, 103, 105, 114, 124, 160, 201, 242, 256, 262
Holiness movements, 256, 261-62
Holy Spirit, 38-41, 48, 56, 58, 61, 64, 66, 74, 76-7, 108-10,

115-16, 135-61, 177, 204, 283-86, 248-49, 250, 271, 278-86
Humanism, 47, 170
Hyper-Calvinism, 281-82
I-Thou theology, 35
Idealism, 4, 68, 140, 148, 161,, 239, 242, 255
Imitatio Christi, 55, 84, 103-4, 107, 108, 112, 118, 125, 128, 134, 183, 212, 214-15, 221, 245, 266
Imputation, 83-8, 109, 133-34, 139, 185, 245
Incarnationalism, 22, 34, 40-2, 56-7, 59-60, 91, 94, 101-8, 113-17, 124-25, 127, 130, 133, 149, 153, 155, 158, 178, 182-83, 186, 187-88, 190-92, 201, 203-17, 223, 229, 242, 246, 254, 260
Individualism, 42, 85
Information, 62, 67, 74-5, 77-9
Innovation, 8, 17, 21, 52, 57, 64, 75, 80, 83, 84, 93, 94, 95, 96, 97, 99, 101, 104, 107, 109-13, 116-18, 121, 123, 126-30, 131-35, 136, 145, 146, 148, 150, 152, 158-61, 165-68, 171-75, 182, 187, 190, 192, 194-95, 201, 205, 211, 214, 218, 220, 221, 225, 226, 229-30, 232, 244, 249, 251-52, 253-64, 279, 283, 287-88, 291, 294
Internalism, 23, 49-57, 64, 68, 74, 77, 91, 93, 102, 104-10, 143-45, 167, 169, 173, 181, 221, 230, 243, 250, 258, 265, 269-70, 272-75
Intuition, 24, 48, 54, 55, 61, 64, 74, 77, 80, 145, 169, 181, 247, 250-1, 292, 293
Irresistible grace, 126, 281
Jesus, life of, 214-17

Judgment, 98, 117, 123, 196, 256
Justification, 37, 69, 81, 83-5, 109, 113, 127-28, 134, 139, 178, 196, 282
Justification by faith, 80-8
Kenosis, 218-19
Keswick conferences, 261-62
Knowledge, 15, 16, 17, 40, 48, 58-61, 65-79, 89, 114, 123, 136-37, 141, 156, 181, 197-98, 204, 214, 241-42, 250, 285-86
Law, 22, 58, 123, 196
Liberalism, 2, 11, 35, 81, 87, 93, 125, 135, 140, 146-47, 151, 155, 158, 159, 213, 215, 219, 220, 223, 224, 226, 237, 242, 255-57, 260-61, 273, 276, 288
Love, law of, 36-7, 54, 59-61, 64-6, 72, 85-6, 212-13, 221, 261, 262
Lux Mundi, 207
Marrow Controversy, 1, 11, 29-30, 97, 145, 211, 286
Mediating theology, 143, 159, 168, 197, 237, 241, 244-46, 251
Methodism, 8, 138,
Miracles, 31, 50-1, 91, 135
Moral atonement, 122-24, 290
Moral exemplarism, 84, 111, 113, 120, 122-24, 135, 144, 211-20, 290
Moral idealism, 211-17, 267
Moral government, 102, 144-45, 289-95
Moral law, 31, 61-2, 168, 183
Moral philosophy, 138, 159, 227, 292-93
Moravians, The, 4, 284
Morning Watch, The, 188
Mysticism, 25, 48, 75, 87, 107-8, 114, 132, 147-48, 161,

Index of Subjects

166-67, 170, 173, 176-80, 245, 246, 247, 252, 262
Natural Theology, 37, 46, 48-53, 64, 68, 75, 135, 138, 146, 170, 181, 254-55, 293
Nestorianism, 214
New England, 49, 269, 279
New Haven, 219, 292-93
Obedience, 23, 37, 57, 70, 72, 75, 84, 129, 153-54
Oberlin, 262
Ordo salutis, 151, 156
Oriel School, The, 227
Oxford movement, The, 9, 12, 211
Pantheism, 25, 143, 230
Patristics, 40, 172-73, 182, 211, 234
Pelagianism, 134, 141, 155, 169, 200, 214, 283-84
Penal substitution, 23, 25, 103-4, 111-13, 117-18, 122, 130, 133, 186, 192, 197, 219
Pentecostalism, 261
Perfectionism, 66, 83
Perichoresis, 43
Perseverance, 154
Personhood, 33, 41
Philosophy, 8, 25, 37, 58, 60, 61, 68, 93, 136-37, 144, 146-48, 159, 161, 170, 194, 195, 212, 225, 228, 232-33, 235, 244, 250-52, 254, 258, 263, 265-66, 292-93
Physical redemption, 105-6
Physiology, 61, 93
Pietism, 4, 8, 83-4, 107, 138, 166, 168, 238, 242
Platonism, 25, 48, 56, 73, 88, 143, 166-67, 177-80, 183-84, 195, 199, 214-15, 221, 246-47, 263, 265-66
Post-mortem salvation, 173-74, 185, 197-98, 201-2, 260
Predestination, 121, 126, 128, 129, 234

Probation, 23, 111, 150, 175
Propitiation, 109, 117-25, 152, 186, 218, 219, 222
Psychology, 33, 46-8, 53, 57, 65, 70, 73, 75, 81, 93, 110-11, 113, 127, 144, 147-48, 212-13, 243, 278, 288, 289, 293
Punishment, 23, 26, 27, 85-6, 88, 94-5, 98, 111-12, 115-21, 133, 154, 182, 196-97, 201
Puritanism, 99
Quakerism, 8, 132, 143, 173, 175-83, 199, 223, 261
Rationalism, 46, 55, 145-49, 159, 168, 177, 230, 238, 241, 244, 246, 255
Reason, 23, 36, 49, 51, 55, 59, 67, 71, 73-4, 78-9, 80, 138, 139, 145-47, 168-70, 197, 212, 239, 241, 247, 250-51, 265
Recipiency, 39-43, 42-3, 62-3, 70, 81, 82-3, 85, 109
Redemption, 68, 101, 105-6, 110, 112-14, 120, 133-34, 159, 175, 178, 183, 186, 191-92, 196, 212, 222, 281
Reformed Theology, 66, 138
Regeneration, 22, 28, 32, 55-6, 61, 65, 91, 111, 127, 137, 139, 141, 144, 149-58, 183, 191, 238-39, 242, 278, 281-82, 288
Relationality, 10, 24-5, 33-6, 41-4, 65, 267
Repentance, 97-8, 113, 151,
Representation, 103-4, 113, 118, 158, 186, 242-43
Reprobation, 127-29, 150, 173, 185, 191
Resurrection, 57-8, 62, 105, 107, 108, 109, 112-13, 118, 133
Retribution, 23, 25, 94, 98, 112, 144, 152, 197, 290

Revelation, 13, 46-93, 129, 135, 138, 146, 148, 168, 170, 180, 204, 206-7, 241, 242, 255-56, 269-70, 277

Righteousness, 24, 62-5, 83, 85-8, 109-10, 115, 118-19, 122, 124, 127, 133-34, 142, 152, 196-98, 223

Roman Catholicism, 85, 139, 198

Romanticism, 8, 25, 28, 33, 46-7, 49, 55, 64, 73, 79, 93, 140, 143, 156, 166-69, 172, 178, 179-80, 184, 194, 195, 199, 217, 225-30, 237, 239, 247, 251-52, 255, 261, 263, 265, 268-69, 271, 272-73

Row movement, The, 13-15, 96, 131, 132, 140, 148-49, 199-200, 258, 280

Sabellianism, 143-44, 146

Sacrifice, 37, 109, 110-19, 186, 192, 204, 213, 217-24

Salvation, 26, 60-1, 66-88, 94-130, 136, 139, 141, 150, 153, 154, 159-60, 175, 185-86, 196, 200

Sanctification, 24, 65, 83-4, 95, 103, 115, 120, 124-25, 137, 139, 140, 153, 157, 178, 185-86, 200, 256, 284

Sandemanianism, 70, 144-45, 278-88

Science, 37, 52, 60-4, 71, 93, 136, 146, 148, 195, 254

Scotland, 9-13, 27, 46, 53, 63-4, 70, 72, 75, 93, 100, 130, 132-5, 165, 195, 205, 223, 225-27, 230, 233-34, 246, 254, 257-59, 264, 274-77, 279-80, 285, 294

Scottish Common Sense, 53-4, 227, 250, 268, 292-93

Sin, 66, 67, 83, 94-5, 99-100, 103, 106-126, 136, 151-54, 175, 196-97, 202, 204, 222, 239, 242, 270

Socinianism, 30, 92, 226

Sonship, 10, 29, 34, 36-8, 81-2, 104, 144, 196, 200

Spectator, The, 2, 4, 124, 207, 231, 257, 259

Spiritual laws, 25-6, 37, 48, 54, 58-75, 82, 93, 156, 174, 201, 220-21, 255, 262

Spiritual order, 22, 25, 41, 48, 58-68, 82, 181-82, 195-203, 206, 209, 212, 221, 223

Spiritualism, 261

Subjectivism, 50, 92, 107-10, 119, 122, 134, 142, 147, 177, 181, 186, 212, 238, 246, 265, 287

Suffering, 26, 85, 88, 108, 110-17, 122, 125, 128, 130, 152, 175, 186, 196, 200, 203, 217-24, 248, 262

Supernatural, 48, 53, 61, 64, 75, 135, 137, 146, 148-49, 179, 241-42, 243, 250, 255, 265, 275

Swiss Réveil, 232, 233-34

Sympathy, 24, 42-3, 70, 83, 84, 112-13, 117, 125, 151, 153, 218, 242, 248-49

Theodicy, 22, 111-17, 120, 130, 174, 200, 217

Theology, reconstruction of, 17, 21, 27, 37, 46-8, 68, 73, 85, 86-7, 92, 93, 98, 103, 108-9, 111-12, 117-19, 123-24, 126-30, 131-39, 152, 154, 159-61, 165-68, 171-75, 194-224, 225-252, 253-64, 277

Theopoiesis, 40

Transcendentalism, 49, 268-69

Trinity, 33-6, 38, 42-3, 139, 144, 146-49, 158, 222, 268

Trust, 41, 69-70, 82-4, 95, 109, 119, 136, 152, 154-55, 196, 208-9, 222

Truth, 47, 50, 56, 59, 61, 67, 71-4, 79, 91, 137, 139, 141, 148, 151, 207, 230, 242, 247, 251, 265, 290
Unitarianism, 30, 35, 55, 92, 111, 173, 183, 192, 214-15, 221, 236, 268-71, 291, 293
Universal atonement, 283, 290
Universal pardon, 24, 69, 72, 84, 88, 96-101, 150, 151, 160, 168, 178, 182, 184, 282-83, 293-94

Universalism, 25, 98, 106, 126, 129, 130, 147, 148, 174, 182, 184, 190-91, 197-98, 201-3, 229, 242, 243, 249, 256, 257, 258, 260, 261, 262, 263
Utilitarianism, 8, 51, 152, 268-71
Wesleyanism, 32, 64-6, 83, 142, 249, 261
Westminster Confession, 11, 27, 100, 133, 259, 276-77
Wittenberg, 240, 244

Index of Persons

Abelard, Peter, 102, 111, 114-15, 120, 122, 212, 213
Arndt, John, 107-8, 177
Arnold, Matthew, 6, 87
Arnold, Thomas, 6, 56, 166, 223
Athanasius, 40, 43, 105-6, 172, 178, 182
Augustine, 173
Baldwin Brown, James, 6
Barclay, Robert, 176, 177
Barth, Karl, 33, 42, 49, 85, 101, 129, 130, 157-58, 237, 239, 245, 263
Bebbington, David, 194, 261
Bellamy, Joseph, 145, 286
Bernard of Clairvaux, 114
Bewkes, Eugene Garrett, 14
Boehme, Jacob, 107-8, 166-67, 179, 180, 184, 191, 230, 235, 246
Bost, Paul Ami, 233
Boulger, James D., 228
Bourignon, Antoinette, 284
Broglie, Duchess de, 4, 5, 274
Brose, Olive, 2
Brotherston, Peter, 15
Brown, David, 27, 189
Brown, Thomas, 227
Browning, Robert, 1, 202
Bulloch, James, 3
Bunsen, Christian Karl Josias von (Chevalier), 227, 237, 245, 274
Burns, Rev. Robert, 133, 284
Bushnell, Horace, 6, 102, 213, 219-20, 222
Butler, Bishop Joseph, 52, 54, 93
Byron, Lord, 226
Caird, Edward, 11
Caird, John, 11
Calvin, John, 78, 100, 211, 280

Campbell, John McLeod, 1, 2, 3, 6, 8, 10, 11, 12, 13-15, 27, 35, 38, 40, 43, 51, 61, 74, 78, 81, 95, 96, 99, 102, 103, 108, 112-13, 117, 125, 131, 165-66, 177, 189, 192, 194, 199, 202, 213, 220, 228-30, 232, 237, 255, 257, 258, 260, 264, 294-95
Nature of the Atonement, 14, 108, 111, 113, 125, 173, 211, 219, 248, 294-95
Candlish, J. Stuart, 11, 96, 138, 144, 145, 195-96, 200, 279-80, 284-85, 287-88
Candlish, Robert Smith, 44, 221-24
Carlyle, Jane Welsh, 5, 30
Carlyle, Thomas, 5, 11, 166, 227, 228, 231, 257
Chalmers, Thomas, 5, 50-1, 54, 98, 99, 119, 132, 149, 223, 228, 234, 259, 279, 280, 290, 293
Channing, William Ellery, 35, 51, 55, 92, 93, 173, 215, 220, 268-71, 292
Cockburn, Henry, Lord, 232, 293
Colenso, Bishop John William, 273-76
Coleridge, Samuel Taylor, 4, 6, 7, 33, 51-2, 78-9, 81, 90, 92, 93, 126, 148, 166, 167, 168, 179, 180, 189, 194, 199, 200, 202, 219, 225, 226-29, 231, 232, 237, 244, 262
Conway, Moncure Daniel, 231
Cox, Samuel, 202
Crawford, Thomas, 44
Cunningham, William, 85
d'Aubigne, Merle, 5

Dante, Aligheri, 235
Darby, John Nelson, 80
Darwin, Charles, 1
Davies, Horton, 101
Dillistone, F.W., 114-15
Dionysius, 177, 246
Dorner, Isaac, 241, 245, 276
Drummond, Andrew L., 3
Drummond, Henry (1851-97), 174
Drummond, Henry (1786-1850), 232, 233
Eckhart, Meister, 167
Edwards, Jonathan, 78, 93, 144, 173, 211, 285-86, 289
Eliot, George, 273
Emerson, Ralph Waldo, 268
Erskine, John, 29, 279, 280
Erskine, Thomas:
  Brazen Serpent, 16, 48, 50, 97, 139, 188, 189, 197, 203, 211, 212, 213, 245, 246, 248, 263
  Doctrine of Election, 50, 67, 80, 119, 126-27, 132, 141, 156, 173, 176, 177-78, 198, 201, 203, 224, 244, 245, 274
  Essay on Faith, 7, 71-3, 132, 136, 141, 280, 287
  Extracts of Letters, 96, 211, 282,
  Gifts of the Spirit, 153
  Internal Evidence, 7, 131-32, 135, 136, 139, 145, 153, 187, 285, 286
  Letters of S. Rutherford, 47, 95, 291
  Spiritual Order, 17, 25, 38, 80, 124, 202
  Unconditional Freeness, 2, 96, 98, 149, 184, 188, 234-35, 263, 293, 294
Ewing, Alexander, 3, 5, 113, 176, 181, 198, 219, 220, 255, 258, 292

Fairbairn, Andrew Martin, 258, 276-77
Fénelon, François, 177
Fergusson, David A.S., 129
Finlayson, Duncan, 70
Finney, Charles Grandison, 6, 261
Forsyth, Peter Taylor, 29, 263
Foster, John, 173-74, 202
Foster, Marian, 179, 231
Fox, George, 177
Franks, Robert S., 2, 3, 241
Fraser, James, of Brea, 11, 211
Fuller, Andrew Gunton, 281, 289-90
Gaussen, Louis, 126, 234
Glas, John, 279-80
Gobat, Bishop Samuel, 173, 234, 240
Goethe, Johann Wolfgang von, 226, 237
Gore, Charles, 158, 186, 207, 214, 216
Gowler, Steve, 3, 4, 6, 228, 231
Groves, Anthony N., 149-50, 153
Gunton, Colin E., 33
Gurney, Emelia Russell, 5, 62, 261-62
Haldane, James A., 132-35, 176, 232, 280, 281, 283-84, 289
Haldane, Robert, 232, 233, 289
Hamilton, William, 15
Hanna, William, 4, 213, 259
Hare, Julius Charles, 227, 228, 232
Harnack, Adolf von, 35, 195
Hart, Trevor, 2, 7, 106, 287
Hegel, G.W.F., 166, 180, 230, 239, 240
Henderson, G.D., 11
Henderson, Henry F., 7, 87, 107, 177, 258, 291
Hervey, James, 145, 286
Heubner, H.L., 240
Hick, John, 175

Index of Persons

Hicks, Peter, 250-55
Hilton, Boyd, 54
Hodge, Archibald Alexander, 290
Hodge, Charles, 179, 232, 233, 237, 250-51
Hofmann, J.C.K. von, 246
Hooker, Morna, 114
Hooker, Richard, 62, 167, 189
Hume, David, 46-7, 50, 51, 53, 58, 71, 73, 74, 84, 93, 292
Hutton, Richard Holt, 205-9
Inge, Dean William Ralph, 180
Irenaeus, 40, 106, 172, 174-75, 178, 182
Irving, Edward, 1, 5, 13, 27, 39, 76, 93, 132-33, 135, 149, 166, 173, 174, 177, 187-92, 204, 209-11, 223, 228-29, 246, 254, 258
Jeffrey, Francis, Lord, 232, 293
Jenkyn, Thomas, 290
Jenyns, Soame, 51
Johnson, Harry, 188
Jowett, Benjamin, 5, 6, 239
Jukes, Andrew, 202, 262
Kant, Immanuel, 1, 8, 15, 22, 23, 25, 33, 46-7, 50, 54, 58, 71, 73, 79, 85, 87, 93, 166, 168-71, 202, 214-16, 226-28, 230, 234, 237, 241, 244, 247, 263, 265-68, 291-92
Kent, John, 6
Kepler, Johann, 71
Kettler, Christian D., 114
Kierkegaard, Søren, 6
Kingsley, Charles, 5, 6, 200, 218, 223
Knight, William Angus, 240
Lampe, G.W.H., 219
Law, William, 8, 40, 56, 66, 74, 87, 93, 96, 128, 166-67, 174-75, 178, 180-92, 202, 230, 245-46, 252, 254, 262
Leckie, J.H., 202
Lessing, Gotthold Ephraim, 220

Lidgett, J. Scott, 44
Locke, John, 33, 50, 70, 73, 184
Logan, John B., 2
Luther, Martin, 178, 211
MacDonald, George, 5, 6, 8, 202, 262
MacEwen, Alexander, 14
Macleod, Norman, 3, 6
Mahan, Asa, 261
Malan, César, 5, 233, 234
Marshall, Walter, 144, 286
Martensen, Hans Lassen, 241
Martineau, James, 173
Maurice, Frederick Denison, 5, 6, 11, 33, 34-5, 43, 46, 81, 82, 86, 102, 124, 128, 165, 176, 179, 189, 197-99, 202, 204, 206, 207, 209-11, 213, 215, 216, 218, 221-24, 226, 235, 241, 242, 246, 249, 255, 256, 266, 270
McCurdy, Leslie, 263
McFarlane, Graham, 39
McGrath, Alister, 122-23
McIntosh, John R., 285
Melbourne, Lord, 72
Menken, Gottfried, 246
Meynell, Hugo, 23
Miller, Hugh, 203
Milman, Henry Hart, 166
Molinos, Miguel de, 177
Moncrieff, Sir Henry, 277
Monod, Adolphe, 5, 56, 261
Monod, Theodore, 261
More, Henry, 179
Mount-Temple, Lord and Lady, 261
Mullin, Robert Bruce, 220
Murphy, Joseph John, 203
Neander, Johann August Wilhelm, 226, 236, 238, 244, 250
Needham, Nicholas, 2, 3, 97, 102, 131, 144, 149, 179, 188, 189, 231, 235, 278-80, 288, 289, 290-91

Newell, Philip, 229
Newman, John Henry, 7, 12, 144-49, 159, 166, 235, 273, 287-88
Newton, Isaac, 2, 52, 60, 63-4, 71
Niebuhr, Barthold Georg, 227, 236
Noel, Gerard T., 173-74, 233, 234
Novalis, 237
Oliphant, Mrs, 7, 9, 189
Origen, 43, 174, 177
Orr, James, 195, 242
Owen, John, 42, 134, 189
Paley, William, 50-1, 168
Pascal, Blaise, 177
Pattison, Mark, 239
Payne, George, 290
Pearsall Smith, Hannah, 261-62
Pearsall Smith, Robert, 261
Penn William, 177
Pfleiderer, Otto, 2, 166, 194, 228, 230-31, 237
Plato, 40, 57, 66, 73, 74, 86, 88, 93, 167, 184, 215
Plumptre, E.H., 4
Porter, Roy, 8
Pusey, Edward, 232, 237, 238
Pye Smith, John, 290
Quincey, Thomas de, 226, 227
Rahner, Karl, 40
Rashdall, Hastings, 102, 213
Rauschenbusch, Walter, 261
Reardon, Bernard M.G., 194, 226, 231
Reid, Thomas, 53, 250, 292-93
Reimarus, Hermann Samuel, 216
Renan, Joseph Ernest, 216, 217, 273-74
Richardson, John, 227
Ritschl, Albrecht, 35, 195, 237, 241, 276
Robertson, Archibald, 8, 182-83

Robertson, Frederick William, 6, 206, 220-22, 246, 258-59
Robinson, Henry Crabb, 226
Rothe, Richard, 102, 236-37, 239-44, 246, 276
Rousseau, Jean-Jacques, 22, 54-5, 93, 169
Rowell, Geoffrey, 174
Ruskin, John, 261
Russell, David, 280
Rutherford, Lord, 5
Salisbury, Dean of, 257
Sandeman, Robert, 144, 279-80, 282-83
Schelling, Friedrich von, 8, 180, 226, 229-30, 241
Schlegel, Friedrich von, 226
Schleiermacher, Friedrich, 4, 6, 11, 15, 25, 43, 47, 49, 50, 51, 52, 56, 57, 82, 83, 87-8, 90-1, 93, 102, 111, 113, 122, 123-26, 143, 145, 146, 154, 166, 168, 169, 172-75, 179, 192, 196, 215, 219, 220, 222, 227, 230, 231, 233, 235-42, 244, 245, 246, 247, 249, 250, 263
Schleusner, J.F., 244
Schweitzer, Albert, 107
Schwenckfeld, Casper, 246
Scott, A.J., 1, 5, 6, 8, 13, 14, 28, 61, 150, 166, 172, 228-29, 236, 258
Scott, Sir Walter, 226, 293
Sell, Alan P.F., 143, 170-71
Shairp, John Campbell, 5, 24, 56, 87, 91, 177, 240, 273, 277
Shelley, Percy Bysshe, 226
Smail, Tom, 115-16, 152
Smeaton, George, 35, 123-24, 143-44, 238, 243, 245-46, 281, 286
Smith, Adam, 248
Smith, John, 179
Smith, William Robertson, 276
Smyth, John, 98, 282-83
Southcott, Joanna, 284

Index of Persons

Staël, Madame de, 226
Stanley, Dean Arthur Penrhyn, 5, 6, 202, 239, 255, 257-58, 262, 277
Stephen, Leslie, 54, 180
Stevens, George, 68
Stewart, Dugald, 227, 292-93
Storr, Vernon, 3, 6, 14, 169, 230
Story, Robert Herbert, 10
Strauss, David Friedrich, 216, 273
Stuart, Charles, of Dunearn, 172, 226, 229, 238, 289-90
Stuart, Moses, 269
Stunt, Timothy, 231, 232
Swedenborg, Emanuel, 246
Tayler, J.J., 173, 236
Taylor, Nathaniel, 292
Tennyson, Alfred, 202
Thirlwall, Connop, 137, 166, 201, 227, 232
Tholuck, Friedrich August Gottreu, 226, 237, 238-39, 241, 242, 244, 250, 262, 276
Thomas à Kempis, 177
Thomson, Andrew, 12, 75, 101, 126, 176, 240, 246
Tindal, Matthew, 52, 167

Toland, John, 52, 138
Torrance, Thomas F., 106, 114, 158, 191, 205
Tulloch, John, 3, 5, 9, 11, 46, 90, 145, 165, 166, 176, 194, 231, 245, 246, 259
Vaughan, D.J., 3
Vinet, Alexandre, 5, 68, 228, 252, 260
Vinet, Madame, 127
Wardlaw, Ralph, 96-7, 280, 290, 294
Warfield, B.B., 102, 246
Watson, Richard, 50, 135-37, 144, 149
Wedgwood, Julia, 1, 5, 9, 13, 36, 59, 62, 182, 194, 240, 256, 262
Wesley, John, 4, 29, 83-4, 93, 143, 180, 282
Williams, Rowland, 239
Wilson, H.B., 239
Winslow, Donald, 14, 36, 38, 43
Woods, Leonard, 269, 294
Wordsworth, William, 180, 217, 226, 232
Young, David, 8

Studies in Evangelical History and Thought
(All titles uniform with this volume)
Dates in bold are of projected publication

Clyde Binfield
The Country a Little Thickened and Congested?
Nonconformity in Eastern England 1840–1885
Studies of Victorian religion and society often concentrate on cities, suburbs, and industrialisation. This study provides a contrast. Victorian Eastern England—Essex, Suffolk, Norfolk, Cambridgeshire, and Huntingdonshire—was rural, traditional, relatively unchanging. That is nonetheless a caricature which discounts the industry in Norwich and Ipswich (as well as in Haverhill, Stowmarket, and Leiston) and ignores the impact of London on Essex, of railways throughout the region, and of an ancient but changing university (Cambridge) on the county town which housed it. It also entirely ignores the political implications of such changes in a region noted for the variety of its religious Dissent since the seventeenth century. This book explores Victorian Eastern England and its Nonconformity. It brings to a wider readership a pioneering thesis which has made a major contribution to a fresh evolution of English religion and society.
2005 / 1-84227-216-0 / approx. 274pp

John Brencher
Martyn Lloyd-Jones (1899–1981) and Twentieth-Century Evangelicalism
This study critically demonstrates the significance of the life and ministry of Martyn Lloyd-Jones for post-war British evangelicalism and demonstrates that his preaching was his greatest influence on twentieth-century Christianity. The factors which shaped his view of the church are examined, as is the way his reformed evangelicalism led to a separatist ecclesiology which divided evangelicals.
2002 / 1-84227-051-6 / xvi + 268pp

Jonathan D. Burnham
A Story of Conflict
The Controversial Relationship between Benjamin Wills Newton and John Nelson Darby
Burnham explores the controversial relationship between the two principal leaders of the early Brethren movement. In many ways Newton and Darby were products of their times, and this study of their relationship provides insight not only into the dynamics of early Brethrenism, but also into the progress of nineteenth-century English and Irish evangelicalism.
2004 / 1-84227-191-1 / xxiv + 268pp

J.N. Ian Dickson
Beyond Religious Discourse
Sermons, Preaching and Evangelical Protestants in
Nineteenth-Century Irish Society
Drawing extensively on primary sources, this pioneer work in modern religious history explores the training of preachers, the construction of sermons and how Irish evangelicalism and the wider movement in Great Britain and the United States shaped the preaching event. Evangelical preaching and politics, sectarianism, denominations, education, class, social reform, gender, and revival are examined to advance the argument that evangelical sermons and preaching went significantly beyond religious discourse. The result is a book for those with interests in Irish history, culture and belief, popular religion and society, evangelicalism, preaching and communication.
2005 / 1-84227-217-9 / approx. 324pp

Neil T.R. Dickson
Brethren in Scotland 1838–2000
A Social Study of an Evangelical Movement
The Brethren were remarkably pervasive throughout Scottish society. This study of the Open Brethren in Scotland places them in their social context and examines their growth, development and relationship to society.
2003 / 1-84227-113-X / xxviii + 510pp

Crawford Gribben and Timothy C.F. Stunt (eds)
Prisoners of Hope?
Aspects of Evangelical Millennialism in Britain and Ireland, 1800–1880
This volume of essays offers a comprehensive account of the impact of evangelical millennialism in nineteenth-century Britain and Ireland.
2004 / 1-84227-224-1 / xiv + 208pp

Khim Harris
Evangelicals and Education
Evangelical Anglicans and Middle-Class Education
in Nineteenth-Century England
This ground breaking study investigates the history of English public schools founded by nineteenth-century Evangelicals. It documents the rise of middle-class education and Evangelical societies such as the influential Church Association, and includes a useful biographical survey of prominent Evangelicals of the period.
2004 / 1-84227-250-0 / xviii + 422pp

November 2004

Mark Hopkins
Nonconformity's Romantic Generation
Evangelical and Liberal Theologies in Victorian England
A study of the theological development of key leaders of the Baptist and Congregational denominations at their period of greatest influence, including C.H. Spurgeon and R.W. Dale, and of the controversies in which those among them who embraced and rejected the liberal transformation of their evangelical heritage opposed each other.
2004 / 1-84227-150-4 / xvi + 284pp

Don Horrocks
Laws of the Spiritual Order
Innovation and Reconstruction in the Soteriology of Thomas Erskine of Linlathen
Don Horrocks argues that Thomas Erskine's unique historical and theological significance as a soteriological innovator has been neglected. This timely reassessment reveals Erskine as a creative, radical theologian of central and enduring importance in Scottish nineteenth-century theology, perhaps equivalent in significance to that of S.T. Coleridge in England.
2004 / 1-84227-192-X / xx + 362pp

Kenneth S. Jeffrey
When the Lord Walked the Land
The 1858–62 Revival in the North East of Scotland
Previous studies of revivals have tended to approach religious movements from either a broad, national or a strictly local level. This study of the multifaceted nature of the 1859 revival as it appeared in three distinct social contexts within a single region reveals the heterogeneous nature of simultaneous religious movements in the same vicinity.
2002 / 1-84227-057-5 / xxiv + 304pp

John Kenneth Lander
Itinerant Temples
Tent Methodism, 1814–1832
Tent preaching began in 1814 and the Tent Methodist sect resulted from disputes with Bristol Wesleyan Methodists in 1820. The movement spread to parts of Gloucestershire, Wiltshire, London and Liverpool, among other places. Its demise started in 1826 after which one leader returned to the Wesleyans and others became ministers in the Congregational and Baptist denominations.
2003 / 1-84227-151-2 / xx + 268pp

November 2004

Donald M. Lewis
Lighten Their Darkness
The Evangelical Mission to Working-Class London, 1828–1860
This is a comprehensive and compelling study of the Church and the complexities of nineteenth-century London. Challenging our understanding of the culture in working London at this time, Lewis presents a well-structured and illustrated work that contributes substantially to the study of evangelicalism and mission in nineteenth-century Britain.
2001 / 1-84227-074-5 / xviii + 372pp

Herbert McGonigle
'Sufficient Saving Grace'
John Wesley's Evangelical Arminianism
A thorough investigation of the theological roots of John Wesley's evangelical Arminianism and how these convictions were hammered out in controversies on predestination, limited atonement and the perseverance of the saints.
2001 / 1-84227-045-1 / xvi + 350pp

Lisa S. Nolland
A Victorian Feminist Christian
Josephine Butler, the Prostitutes and God
Josephine Butler was an unlikely candidate for taking up the cause of prostitutes, as she did, with a fierce and self-disregarding passion. This book explores the particular mix of perspectives and experiences that came together to envision and empower her remarkable achievements. It highlights the vital role of her spirituality and the tragic loss of her daughter.
2004 / 1-84227-225-X / approx. 360pp

Ian M. Randall
Evangelical Experiences
A Study in the Spirituality of English Evangelicalism 1918–1939
This book makes a detailed historical examination of evangelical spirituality between the First and Second World Wars. It shows how patterns of devotion led to tensions and divisions. In a wide-ranging study, Anglican, Wesleyan, Reformed and Pentecostal-charismatic spiritualities are analysed.
1999 / 0-85364-919-7 / xii + 310pp

November 2004

Ian M. Randall
Spirituality and Social Change
The Contribution of F.B. Meyer (1847–1929)
This is a fresh appraisal of F.B. Meyer (1847–1929), a leading Free Church minister. Having been deeply affected by holiness spirituality, Meyer became the Keswick Convention's foremost international speaker. He combined spirituality with effective evangelism and socio-political activity. This study shows Meyer's significant contribution to spiritual renewal and social change.
2003 / 1-84227-195-4 / xx + 184pp

James Robinson
Pentecostal Origins (1907–c.1925): A Regional Study
Early Pentecostalism in Ulster within its British Context
Harvey Cox describes Pentecostalism as 'the fascinating spiritual child of our time' that has the potential, at the global scale, to contribute to the 'reshaping of religion in the twenty-first century'. This study grounds such sentiments by examining at the local scale the origin, development and nature of Pentecostalism in the north of Ireland in its first twenty years. Illustrative, in a paradigmatic way, of how Pentecostalism became established within one region of the British Isles, it sets the story within the wider context of formative influences emanating from America, Europe and, in particular, other parts of the British Isles. As a synoptic regional study in Pentecostal history it is the first survey of its kind.
2005 / 1-84227-329-9 / approx. 424pp

Geoffrey Robson
Dark Satanic Mills?
Religion and Irreligion in Birmingham and the Black Country
This book analyses and interprets the nature and extent of popular Christian belief and practice in Birmingham and the Black Country during the first half of the nineteenth century, with particular reference to the impact of cholera epidemics and evangelism on church extension programmes.
2002 / 1-84227-102-4 / xiv + 294pp

Roger Shuff
Searching for the True Church
Brethren and Evangelicals in Mid-Twentieth-Century England
Roger Shuff holds that the influence of the Brethren movement on wider evangelical life in England in the twentieth century is often underrated. This book records and accounts for the fact that Brethren reached the peak of their strength at the time when evangelicalism was at it lowest ebb, immediately before World War II. However, the movement then moved into persistent decline as evangelicalism regained ground in the post war period. Accompanying this downward trend has been a sharp accentuation of the contrast between Brethren congregations who engage constructively with the non-Brethren scene and, at the other end of the spectrum, the isolationist group commonly referred to as 'Exclusive Brethren'.
2005 / 1-84227-254-3 / approx. 318pp

James H.S. Steven
Worship in the Spirit
Charismatic Worship in the Church of England
This book explores the nature and function of worship in six Church of England churches influenced by the Charismatic Movement, focusing on congregational singing and public prayer ministry. The theological adequacy of such ritual is discussed in relation to pneumatological and christological understandings in Christian worship.
2002 / 1-84227-103-2 / xvi + 238pp

Peter K. Stevenson
God in Our Nature
The Incarnational Theology of John McLeod Campbell
This radical reassessment of Campbell's thought arises from a comprehensive study of his preaching and theology. Previous accounts have overlooked both his sermons and his Christology. This study examines the distinctive Christology evident in his sermons and shows that it sheds new light on Campbell's much debated views about atonement.
2004 / 1-84227-218-7 / xxiv + 458pp

Martin Wellings
Evangelicals Embattled
Responses of Evangelicals in the Church of England to Ritualism, Darwinism and Theological Liberalism 1890–1930
In the closing years of the nineteenth century and the first decades of the twentieth century Anglican Evangelicals faced a series of challenges. In responding to Anglo-Catholicism, liberal theology, Darwinism and biblical criticism, the unity and identity of the Evangelical school were severely tested.
2003 / 1-84227-049-4 / xviii + 352pp

November 2004

James Whisenant
A Fragile Unity
Anti-Ritualism and the Division of Anglican Evangelicalism in the Nineteenth Century
This book deals with the ritualist controversy (approximately 1850–1900) from the perspective of its evangelical participants and considers the divisive effects it had on the party.

2003 / 1-84227-105-9 / xvi + 530pp

Haddon Willmer
Evangelicalism 1785–1835: An Essay (1962) and Reflections (2004)
Awarded the Hulsean Prize in the University of Cambridge in 1962, this interpretation of a classic period of English Evangelicalism, by a young church historian, is now supplemented by reflections on Evangelicalism from the vantage point of a retired Professor of Theology.

2005 / 1-84227-219-5

Linda Wilson
Constrained by Zeal
Female Spirituality amongst Nonconformists 1825–1875
Constrained by Zeal investigates the neglected area of Nonconformist female spirituality. Against the background of separate spheres, it analyses the experience of women from four denominations, and argues that the churches provided a 'third sphere' in which they could find opportunities for participation.

2000 / 0-85364-972-3 / xvi + 294pp

Paternoster
9 Holdom Avenue
Bletchley
Milton Keynes MK1 1QR
United Kingdom

Web: www.authenticmedia.co.uk/paternoster

November 2004